Globa

Global Politics

Globalization and the Nation-State

Anthony G. McGrew, Paul G. Lewis et al.

Polity Press

Copyright © this edition Polity Press 1992

Copyright Parts I, II, III The Open University 1988; Part IV The Open University 1989

First published 1992 by Polity Press in association with Blackwell Publishers Ltd
Reprinted 1993, 1995

Editorial office:
Polity Press
65 Bridge Street,
Cambridge CB2 1UR, UK

Marketing and production:
Blackwell Publishers Ltd
108 Cowley Road,
Oxford OX4 1JF, UK

Blackwell Publishers Inc.
238 Main Street
Cambridge, MA 02142, USA

ISBN 0 7456 0755–1
ISBN 0 7456 0756–X (pbk)

A CIP catalogue record for this book is available from the British Library and the Library of Congress.

Typeset in 10 on 12 pt Ehrhardt
by Photo·graphics, Honiton, Devon
Printed in Great Britain by T J Press, Padstow

This book is printed on acid-free paper.

Contents

vi   Contents

Preface

This volume has its origins in an Open University course entitled D312 Global Politics. Indeed all the chapters in this work are substantially revised versions of papers originally published as part of the teaching package for Global Politics. We would therefore like to thank the Open University for granting us permission to utilize elements of the existing teaching texts.

During the writing of this volume we were saddened to learn of the death of John Vincent, a highly regarded scholar in the British international relations community and a valued contributor to the original D312 course team. We would like to dedicate this volume to his memory.

Paul Lewis
Tony McGrew
The Open University

Acknowledgements

The authors thank the following for giving their permission to include previously published material in this work: *Yearbook of International Organizations*, for figures 1.4, 1.6, tables 1.1, 1.2; *Transnational Associations*, Brussels, 1978, for table 1.3; *International Organization*, for figure 1.6; International Institute for Strategic Studies, *The Military Balance*, for tables 5.1, 5.2, 5.5, figure 5.1; Stockholm International Peace Research Institute *Yearbook*, for tables 5.6, 5.7, 5.8, figure 5.2; *International Organization*, for figure 6.1; the OECD, World Bank *Development Report* and EEC *Statistics*, for tables 9.1, 9.2, 9.3; Buzan, B. (1987) *Strategic Studies*, London: Macmillan; Mackenzie, D. (1990) *Inventing Accuracy*, London: MIT Press; Axelrod, R. (1984) *The Evolution of Co-operation*, New York, Basic Books, for figure 6.2; Keohane, R. (1984) *After Hegemony*, Princeton: Princeton University Press, for table 9.5; Gilpin, R. (1987) *The Political Economy of International Relations*, Princeton: Princeton University Press, for table 9.6; *International Organization*, for table 9.7; Lewis, W.A. (1984) *The Rate of Growth of the World Economy*, Taipei: Institute of Economics, for figure 9.1; Rosenau, J.S. (1990) *Turbulence in World Politics*, London: Harvester Wheatsheaf.

List of Contributors

Dr B. Beeley, Staff Tutor in Geography, The Open University

Dr R. Bessel, Senior Lecturer in History, The Open University

Dr P. Lewis, Senior Lecturer in Government, The Open University

Dr A. McGrew, Senior Lecturer in Government, The Open University

Dr J. Mitchell, Lecturer in Government, The Open University

Professor D.C. Potter, Professor of Political Science, The Open University

Professor M. Smith, Professor of International Relations, Coventry Polytechnic

Dr N. Swain, Research Fellow in Economic History, Liverpool University

Dr G. Thompson, Senior Lecturer in Applied Social Sciences, The Open University

Professor R. Tooze, Professor of International Relations, Nottingham Polytechnic

The late John Vincent, Montague Burton Professor of International Relations, London School of Economics

Dr J. Vogler, Principal Lecturer in International Relations, Liverpool Polytechnic

1

Conceptualizing Global Politics

ANTHONY G. McGREW

INTRODUCTION

As the Cold War era of conflict and rivalry fades it is being replaced with an expanding awareness of global independence. This is reflected in the language of contemporary politics which is increasingly suffused with references to global problems, appeals to universal values and visions of a global community. Equally it finds expression in the academic study of politics, most visibly in the fascination with the future viability of the modern nation-state in an increasingly interdependent world system. Certainly the fact that no modern society can insulate itself from the vagaries of the world market, or transnational movements of capital, ideas, beliefs, crime, knowledge and news, seems evidence enough of the emergence of a truly global society. Moreover our everyday existence, as a glance in any kitchen cupboard will confirm, is to varying degrees sustained by a complex web of global networks and relationships of production and exchange of which we remain largely unaware. Because of this, events and actions in one part of the world can come to have significant ramifications for communities in quite distant countries. When Iraq entered Kuwait on 2 August 1990, causing a steep rise in oil prices, the headline in a Coventry paper read 'Iraq invades Kuwait – bus fares in Coventry set to rise'. More significant than the humorous nature of this headline is the unstated assumption that the paper's audience readily understood: namely that, in an interdependent world, domestic matters are in some mysterious way partly governed by external factors. As McLuhan remarked many years ago, one of the defining characteristics of the modern age is the developing realization that we live in a 'global village' (1969, p. 302). Yet the world still remains organized into over 170 separate nation-states each jealously guarding its national independence. Accordingly, whilst few would doubt that within the Western political imagination there is a widespread belief that the world is becoming progressively more interdependent, the actual evidence warrants a more critical and substantive interrogation. That in part is the purpose of this volume.

Constituent Features of Global Politics

The apparent emergence, in the late twentieth century, of an increasingly tightly interconnected and self-conscious global community does not necessarily imply, as some have argued, the arrival of some kind of world society. Whilst the infrastructure of a global social system may be evident, most visibly in the globalization of communications, the media and production, the fact remains that the world is organized into sovereign nation-states. Although historically only a relatively modern phenomenon, the nation-state is today the supreme territorial, administrative and political unit which defines the 'good community'. National sovereignty and the territorial integrity of the nation-state are jealously guarded, most particularly in the Third World where the struggle to achieve independent statehood is still fresh in the collective consciousness. War and permanent preparation for war, political fragmentation, cultural diversity, and the immense gap between the advanced states and the poorest states remain central features of the contemporary global system. Accordingly, whilst from the vantage point of the affluent West there is a temptation to view the world in terms of intensifying patterns of global interconnectedness, at best this is only a partial and superficial perspective. Nor is there any overwhelming evidence to support the frequently asserted proposition that processes of globalization are precipitating a 'crisis of the territorial nation-state' (Hertz 1969). On the contrary, the preponderance of the nation-state as the primary unit in world politics is itself a product of globalizing forces.

What seems somewhat less contentious is the observation that political processes, events and activities nowadays appear increasingly to have a global or international dimension. In an age of rapid communications it is fairly commonplace for political events or developments in one part of the world to impinge directly or indirectly on the political process in quite distant communities. Such linkage is articulated most acutely in crisis situations, like that of the 1991 Gulf War or the 1962 Cuban missile crisis, where distant events come to acquire a powerful hold over domestic politics in scores of nations and where the actions of only a handful of decision makers can have truly global consequences. Yet equally significant, although certainly less sensational, are the enormous transnational flows of finance, capital and trade which bind together the well-being of communities spread across the globe. During the early 1990s, for instance, the virtual ending of coal mining in Wales could be attributed in part to the import of more cheaply produced Australian and South African coal. The interconnection between the local, national and global political economy of coal is a vital element in understanding the decline of the Welsh coal industry. But the globalization of markets is only one, albeit important, determinant of the globalization of political life. Of equal significance is the internationalization of the state itself. In the post-war period especially there has been an enormous expansion in both the numbers and the functional scope of international institutions, agencies and regimes. This expansion has been engineered in part by governments recognizing that, in a highly interconnected world system, simply to achieve domestic policy goals requires enhanced levels of international cooperation. In the post-war period the growth of the welfare state and the intensification of patterns of international cooperation were intimately related. Moreover, the revolution in communications and transport technologies has facilitated greatly the global interplay of cultures, values, ideas, knowledge, peoples, social networks, elites and social movements. That this is a highly uneven and differentiated process does not detract from the underlying message that societies can no longer be conceptualized as bounded systems, insulated from the outside world. How could one possibly account for the contemporary drugs problem in most major cities without acknowledging the role of global networks of organized crime and the global trade in narcotics? In modern society the local and the global have become intimately related.

Writing some years ago Rosenau observed that, in the modern era, 'Politics everywhere, it would seem, are related to politics everywhere else . . . now the roots of . . . political life can be traced to remote corners of the globe' (in Mansbach et al. 1976, p. 22). In identifying the globalization of the political arena, as a distinctive feature of contemporary politics, Rosenau articulated what can be observed almost daily, namely the declining significance of territorial boundaries and place as the definitive parameters of political life. Politics within the confines of the nation-state, whether at the neighbourhood, local or national levels, cannot be insulated from powerful international forces and the ramifications of events in distant countries. In the late twentieth century, politics can no longer be understood as a purely local or national social activity but must be conceived as a social activity with a global dimension. This invites abolition of the traditional distinction between domestic and international politics, between the foreign and the domestic. It also demands a certain conceptual readjustment: thinking of politics as an activity which stretches across space (as well as time) rather than as a social activity which is confined within the boundaries of the nation-state, or at the international level as an activity confined to interactions between governments. Such a readjustment is realized in the concept of global politics.

To talk of global politics is to acknowledge that political activity and the political process, embracing the exercise of power and authority, are no longer primarily defined by national legal and territorial boundaries. In the twentieth century there has occurred a *stretching* of the political process such that decisions and actions in one part of the world can come to have world-wide ramifications. Associated with this stretching is also a *deepening* of the political process such that developments at even the most local level can have global ramifications and vice versa. Moreover, the stretching and deepening have been accompanied by a *broadening* of the political process. 'Broadening' refers to the growing array of issues which surface on the political agenda combined with the enormously diverse range of agencies or groups involved in political decision-making processes at all levels from the local to the global. The concept of global politics thus transcends the traditional distinction between the international and the domestic in the study of politics, as well as the statist and institutionalist biases in traditional conceptions of the political. It also suggests that there is an identifiable global political system and global political process which embraces a world-wide network of interactions and relationships between 'not only states but also other political actors, both "above" the state and "below" it' (Bull, 1977, p. 276).

George Modelski (1974) has devised a useful analogy for thinking through some of the distinctions and the connections between different levels of political interaction and activity in the contemporary world. His layer cake model provides a powerful heuristic device for simplifying the complex patterns of political interaction which define global politics. There are, he suggests, three distinct layers of political activity, from the local through the national to the global. To this might be added a fourth, the regional, which sits between the global and the national (see figure 1.1). Each layer, he argues, constitutes a defined political community with its own particular aspirations and needs. Each also embraces an identifiable set of political processes and

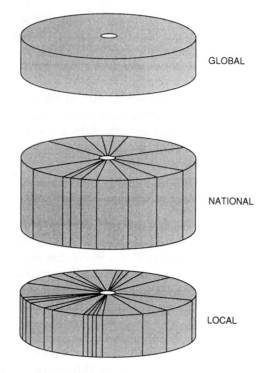

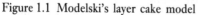

Figure 1.1 Modelski's layer cake model

institutions which exist to facilitate the taking of authoritative decisions. Whilst there are discontinuities between each of these layers, Modelski's model points to the systemic interdependencies between them; they are porous membranes rather than impermeable barriers to political interaction.

Media reports bring to public attention almost daily the evidence of the linkages between these different layers of political activity. When, in early 1991, the German Bundesbank raised domestic interest rates in response to the problems created by reunification, the consequences were felt not just in Europe but globally too. Because of Britain's membership of the European exchange rate mechanism, such a move meant sustaining high interest rates, exacerbating an already dire picture of rising domestic bankruptcies, unemployment and a housing slump. In the US the same event triggered a run on the dollar, requiring coordinated international action by the world's major central banks to prevent a further slide which would have had serious ramifications for the American economy. In 1988 the British novelist Salman Rushdie published *The Satanic Verses* which, because of its characterization of Muhammad, provoked a wave of street protests within Muslim communities across Europe, Asia and the Middle East. Many deaths were reported in these incidents, and the furore led to a Fatwah being issued by the Ayatollah Khomeini in Iran calling for the assassination of Rushdie. This instigated a major diplomatic confrontation between Western governments and Islamic states, resulting in the termination of Britain's diplomatic relations with Tehran. The Rushdie affair was a clash of cultures and civilizations and played out across the globe, from the street level to the General Assembly of the United Nations. Both of these illustrations give some insight, albeit partial, into the nature of global politics as well as the complex interactions between the layers in Modelski's layer cake model. Some further systematic exploration of the terrain of global politics is therefore warranted.

Isolating the global layer in Modelski's model requires us to distinguish between two particular forms of political interaction: interstate or international relations, and transnational relations. Since, as noted earlier, nation-states are the predominant form of political and legal organization in the modern world, the first step towards understanding the dynamics of global politics brings into focus the interactions and relations between sovereign nation-states, or more simply put *international relations*. In effect, since nation-states are taken to be synonymous with the governments or regimes which rule them, international relations are conventionally understood as the official relationships and diplomatic interactions between national governments, including relations between governments and intergovernmental organizations such as the United Nations. This is the domain of foreign and defence policy and the preserve of foreign ministries and diplomats. It is also a domain which is inherently political because it involves the exercise of influence, power and force by governments in the pursuit of their own national interests. *International politics* can therefore simply be defined in terms of conflict and cooperation between sovereign nation-states. This definition clearly embraces international organizations in so far as these have become the new arenas within which governments bargain and negotiate with one another (see figure 1.2).

The contemporary world order is historically unique because there now exists a truly global interstate system. In the post-war period, the nation-state has become the dominant form of political organization at the world level. One of the consequences of this globalization of the nation-state form has been the creation, as Bull suggests, of a global political system:

> What is chiefly responsible for the degree of interaction among political systems in all continents of the world, sufficient to make it possible for us to speak of a world political system, has been the expansion of the European states system all over the globe, and its transformation into a states system of global dimension.
> (1977, pp. 20–1)

Bull's argument is that the emergence of a global states system, replacing a bifurcated system of states and colonies, has exposed in a very tangible form the ways in which the actions or decisions taken by one government can easily intrude upon the interests and policies pursued by other governments. As a consequence, relationships and issues can be instantly politicized and opposing political coalitions of states readily mobilized. A global states system inevitably entails a high degree of sensitivity among its constituent units to the actions of each other, a situation which Morse (1976) has referred to as strategic interdependence (as opposed to economic, technological or other forms of interdependence). An interesting illustration of this kind of primitive politics amongst states, which exposes the strategic interdependencies between governments, is the case of international economic sanctions against South Africa.

In the mid 1980s the international controversy about how the world community should deal with apartheid in South Africa reached a critical watershed. A significant majority of states within the United Nations desired the imposition of international economic sanctions, whilst many of the more powerful Western states opposed such

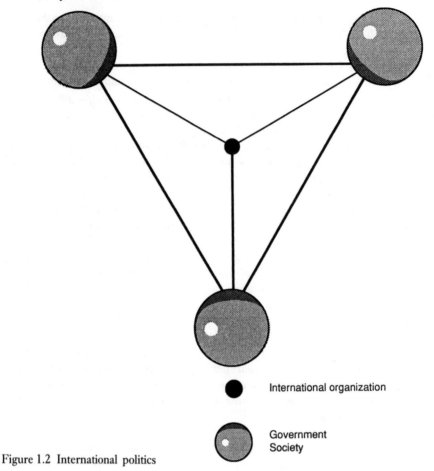

Figure 1.2 International politics

action. Using bilateral and multilateral diplomacy within many different international forums, such as the UN, the EC and the Commonwealth, black African states, together with their supporters, put international sanctions on the global diplomatic agenda. Those governments pressing for international sanctions recognized that without coordinated international action their own policy objectives could never be achieved. Despite the opposition of the United States and the UK governments, vigilant and concerted political action brought limited success with a combination of nationally imposed and internationally agreed economic sanctions against the Pretoria government. By the early 1990s, with the beginnings of the abandonment of apartheid in South Africa, the debate on sanctions had been transformed into the issue of whether or not they should be sustained. This new debate was as acrimonious as the original controversy over the imposition of sanctions, although the politics were decidedly more complicated. Both cases are instructive examples, not only of politics between states, but also of strategic interdependence between states in a global states system. Moreover, the sanctions issue vividly illustrates the interconnections between the domestic (apartheid) and the global (sanctions diplomacy), a connection which Bull's remarks suggest is itself a product of the globalization of the states system. Finally, the sanctions issue is also revealing because it cannot be fully understood or explained without reference to transnational relations – the other strand of political activity encompassed within the global layer in Modelski's layer cake model.

Transnational relations describe those networks, associations or interactions which cut across national societies, creating linkages between individuals, groups, organizations and communities within different nation-states. A distinguishing feature of transnational relations is that in effect they bypass governments because they operate within the societal domain and beyond direct state control (see figure 1.3). It is no longer simply the case that only governments interact with one another at the international level; the revolution in transport and communications technologies supports a staggering array of transnational activity. Modern societies display an incredible permeability to trans-national forces, as evidenced in the massive flows of goods, ideas, knowledge, people, capital, services, crime, cultural tastes, values, fashions, social movements and even social problems, which cut across or fail to respect national territorial boundaries. Where such transnational interaction or activity has deliberate or unintended political consequences it is normally described as transnational politics. Indeed, *transnational politics* refers to all those relationships, associations, networks, interactions and organiza-tions which cut across national societies and which intervene deliberately or uninten-tionally in domestic and international political processes (see figure 1.3). The global environmental movement, exemplified by Greenpeace, comes to mind here as a signifi-cant transnational force in contemporary politics both domestically and internationally.

Whilst many transnational networks and relationships operate in a rather informal or unofficial manner, many others are institutionalized. It is possible to identify a vast array of transnational organizations operating simultaneously across and within many nation-states (see figure 1.4). *Transnational organizations* are non-governmental bodies operating 'across national boundaries, sometimes on a global scale, which seek as far as possible to disregard these boundaries, and which serve to establish links between different national societies, or sections of those societies' (Bull 1977, p. 270). Good examples of transnational organizations are multinational or transnational corporations, such as General Motors, Ford, IBM, Lonrho, ICI, Nestlé, Unilever or Shell, which

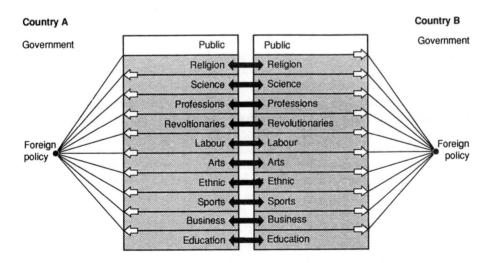

Figure 1.3 Transnational politics

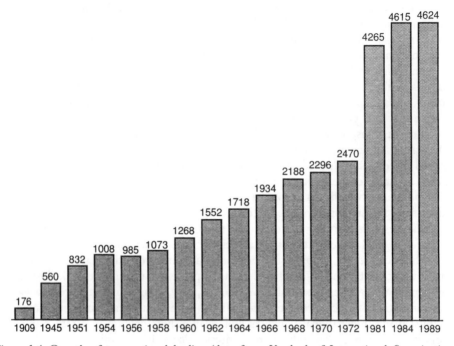

Figure 1.4 Growth of transnational bodies (data from *Yearbook of International Organizations*, 19th edn, 1981)

conduct their operations in many states and organize production on a transnational basis. Besides corporations, there are also a whole host of other types of transnational organizations: political bodies, such as the Inter-Parliamentary Union which links members of national legislatures across the world; environmental pressure groups, such as Greenpeace and Friends of the Earth; professional associations, such as the International Political Science Association and the International Chamber of Commerce; trade unions, such as the International Confederation of Trade Unions; religious bodies, such as the World Council of Churches, the Catholic Church, the World Muslim Congress and the International Council of Jewish Women; sports organizations, like the International Olympic Committee and UEFA; welfare organizations, such as the International Red Cross, Cafod and Oxfam; and scientific bodies, such as the International Association on Water Pollution Research and the International Union of Nutritional Sciences. Throughout the post-war period, there has been an exponential growth in the number of transnational bodies. As figure 1.4 illustrates, since 1958 alone their number has increased at least fourfold. They also cover, as table 1.1 shows, every single aspect of social life. Despite this phenomenal growth, they tend towards a certain geographical and functional concentration. As tables 1.2 and 1.3 indicate, the Western developed states are the home of many of these bodies, even though their activities may be global in scope.

Alongside transnational relations, there exists also the phenomenon of transgovernmental relations. *Transgovernmental relations* refers to those networks of direct contacts between departments within different national governments that are not under complete central control (see figure 1.5). For example, direct contacts exist between the environ-

Table 1.1 Transnational organizations by sector
of activity

Bibliography, press, documentation	72
Religion, morality	112
Social sciences	10
International relations	144
Politics	27
Law, administration	58
Social aid	104
Employers' organizations	119
Trade unions	70
Economy, finance	47
Commerce, industry	251
Agriculture	88
Travel	89
Technology	133
Science	184
Health, medicine	256
Education, youth	116
Arts, literature, radio	89
Sports, leisure	110
Occupational groups and commerce in the EC and EFTA	283
Total	2,456

Source: *Yearbook of International Organizations*, 15th
edn, 1974

mental agencies of national governments, between the central banks and between the education departments. The complexity of modern government sometimes requires officials from government bureaucracies to be in frequent contact with their opposite numbers in other foreign governments in order to acquire information, coordinate responses to common policy problems, or harmonize national policies where this has been agreed at a higher political level. The British Treasury and the Bank of England, for instance, are in constant contact with their opposite numbers in other Western industrialized states in order to maintain stability in the currency markets and alert each other to official changes in interest rates, exchange rates etc. These functional bonds between officials are facilitated by the phenomenal expansion in the number and coverage of international governmental organizations (IGOs) (see figure 1.6). IGOs provide forums within which bureaucratic contacts and networks are cultivated and strengthened. Thus, for instance, the finance ministers of all the major Western industrial states meet at least twice a year under the auspices of the International Monetary Fund and the World Bank to discuss and agree on cooperative action on common policy problems. Governments in reality do not appear as coherent, monolithic actors on the world stage, but rather more frequently as incoherent associations of bureaucratic agencies pursuing their own conceptions of the national interest in concert with their opposite numbers abroad.

Table 1.2 Countries represented in over 1000 transnational organizations

France	1,898
West Germany	1,820
UK	1,796
Belgium	1,739
Italy	1,734
Netherlands	1,706
Switzerland	1,554
Denmark	1,467
Sweden	1,449
Spain	1,410
USA	1,366
Austria	1,360
Norway	1,283
Finland	1,256
Canada	1,219
Japan	1,111
Australia	1,062
Total	25,230

Source: *Yearbook of International Organizations*, 19th edn, 1981

Of course, the strength of these transgovernmental networks can vary from policy sector to policy sector, and from issue to issue. On some occasions, professional and functional bonds can override the central organs of national foreign policy. During the 1982 Falklands War, for instance, the Pentagon provided direct assistance to the UK Ministry of Defence and the British armed forces, even though this contravened official State Department policy, and was without the endorsement of the British War Cabinet or the US President. Transgovernmental networks also facilitate the emergence of *transgovernmental coalitions* on policy issues, in which the common interests of ministers or officials from different national governments lead to mutual support in their respective bureaucratic struggles over policy. According to one study of British foreign policy:

> Foreign governments intervene in Whitehall discussions, supporting some ministers or departments, combating the arguments of others. Coalitions of interest occasionally cut across the formal barriers of national sovereignty and evade the apparatus of central coordination; the common interest of finance or of defence ministers and their subordinate officials has often proved strong enough to support intervention in each other's domestic discussions.
>
> (Wallace 1977, p. 270)

We have now sketched in the salient features of the global layer in Modelski's layer cake model. Trying to assemble these features into a meaningful pattern or picture is not easy, but there is one striking image which can capture the complexity we are seeking to portray: the image of a cobweb (Burton 1972). As we have described it, the

Table 1.3 Congresses held by transnational organizations, 1976

By continent	
Europe	2,327
America	791
Asia	360
Africa	146
Australasia	75
	3,699
By country	
USA	467
France	384
UK	349
Switzerland	218
West Germany	170
Belgium	169
Canada	140
Austria	138
Netherlands	85

Source: *Transnational Associations*, Brussels, February 1978

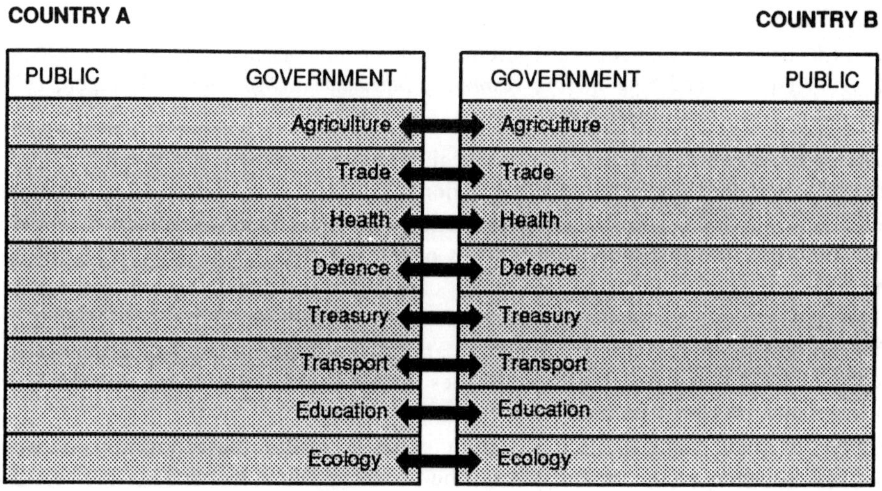

COUNTRY A   **COUNTRY B**

PUBLIC	GOVERNMENT	GOVERNMENT	PUBLIC
	Agriculture ⬌	Agriculture	
	Trade ⬌	Trade	
	Health ⬌	Health	
	Defence ⬌	Defence	
	Treasury ⬌	Treasury	
	Transport ⬌	Transport	
	Education ⬌	Education	
	Ecology ⬌	Ecology	

Figure 1.5 Transgovernmental relations

Number of IGOs

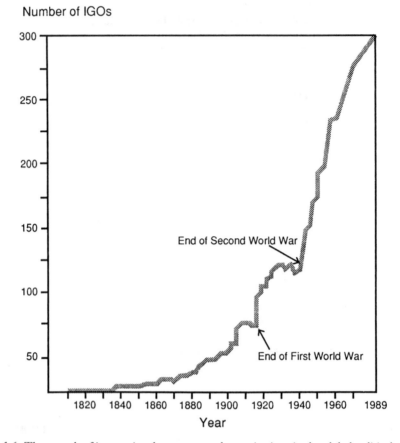

Figure 1.6 The growth of international governmental organizations in the global political system, 1815–1989 (Wallace and Singer 1970; *Yearbook of International Organizations*, 15th edn, 1974)

global layer encompasses not just political relations between states, and relations between states and international organizations, but also a vast array of transnational interactions which cut across national societies, as well as transgovernmental relations which permeate the institutional structures of the state itself. One way to picture the incredible variety of political activity which constitutes the global layer is as a cobweb of interactions and relations which cut across national boundaries and which are superimposed upon the already complex pattern of global interaction between states (see figure 1.7). This cobweb image provides three valuable insights into the dominant characteristics of global politics.

Firstly, in highlighting the richness and complexity of the interconnections between states and societies in the global system, the image makes more tangible the fact that developments or decisions in one part of the globe can come to have significant reverberations elsewhere. A particularly good illustration of this is the way in which Iraq's invasion of Kuwait in 1990 created short-term instabilities in world oil and financial markets which in turn had serious economic and welfare consequences for many countries but especially the world's poorest nations.

Secondly, the image of a cobweb, with no single focal point around which relations

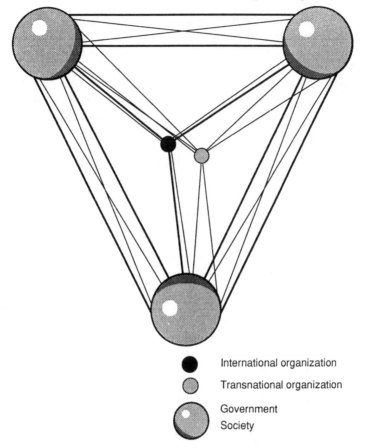

International organization
Transnational organization
Government
Society

Figure 1.7 The cobweb image of global politics

and interactions revolve, well describes the decentred character of global politics. This process of decentring has been articulated in a number of domains:

1 With the demise of the Cold War and the relative decline of both the US and the Soviet Union, the superpower era is coming to a close. Accordingly the notion that there are only two centres of power which count in global politics, namely Washington and Moscow, no longer rings true. New concentrations of power, such as Germany and Japan, are emerging and represent a transformation in the global power structure. This, together with the increasing importance of economic and industrial power, is beginning to erode the conventional conception of international politics as an activity centred around or contingent upon the actions of the two superpowers.
2 Although governments remain powerful actors in the global system, they share the stage with a vast array of other agencies and organizations. Above the state there stand quasi-supranational institutions like the EC, whilst alongside it there exist an enormous number of intergovernmental organizations, agencies and regimes which operate at the global level. Moreover, non-state actors such as multinational corporations, transnational pressure groups and transnational professional associations participate intensively in global politics. Below the state too the activities of a

considerable range of subnational actors, such as city governments, local authorities, national political parties and national pressure groups, can spill over into the international arena. Accordingly the global arena is best described as a mixed-actor system. This implies that states should no longer be conceived as the primary or dominant actors at the global level. Such a conclusion directly challenges the conventional characterization of the global political system as essentially state-centric.

3 Technological changes combined with economic and political developments have thrust a whole new set of problems on to the global agenda. Pollution, drugs, space, human rights and terrorism are amongst an increasing number of transnational policy issues which cut across existing global political alignments and which demand international cooperation.

Thirdly and finally, the cobweb image underlines the permeability of the nation-state to external influences. In doing so it challenges the traditionally held distinction between the domestic and the international, since developments abroad may be inserted into the domestic political process whilst, alternatively, even local actions may come to have significant repercussions abroad.

To illustrate these three points and the heuristic value of the cobweb image, we shall return to the case of economic sanctions against South Africa. It has been noted already that the imposition and maintenance of international economic sanctions against Pretoria in the 1980s and early 1990s deliver a striking example of how a primarily domestic matter, namely apartheid, has become a significant global political issue. Indeed it provides unambiguous evidence of how any attempt to separate politics within states from politics between states is nowadays fraught with such conceptual difficulty. But equally as important, it demonstrates the significant role of transnational networks, organizations and forces in global politics.

Throughout the early 1980s, the Anti-Apartheid Movement in Britain and the anti-apartheid lobby in the US (which is a coalition of organized interests) sought to undermine, both domestically and in international forums, their own governments' official opposition to sanctions. This was done by forcing sanctions on to the domestic political agenda, raising public consciousness about Western corporate investment in South Africa, and supporting those pressing for sanctions in Congress, Parliament and within international forums, such as the Commonwealth, the UN and the European Parliament. In addition, Western anti-apartheid organizations were assisted and supported in their efforts by black South African anti-apartheid organizations, such as the ANC. Equally, the strong transnational connections between the established churches in South Africa and their 'sisters' abroad provided a further channel for influencing public opinion and the policies of foreign governments. Church leaders, like Archbishop Desmond Tutu, became significant players at the global level. Transnational corporations and banks too were implicated in the politics of sanctions and could not remain neutral, with the consequence that a number of major US corporations, such as Ford, took the opportunity to divest themselves of their South African subsidiaries, whilst others introduced non-discriminatory policies in an effort to look clean at home. And the media, despite the imposition of reporting restrictions by the South African government, continued to fuel the global awareness of political developments in the country and the internal divisions concerning the Western threat to impose economic sanctions.

The politics of economic sanctions thus does not fit neatly into any preconceived categories of international or domestic politics. Rather, it cuts across these conventional distinctions. Moreover, it is not an issue on which states were the only, or the dominant, political actors. On the contrary, it involved domestic pressure groups with transnational ties, transnational banks, churches, church leaders, transnational corporations and the media, as well as international organizations such as the UN, the Commonwealth and the EC. Even within governments, there were major policy differences between different arms of the state, as well as between different departments of government. All this underlines the importance of a global perspective in attempting to describe the complex politics of economic sanctions against South Africa. But the unwillingness of the key actors, namely the US and the UK governments, to adopt economic sanctions, despite the overwhelming and united global pressure for them to do so, raises the fascinating issue of the relationship between power and politics in the global arena.

Although our short diversion into the global politics of apartheid illustrates vividly the global side of the global politics equation, it provokes an equal fascination with the politics side of the equation. Like the TV advert which poses the question 'Who put the T in Typhoo?', we need here to ask: what form does the 'politics' in 'global politics' actually take? Is it somehow different in kind or nature from politics at the neighbourhood, local and national levels with which we are all familiar? Does it distinguish itself purely by its defiance of territorial boundaries, or is it somehow qualitatively and historically different from our traditional understanding of what politics is about?

As one might expect, the answers to these difficult questions are contingent upon the theoretical framework of enquiry which one adopts. There is no universally accepted definition of politics, since it is both a highly contested concept and one which is conditioned by normative considerations, i.e. questions of value, or what should be as opposed to what is the case. Throughout this volume we therefore offer three distinctive, but by no means mutually conflicting, paradigms or traditions of enquiry as modes of interpreting and explaining the substance of global politics. These three paradigms, which in the academic literature are often referred to as realism, liberal-pluralism and neo-Marxism, have deep intellectual roots in the three major strands of modern (as opposed to classical) political theory: conservatism, liberalism, and Marxism. Indeed, since they represent different traditions in the study of politics, it seems perfectly natural to exploit them as we attempt to map the relatively new terrain of global politics.

Realism starts from the assumption, to paraphrase its now deceased but leading exponent, Hans Morgenthau, that politics is conceived as interest defined in terms of power. With power comes the ability of the state to protect and promote its national interest, and if necessary to impose its will on others. For realists, national power is particularly crucial to the defence of national interests since, in a world which is constituted by sovereign nation-states, no single state can rely on any others to promote its interest. The global states system is consequently one in which self-help dominates, because there is no body above the state to ensure its interests are defended, or even to guarantee its survival or existence. In realist terms then, the politics in global politics can be viewed essentially as a struggle between states to protect and defend the national interest in the global system. This may involve bilateral and multilateral diplomacy, processes of negotiation and bargaining, as well as the use of military force, and it is this latter fact that for realists distinguishes global politics from all other forms of politics. For the use of force by the state to protect its core interests is an insti-tutionalized feature of the global states system. The political element in global politics thus revolves around the exercise of power by states to promote and defend their national interest in the global arena.

Returning to our discussion of sanctions against South Africa, a realist analysis would highlight that the real politics concerned the conflict between states, underwritten by their very different national interests. Although realists would accept that there were many players, other than governments, trying to shape international policy on this issue, they would argue that only the states were the significant players, since only the states involved had any effective power to determine the political outcome. What for the realist is therefore political about the global activity which surrounds the issue of international sanctions against South Africa is that it involves conflict and cooperation between governments, each pursuing its own national interests. *Global politics thus concerns conflict and cooperation between sovereign states, in which national power is a crucial variable.*

A rather different interpretation of this same case would be given from within the *liberal-pluralist* paradigm. Politics in this paradigm is centrally about authoritative decision making or 'who gets what and why', so that few distinctions are made between local, national and global politics. Although the global system lacks any form of world government, liberal-pluralists would argue that the increasing degree of interconnection between societies has led to the creation of a vast array of international organizations and international arrangements for managing the consequences of high levels of interdependence. Global politics, like national politics, is thus conceived essentially as pressure group politics. The political world is conceived as a complicated patchwork of issue areas or policy sectors, such as trade relations, monetary relations, North–South relations, human rights etc., within which there are a multiplicity of groups (states, bureaucratic fragments of states, transnational corporations, transnational organizations, international organizations, individuals etc.) attempting to influence the direction of international policy outcomes. Since, in this view, power is fragmented amongst a plethora of states, transnational organizations, international bureaucracies, national pressure groups, transnational corporations etc., politics involves a process of bargaining, mutual adjustment of interests, and the making of authoritative decisions legitimized largely through an acceptance of consensual modes of decision taking. *Global politics is thus cast in terms of pressure group activity and authoritative decision making within a pluralistic (polyarchical) global system.*

This liberal-pluralist conception of the political would find in our chosen case of economic sanctions an almost perfect illustration of global politics. For, as we have noted previously, here is a global issue which involved an enormous variety of governmental and non-governmental, national and transnational organizations, each attempting to influence the outcome of international policy making on the sanctions issue and the subsequent implementation of any policy. The global politics of sanctions is thus the politics of pressure and influence amongst the complex array of participants in the global policy process on this specific issue.

Finally, we conclude this exploration of the political by reviewing the *neo-Marxist* conception of global politics. Whilst neo-Marxists would not discount the existence at the global level of a plethora of actors other than the state, what they would regard as quintessentially political about global politics is rather different from that suggested by the other two paradigms. For the neo-Marxist paradigm stresses the underlying conflicts and contradictions between the global economic order, in which capitalism is increasingly organized on a transnational basis, and the political order which is still organized (vertically) into a myriad of nation-states. Global politics is thus conceived as a product of global economic forces, which generate conflict and contradictions between national and transnational capital, between national and emerging transnational class forces, and between states and emerging supranational state structures. It is concerned with the ideological, material and institutional forces by which capital continuously extends the boundaries to, and sustains the legitimacy of, a global economic order which is essentially exploitative of the majority of states and a significant proportion of the world's population. In simple language, *global politics is about how far and in what ways capital has come to rule at the world level*, and in this sense the explanation differs little from neo-Marxist interpretations of local or national politics.

Returning briefly to the case of sanctions, a neo-Marxist interpretation would cut through the surface appearances of conflicting national interests and pressure group activity, given so much credence by the other paradigms, to reveal the real forces determining the political outcomes on this issue. The politics here, it would be argued, reflect the underlying structure of power relationships between the states involved and transnational, as well as national, capital. In this particular case, the interests of capital seem to have prevailed. But neo-Marxists would not consider this was in any sense inevitable. What they would argue is that the states involved operate under the structural *constraints* imposed by the workings of transnational and national capitalism. Within these constraints, each state can act relatively freely, even ignoring the demands of any particular sector of capital. It is the tensions and contradictions resulting from the disjuncture between global capitalism and the existence of a global states system which is, for neo-Marxists, the essence of global politics.

THE ANATOMY OF GLOBAL POLITICS

Attempts to offer a coherent account of the dynamics of global politics risk the twin danger of oversimplification and reification. Yet simply to identify the important features of global politics requires some implicit or explicit conceptual framework of enquiry. This poses a real intellectual dilemma for the student of global politics. One strategy for managing, although by no means resolving, this dilemma is to explicate the theoretical traditions which frame the study of global politics. For pedagogic reasons this is the strategy already adopted here. However, before a more systematic overview of the three traditions introduced above – namely realism, liberal-pluralism and neo-Marxism – is offered, a few important caveats must be voiced.

In the 1980s social science was permeated by a new brand of relativism best described as the doctrine of competing perspectives. Underlying this doctrine was a particular approach to explanation in the social sciences, an approach which emphasized the impossibility of establishing a single valid explanation of social phenomena because of the diversity of theoretical traditions. At its crudest it contributed to the rather formulaic response to the question of explanation: 'It all depends upon the theoretical perspective one uses.' More sophisticated analyses recognized that the existence of competing explanations did not deny the possibility of establishing criteria for judging between them even if such judgements were of a relative nature, i.e. explanation x is better than explanation y. This is a line of reasoning with which the authors in this book have much sympathy. However, in wishing to ensure that the pedagogic approach adopted here (and throughout this book) is not misinterpreted or misconstrued as the cruder version of relativism, some vital points need to be aired. More specifically, the approach adopted here is guided by a particular set of assumptions about the nature of paradigmatic enquiry. These assumptions include:

1 A recognition that the three traditions or theoretical paradigms elaborated in this chapter should not be conceived as hermetically sealed intellectual discourses posed in complete opposition to one another. Rather they are quite open disquisitions, in dialogue and debate with each other. Moreover, in some areas their theoretical concerns and conclusions overlap although their reasoning and basic assumptions may fundamentally differ.
2 An acknowledgement that within each of the three traditions there is a considerable theoretical diversity and even debate between alternative theoretical positions. However, despite such diversity intellectual disagreements within each paradigm operate within a context of shared assumptions about the social world and shared concepts; each paradigm can be said to embrace a distinctive meta-narrative (theoretical storyline).
3 An emphasis upon the dynamic nature of these paradigms and traditions. They are not static theoretical entities but evolve in relation to changing objective conditions in global politics. Moreover, the intellectual dialogue within and between paradigms represents a constant pressure for critical thought and conceptual refinement.
4 An acceptance that realism, liberal-pluralism and neo-Marxism do not exhaust all the potential traditions in the study of global politics. However, they do represent the dominant traditions in Western thinking. In addition these traditions have operated as powerful guides to political praxis in the global arena.
5 A recognition that paradigmatic explanations of global political phenomena can be evaluated according to certain strict criteria.

Accepting that this particular set of assumptions prefigures the pedagogic approach adopted here, the next step demands the unfolding of the paradigms themselves. Each of the paradigms will be reviewed with regard to its characterization of global politics and the presuppositions embedded in its meta-narrative concerning the four critical parameters of the global system: the nature of the *actors*; the nature of the *global political process*; the characterization of the *global political order*; and the characterization of the dominant forms of *global power relations* and *processes of globalization*.

Realism and Neo-realism

Realism asserts the primacy of the state in global politics. Although realism acknowledges the existence of other actors in the global system, such as international organizations, multinational corporations and individuals, it posits that states are the dominant actors. The reason for this is simply that realists attach great importance to sovereignty: the ultimate legal authority which a state exercises over a defined territory and the people within it. There is thus no authority above the state, no equivalent of domestic government, which can require states to act in certain ways. Even international organizations are regarded as subservient to states, since they are creatures of states. All other actors in the global system too, realists argue, must either work through states or influence state policy if their interests are to be fulfilled. For realists, the global system is a global states system.

If states are the dominant actors, realists would argue that the political process at the global level involves competition, conflict and cooperation between the representatives of states. With no overarching authority in the global system, a situation of anarchy exists in which states must acquire power to defend and protect their vital interests. Politics between states thus takes on the requirements of a struggle for power. But this does not mean that war and conflict are necessarily the only means through which states can pursue their interests. On the contrary, realists emphasize that, through diplomacy and negotiation, states cooperate to achieve common ends.

Although they stress the absence of government in the global system, realists nonetheless argue that political order is maintained through various mechanisms. The struggle for power does not lead to all-out conflict, since peace and stability is established through the mechanisms of global and local balances of power. In addition, *neo-realism*, which has emerged recently as an attempt to update classical realism, gives particular weight to the role of hegemonic powers (dominant powers such as the United States or the Soviet Union) in establishing and maintaining order in the global system. For instance, both superpowers attempt to police their own spheres of influence and to control their subordinates' actions where these threaten to undermine global peace and security. And, in the post-war period, the US, as the world's hegemonic economic power, established (as we noted earlier) the basic framework of international economic order which has to this day shaped the conduct of global economic relations. Neorealism stresses the significance of the structure of power in the global system in shaping the character of the political order which exists. Thus, a world of only two great powers has a more stable political order than a world in which there are three or more powers, since the Soviets and the Americans are in no doubt as to whom to defend themselves against. The structure of power is thus important to the durability of the global political order.

Furthermore, states have institutionalized cooperative relations, where the national interest dictates, through the creation of a vast array of international organizations. It is therefore possible, most realists would suggest, to conceive of the global states system as very much a society of states. It is a society because, as Bull (1977) argues, there are agreed rules, principles, norms, laws, mechanisms and institutions for creating and maintaining order amongst its members.

Finally, realism places great stress upon the significance of military power in shaping global politics. Since there is no overarching authority in the global system, states are reliant upon their own resources to ensure their security and survival. In the end, military power becomes the essential ingredient of state power, since without it states cannot defend their own core interests. The acquisition and the exercise of military and coercive power are thus essential ingredients of the realist interpretation of global politics. Similarly, in terms of the dominant processes of globalization, realists stress the significance of the competition and struggle for power between all states as being a crucial factor in creating a more politically interdependent world. In particular, the emergence of global rivalry between the superpowers has transformed the world into one unified strategic arena in which political developments everywhere are interpreted by the superpowers and their allies in terms of how they may affect the global balance of power. Politics everywhere thus takes on a global dimension.

Liberal-Pluralism

A rather different conception of global politics is proffered from within the liberal-pluralist paradigm. Although not as coherent a body of theory as realism and neo-realism, liberal-pluralism starts from the assumption that the state is no longer the primary actor on the world stage. Rather, the growth of transnational relations points to the significance of non-state actors, such as multinational corporations, and a myriad of other transnational associations. Alongside these actors, liberal-pluralism also stresses the importance of international organizations which are considered actors in their own right and not simply creatures of states. Indeed, the state itself is conceived as a rather fragmented entity, constituted by an array of bureaucratic organizations and institutions, each of which has the potential to become a player in the global political process. As a consequence, liberal-pluralists often describe the global system as a polyarchical, mixed-actor or complex conglomerate system to denote the incredible variety of actors.

Rather than viewing the global political process as one which only embraces states, liberal-pluralists argue that it involves processes of bargaining and the exertion of influence amongst a variety of actors, each pursuing its own interests. The global system is viewed as an agglomeration of different issue areas or policy sectors, such as trade, finance, energy and human rights, in which domestic and international policy processes, because of growing interdependence, merge into one another. The political process is therefore largely concerned with the management of global interdependencies, and takes the form of bargaining, negotiation and consensual decision making amongst the participants in each issue area.

For liberal-pluralists, order is maintained in the global system not through states or the balance of power. Rather, as in domestic society, order is maintained through commonly accepted values, a recognition of a high degree of interdependence between national societies, and the existence of accepted rules and norms of behaviour, as well as institutions or processes of governance. Great significance is attached to the existence of the vast array of international organizations and regimes which govern every single sector of global activity, from military relations to monetary relations. Order is thus achieved and maintained through a complex web of criss-crossing governing arrangements which bind states and societies together.

Finally, liberal-pluralism identifies technological and economic forces as the most important harbingers of global interdependence. Technology, particularly the revolution in communications and transport technologies, is regarded as being responsible for the growing insignificance of territorial boundaries. Linkages and channels of communication between societies have now become so extensive that every state is penetrated by external forces and pressures. Also, the emergence of a world-wide system of production and exchange has enmeshed all states in webs of complex interdependence over which individual national governments can exert little control. For liberal-pluralists, therefore, economic forces and technological forces are regarded as primarily responsible for bringing about increasingly higher levels of global political interdependence. Not surprisingly, they also identify economic and technological power as the most crucial forms of power in the global system.

Neo-Marxism

Whilst neo-Marxism, as an explanation of global politics, shares some common ground with realism and liberal-pluralism, it also has many quite significant points of divergence. Whereas classical Marxism conceived of capitalism largely in terms of separate national capitalisms, which had to engage in foreign trade and investment (colonialism and imperialism) in order to overcome their own internal contradictions, neo-Marxist theorists have come to view the world in terms of a global capitalist system. Moreover, neo-Marxists consider that the structure of this global capitalist system imposes its own constraints upon the behaviour of all the key actors in the global system: states, classes, international economic organizations and transnational corporations. But unlike realism, which considers that the state acts in the national interest, neo-Marxism considers that states and international organizations are largely the expressions of dominant class interests at the world level. This does not mean that states, or bureaucratic fragments of states, or international organizations cannot operate independently of dominant class interests, but rather that they are subject to strong structural requirements to ensure that the long-term interests of transnational capitalism are met, i.e. sustaining a hospitable environment for global capital accumulation and expansion. But these structural requirements have to be balanced against the need of states and international organizations to be seen to be acting in the national or international interest. Neo-Marxist analyses of global politics (unlike classical Marxist theories) therefore stress the scope for states and international economic institutions to act relatively autonomously from the demands of capital, whether national or transnational.

Neo-Marxists conceive of global politics as constrained by the needs of transnational capitalism, with the consequence that the dominant *political processes* at the global level are viewed essentially as expressions of underlying class conflicts on a world scale. Obviously the situation is far more complex than this, and most neo-Marxists would accept that conflicts and tensions between national and transnational capital also shape the political process. Moreover, they also share with liberal-pluralists a recognition of the importance of international organizations and regimes, and thus of the processes of collective decision making which they embody. However, the difference is that these governing arrangements are considered by neo-Marxists to reflect the requirements of transnational corporate capitalism. This brings us directly to the question of the global order.

Like their neo-realist and liberal-pluralist counterparts, neo-Marxists also share the belief that the global system is highly ordered. But, unlike neo-realists, they do not conceive of that order as based upon the structure of military power; nor do they accept that it is sustained by webs of interdependence as do liberal-pluralists. Rather, neo-Marxist analyses assert that the prevailing world order is a capitalist order based upon a global structure of production and exchange established by transnational corporations. One of the dominant characteristics of this order is the structural differentiation of the world into core, peripheral and semi-peripheral centres of economic power: in simple terms, the division between North, South and the Eastern bloc. This structure is mirrored internally within states in the polarization between those sectors of national society integrated into the transnational capitalist system and those sectors which are marginalized. Thus, the expansion of transnational capitalism contributes directly to the combined processes of global integration and national disintegration.

Global order is maintained through the hegemonic capitalist state, international state agencies, transnational corporations, international regimes and international networks, and is legitimized through the global diffusion of a dominant ideology of liberalism and Western-type modernization.

Finally, it will come as little surprise to learn that, in explaining the regularities and patterns in global politics, neo-Marxist interpretations give primacy to economic determinants. In particular, such interpretations stress the significance of economic power in accounting for global politics. Similarly, they identify the global spread of capitalism and the ideology of modernization as the primary processes of globalization.

Although each of the paradigms has been described here in a somewhat impressionistic manner, nonetheless it should be evident that each delivers a quite distinct account of global politics (see table 1.4). But even these accounts have to be supplemented by an appreciation of the dominant processes of globalization which nurture global politics.

Table 1.4 A summary of the three paradigms

	Realism and neo-realism	*Liberal-pluralism*	*Neo-Marxism*
Dominant actors	States	Mixed-actor system, e.g. states, corporations, international organizations	States, classes, transnational corporations International economic organizations
Political process	Competition, conflict, bargaining, negotiation and diplomacy between states	Polyarchy, issue areas, global policy processes, and consensual and authoritative decision making	Class conflict mediated through states Conflict between national and transnational capital
Global order	Balance of power Hegemonic powers Structure of power Society of states	Global management International organization and regimes	Global structure of production and exchange Rule of capital
Dominant forms of power and processes of globalization	Military power Struggle for hegemony between great powers	Technological and economic progress Technological and economic power	Economic power and ideological power Transnational capitalism Capitalist modernization

PROCESSES OF GLOBALIZATION

To talk of global politics is to assert that there are processes of globalization at work which in some way contribute to the globalization of political activity. Globalization refers to the multiplicity of linkages and interconnections between the states and societies which make up the modern world system. It describes the process by which events, decisions, and activities in one part of the world can come to have significant consequences for individuals and communities in quite distant parts of the globe. Globalization has two distinct dimensions: scope (or stretching) and intensity (or deepening). On the one hand it defines a set of processes which embrace most of the globe or which operate world-wide; the concept therefore has a spatial connotation. Politics and other social activities are becoming stretched across the globe. On the other hand it also implies an intensification in the levels of interaction, interconnectedness or interdependence between the states and societies which constitute the world community. Accordingly, alongside the stretching goes a deepening of global processes.

Far from being an abstract concept, globalization articulates one of the more familiar features of modern existence. As noted earlier, a moment's reflection on the contents of our own kitchen cupboards or fridges would underline the fact that, simply as passive consumers, we are very much part of a global network of production and exchange. But of course globalization does not mean that the world is becoming more politically united, economically interdependent or culturally homogeneous. Globalization is highly uneven in its scope and highly differentiated in its consequences. For example, urban life in the capital cities of most Latin American countries is perhaps much more deeply implicated in global processes than, for instance, is rural life in the Orkneys or the Shetland Islands. Moreover, far from being a completely novel or primarily twentieth-century phenomenon, a globalizing imperative has been evident in many previous periods of history, and is perhaps most powerfully visible in nineteenth-century imperialism (see chapter 13).

It would also be inaccurate to conceive of globalization as some kind of teleological process or set of processes. The idea that globalization incorporates some predetermined historical logic which is leading inexorably either to the creation of a world society or to some form of world government is simply not tenable. The historical evidence is ranged against it. For globalization stimulates forces of opposition which may just as readily lead to an increasingly fragmented world, since greater mutual awareness and interconnections between different societies may simply sow the seeds of conflict and tension. As Bull observes: 'awareness of other societies, even where it is "perfect", does not merely help to remove imagined conflicts of interest and ideology that do not exist; it also reveals conflicts of interest and ideology that do exist' (1977, p. 280). In many respects globalization can be conceived as a dialectical process (or set of interlinked processes) which is also highly uneven and highly differentiated in its impact across different societies and within different policy domains. Globalization should be construed neither as a historically unique process nor as the harbinger of a world society.

In any review of the literature on globalization, a number of key processes recur in discussions of the apparent intensification of global interdependence in the post-war epoch. These can be distilled into four fundamental processes of globalization, characterized respectively as: great power competition; technological innovation and its diffusion; the internationalization of production and exchange; and modernization, or as Giddens more accurately labels it, the 'dynamism of modernity' (1990, p. 16). But in what sense are these fundamental processes of globalization? How do they connect to the globalization of politics? And how does each condition the nature and dynamics of global politics? Such questions can only be answered by exploring a little more deeply each of these four globalizing forces.

Superpower Rivalry

One of the dominant realities of the twentieth century has been the competition between the great powers of the day for global hegemony. The two world wars were hegemonic conflicts with the combatants vying for political and military dominance. But in the post-1945 epoch the struggle for hegemony was expressed as a Cold War between two rivals whose power capabilities completely outweighed those of any other states or even coalition of states. Superpower rivalry imposed its own logic on global politics for, as Waltz observed,

> In a bipolar world there are no peripheries. With only two powers capable of acting on a world scale, anything that happens anywhere is potentially of concern to both of them. Bipolarity extends the geographic scope of both powers' concern. It also brackets the range of factors included in the competition between them.
>
> (1979, p. 171)

In effect Waltz is suggesting that superpower rivalry transformed the globe into a single strategic arena. In the process, time and space have been collapsed. Superpower rivalry has therefore been one of the most significant factors in the globalization of politics in the post-war period.

Although the intensity of superpower rivalry has varied from the *détente* of the 1960s and 1970s to the Second Cold War of the 1980s, its dynamic has structured the politics between states in the global system as well as politics within states and regions across the globe. Despite its globalization, the impact of superpower rivalry has been unevenly experienced, with some regions and states more deeply implicated in its dynamics than others. Moreover, with the ending of the Cold War in the early 1990s it might be argued that superpower rivalry will no longer remain a significant globalizing tendency in the world system. But this is to ignore the critical importance of the unassailable military supremacy of the United States and the Soviet Union, a position which will continue to sustain their interest and involvement in developments around the globe. Additionally the prospect of some kind of superpower condominium cannot be ignored. But even if a more multipolar global system emerges in the 1990s, this will not negate the continuing significance of great power rivalry, whatever form it may take, as a globalizing process. To deny this is to confuse the ending of superpower rivalry – the Cold War – with the ending of great power rivalry *per se* as a characteristic feature of the future international system.

Technological Innovation and its Diffusion

Since the turn of the century, the revolution in communications and transport technologies has shrunk the globe. Time and space have been compressed, with the result that politics now takes place in a 'global city'. Technological innovation and its diffusion is therefore considered one of the most powerful engines of globalization in the twentieth century. In the military arena it has created a truly global battlefield and a truly global military order in which the most advanced states set the technological standards for all other states. But it is not only military technology which has global ramifications. Civil technologies have thrust new issues on to the global agenda, problems which demand global management or at least global regulation. Pollution, as the problems of acid rain and the ozone layer demonstrate, is a technologically induced transborder matter which cannot always be resolved by national action; exploitation of the airwaves too requires some form of global regulation, since without it international communications would be well-nigh impossible. Moreover, the diffusion of technologies and technological know-how creates new levels of interconnectedness between societies and communities. It also transforms the nature of societies, propelling them along similar but far from identical trajectories of modernity. Indeed, the process of techno-logical innovation has the appearance of operating as a quasi-autonomous force beyond the confident control of political authorities and social institutions. Accordingly, tech-nology is regarded as one of the decisive agents of globalization.

The Internationalization of Production and Exchange

As the global stock market crash of 1987 illustrated, national economies can no longer be insulated from the instabilities and vagaries of the global market-place. In the post-1945 period the process of global economic integration appears to have accelerated such that it has become possible, particularly since the collapse of socialist economies, to argue that there now truly exists a single world capitalist economy. With production and finance organized on a transnational basis and a constantly evolving international division of labour, strategies of national economic management appear to be under increasing strain. Governments have therefore recognized the importance of inter-national and regional structures of economic management as mechanisms for securing domestic prosperity in a more interconnected global economic system. But the process of global economic integration is also extremely uneven in its scope and is juxtaposed with powerful disintegrative tendencies arising from competitive pressures, conflicts over resources, and moves towards regional trading blocs within the global system. Despite this, the globalization of economic and industrial activity remains a critical determinant of the globalization of politics.

Modernization

Modernization is a deeply problematic concept. On the one hand it is largely discredited because of its association with notions of convergence, i.e. that 'progress' is good and is synonymous with the Western capitalist lifestyle. On the other hand it is a useful umbrella label for the interrelated processes of economic, industrial, technological, social, cultural and political development which define the transition from traditional to modern societies. It also captures the notion that becoming modern is very much a global historical process since the effects of modernity are experienced throughout the globe. Modernization is clearly associated with Westernization and the imposition of Western forms of the modern upon societies across the globe. But modernization stimulates powerful reactions and forms of resistance to 'progress' within all societies;

the emergence of the Greens in advanced industrial states and the rise of religious fundamentalism in many Third World states demonstrate this point quite dramatically. Indeed modernization is a source of conflict and tension since it thrusts different cultures and value systems into direct contact with each other. Accordingly modernization does not imply the emergence of some kind of world society in which cultural homogeneity or cosmopolitanism prevails. Rather, because its effects are unevenly experienced throughout the globe and because it promotes resistance wherever it permeates, it is more accurate to conclude that modernization reinforces the tendencies towards both integration and disintegration in the contemporary global system. Despite the limitations of the concept, modernization is a functional expression for those interlinked processes of secular social, political, economic and cultural change (such as industrialization, democratization, bureaucratization and urbanization) whose effects are experienced world-wide, albeit in a highly uneven way. Modernization can thus be considered a significant globalizing tendency in the modern world.

EXPLORING GLOBAL POLITICS

In the chapters which follow, each of these four key processes of globalization will be analysed in a more substantive and critical manner than space has allowed here. This task will involve exploring whether these processes are intensifying or decelerating, as well as how each relates to the globalization of politics in the late twentieth century. But these processes will also structure our exploration of global politics since they define the framework of enquiry adopted in this volume. For parts I to IV map directly on to each of the four key processes of globalization outlined in the previous section.

Part I focuses upon the globalization of superpower rivalry and how it has shaped the globalization of political life. It will examine the rise and decline of the Cold War and the extent to which it was and is central to the globalization of politics. This will be achieved through an examination of the underlying causes of the globalized rivalry between the two superpowers (chapter 2). Complementing this discussion are two further chapters which investigate how far the politics of three quite distinctive regions in the world (South Asia, Southern Africa and Central America) has been (and continues to be) fashioned by the great contest between the United States and the Soviet Union (chapters 3 and 4).

Part II examines the globalizing tendencies of technology in both the civil and the military spheres. It investigates the superpower arms race and its global ramifications, embracing a discussion of the transformation of interstate and domestic politics associated with the military technological revolution in the post-war period (chapter 5). Shifting to civil technologies, it critically analyses the threats posed to state sovereignty and autonomy by the global diffusion and exploitation of modern technologies. In this context chapter 6 discusses the relationship between technological innovation and the creation of a new agenda of global issues, such as pollution, the colonization of space and the exploitation of the oceans, which appear to demand increasingly extensive and intensive forms of international cooperation between states. Chapter 7 examines how the global information technology revolution challenged state autonomy and legitimacy in Eastern Europe, contributing to the region's political transformation in the late 1980s.

Part III concentrates upon the relationship between the dynamics of the world capitalist economy and the dynamics of global politics. It is concerned with the question of how far the globalization of economic relations is responsible for the globalization of political activity. Exploiting a historical perspective, this part provides a succinct overview of the development of the modern global economy from the inter-war period to the present day (chapters 8 and 9). In doing so, particular attention is given to the changing nature of the global economy and the evolution of global structures of economic management. Two further chapters explore how the interdependent character of the modern world economy severely tests the capacity of both advanced industrial states (chapter 10) and Third World countries (chapter 11) to manage their own internal economic affairs. The final chapter in this part contrasts the insights provided by each of the three paradigms into the question of the relationship between the global economy and global politics (chapter 12).

Part IV analyses the interrelationships between modernization, globalization and the future of the nation-state in global politics. It is concerned with the ways in which modernity and reactions against it may be transforming the nature of global politics, and in particular the role and continuing viability of the nation-state in a now highly interconnected global order (chapter 13). Through examinations of human rights (chapter 14) and Islam (chapter 15), evidence is offered of the extent to which modernity fashions a globalization of values and ideologies which transcend the nation-state. The part concludes with a discussion of how processes of globalization are deconstructing and reconstituting the role and authority of the nation-state in the global system (chapter 16). This final chapter embraces an overview of the terrain of contemporary global politics whilst also cautiously identifying a range of alternative future world orders implied by contemporary trends and tendencies.

Slicing through each of these parts in this volume are three overarching themes. These can be conceived as intellectual pathways guiding the student through the complex and unfamiliar cosmos of global politics. The first theme or pathway concerns processes of globalization. Throughout the volume particular attention will be given to the question of whether, in the contemporary epoch, processes of globalization are intensifying, stabilizing or decelerating. This connects with the broader issue of how far such processes are fuelling greater political integration or political fragmentation within the world community. The second theme derives from a fascination with the future of the nation-state in a more interconnected global order. Accordingly each of the parts reflects a concern with the consequences of globalizing processes for the modern nation-state. This is articulated in the question of whether processes of globalization enhance, transform or undermine the power and autonomy of the modern nation-state. Thirdly, and finally, there is the matter of theory and explanation in global politics. The triptych of theoretical traditions introduced in this chapter is deployed throughout the volume, more explicitly in some contributions than others, in an attempt to move beyond empirical description towards generating explanatory accounts of global politics. Such accounts may then be more generally applied to global issues outside the scope of this volume. Accordingly, each part contributes to a progressively deeper appreciation of the realist, liberal-pluralist and neo-Marxist traditions in the study of global politics.

Global politics is a focus for intellectual curiosity because it cuts across the traditional boundaries which separate the study of international politics from the study of domestic politics, comparative politics and political economy. Reinforcing this curiosity is a recognition that globalization (and its consequences) is one of the essential features of modernity (Giddens 1990). To acquire even a limited knowledge of global politics is therefore to obtain some understanding of the powerful forces which define the conditions of human existence in the late twentieth century.

References

Bull, H. (1977) *The Anarchical Society*. London: Macmillan.
Burton, J. (1972) *World Society*. Cambridge: Cambridge University Press.
Giddens, A. (1990) *The Consequences of Modernity*. Cambridge: Polity Press.
Hertz, S. (1969) The territorial state revisited. In J.N. Rosenau (ed.), *International Politics and Foreign Policy*. New York: Free Press.
Mansbach, R.W., Ferguson, Y.H. and Lampert, D.E. (1976) *The Web of World Politics*. New York: Prentice-Hall.
McLuhan, M. (1969) *Understanding Media: The Extension of Man*. New York: New American Library.
Modelski, G. (1974) *Principles of World Politics*. New York: Free Press.
Morse, E.L. (1976) *Modernization and the Transformation of International Relations*. New York: Free Press.
Wallace, M. and Singer, D. (1970) Intergovernmental organization in the global system, 1815–1870. *International Organization*, 24, 239–87.
Wallace, W. (1977) *The Foreign Policy Process in Britain*. London: Allen and Unwin.
Waltz, K.N. (1979) *Theory of International Politics*. New York: Addison-Wesley.

Part I

Great Power Rivalry
and
Globalized Conflict

2

Superpower Rivalry and the End of the Cold War

PAUL G. LEWIS

THE NATURE OF SUPERPOWER RIVALRY AND THE COLD WAR

Ronald Reagan could claim several achievements during his eight-year stint as US President. He was the first to win two presidential contests since the time of General Eisenhower and the high point of post-war American power in the 1950s. He remained politically unscathed by the Iranian arms scandal and the investigation of a range of dubious practices that had been undertaken in Central America to further the aims of his administration. He did not even seem to incur in any significant measure the displeasure of the American public for his forgetfulness about matters of state and apparent inability to concentrate on the political business over which he was supposed to be presiding. When asked what he himself regarded as his greatest achievement, though, he was reported to have replied 'People tell me I won the Cold War'. Whether or not that claim was accurate (Mikhail Gorbachev's initiative in warming up the political climate, and Leonid Brezhnev's record in running the Soviet economy into the ground and then invading Afghanistan, should also deserve a mention) there is no doubt that the change in superpower relations was one of the major global developments of the late 1980s.

Whatever the causes of the change, it did signal a major shift in the pattern of international conflict and cohesion and suggested the erosion of a relationship that had provided a basis for the post-war global political order. Signs of further movement in this direction multiplied during the first year of the Bush administration. Finally, when the Berlin Wall began to crumble on 9 November 1989, 41 years after the Berlin crisis that had been a major sign of the militarization of the post-war East–West conflict, the ending of the Cold War took on more visible form. It became clearly evident that the joint commitment of the superpowers to maintaining their established spheres of influence had significantly weakened. Self-determination for Eastern Europe, declared not long previously to be the 'principal requirement for the end of the Cold War', suddenly materialized and it was clear that a major political change had occurred (Mandelbaum 1989, p. 21). At a meeting held in Paris in November 1990 the leaders of NATO and the Warsaw Pact countries declared that they were no longer adversaries, pledged that they would not use force against one another, and signed a treaty which effectively brought the Cold War to an official end.

A number of factors lay behind this significant development in global politics and the associated weakening of superpower rivalry. We shall examine them in this chapter in the attempt to chart recent developments in superpower relations and their implications for future patterns of global politics. First, though, we shall consider the nature of superpower rivalry in the post-war world. Superpower rivalry and associated activities have become identified with the development of nuclear weaponry and the dominant role it has occupied in modern global politics. It also took the form of ideological conflict, an aspect strengthened once more during the early years of the Reagan administration but one which had various roots predating the immediate post-war period and which showed considerable differentiation following the onset of the intensified post-war conflict. In its different forms, superpower rivalry has been one of the dominant political features of the post-war period and the very idea of a superpower one of the characteristic concepts of modern political life.

The first use of the term was made in 1944, just before the end of World War II and the onset of the multifaceted conflict that developed between East and West. A superpower in this context referred to a power whose reach was of great international scope and whose armed force was so extensive and mobile that it could be deployed in any strategic theatre. This was contrasted with a power whose interests and influence were great in only a single regional theatre of power conflict (Fox 1944, p. 20). We generally tend to associate the idea of a superpower with the possession of a major arsenal of nuclear weapons which, with the assistance of missiles and sophisticated technology, can be deployed virtually anywhere on the globe. Yet the original conception of the superpower predated the nuclear age and actually included Great Britain as one of its three examples. This was soon shown to be a mistake, as became evident in 1947 when the British made clear to the Americans their inability to maintain a dominant role in Greece and handed over responsibility for that area in the US.

Great Britain too soon became a nuclear power; however, unlike the Soviet Union, it did not have the incentive, the resources or the degree of commitment to the nuclear race needed to keep up with the leading position taken in that competition by the United States. The Soviet Union exploded its first atomic bomb in 1949, four years after the first American use over Japan. The first test of an American thermonuclear superbomb (hydrogen bomb) took place in October 1952, and that of a comparable Soviet device in November 1955. The launch of Sputnik 1 in October 1957 suggested that Soviet nuclear capacity might be associated with the ability to deploy that power globally using long-range missiles. But the gap between the Soviet Union and the US in terms of military technology remained very significant. Only four of the launchers that put the Sputnik into orbit were ever deployed militarily (Holloway 1984, p. 43). Lacking effective long-range bombers, the Soviet Union was not able to mount an effective threat to the American heartland until late in the 1960s – although the situation was quite different with regard to Western Europe and America's major allies.

For at least two decades after World War II, then, superpower competition was far from being embedded in a context of comparable power balance or military equivalence in terms of the capacity to mount a similar kind of nuclear threat. From the early post-war period, nevertheless, superpower relations became effectively synonymous with a pattern of global bipolar politics and East–West rivalry, predominantly expressed in the level of antagonism that existed between the United States and the Soviet Union.

It also took on a major ideological dimension, although this was by no means a new element in international relations (as global ideological conflict and its formal expression had been a significant part of the scene since the Russian revolution of 1917), and the form of this ideological content changed significantly during the Cold War period. Superpower rivalry, then, soon settled into the bipolar pattern, which has been recognized for its significance as the 'first true polarization of power in modern history' (Gaddis 1986, p. 107).

It developed a close association with both the nuclear arms race and ideological competition, although the degree to which the superpowers participated in the nuclear relationship and the way in which ideological conflict gained expression were subject to considerable variation. In the public mind as well as amongst major decision-making circles in both superpowers, this pattern of conflict and competition became associated at an early stage with the idea of a Cold War. It was a term that gained currency among American political journalists in 1946 and 1947 and become particularly associated with the writings of Walter Lippman. Its use, however, could be traced back much earlier than that. It is found in the writings of the fourteenth-century Spanish writer Don Juan Manuel, referring to a situation where conflict not just had a political and potentially military character but also involved a clash of different world views (and those of a non-worldly character), of fundamental social values and ways of life (Halliday 1986, p. 5).

That kind of international conflict – one that was at once economic, social, political, religious and civilizational – ceased, it has been suggested by one influential theorist of international affairs (Gilpin 1981, p. 111), with the subsequent triumph of the West over Islam and the Treaty of Westphalia in 1648, which laid the foundations of the modern European state system. Yet the form taken on the international plane by the general globalized conflict apparent between capitalism and socialism, liberal-democracy and communist political dictatorship, which followed the formation of a consciously revolutionary state in Russia after October 1917, in some ways reflected the premodern rivalry between Western Christendom and the Muslim East. It is important to recognize that the modern Cold War contained elements which went considerably further than military or even political conflict, introducing new factors into the course of modern politics but also recalling others which were of more ancient provenance.

In general use, the term has come to be applied to a certain set of relations that developed between the superpowers and their allies after World War II. The Cold War in its original and classic manifestation is normally situated in the period from 1946, at the beginning of which Stalin made his first major post-war speech on foreign policy, stressing the irreconcilability of the two camps, which was followed by Churchill's description of the Iron Curtain that had descended in Europe, to 1953, when the Korean War ended, a new US president took office and Soviet leaders sought new relations with the West following the death of Stalin. Some, however, see the Cold War in its classic phase continuing until the beginning of a more formal *détente* in the late 1960s. Reference to a new or Second Cold War became prevalent following the Soviet invasion of Afghanistan and during much of Reagan's period in the White House. Soviet–US relations steadily worsened in the early 1980s until all arms control talks were suspended in December 1983, the first time in 25 years that the superpowers were not engaged in any formal arms control negotiations.

But the Second Cold War was not just a rerun of the original version, and the worsening of superpower relations did not mean a direct return to the kind of stand-off that had developed in the immediate post-war period. The degree of ideological conflict was less intense and the US stance more anti-Soviet and opposed to specific Soviet actions and policies than anti-communist in a general sense; the effects of the Sino–Soviet split were important here, and the United States' *rapprochement* with China meant that it had to be more specific in its criticism. Even Reagan's well-known attack on the 'evil empire' suggested distaste for a kind of state formation rather than for the principles that underlay it. Further, despite the breakdown of arms control negotiations in 1983, other forms of East–West agreement remained in place and there was still some shared framework for crisis management. Neither was there the level of internal repression that had developed in the early 1950s or the witch-hunts that were mounted against internal enemies, foreign agents and spies.

The new Cold War tended to remain in the domain of external relations and foreign policy rather than to form part of domestic social life. The Cold War that persisted and even intensified in the 1980s was therefore somewhat different from the conflict that developed in the 1940s. As the original variant it has been defined (Halliday 1986, pp. 8–9) in terms of the following characteristics: military buildup, with a special emphasis on nuclear weapons; intense propaganda campaigns between the two camps involving direct ideological conflict; the absence of effective negotiations and a climate of confrontation along some kind of iron curtain; revolutionary situations in intermediate areas (the Third World) expressing the underlying ideological conflict; the construction of military blocs and the tightening of internal controls; and emphasis on mobilization for the confrontation, and recognition of its primary significance for the society as a whole.

ORIGINS OF THE COLD WAR

The original Cold War developed out of the situation that took shape towards the end of World War II and the years immediately following its conclusion. This clearly marked the specific form it took and meant that any intensification of superpower rivalry that occurred during other periods, notably during the late 1970s and early 1980s, was hardly likely to take the same form. The original nature of the Cold War was, moreover, marked by the character and outlook of the leading politicians and statesmen who were involved in its creation, a feature lent greater significance by the enhanced role of individual leadership under wartime conditions and hardly minimized by the participation of personalities like Soviet leader Joseph Stalin in the process. The development of Cold War relations, of course, also had roots which went far deeper. One strand was the ideological conflict between capitalism and communism, liberal-democracy and Marxism-Leninism, which had been present in international affairs since 1917.

A further element was the disastrous course that developments took in Europe following the end of World War I, with economic instability and collapse followed by the demise of democracy and constitutional government in Germany, Italy, Spain and several countries in Eastern Europe, a process which led to the horrors of fascist aggression. President Wilson's passion for democratic state formation towards the end of World War I, succeeded by American non-involvement in European developments, contributed to the context in which these events were made possible. The exclusion of the Soviet Union from traditional channels of international diplomacy and its primary concern with building 'socialism in one country' also helped sustain the power vacuum that facilitated the extension of Nazi influence throughout the European continent. The involvement by the end of 1941 of all the major powers in a global conflict once more brought with it a heightened awareness of the dangers of disengagement from the European mainland, accompanied by a recognition of the need to keep future security objectives in mind at the same time as the war was fought to its conclusion.

The lessons learnt from the inter-war experience, and the *post bellum* security objectives quite reasonably brought by the Allied participants to the hostilities of World War II, were however not easily accommodated to the short-term exigencies of the alliance or the tactical demands of military operations. The ideological incompatibilities of the communist and capitalist Allies also caused strain, despite the efforts of public relations specialists to promote the benevolent and military qualities of 'Uncle Joe Stalin' and the care taken by Uncle Joe himself to enlist the sympathies of fellow democrat Roosevelt for his distaste of both fascist aggression and British imperialism. The interests of minor Allies produced further problems and, while those of Poland (which had been invaded from the east by the Soviet Union 16 days after the Nazi onslaught in September 1939) were clearly subordinated to those of the Big Three, Western attempts to secure vestigial rights for the Poles were an early bone of contention among the Allies.

Soviet aspirations in Eastern Europe, particularly those which clashed with the interests of formal Allies, created problems for the alliance at an early stage. While it has become part of accepted historical opinion that Stalin did not actually have in mind any blueprint for world revolution, his tactical ambitions did appear to be virtually unlimited (Gaddis 1983). These ambitions were particularly difficult to resist whilst the bulk of German forces was concentrated on the eastern front, Soviet citizens formed the greatest single source of Nazi victims, and the Western Allies were unable to satisfy Stalin's demand for a second front. Fears among both Western and Eastern Allies that one side might make a separate peace with the Germans contributed a further element of insecurity and suspicion. Stalin appeared to gain British and US acquiescence to his territorial demands at the first meeting of the Big Three in Tehran and received further satisfaction with the opening of the much-awaited second front in Normandy during June 1944.

Soon after, the Kremlin was pursuing its objectives in the Balkans with even greater vigour while, throughout September, Soviet forces were content to wait and see the Warsaw Uprising put down by Nazi forces. Already by the autumn of 1944 Western representatives had become convinced that some fundamental change of policy had taken place in Moscow, and the British military came to the conclusion that the Anglo–Soviet alliance no longer took the form of a credible partnership (Mastny 1979, p. 212). The course of discussions the following year at Yalta and Potsdam only served to confirm the impression, as did Soviet actions in occupied Germany. All this tended to place the roots of Cold War relations well before the end of the German surrender, although the public expression of the conflict and its full reflection in the diverse aspects of international relations took some time to be apparent. But while they undoubtedly played a major role in producing the intermediate causes of the Cold War, excessive emphasis should not be placed on Soviet wartime policy and the attitude of Joseph Stalin.

His attitude over Poland, the most contentious issue to arise between the Allies concerning the future of Eastern Europe, which itself provided the central battleground on which the Cold War emerged, could equally well be interpreted in terms of historical factors. These might include the experience of June 1941, when the Soviet Union was brought into the war; Russian sentiments of insecurity and vulnerability to attack throughout the centuries; and historical precedence in view of the regional status of Russia as a dominant force and the territorial uncertainties that remained after World War I. The major sources of conflict lay in the fact that the wartime alliance was the product of necessity forced on its participants by Axis aggression, and that their community of view did not extend much beyond the necessity of defeating Nazi Germany in Europe. There was, too, a common interest in a lasting peace and stable political order in Europe – but ideology, experience and viewpoint meant that the Allies' vision of the form it might take was fundamentally different.

It might be argued more appropriately that the Cold War originated less in the breakdown of the wartime alliance than in the fact that the demands of global warfare had pressed very different powers into an otherwise unnatural and unstable alliance which had the effect of increasing the likelihood of conflict between them. It was, rather, the unusual degree of isolationism that had developed in the inter-war period that had kept conflict of a Cold War character at arm's length. These divergences became more prominent as the conclusion of hostilities grew closer and their expression more stark as the separation of the two camps became more clearly drawn. This became more prominent with the growing salience of structures of bipolarity. The dominance of the United States within the Western camp in terms of political, economic and military power became stronger with the growing signs of British weakness and problems experienced by all European countries during the immediate post-war period. Bipolarity itself, however, brought a further logic to superpower relations which contributed to the development and extension of Cold War relations.

The rapid emergence of a bipolar world in the immediate post-war period imposed a particular structure on superpower competition. The existence of two superpowers with distinct interests and differing political approaches facilitated the development of an adversarial relationship, while the enormous economic and technological power of the United States and the large military presence of the Soviet Union – considerable portions of which were now stationed in advanced positions in Central Europe – combined to accentuate feelings of insecurity and potential threat. The logic of bipolarity was itself a logic of insecurity (Bowker and Williams 1988, p. 11), according to which the actions taken by one side to enhance its security could all too easily be seen as a threat to the interests of the other. The different ideological orientations of the superpowers made a further contribution to this, while the proximity of the Soviet Union to contested areas of Central and Western Europe and the distance of the United States from them brought additional elements to the pattern of superpower relations. The structural inclinations and historical ingredients for the Cold War were already well to the fore without any aggressive intentions or designs for dominance on the part of either participant.

The adversarial relationship was in place by the end of 1944, and the summit meetings held during 1945 in Yalta and Potsdam already took the form rather of a major political contest than of the deliberations of victorious allies contemplating future joint action. Public statements of both sets of leaders clarified their respective outlooks the following year, while the consolidation of the two camps underwent further development in 1947 with the launching of the Marshall Plan, the enunciation of the Truman Doctrine and the establishment of the Cominform. The communist takeover in

Czechoslovakia and the trial of strength initiated by the Berlin crisis in 1948 underlined the division of Europe and confirmed the strength of the superpowers in their sphere of influence – and the difficulties each would encounter if a serious challenge was made to the power of the other. Tension eased following the death of Stalin and the end of the Korean War, although progress in superpower relations was halted with the Suez crisis and the Soviet invasion of Hungary. Relations became increasingly critical with the resumption of the Berlin crisis, which culminated in the building of the Wall in 1961, and the Cuban missile crisis of 1962. In the years that followed, though, relations became more stable and less threatening.

DÉTENTE AND DISILLUSION: FLUCTUATIONS IN SUPERPOWER RIVALRY

In June 1963 Kennedy and Khrushchev agreed to install a direct communications link, the hot line, and signed the Partial Test Ban Treaty in August of that year. Trade relations were developed, and America began the sale of grain to the Soviet Union in October 1963. Changes in the approach of European Allies also played a part and, while France opted out of NATO's integrated command structure, West Germany began to move away from its implacable hostility to *détente* and come to terms with the implications of the Soviet presence in Eastern Europe. But although superpower relations improved in the 1960s, the changes that occurred were largely of an incidental and uncoordinated nature. It was only towards the end of the decade that the framework for a more systematic process of *détente* began to emerge. Growing Soviet strength produced a more confident view of the role of the East in international affairs, while the need for caution in the face of capitalist insecurities and instability was also well recognized. But the declining rate of Soviet economic growth was another major factor. Soviet GNP grew by 6.4 per cent between 1950 and 1958, by 5.3 per cent between 1958 and 1967, but by only 3.7 per cent between 1967 and 1973. The rate of growth in industrial labour productivity was declining, while American grain imports continued to be necessary to feed the Soviet people. As Brezhnev's position within the leadership strengthened, Soviet policy became more firmly committed to the view that the development of foreign trade relations was a fundamental component in the improvement of domestic economic growth, while the dramatic worsening of relations with China suggested the advisability of moderating conflict with the West. The arrival of the Nixon administration brought with it a conviction of the need to adapt strategic thinking to cope with the new global power of the Soviet Union and help in disentangling the United States from its increasingly painful involvement in Vietnam. America was also aware of the economic challenge posed by Japan and a more powerful Western Europe, while suffering itself from a worsening balance of payments. Improved opportunities for East–West trade were seen as a definite advantage in this situation. The interests and objectives of the superpowers thus showed a significant degree of coincidence in the late 1960s and led them to re-establish their relationship within a new framework of *détente*.

Strategic differences were never absent, however, and from the beginning entered into the conceptions held of *détente*. The relationship was perceived by the Soviet Union as a new way of exercising its enhanced power and pursuing its objectives under conditions of improved security. Neither did it mean the abandonment by the United States of the policy of containing Soviet power and restraining its influence in contested areas. These objectives were rather to be pursued by different means and, in fact, built into Soviet conduct through linkage and the establishment of a new kind of framework for more complex interaction and self-restraint. These differing perceptions contributed to the shortness of the period of *détente* in superpower relations and the resurgence of features of the original Cold War conflict towards the end of the 1970s. They emerged with their full clarity when the Soviet Union invaded Afghanistan on Christmas Day 1979. The United States took cognizance of the failure of its strategy of containment through *détente*, and returned to reaffirm the priority of the security concerns it had developed during the years that followed World War II.

Yet the Soviet invasion was by no means the finely planned manoeuvre and the culmination of a policy of expansion under the guise of *détente* that many Americans perceived it to be. There were few signs of Soviet involvement in the political changes within Afghanistan during the 1970s, and concern had grown in the Kremlin at the turn affairs were taking under the leadership of the communist Hafizullah Amin following the coup of April 1978. Soviet sponsorship of a plan to replace Amin failed and Soviet fears of turmoil and insecurity grew. The invasion was prepared primarily, it seems, with the intention of establishing a more popularly based government and stabilizing the situation. The region was not one where the United States had any direct interests – and was even less one where it had a capacity for intervention. Even so, the decision appeared to be a difficult and controversial one for the Soviet leadership. The invasion was, nevertheless, the first military action undertaken by the Soviet Union outside its own borders since the crushing of the Czechoslovak reforms in 1968. The action was certainly difficult to comprehend within the framework of a *détente* policy, and Brezhnev's attempt to justify it was both crude and unconvincing. Its effect was to undermine the position formerly taken by President Carter, who had been campaigning unsuccessfully for Congress to ratify the SALT II arms control agreement, and to push to the fore the views of those who argued that Soviet power should be confronted and all moves to extend its territorial reach directly countered. After Afghanistan it was the rhetoric of the Cold War that took the high ground of American politics and helped Ronald Reagan along the road to the White House.

But the ground for this had also been prepared earlier, and US military expenditures had begun to rise before 1977, well before any signs of Soviet intervention in Afghan affairs (Halliday 1986, p. 123). The roots of the Second Cold War, therefore, lay within the *détente* period and in the tensions and contradictions that had resided within that conceptualization of superpower relations. By the early 1980s US–Soviet rivalry appeared to have reverted to the Cold War mode that had come to prevail in the 1940s, although this was initially more evident on the American side. But the Second Cold War did not replicate all the features of the First, and many channels of international exchange and cooperation had become too well established under overall conditions of modified superpower rivalry to be interrupted at will. It did not involve the same degree of ideological commitment and remained an affair within the domain of foreign affairs rather than one involving domestic mobilization. Neither was it accompanied by the kind of direct military confrontation between the two camps that had occurred during the Korean War. The Soviet Union remained embroiled in hostilities within Afghanistan, in which the United States participated only to the extent of maintaining strong support for Pakistan and assisting the anti-Soviet forces. The Soviet Union provided some support for Nicaragua, which became a major obsession during the Reagan administration, although its commitment in military terms and implications for US security were certainly far less than American representatives often chose to claim.

In general terms, the level of direct military confrontation was considerably below that of the 1940s and 1950s – or even, in the context of the Cuban missile crisis, of the 1960s. The enhanced rivalry of the early 1980s also seemed to vanish as quickly as it had appeared, suggesting that perceptions were as much the stuff of contemporary politics as seemingly more tangible issues and conflicts. Not only did the atmosphere of greater superpower antagonism and increased rivalry evaporate, but the Cold War itself soon appeared to be on the way out and, by the time of President Reagan's departure from the White House, could unconvincingly be declared to have ended. One reason for this was undoubtedly the accession of Mikhail Gorbachev to the leading position in the Soviet Union and the initiatives he launched in both the domestic and the international fields. Ronald Reagan also seemed to show a strong personal commitment to the process of arms control and the reduction of existing stocks, which stood in some contrast to his earlier views and pronouncements on the Soviet menace. Attitudes thus changed, but so did other factors which had made a major contribution to the development of superpower relations.

ASPECTS OF A NEW GLOBAL ORDER: THE END OF THE COLD WAR

The environment in which superpower rivalry was now pursued was different from that of earlier periods. The integration of the blocs that had earlier been formed was now loosened and the structure of bipolarity had been considerably weakened. The Sino–Soviet split was one obvious sign of this, but the growing strength of Western Europe and Japan was also important. The world was increasingly a multipolar one. International politics and relations between states were more diverse and complex, not least because there were simply a lot more states around towards the end of the twentieth century. Fewer than 50 states had participated in the newly formed United Nations Organization (although some others soon joined); by 1980 it had 157 members, and the number had risen to 170 by the time of the accession of Namibia. The importance of ideology had also declined, as suggested by Reagan's change of tone from the 'evil empire' discourse and Gorbachev's espoual of 'new thinking' in domestic and international relations.

The relationship between formal Soviet ideology and the organization of international communism had always been a major aspect of Soviet foreign policy, and the decline of the former had a particular practical significance for the exercise of Soviet influence as the fortunes of world communism underwent 'drastic decline as a political force' (Wrong 1989, p. 194). Additional factors derived from the economic background which, not surprisingly, continued to be of great significance. The slowing rate of economic growth had been, as we have seen, an important factor in bringing the Soviet Union to accept the framework of *détente* in the 1960s. The consequences of *détente* for the Soviet economy were, however, far from as positive as the Brezhnev leadership had hoped. In a speech to the plenum of the CPSU Central Committee in February 1988 Gorbachev stated that, in the 20 years prior to his accession to power in March 1985, Soviet national income did not increase in real terms at all – with the exception of the production of alcohol. Moreover, Brezhnev had used *détente* actively to pursue Soviet aims in the Third World and elsewhere and had continued to build up the military strength of the USSR the better to do this. The Soviet Union had been seeking parity with the United States and all 'opposing powers', including China and Japan, an objective later described by Soviet spokesmen as being without historical precedent, 'ruinously costly' and bound to fail in view of the fact that the gross national income of the NATO countries alone was four times that of those which adhered to the Warsaw Pact. The commitment of Soviet forces to Afghanistan added further to this burden and increased the cost of military activity. The *détente* period, then, did not see any improvement in the Soviet economic situation; rather there was an extension of Soviet military commitments, which had the reverse effect. The more vigorous pursuit of foreign trade links was, too, quite inadequate to contribute significantly to the solution of declining productivity and the structural problems afflicting the Soviet economy.

It took Gorbachev to cut back on Soviet military commitments, raise superpower relations to a new plane and launch radical policies of *perestroika* and *glasnost* in the domestic sphere in order to produce the conditions under which reform could be more realistically pursued. But it still took four years before it became apparent that the Gorbachev leadership was actually prepared to take concrete steps to cut back on defence outlays (Holloway 1989–90, pp. 10–11). Even the civil changes on the scale contemplated had precious little effect on the state of the Soviet economy during the first five years of Gorbachev's rule, and there were few signs of it breaking out of the solidly entrenched state of stagnation into which it had begun to move a matter of decades previously. Particularly important, however, was less the fact of persistent Soviet economic weakness than the growing salience of global economic processes for all countries, the general character of contemporary pressures for closer economic integration, and the particular problems which face a centralized bureaucratic system when it confronts these pressures. While Soviet economic weakness was a major factor, it was the global context that placed stagnation under a wholly different light and lent it a determinant significance (Halliday 1990, p. 17). Gorbachev's approach to the problem reflected awareness of this and involved a radical revision of Soviet views on the underlying nature of the patterns of global economic development and the appropriate relationship to be established with them by the Soviet Union. Changes in this area went far beyond Brezhnev's recognition of the value to be gained from improved foreign trade relations. Following this line, Gorbachev stressed in July 1989 that *perestroika* was 'inseparable from a policy of full participation in the world economy' (Kaser 1989–90, p. 92). A publication of the Soviet Foreign Ministry during 1989 declared that the idea of the world as an arena for international class struggle was now anachronistic, and acknowledged that most developing countries already followed a Western model of development and suffered not so much from the mechanisms of capitalism as from their absence.

All this had major implications for the present status and future prospects of the Soviet Union, which had only harmed itself and reduced the capacity to pursue its interests by cutting itself off from the main current of global economic development and the benefits of capitalist growth. What was now recognized to have been an incorrect perspective that had become dominant in the Kremlin had led it to ignore the revolution in science and technology and the impact it had had on the world economy. The level of cooperation with capitalist countries and integration with global economic processes that was now accepted to be necessary for the Soviet Union spelt the phasing out of any fundamental superpower rivalry, more intensive development of global economic links and technological cooperation, and the improvement of relations with the United States to the extent that the end of the Cold War was now on the immediate agenda. While the economic situation in the Soviet Union had developed into a major crisis and led the Gorbachev leadership to a thoroughgoing reappraisal of the Soviet Union's global position, the condition of the US economy – while clearly less critical than that of the Soviet Union – also prompted a major rethink and the adoption of policies that contributed to the decline of Cold War tensions. The programme of increased military expenditure undertaken by President Carter was followed through and extended by Ronald Reagan under the impetus of the enhanced superpower rivalry and climate of suspicion that followed the Soviet invasion of Afghanistan. This, in association with other economic and financial changes that occurred during the early years of the Reagan administration, led to greatly increased levels of debt. Domestic US government debt rose from $1 trillion in 1980 to $2.7 trillion in 1989, while foreign debt, from a positive US balance in 1980, had reached $500 billion by 1989. This suggested, among other things, that the enhanced military strength of the United States was also achieved at a significant domestic cost and at the expense of economic stability. It tended to qualify the image of superpower strength and muted the contribution of higher spending levels to the credibility of US military power. It was associated with important domestic disagreements and resistance to this direction of policy from Congress which, in the words of an influential American academic, was 'curiously impervious to the logic of trying to exhaust the Russians by tripling our own national debt' (Williams 1989, pp. 278–9).

This level of indebtedness served to underline the growing economic role of Japan and Western Europe and reinforced the transition from bipolarity to a multipolar world, a development given further impetus by China's shifting alignment and the development of a distinctive West European approach to relations with the Soviet Union. This had clear implications for America's superpower status which were recognized in leading political circles. In an open letter of advice to Reagan's as yet unknown successor as US president, former Secretaries of State Kissinger and Vance jointly observed that 'America's role in the world has become directly dependent on the strength and performance of the US economy' and concluded that the 'US is no longer in the economic position to play the Western superpower role in which it has been cast since the end of World War II'. A year after the election of President Bush, his position was compared with that of British Prime Minister Macmillan in the 1950s as the US appeared to be 'clinging by its fingertips to its superpower status, too poor to hang on but too proud to let go' (*The Guardian*, 10 November 1989).

By no means all were convinced of the significance of these developments for relative US decline, and American problems were certainly not as critical as those which were clearly evident in the Soviet Union (Huntington 1989). Nevertheless, they did suggest the common problems involved in maintaining superpower status and the general tendencies encouraging and even compelling a move towards the end of Cold War politics. The plain conclusion appeared to be that the kind of superpower rivalry that had laid the basis for the Cold War, and further intensified under the conditions that had been established by it, was not sustainable within the framework of the global political and economic order that had emerged during the post-war decades. The pursuit of security in terms of military supremacy imposed an intolerable economic burden on both parties in the context of global political divisions, the diverse sources and forms of potential political conflict, and the current rate of technological development.

The imperatives of Cold War rivalry tended to produce in both camps the forms of a national security state and a degree of economic dislocation that threatened the overall viability of the participants' social systems and capacity to act as states in the arena of more conventional international relations. Neither did the practice of super-power rivalry or the pursuit of supremacy within the terms of the Cold War relationship appear to be meaningful or sensible in terms of the goals set and the values articulated within the contemporary political life of the United States and Soviet Union. The overriding priority for the Soviet population was the establishment of a viable material basis for social life, and the replication and exploitation of the achievements of the leading capitalist countries rather than their domination or destruction. Less than the nebulous threats of world communism or Soviet aggression it was, for the United States, terrorism and the economic competition presented by growing Pacific powers and the rise of an increasingly integrated Western Europe that were perceived to be the sources of greatest external insecurity, while signs of social dislocation and the consequences of domestic disorder provided a more potent challenge to American values and the American way of life than any ideological challenge from without.

The brief course of the Second Cold War of the 1980s served to reinforce the importance of these factors and facilitate their recognition by decision makers in West and East. The resurgence of intensified superpower rivalry, it may be argued, soon had the effect of encouraging the initiation of a radical move away from traditional policies in the Soviet Union and a significant reappraisal of strategy and priorities in the United States. The Second Cold War, in its turn, had largely been the result of the earlier move into a *détente* relationship by both parties without their relinquishing or modifying primary objectives pursued in the established conflict. Signs of superpower decline and weakness in the performance of globally dominant roles had, therefore, become evident at a relatively early stage of superpower rivalry and played a part in the initiation of *détente* – although their signal importance and relationship to major changes in the global political and economic order were not fully recognized or acted on.

From a broader perspective, the years of heightened superpower tension from the late 1940s to the 1960s, and its brief resurgence in the 1980s, may well be judged to have been an exceptional phase in Soviet–US relations. The initial *détente* of the 1970s that came between them was premised on a limited change in superpower perceptions which did not modify the basic superpower objectives which had developed following World War II. From the end of 1988, though, the conviction came to be held with growing firmness that a fundamental change in superpower relations was under way, a view that became stronger through 1989 with the defection of the Soviet satellites in Eastern Europe and the expression of Soviet willingness to consider the reduction or even removal from that region of Soviet military forces. The feeling grew that the Cold War relations which had persisted in some form ever since the end of World War II were also on their way out and that the reserves of superpower antagonism were becoming exhausted.

The learning process had been a long one not just because of the tensions that developed in the post-war world but also because of the legacy of earlier developments. These included the conflicts that had developed during the enforced intimacy of the wartime alliance and the unusually distant relations that had existed between the two great powers during the inter-war years, as the Soviet Union worked out its revolution-ary fate in Stalin's formulation of 'socialism in one country' and the United States remained isolated from developments across the Atlantic. Relations between the United States and Russia in its post-revolutionary, Soviet guise had therefore been characterized by an unusual distance until the acquisition of a common enemy in 1941, were succeeded by the problems of political as well as military alliance, and then underwent a lengthy process of adjustment as the several areas of potential conflict between them were explored and tested by both powers over the years.

The process of accommodation was not made easier by the rapid pace of technological development, not least in the nuclear field, and the post-war capitalist boom – which was both an object of envy and a source of threat to the socialist camp. These, as well as other factors, played an important part in the development of superpower relations and helped bring closer the end of the Cold War. Military expenditure crippled the Soviet economy and began to pose major problems for the United States. Economic processes increasingly took on a global pattern which exerted further pressures on even the larger national economies. New technological developments affected both processes and had an increasingly solid base in the new Asian economies, which were outside the control of both superpowers yet whose influence they were unable to resist. The bipolarity that had sustained and encouraged Cold War rivalries thus began to break down in the face of growing global complexity and the rise of alternative, more specialized sources of power which increasingly qualified the military basis of superpower rivalry.

But the erosion of bipolarity and the spread of new thinking, which involved a conception of the world as a community of interdependent states with a joint interest in cooperation, although rejecting the use of force as an effective guarantee of security, by no means carried the promise of collaborative relations or the strengthening of tendencies for international peace (Cox 1990, p. 36). The diminished power of the Soviet Union threatened growing instability, with signs of a loss of control by the reforming Soviet elite. The reformist drive entered a dangerous half-way phase, Gorbachev's authority having been sufficient to come to terms with the realities of the external environment but apparently inadequate to overcome the rigidities of the Soviet system or carry through domestic reform to any effective conclusion. The qualification of the US global role, considerably less pronounced than that of the Soviet Union, could also reduce prospects for stability, as it was by no means clear that it was able to perform the imperial or hegemonic role that might be necessary to replace the progressively dismantled structures of bipolarity. The start of the Gulf War, less than a year after the end of the Cold War, provided a graphic example of this tendency as the invasion of Kuwait by Iraq, the major Soviet ally in the Middle East, prompted the formation of a US-led coalition in the name of the United Nations to counter the aggression. The least that can be said on this subject is that any solution achieved was neither easy to arrive at nor gained by peaceful means.

References

Bowker, M. and Williams, P. (1988) *Superpower Détente: a Reappraisal*. London: Sage.
Cox, M. (1990) From the Truman Doctrine to the second superpower détente: the rise and fall of the cold war; *Journal of Peace Research*, 27 (1), 25–41.

Fox, W. (1944) *The Super-Powers*. New York: Harcourt Brace.

Gaddis, J. (1983) The emerging post-revisionist synthesis on the origins of the cold war. *Diplomatic History*, 7, 171–90.

Gaddis, J. (1986) The long peace. *International Security*, 10, 99–142.

Gilpin, R. (1981) *War and Change in World Politics*. Cambridge: Cambridge University Press.

Halliday, F. (1986) *The Making of the Second Cold War* (2nd edn). London: Verso.

Halliday, F. (1990) The ends of cold war. *New Left Review*, 180, 5–23.

Holloway, D. (1984) *The Soviet Union and the Arms Race* (2nd edn). New Haven: Yale University Press.

Holloway, D. (1989–90) State, society and the military under Gorbachev. *International Security*, 14 (3), 5–24.

Huntington, S. (1989) The United States: decline or renewal? *Adelphi Papers*, 235, part I, 63–80.

Kaser, M. (1989–90) Economic dimensions of east–west relations. *Adelphi Papers*, 247, part I, 92–103.

Mandelbaum, M. (1989) Ending the cold war. *Foreign Affairs*, 68 (2), 18–36.

Mastny, M. (1979) *Russia's Road to the Cold War*. New York: Columbia University Press.

Williams, P. (1989) US–Soviet relations: beyond the cold war? *International Affairs*, 65, 275–88.

Wrong, D. (1989) The waning of the cold war. *Dissent*, Spring, 192–7.

3

Superpower Rivalry in South Asia and Southern Africa

DAVID POTTER

Superpower rivalry is a global phenomenon involving both military power and ideological conflict. As a global phenomenon it can be said to have both horizontal and vertical dimensions: it may spread out horizontally into all parts of the globe; it may also reach down vertically into regional and domestic levels of society and limit their freedom of policy choice. This rivalry clearly does spread horizontally into South Asia and Southern Africa, although why the superpowers are there is a matter of debate (Rais 1986, pp. 1–12; George 1990). The main question in this chapter relates to the vertical reach of the subject: *to what extent has superpower rivalry constrained the foreign policies of states in South Asia and Southern Africa?* In addressing this large question, I must restrict myself in this short chapter to sketching a terrain of inquiry and noting some of the minefields in the area.

MODELS OF SUPERPOWER RIVALRY

Any answer to the main question is going to be shaped by the particular model of global political relations being used – realist, pluralist, Marxist. The literature of international relations is full of comparative evaluations of these and other models. I cannot go into these debates in detail here. The importance of models for the question being asked here can be illustrated, however, by comparing what I would call a tight model with a loose one.

An example of a comparatively tight model is used in Halliday (1986). It is not easy to locate this book in a particular model; it seems to combine both realist and Marxist features. However, if one must, then it is probably most useful to identify it as close to some form of neo-Marxism. Marxists tend to start their analyses with modes of production (the general way that people produce the goods and services they require for survival) and the class formations that results from such modes; realists by contrast tend to start with sovereign states. Halliday may be said to be closer to the former position because his characterization of the international political system is framed fundamentally by the military and ideological struggle between the capitalist West led by the USA and the communist East led by the USSR, with these two domains resting (at least implicitly for Halliday) on contrasting economic bases or modes of production (i.e. capitalism and communism). My own summary sketch of Halliday's model singles out six main propositions as characterizing the present international political system:

1 The present system is unique. It was born in 1945–6 and there was nothing like it previously.
2 The present system is dominated by the capitalist–communist rivalry and the arms race.
3 That rivalry is bipolar. It is essentially a conflict between the capitalist domain led by the USA and the communist domain led by the USSR. The USA and the USSR emerged as dominant forces in their respective domains at the end of World War II.
4 The rivalry is systemic. The rivalry is between two fundamentally opposed and interdependent socioeconomic orders such that the rivalry between them cannot be permanently resolved.
5 The rivalry is globalized. As Halliday emphasizes, 'it involves the whole world in its political and military dynamics' and, whilst the superpowers are 'unable to control or programme much of world events', they 'nonetheless tend to impose their own competitive logic upon them' (p. 31).
6 The rivalry is dynamic. Its intensity has changed through time. There have so far been four phases: the First Cold War (1946–53), oscillatory antagonism (1953–69), *détente* (1969–79) and the Second Cold War (1979–86).

Halliday's model of the present international political system strikes me as fairly tight in conception in that the whole system is 'dominated' (his word) by the superpower rivalry and by the arms race, which involves the whole world in its political and military dynamics and imposes the logic of the superpower conflict upon world events. Halliday is not entirely consistent about the global reach of this system. He can say sensibly that 'there are many factors in world affairs which are beyond the control of Moscow and Washington' (p. 27), and yet later refer to 'the bipolar dynamic that grips the Third World' (p. 260). On the whole, however, the global reach of this system can be fairly long. The system can move in tight on political events and processes around the world, then move back. Its reach will vary over time. For example, when the superpower rivalry is more intense, the reach can be longer. Using this model, one might be drawn to the conclusion that the superpower rivalry has been a major determinant of political relations around the world, especially during the First and Second Cold Wars. That general position has an effect on any answer to the main question here. Thus, using this model, it looks like the superpowers are able (particularly during periods of intense superpower antagonism) to limit generally the capacity of states to pursue their own policies.

For purposes of comparison, it is worth looking at another model which is comparatively loose. One such has been outlined by Hoffmann (1985). It has a number of pluralist features. My own summary sketch of Hoffmann's model includes five features characterizing the present international political system:

1 The present international political system is original (unique). It differs from previous bipolar and balance of power systems.

2 The present system is structurally heterogeneous in terms of power. There are different kinds of power relations in the system: diplomatic-strategic, military, monetary, industrial etc. In classic bipolar systems, the strategic-diplomatic power game is by far the most important in determining interstate relations; in the current system, however, 'there are other important games, and they are not bipolar.'

3 The present system is fragmented vertically into partly separate arenas, each with its own separate hierarchy of persons (actors). The different power games within the system have different sets of players.

4 The present system is fragmented horizontally into a variety of regional subsystems, together with one 'core contest' involving the superpowers which is truly global. Thus in the present system there is both 'one world-wide contest, the superpowers' rivalry, and tenacious local rivalries or configurations that can be used by the superpowers for their competition (and whose actors call in the superpowers for their own purposes) but which also have a life of their own and their own rules'. The system as a whole can also be said to contain a core and a periphery of distinct regions containing legally independent actors, and 'the relative autonomy of regional concerns dampens the superpowers' contest, or divides it into reasonably separate compartments.'

5 The present system is dynamic. The intensity of core confrontations as they affect the various subsystems of the periphery keep changing, e.g. the two tense periods in Central America have been the early 1960s and the mid 1980s. There is also now the possibility of major changes in the system in that the core contest may 'spill over into the peripheries and become truly global; i.e. that in each subsystem there would be a struggle for dominance, so to speak, between the truly local (internal and interstate) factors of conflict and the Soviet–American "relation of major tension", which the latter would win.'

Hoffmann's model of the present international political system strikes me as fairly loose in conception, in that it is marked by structural differentiation and by vertical and horizontal fragmentations. There is a core confrontation in the strategic-military arena that ties nearly all actors in that arena within the system to that central core. But there are additional arenas of importance in the system played by other actors according to rather different rules, and the core confrontation may only barely affect them. Using a model like this, one might be drawn to the conclusion that the bipolar superpower rivalry has been less significant in shaping patterns of politics in South Asia and Southern Africa. The model suggests instead that a variety of factors may jointly be at work – international, regional, domestic – and that the relative importance of these factors might vary depending on the arena of international relations being examined. Hoffmann's answers to the main question in this chapter would tend to look rather different from Halliday's answers. Are the superpowers able to limit the capacity of states to pursue autonomous policies? Hoffmann's answer: it depends on the policies (there are different policy arenas) and regional or local configurations at the time. In many policy arenas, most of the time, the superpowers do not effectively limit the autonomy of state policy making. Broadly, for Hoffmann, states tend to have a lot of autonomy outside the core confrontation.

One of the things that stands out in Hoffmann's model, as distinct from Halliday's, is the importance of regions. There is, says Hoffmann, 'one world-wide contest' involving the superpowers, but there are also regional rivalries that 'have a life of their own and their own rules'. The importance of regions has been emphasized by Buzan (1986). Three points deserve emphasis.

First, according to Buzan, there are a number of regional security complexes in the world making up a level of global politics between the 'supercomplex' involving the superpowers and the level of individual nation-states. Buzan gives us a way of distinguishing one such region from another. South Asia is a regional security complex because there is a set of contiguous states linked closely together by patterns of intense enmity and amity as regards their perceptions of their own security. The Middle East is another regional security complex for the same reason. What distinguishes the South Asia complex from the Middle East complex is that, whereas the interdependencies are intense within each region, there is comparatively little interaction between the two regions as regards the security perceptions of the states involved. The wars of the Middle East have not had repercussions in South Asia, nor have the wars in South Asia spilled over into the Middle East.

Secondly, however, according to Buzan there are roughly two types of regional security complex. One is the sort just indicated, involving basically a set of local states only. The other type also contains great powers like the USA, the Soviet Union or China. In this second type, the relation between the set of local states and the great power (or powers) may be lopsided; Buzan gives the example of China being a major security concern for India, but India not being a security concern for China.

That example leads to the third point. Great powers, including the superpowers, can limit substantially the security perceptions and foreign policies of states in some regional complexes, whereas in other cases they can have comparatively little effect on policy. Similarly, Buzan tells us that the security relations between the superpowers are intense and they 'penetrate in varying degrees into the affairs of the local [regional] complexes'. All this is useful as a framework within which to explore the main question here, but the phrase 'penetrate in varying degrees' is rather vacuous as it stands, and needs sharpening on specific cases.

The two regions considered here are not ones where the superpowers' vital interests are engaged, as in the Middle East. Southern Africa is a region in which the superpowers have quite modest interests. In the case of South Asia, a region of modest interest for the superpowers has recently changed to one of considerable importance. Partly for this reason, I shall give rather more attention here to South Asia, and within South Asia to relations between India and Pakistan and the extent to which superpower rivalry has affected these relations.

INDIA, PAKISTAN AND SUPERPOWER RIVALRY: A THUMBNAIL SKETCH

Recently I looked at some of the international relations literature on the superpower rivalry in South Asia. I tried to find a few analyses which together threw light on the main question from different perspectives. Six studies particularly attracted my attention. One was by Anita Inder Singh (1986); she was at the time a research scholar at the Institute of International Affairs in Stockholm. Three papers indicated views on the subject from within the foreign policy establishments of the two superpowers. One was by Alexander Chicherov (1984), who was at the time Head of the International Research Department, Institute of Oriental Studies, Moscow. Two others suggested the kinds of views that circulated in Washington in the mid 1980s: one by Robert

Wirsing (1985), the other by Selig Harrison (1986). Wirsing was a visiting Professor at the School of International Studies, US Army Special Warfare Center; Harrison was a senior associate of the Carnegie Endowment Fund. The last two studies were from work by left-wing scholars: one by Lawrence Lifschultz (1986), the other by Srikant Dutt (1984). Lifschulz was an American academic, Dutt a young Indian academic tragically killed in a motor accident while his book was being published.

Amongst other things, these six studies provide a basis for a thumbnail sketch of the history of superpower relations *vis-à-vis* South Asia since the 1940s. The history is interesting because it suggests that the looser model may be more helpful in the case of South Asia than the tighter one.

When superpower rivalry commenced in the 1940s, the British Empire in India was breaking up. As is well known, India and Pakistan were almost immediately at war over Kashmir. Ever since that traumatic time, serious instability in the South Asian region has mostly concerned India–Pakistan relations. It is important to appreciate that the origins of this conflict had nothing to do with superpower rivalry.

India, the largest new state in the region, received early Western encouragement in the latter part of the 1940s to play a key nation role in South Asia as a sort of global imperialist there. Kuomintang China and Brazil were encouraged to play similar roles in their regions. But this loose Western conception disintegrated by the end of the 1940s as India opted for non-alignment and 'was steered into a more equidistant position between the superpowers'. This more balanced position 'helped India to gain a measure of autonomy in its foreign policies and [later] increased assistance for its ambitious industrial projects' (Dutt, 1984, p. 10). At the same time, initiatives by Pakistan and India to obtain arms took their conflict outside the regions, and these initiatives were met by initiatives from the USA attempting to contain world communism. Washington began to supply Pakistan with military assistance in 1954, with the signing of the Mutual Defence Assistance Agreement. Military assistance continued to flow to Pakistan throughout the 1950s, much to the irritation of the Indian government. However, considerable economic aid flowed into India from the West during this period.

The Soviet Union began to 'promote India' after the Sino–Soviet split in the late 1950s. This support continued through the period of the China–India War in 1962 when severe economic dislocations occurred and India 'became temporarily even more dependent [economically] on the West' (Dutt, 1984, pp. 10–11). By 1964, American strategic dominance in the Indian Ocean area (including Iran) was such that the Soviet Union was led to attempt to have the area declared a nuclar-free zone. This proposal was rejected by the USA, and since then Soviet naval buildup in the area has been substantial. As part of this strategic buildup, Soviet support for India's need for an improved defence capability began in earnest. By the late 1960s the Soviet Union had become India's primary arms supplier (Wirsing, 1985, p. 266).

The most serious regional security crisis of the entire period occurred in 1971 with the India–Pakistan War, when East Pakistan became the independent state of Bangladesh. The superpowers had no direct bearing on these actions. The USA sent the warship *Enterprise* to the Bay of Bengal at the time, but this was 'largely to impress China, not to save Pakistan by getting involved in what it saw as a local conflict' (Inder Singh 1986, p. 222). The war not only diminished Pakistan; it also strengthened India. It gave back to the Indian ruling classes 'some of the old self-confidence', and their aspirations for world influence revived during the 1970s: 'nuclear power, missiles, satellites, aircraft, electronics, and an indigenous arms industry are all there to back up the ruling class's image of itself as an important world power' (Dutt 1984, p. 10). During the same period, Washington's interest in South Asia declined, as measured by the 'virtual termination of its own arms assistance program in the region' (Wirsing 1985, p. 266). The view from Washington was that India 'is rapidly emerging as a major industrial and military power' and 'is determined to achieve a dominant position in South Asia commensurate with its overwhelming preponderance of population, resources, and economic strength' (Harrison 1986, pp. 126, 129).

By the beginning of the 1980s, superpower rivalry in South Asia had entered a new phase. Two events in 1979 triggered it. One was the overthrow of the Pahlavi regime in Iran, with the result that the USA lost its closest ally in the Middle East along with its bases there. The second was the Soviet occupation of Afghanistan. These two events were immediately followed by the election of Ronald Reagan. This led to more 'aggressive militarist trends in US foreign policy'; any 'local processes' in South Asia or elsewhere unfavourable to the US were 'now viewed only through the prism of global military confrontation with world socialism' (Chicherov 1984, p. 1121). The USA and the Soviet Union immediately became 'engaged for the first time in simultaneous, massive and directly competitive arms supply activity with their respective South Asian clients' (Wirsing 1985, p. 266).

American support for Pakistan took a quantum leap forward. With the loss of Iran, Pakistan was a favourable alternative. There was its 'strategically suitable coastline in Baluchistan'. Its political regime was able to crush any opposition in the country. Pakistan was also the perfect place from which to supply military aid for the Afghan resistance movement fighting Soviet armed forces in Afghanistan. There was a huge and unparalleled increase (of at least 500 per cent over previous decades) of US military and economic assistance to Pakistan (Lifschultz 1986, p. 75). When the US Central Command (CENTCOM) was set up in January 1983, Pakistan became involved. CENTCOM began trying 'to draw Pakistan into a network of understandings' regarding use of bases, overflight rights, support agreements and so on. Soon, US P-3 Orion aircraft were using Pakistan air bases as 'part of the global US network' tracking Soviet nuclear submarines, and construction of additional base facilities in Baluchistan and elsewhere was apparently under way (Lifschultz 1986, pp. 71, 73, 75). In exchange, Pakistan became the recipient of 'huge supplies of modern offensive weapons' and enough economic aid to bail Zia ul-Haq out of potential economic crises and stabilize his regime (Chicherov 1984, p. 1128). The strengthening of Pakistan–USA military relations, however, did not offer Pakistan any guarantee of US support in the event of a Soviet threat to its territorial integrity, and Pakistan's main arms supplier continued to be China, not the USA (Inder Singh 1986, p. 217).

India was affected by this USA–Pakistan escalation, and started buying new weapons from the Soviet Union. As the arms race between India and Pakistan escalated, Indian distrust of American intentions increased (Harrison 1986, p. 127). Indira Ghandi expressed 'disappointment' with Reagan's foreign policy because it 'nurtures dictatorships in many parts of the world while displaying "indifference and hypocrisy" towards India – "the greatest democracy in the world"'. Nevertheless, the Reagan administration did try to improve relations with India 'at the expense of Soviet–Indian relations', and the volume of trade between the two countries grew substantially (Chicherov 1984, pp. 1126–7). When Indira Gandhi was assassinated in 1984 and her son Rajiv came to power, he initially preferred closer links with the USA, but that was 'eroded by a series of irritations, notably Washington's lavish arms aid to Pakistan'; there was an incredibly swift buildup, with huge budgets, of CENTCOM as a whole, which by 1986 was 'considered to be on a par with NATO in Europe' (Lifschultz 1986, p. 72). For India, Pakistan being centrally implicated in CENTCOM posed a threat to India's position as the regional superpower in South Asia.

Furthermore, the arms race in South Asia had a distinctly nuclear flavour by the mid 1980s. India made it clear it had a 'workable nuclear device' in the 1970s when it was reported that tests had been carried out. By the mid 1980s Pakistan was apparently 'two screwdriver turns away' from also having such a device. The Pakistanis had been careful to stop there and not go on to complete the job and test it because 'all the aid packages offered to Pakistan by the US have had one condition attached to them – thou shalt not make the bomb'. The reason?

> The main opposition by the US to Pakistan's making a nuclear bomb is precisely because it is the Islamic Bomb, i.e. Pakistan will become the first Muslim nation to have such a device. Furthermore, when Libya and Pakistan were friends, the Libyans had plans to 'buy' the bomb and use it against Israel. This is something the Americans will never permit, come what may. They will use all possible means to stop Pakistan making the bomb, although Pakistan has in a sense already made it. The most likely scenario is that Pakistan will not publicly test the device as long as aid comes in, but will only test it in case of war with India.
>
> (Babar Ali 1987, p. 590)

The extent of India's nuclear arsenal by the mid 1980s was not known, although presumably it had gone beyond one or two nuclear devices. By 1988, India had acquired a nuclear powered submarine – named the INS *Chakra* – from the Soviet Union.

One of the striking things revealed by this thumbnail sketch is the apparent mismatch between the intensity of superpower rivalry and the intensity of the India–Pakistan conflict during the period. According to Halliday (1986), the most intense periods of superpower conflict have been during the First Cold War (1945–53) and the Second Cold War (1979–86). We might expect, using Halliday's model, that the global reach of the superpowers would be longest during those periods, in the sense of being able to reach a long way into South Asia and profoundly limit the policy making there. Similarly, when their rivalry was less intense, the superpowers would have a less important effect on policy.

This would be particularly so during the period of *détente* (1969–79). Clearly, however, the most severe conflict in South Asia occurred in 1971 during the India–Pakistan War, leading to the dismemberment of Pakistan and the creation of Bangladesh. But this was the period of superpower *détente*. Provisionally, then, the evidence suggests that Halliday's tight model may be less useful as a framework for examining the effect of superpower rivalry on the foreign policy choices of India and Pakistan than Hoffmann's looser model.

THOUGHTS ON THE MAIN QUESTION IN RELATION TO SOUTH ASIA

To what extent have the states of India and Pakistan had the freedom to choose their own foreign policies without being limited by the military or ideological power of the USA or the USSR?

For one thing, it is clear that the military aspect of superpower rivalry has extended into the South Asian region and had an influence there. That it existed in the 1980s is undeniable, despite the fact that 'South Asia is not a major bone of contention between the superpowers' (Inder Singh 1986, p. 218). There was in the 1980s an immense buildup of strategic weapons in the area, particularly Soviet nuclear submarines and the American armaments involved in the setting up of CENTCOM. At this level, there was what General Kingston (for CENTCOM) referred to as 'the military conception of a free-standing "area of operations"' (Lifschultz 1986, p. 78). Superpower relations in South Asia, when considered in relation only to this free-standing area of operations, were dominated by military competition.

Such free-standing relations, however, were unreal. The world wasn't organized politically that way. As General Kingston pointed out, in his testimony before a Congressional Committee in February 1984, there was an essential conflict 'between the military conception of a free-standing "area of operations" and the actual existence of local populatoins with their own political institutions and nationalist sentiments' (Lifschultz 1986, p. 78). He informed the Committee that he required facilities in Pakistan and elsewhere to 'facilitate attainment of my power projection objectives' (pp. 76–7) (did he really talk that way?!) but that he had not so far approached Pakistan for a 'forward headquarters' for CENTCOM because 'it's very touchy' (p. 78). One sees here how, for a superpower, it is not enough to have a free-standing presence above South Asia; the superpowers were drawn down into South Asian politics in pursuit of their strategic objectives. For the USA, reaching down into Pakistan politics was 'touchy'. Why?

Part of the answer is the one given by General Kingston: the existence of sentiments of national determination over which the USA could not just ride roughshod. Also important was another factor: China, a major power but not a superpower, and a considerable supplier of arms for Pakistan. If the USA pushed too hard, Pakistan could turn increasingly to China. That was another reason why, for the USA, Pakistan was 'touchy'. The China factor enters in because of the Sino–Soviet regional rivalry in Asia. So we have three levels of strategic-military conflict in South Asia:

1 The free-standing superpower military rivalry
2 The military rivalry between USA–Pakistan–China and USSR–India
3 The regional rivalry between India and Pakistan.

That is why Inder Singh (1986) could say, following Buzan (1986), that 'Sino–Soviet regional rivalry in Asia and the Soviet–American global conflict are therefore two separate, if parallel, dynamics' affecting South Asian security (p. 227). In short, superpower rivalry is not the (only) global phenomenon affecting the security of regions of the world; there are also other major rivalries involving non-superpowers like China that can have an effect on the security of particular regions.

It is worth noting in passing non-military aspects of superpower rivalry in South Asia. Inder Singh (1986) summarizes the position: 'Superpower penetration of the subcontinent has taken economic, cultural, political and military forms' but 'the effect of non-military penetration has been limited in the sense that it has not affected or altered the internal structure of either country' (India or Pakistan) (p. 216). Both superpowers have tried to draw the South Asian states into their orbit economically. Chicherov's (1984) article illustrates this multifaceted nature of Soviet activity in South

Asia (especially pp. 1121–5). Neither superpower has had much success. It does seem to be the case that the military aspect of superpower rivalry is the predominant one. In particular, it has been the superpower contribution to the arms race between India and Pakistan that has 'exacerbated the dynamics of the local rivalry'. It aggravated a conflict already in existence. The India–Pakistan conflict was already in existence before there was superpower rivalry, and the history of that conflict is best explained with reference to regional dynamics, not superpower penetration. We noticed earlier, for example, that the superpowers did not set off the Indo–Pakistan War of 1971, nor did their presence have an effect on the outcome. But the superpower rivalry did exacerbate the conflict by stoking the arms race between India and Pakistan, which clearly made their ongoing conflict more intense.

As for limits on policy making, the views from Moscow and Washington seemed to be similar. Chicherov (1984), for example, viewed Indian foreign policy as virtually independent of superpower restrictions. He identified the 'positive thrust of India's foreign policy reflected in its basically anti-colonial and anti-imperialist stand'. There were 'profound differences and divergence between the foreign policies of India and US' and, although Soviet and Indian 'foreign policy moves' were 'close', the basic position was that 'India's foreign policy is neither pro-Western, nor pro-Soviet, but pro-Indian' (p. 1126). Harrison's (1986) view implicitly was that Indian policy making was not restricted by the USA. India 'is rapidly emerging as a major industrial and military power' and is 'determined to achieve a dominant position in South Asia' (pp. 126, 129). At the same time, as the possibility of American military involvement in South Asia grew, resentment of the USA 'is building up among key military and political figures who are shaping India's regional military role in the decades ahead' (p. 130). There is no indication in Harrison's and Chicherov's articles that either superpower could restrict the capacity of India's military and political policy makers to shape India's military role in the region.

Inder Singh's (1986) view was somewhat different from those of the policy advisers in Moscow and Washington. She concentrated more on the structure of power, the overall effect on India's foreign policy of Indian perceptions of what the superpowers could do. She concentrated primarily on the potential power of the USA. 'Today,' she said, 'the US Seventh Fleet can reach Bombay in three days from Diego Garcia, at a time when the Americans are arming both India's antagonists' (Pakistan and China). She went on:

> The Indians cannot discount the possibility of coercive diplomacy by the US in the future. India does not have the resources to challenge superpowers or to halt the arms race in the region, so Soviet naval deployments have a deterrent value against the US capabilities in the Indian Ocean. With India and Pakistan unable to resolve their local disputes, superpower naval competition in the Indian Ocean will, on the whole, reinforce the existing structure of the South Asian [security] complex. (p. 221)

Dutt's (1984) approach was also rather different. He did not start with relationships between the superpowers and India as state actors. He started with the structure of the world economy. India was 'tremendously dependent on the outside world for finance and technology', yet it also had built itself 'into a state with its own capital and technology' (p. 9). India's quest for great power status had been determined primarily by 'the ruling classes within India itself', and their aspirations and perceptions, which determine their policy making, 'occur against a background of economic forces, which are the very underpinnings of their position' (p. 11). They worked with a state-capitalist system, in which the public and private sectors of the economy were intertwined. Like other capitalisms, this one stagnates unless it expands. And there have been 'chronic problems' of underutilization of capacity, lack of internal demand, lack of new investment – all due in part to a huge, impoverished peasantry not providing an outlet for India's industrial goods. The 'capitalist solution' inevitably has been 'to go abroad . . . open up new markets, exploit productive forces in other countries' (p. 12). Dutt then goes on to describe India's economic expansion into other Third World countries. India is therefore a second-tier imperialist power – a state which has 'some autonomy and whose foreign policies may sometimes even conflict with imperial centres although, at the same time, they remain basically dependent' within the world economy. Relative autonomy in policy making, 'not total subordination, has been the real position of India since 1947' (p. 12). For example, 'the Indian state has some autonomy *vis-à-vis* the superpowers, Indian missiles are being built to enforce an Indian, not a Soviet or an American, strategic policy' (p. 9).

As for Pakistan, Inder Singh and Chicherov clearly suggested that the USA propped up General Zia ul-Haq's regime in the mid 1980s, and therefore had a major influence on the country's foreign policy and domestic politics. Inder Singh (1986) argued that 'the US alliances with Pakistan did not end that country's search for security', nor did they serve her primary purpose in foreign policy – 'security against disintegration through Indian intervention' (p. 217). In the circumstances, Pakistan opted to seek and obtain arms from China. It was American and Chinese arms that made it possible for the Pakistan military to shore up its weak position in domestic politics as the only force capable of governing without a popular mandate. The Soviet invasion of Afghanistan also 'enabled General Zia ul-Haq to continue martial law and has legitimized his political regime' (p. 217). Chicherov (1984) echoed these arguments in a general way when he said that US military aid was used by General Zia 'to stabilize his repressive military dictatorship and suppress the opposition' (p. 1128). With these huge supplies of modern arms to Pakistan, the USA 'contributes to the "survival" of the antidemocratic military regime' and 'disrupts the emerging trend toward stability on the subcontinent' (p. 1124).

Lifschultz (1986) agreed that this 'American patronage has been politically crucial in stabilizing Zia's own position within the Army's unsettled officer corps and in securing the junta's dominance over the body politic' (p. 75). It did not follow, however, that Pakistan's policy makers were merely US puppets. Lifschultz reported General Kingston as saying 'it's very touchy' to even think about approaching the Pakistan government at that time (1984) for a policy decision to allow a CENTCOM forward headquarters on Pakistan soil. He also reported that the Pakistan Bar Association had passed resolutions calling upon the government not to enter into agreements granting access to US forces (p. 77). The USA's CENTCOM was also described as *trying* 'to draw Pakistan into a network of understanding' regarding bases, overflight rights etc. (p. 73). All this conveys the impression that Pakistan's policy makers had some autonomy *vis-à-vis* the USA in the 1980s.

One other example: Harrison (1986) urged the USA to detach itself 'from all forms of direct involvement in a military rivalry' (between India and Pakistan) 'that it cannot control' (p. 134). Cannot control? Pakistan's policy makers, it seemed, may have been able to some extent to control the types of military equipment received. From the American point of view, the purpose of military assistance was to equip Pakistan for purposes of defence against a possible Russian advance across the Afghan frontier, and more broadly to integrate Pakistan firmly into American military planning. The appropriate equipment would have been things such as interceptor aircraft, light tanks, and 105 mm howitzers useful in mountain terrain. Instead, Pakistan had arranged it so that the equipment included, amongst other things, F-16 long-range fighter bombers, heavy tanks, and 155 mm howitzers designed for plains warfare. In short, Pakistan's policy makers in the armaments arena had prevailed at least to some extent: arms were obtained from the USA, then aimed at India.

Seven more general points strike me about this literature related to possible super-power constraints on foreign policy choices in South Asia. First, the foreign policies of India and Pakistan have been preoccupied with security issues *vis-à-vis* each other. The origins of that conflict and the foreign policy positions adopted at that time had nothing to do with the superpowers. Furthermore, foreign policy decisions to go to war in 1971, or to ease the conflict in 1966, were not prompted or limited by the superpowers. It is clear that the superpowers did not want to 'get involved' in what they saw as a local dispute. So, in these ways, India and Pakistan to some extent have been free to choose. But their choices have been framed and shaped by the military capability of the adversary which the superpowers and China have helped to establish. Also the superpowers, by their sheer presence in the region, virtually rule out certain foreign policy options that India or Pakistan might conceivably want to make. To put this vital structural point as bluntly as possible: for India or Pakistan to launch sudden all-out war against the adversary is not a likely option because they anticipate that the USA or the USSR or both would then move in, and the outcome of that scenario is so uncertain that neither India nor Pakistan would want to risk the possible consequences.

Second, superpowers can constrain foreign policy by affecting domestic politics. India and Pakistan appear to differ on this score. The Indian state has been centrally involved in efforts since 1947 to develop into a major economic power. One gains the impression from reading Harrison (1986), Chicherov (1984) and other foreign policy advisers outside India that the superpowers are essentially onlookers in this domestic policy arena. As regards Pakistan, however, the USA through its military assistance and in other ways does appear to help to keep in power the present military regime in Pakistan. It may not control Pakistan's domestic policies directly, but it makes it very clear to everyone that it would not like to see the present regime replaced by a revolutionary one. To that extent the USA is involved in domestic politics and thereby limits foreign policy choices by setting certain limits to political change in Pakistan. Certainly any political change in Pakistan would be of direct significance to the United States.

Third, the main question in this chapter is worded in such a way that one might be led to assume that foreign and domestic policies are constrained either by superpowers or by internal domestic forces, or by a combination of both. The South Asia literature shows clearly that this formulation is too narrow. There can be important regional considerations involved. Buzan (1986) shows us how to identify a regional security complex, and Inder Singh (1986) employs that framework in her analysis of policy making in India and Pakistan. Without bringing in the regional dimension, the import-ance of the China factor in South Asian security and foreign policy could easily be missed.

Fourth, the question begins 'to what extent has superpower rivalry constrained', and unless one is careful it would be easy to slip into assuming that the two superpowers are equally able to constrain, or not able to constrain, as the case may be. A moment's reflection makes one realize that one superpower may be more able to constrain than the other. The South Asia case suggests that the USA may be more able to constrain Pakistan's policy making than the USSR. More generally, Chicherov (1984) suggests that the Soviet Union has tended to take a more relaxed attitude towards South Asian states than the USA.

Likewise, fifth, each local state in a region may not have an equivalent amount of policy-making autonomy *vis-à-vis* the superpowers. A superpower may be very influential in one state's policy-making processes, much less so in another. For example, the superpowers may have been more influential in Pakistan's domestic politics (e.g. legitimating General Zia's regime) in the mid 1980s than was the case with India.

Sixth, the main question has been explored through literature which concentrates primarily on the superpowers and two South Asian states. The terrain is international relations. That literature does throw useful light on the question, as I have tried to suggest, but it does seem that a great deal of what we want to know in order to explain foreign policy making is left out. That is, the readings suggest on the whole that one cannot explain policy making very well by reference only to the constraints of superpowers. But this literature does not (except for Dutt 1984) go much into what presumably is important in explaining South Asian policies – that is, the constraints of domestic social and political forces. Analyses of bureaucratic politics within relevant ministries would also come in here.

Finally, exploring this question on the basis of this literature on South Asia has raised questions about the possible limitations of the question. The question seems limited to possible restrictions imposed directly by superpower states. But there is more broadly an international economic environment, of international economic forces, that may well also restrict them. Dutt (1984) in particular draws attention to such international economic constraints, arguing that India's policy makers 'have some autonomy' but remain 'basically dependent' on 'imperial centres' (p. 12). Presumably one of the superpower states, the USA, is a major force within such an imperial centre, which would include non-state agencies like multinational corporations, the International Monetary Fund and the World Bank. But to speak of imperial centres rather than superpower states takes us beyond the bounds of the question.

SUPERPOWER RIVALRY AND SOUTHERN AFRICA

Is South Asia's relationship with the superpowers unique? If it is, then the preceding discussion may be considered perhaps interesting but not a very reliable guide to an understanding of the extent to which superpower rivalry constrains Third World states. We need to check, if only very briefly, the South Asia case against another similar area of the Third World – similar in the sense that the region, like South Asia, was of only modest interest to the superpowers up to the end of the 1970s and then appeared to become somewhat more important than previously. Southern Africa – Angola, Zambia, Malawi, Zimbabwe, Mozambique, Botswana, Namibia, South Africa, Lesotho, Swaziland – will do very nicely. Such a brief comparative check should enable us to speak somewhat more confidently about superpower rivalry in relation to Third World states in regions perceived by the superpower to be less than vital to their interests. This brief discussion of Southern Africa relies primarily on the work of Berridge (1990) and MacFarlane (1990).

Until the mid 1970s, Southern Africa was barely visible to the policy makers in Washington. Britain had traditionally been a paramount power in the region on whom the USA could rely to deal with any strategic regional problems. To a lesser extent Portugal, as another NATO ally, had also performed this function. By the early part of the 1970s, however, Portuguese colonial rule in Angola and Mozambique had ended and British influence in the region was continuing gradually to wane, owing importantly to developments in Southern Rhodesia (later Zimbabwe). Into this situation stepped the Soviet Union and Cuba. Weapons and combat troops began to be supplied to the Popular Movement for the Liberation of Angola (MPLA), and Soviet influence in Mozambique increased significantly. By the early 1980s, every state in the region except Malawi, Swaziland and South Africa had a Soviet embassy (there was even one in Zimbabwe despite Moscow having backed Joshua Nkomo in the Rhodesian civil war) and most states also hosted diplomats from Cuba, Vietnam, North Korea and Eastern European countries (Berridge 1990, p. 207).

The United States did not respond immediately in the 1970s to this growing Soviet presence in Southern Africa; the reasons are complex, but important factors were domestic political pressure in the USA against becoming engaged after the Vietnam War in foreign entanglements and the domestic political danger of appearing to support apartheid in South Africa. With the arrival of the more conservative Reagan administration in 1980–1, however, the American government's interest in Southern Africa appeared to escalate. A prominent US policy adviser on Southern Africa described American interests there as 'important' and 'exposed' (Crocker 1980–1, p. 346). But such remarks were somewhat misleading; a careful analysis of American interests in Southern Africa during the 1980s suggests that strategically and economically the area remained relatively unimportant, and the only thing that was really important to the Americans was 'the diplomatic, Cold War interest in expelling Soviet influence in the region' (Berridge 1990, p. 211). By the end of the decade, however, even that aim was no longer apparent from US government policy statements. There was a more relaxed view about even the notionally Soviet aligned states of Angola and Mozambique, for it had become clear then 'that such regimes are not "irredeemable", that their emergence has no obviously detrimental impact on US interests, and that Third World radicalism does not necessarily advantage the USSR in a concrete and significant sense' (MacFarlane 1990, p. 22).

The main reason for this more relaxed view was the growing recognition in Washington that the Soviet Union was unable to exercise much control even over its client states like Angola and Mozambique, let alone other states in Southern Africa. To the question 'To what extent do the superpowers constrain the policies of states in Southern Africa?', the answer seems to be 'Not very much'. Berridge (1990, pp. 215–16) gave six reasons for the Soviet Union's weakness in relation to Angola and Mozambique at the end of the 1980s:

First of all, suspicion of Soviet motives on the part of almost all African politicians is at least as deep as suspicion of Western motives, and most of them share a strong attachment to non-alignment. The Angolan and Mozambique governments are stiffened in this regard by neighbouring leaders with high prestige in the non-aligned movement, Kenneth Kaunda of Zambia and Robert Mugabe of Zimbabwe. Secondly, the Soviet bloc has been manifestly incapable of providing the economic assistance so badly needed by Angola and Mozambique, and both have been turning for this increasingly to the West ... Thirdly, the Soviet bloc has no monopoly on the supply of military equipment or advice in the latter half of the 1980s. Mozambique accepted military advisers from Britain and Portugal, while Angola began purchasing weapons from Western Europe. Fourthly, the Soviet Union does not have a monopoly on the supply of troops for internal security either. Mozambique, for example, whose need in this respect is particularly urgent in view of the extensive activities of the South African backed Renamo 'bandits' (the Mozambique National Resistance), has since July 1985 come to rely increasingly on the large and well-trained Zimbabwe army (plus a small complement of Tanzanian troops), especially for defence of the vital Beira Corridor. Following an agreement of December 1986, defence of the Nacala route by the Chissano government was assisted by troops from Malawi. Fifthly, the Soviet Union cannot marshal military and economic power in the region comparable to that of South Africa. And, finally, it has no influence over the South African government or even (since 1956) formal diplomatic relations with it; consequently, it cannot plausibly offer to put pressure on Pretoria in the interests of any of its clients.

Soviet weakness in relation to its clients in Angola and Mozambique is almost certainly not due only to the particular reasons mentioned above. More generally, Marxists from all over Africa met at a conference in Accra at the end of the 1980s and 'concluded that the South could not depend on the USSR for meaningful assistance in the transition to socialism' (MacFarlane 1990, p. 25).

What about the United States in relation to its principal client state in the region – South Africa? Even to call it a client state is probably a misnomer. Certainly the USA has been unable to constrain in any fundamental way South Africa's foreign policies. Berridge (1990, pp. 216–17) suggested that at the end of the 1980s the USA 'has failed to end South African prevarication over Namibia, has failed to halt the Republic's nuclear weapons' programme, and has failed to curb the ferocity of its regional "destabilisation" policies – including even attacks on the capital of Western-inclined Botswana and American-owned oil installations in Northern Angola'. Why?

Firstly, there is the adequacy of the Republic's military strength relative to the threats which it believes it faces. Unlike Israel, South Africa does not need a constant supply of advanced heavy weapons from the United States or anyone else in order to protect its security. However, it is important to note that this may change because, as far as can be told, the South Africans cannot build jet fighters of their own without smuggling in components from abroad and there is evidence that they are reluctant to commit their ageing squadrons in combat against Angola's modern Soviet-supplied fighters and air defence systems. Secondly, there is the knowledge that South Africa has powerful friends as well as powerful enemies in Washington, with the constant promise which this provides that hostility from America is never likely to be pushed too far and, in any event, may tomorrow turn into discreet friendship. Thirdly, there is the Republic's well-developed siege economy, which makes it highly resistant to economic pressure.

Fourthly, there are other states to which South Africa can turn for commercial, financial and military/technical assistance, such as Israel and Taiwan – though it is true that, on 19 March 1987, under pressure from the US Congress, the Israeli government announced that it would enter no *new* military contracts with South Africa. And, amongst other factors, there is the ideological certainty which the ruling National Party has at any rate until recently displayed.

It is for reasons such as these that South Africa avoids being manipulated by the dictates of superpower rivalry in the region. By the end of the 1980s this was matched by a growing recognition in the United States government that 'Cold War competition in the Third World is receding, that conflicts in the Third World are rooted in local causes and that dominoes do not necessarily fall' (MacFarlane 1990, p. 20).

CONCLUSION

It should be clear that we are not in a position to frame by way of conclusion a 'correct' answer to our main question: to what extent has superpower rivalry constrained the foreign policies of states in South Asia and Southern Africa? Nevertheless, the discussion has identified a number of aspects that need to be borne in mind when trying to cope with the question:

1 There are different models of global political competition, each of which is at least loosely related to the three main paradigms – realist, liberal-pluralist, neo-Marxist. Each model tends to produce a somewhat different answer to the main question.
2 It is useful, when dealing with this question, to build in the idea of regional security complexes as they affect relations between superpowers and individual states.
3 Superpower rivalry does extend to regions like South Asia and Southern Africa even though such regions may be less strategically important for the superpowers than other regions.
4 The intensity of superpower rivalry has changed through time, and by the end of the 1980s such Third World states appeared to be less susceptible to superpower control than at the beginning of that decade.
5 Superpower rivalry can exacerbate local rivalries that already have a logic of their own.
6 One superpower may be able to constrain a state in South Asia or Southern Africa more than the other superpower, and one such state may be more or less autonomous from a superpower than another.
7 States in South Asia and Southern Africa can have considerable autonomy regarding making their own foreign policies, although the existence of superpowers in a region tends to rule certain policy options virtually out of the question.
8 Superpower rivalry, or the presence of superpowers in a region, can establish a structure of power that limits states even though one or both superpowers may do nothing by way of exercising their power.

Finally, there has been what amounts to a general line taken on the usefulness of realism, pluralism and Marxism as frames of reference for exploring the impact of the superpowers on the states of South Asia and Southern Africa. In sum, a Hoffmann-like, pluralist framework appears in this chapter to have been more helpful than others. One reason for this is that the chapter has given prominence to regions, à la Buzan (1986) and others, and regional considerations figure more importantly in pluralist analyses than in others. The chapter has taken this pluralist-type focus because relevant literature does suggest that these regional considerations have an important bearing on explanations of the foreign policies of South Asian and Southern African states. It is essential, however, to appreciate that this pluralist frame of analysis has been found useful in exploring this particular question regarding the impact of the two superpowers on South Asian and Southern African states. Other paradigms may be more useful when exploring other questions. Indeed, I shall argue later in this book (chapter 11) that a particular form of neo-Marxist theory may be more useful than others when examining different questions about the relative autonomy of Third World states within the global economy.

References

Babar Ali (1987) Pakistan–US military relationships in the 1980s. *Economic and Political Weekly*, XXII (14), 588–90.

Berridge, G.R. (1990) The superpowers and Southern Africa. In R. Allison and P. Williams (eds), *Superpower Competition and Crisis Prevention in the Third World*, Cambridge: Cambridge University Press.

Buzan, B. (1986) A framework for regional security analysis. In B. Buzan et al. *South Asian Insecurity and the Great Powers*, London: Macmillan, 3–33.

Chicherov, A.I. (1984) South Asia and the Indian Ocean in the 1980s: some trends towards changes in international relations. *Asian Survey*, XXIV (II), 1117–30.

Crocker, C.A. (1980–1) South Africa: strategy for change. *Foreign Affairs*, 59 (winter), 323–51.

Dutt, S. (1984) *India and the Third World: Altruism or Hegemony*. London: Zed Books.

George, A.L. (1990) Superpower interests in Third Areas. In R. Allison and P. Williams (eds), *Superpower Competition and Crisis Prevention in the Third World*, Cambridge: Cambridge University Press.

Halliday, F. (1986) *The Making of the Second Cold War* (2nd edn). London: Verso.

Harrison, S.S. (1986) South Asia: avoiding disaster: cut a regional deal. *Foreign Policy*, 62 (spring), 126–47.

Hoffmann, S. (1985) The future of the international political system: a sketch. In S.P. Huntington and J.S. Nye (eds), *Global Dilemmas*, London: University Press of America.

Inder Singh, A. (1986) The superpower global complex and South Asia. In B. Buzan et al., *South Asian Insecurity and the Great Powers*, London: Macmillan.

Lifschultz, L. (1986) From the U-2 to the P-3: the US–Pakistan relationship. *New Left Review*, 159 (September–October), 71–80.

MacFarlane, S.N. (1990) Superpower rivalry in the 1990s. *Third World Quarterly*, 12 (1), 1–25.

Rais, R.B. (1986) *The Indian Ocean and the Superpowers*. London: Croom Helm.

Wirsing, R.G. (1985) The arms race in South Asia: implications for the United States. *Asian Survey*, XXV (3), 265–91.

4

Superpower Rivalry and US Hegemony in Central America

ANTHONY G. McGREW

INTRODUCTION

Speaking to a specially convened joint session of Congress in April 1983, President Ronald Reagan issued a dire warning of an unparalleled threat to national security:

> If Central America were to fall, what would be the consequences for our position in Asia, Europe, and for alliances such as NATO? If the United States cannot respond to a threat near our own borders, why should Europeans or Asians believe that we're seriously concerned about threats to them? If the Soviets can assume that nothing short of an actual attack on the United States will provoke an American response, which ally, which friend will trust us then? ... The national security of the Americas is at stake in Central America. If we cannot defend ourselves there, we cannot expect to prevail elsewhere.
>
> (quoted in Schoultz 1987, p. 269)

What had provoked this obsessive concern with Central America was the consolidation of the socialist Sandinista regime in Nicaragua, a regime which the administration perceived as both communist and pro-Soviet. The expressed fear was that, if allowed to prosper, Nicaragua would become a base for communist subversion in Central America, igniting a fuse of political revolution which could spread right up to the Mexican–American border (figure 4.1). Not since the revolutionary wars, Americans were warned, had the republic faced such a direct potential threat to national security so perilously close to home. As Halliday remarks, the Sandinista victory in Nicaragua 'brought the threat of Third World revolution geographically much closer to the USA' (1987, p. 96). The American response to this unprecedented challenge to national security was unambiguous: it sought, throughout the 1980s, to enforce its hegemony over the states in the region by exercising its military and economic power to contain the spread of revolution in its own back yard.

This chapter explores the globalization of Cold War rivalry and competition. It gives prominence to the processes and logic which compelled both superpowers into

Figure 4.1 The Americas

globalizing their rivalry – as if the world was akin to a giant chess game in which they controlled the movement of the pieces and established the rules of play. In attempting to understand the imperialistic imperatives which condition the behaviour of dominant states towards subordinate states, this chapter will rely heavily upon realist and neo-Marxist analyses. Why these two paradigms? Primarily because both have much to say about the expansionary drives which govern great power behaviour. Both paradigms

therefore provide a useful starting point for analysing the factors shaping US interventionism in Central America throughout the 1980s. By critically evaluating the
explanations which both these paradigms offer of US hegemony in Central America,
we may be in a stronger position to provide a more generalized account of the
globalizing imperatives underlying great power behaviour.

UNDERSTANDING RELATIONS BETWEEN THE US AND CENTRAL AMERICA: THE LEVELS OF ANALYSIS PROBLEM

When a social scientist attempts to explain the underlying causes of any social phenomenon, whether it be unemployment or voting behaviour, s/he can approach it at two
distinct levels – the micro and the macro. Thus unemployment can be explained, as
it often is, as a consequence of individual attributes (e.g. lack of relevant skills, age,
level of education etc.), or as a consequence of the dynamics of the economic system,
i.e. economic recession or structural change in the national economy. In one case we
focus on the characteristics of the parts which make up the whole, whereas in the
other case we concentrate upon the characteristics of the whole. These two distinct
levels of analysis – the micro and the macro – offer different approaches to interpreting
and explaining the same phenomenon. But they are not in any sense mutually exclusive.
On the contrary, they intersect and complement one another. Let's explore this issue
a little further by focusing specifically upon relations between the US and Central
America.

For much of the post-war period the US has taken a considerable interest in the
domestic and foreign affairs of its Central American neighbours. At various times US
presidents have authorized direct or indirect intervention in the politics of individual
states to protect American interests. In 1954 the Central Intelligence Agency (CIA)
assisted in the overthrow of the socialist Arbenz regime in Guatemala, whilst in 1977
President Carter cut off all military aid to the same country because of its human
rights record. Whatever the motives for intervention, the form that it takes or the
instruments used, there is no doubt that the character of US policy towards Central
America, particularly in the post-war period (but also for much of this century), has
been decidedly interventionist. How can we make sense of this apparent pattern or
regularity in US behaviour?

Any state's foreign policy can be viewed from two distinct levels of analysis: the
systemic (macro) and the state (micro). At the *systemic level of analysis* the focus is upon
the global system and how it conditions, constrains and even determines state behaviour.
This approach gives particular emphasis to the ways in which external conditions and
factors prefigure the choices which decision makers are able to take. Moreover, it
stresses a holistic view since it suggests that a state's behaviour can only be understood
by reference to the characteristics and structure of the global system of which it is
part. Accordingly, one explanation for the interventionary style of American policy
towards Central America is that it arises as a natural product of its systemic rivalry
with the Soviet Union, which requires it to operate according to a balance of power
logic by preventing Soviet gains (even perceived gains) in any part of the world.
Alternatively, US actions can be interpreted as a product of its hegemonic role in the
world capitalist system. Such a role, it is often argued, demands an interventionary
policy on the world's periphery in order to prevent the consolidation of socialist-type

regimes, such as that in Nicaragua, which challenge the prevailing world capitalist order. Although these are quite radically different interpretations of the underlying causes of US behaviour, what links them is a common emphasis upon a holistic, systems level explanation. US behaviour is conceived as a response to systemic requirements.

The alternative to this systems level approach is to focus upon the nature and internal characteristics of the nation-state. Rather than view a state's behaviour as determined by systemic forces, a *nation-state level of analysis* considers it the resultant of the domestic structure and decision-making processes of the state. Thus US behaviour towards Central America can be explained in terms of why the decision makers came to define the national interest in terms of an interventionary policy. Alternatively, the same behaviour could be interpreted as a response to the particular needs and demands of American capital to protect its corporate investments in the region. Whatever the validity of these different explanations, they both nonetheless share a common methodological focus: the nature of the state and its internal policy processes.

In attempting to explain the origins and nature of US policy towards Central America in the 1980s, this chapter deliberately exploits both a systems level and a nation-state level of analysis. One of the reasons for this is simply that to understand such complex behaviour the insights of both are necessary, for one complements the other. Both slice into reality at distinctive angles, yet the image each provides of that reality overlaps and intersects with the other. A further important reason for utilizing both levels of analysis is to demonstrate their crucial significance for ordering and introducing rigour into our enquiry of global politics. For in any social scientific enterprise we need to be very clear about how we approach the subject matter before we can even begin to select the appropriate theoretical tools and evidence. As Singer has noted in a seminal article bringing the level of analysis problem to the attention of foreign policy analysts:

> For a staggering variety of reasons the scholar may be more interested in one level than another at any given time and will undoubtedly shift his orientation according to his research needs. So the problem is not one of deciding which level is most valuable . . . Rather it is one of realizing that there is this preliminary conceptual issue and that it must be temporarily resolved prior to any research undertaking.
>
> (1969, p. 28)

This is an important methodological point, for it impacts directly upon not just how we approach our study of global politics but also the very theoretical tools we study with. For some theories may be more or less relevant according to whether we are interested in system-wide explanations or alternatively explanations which derive from a focus upon the nature of the key actors, be they states, transnational corporations or classes. It is therefore essential in our enquiry here that the two levels of analysis are not confused, since any sensible attempt to evaluate explanations of behaviour must start from the premise that they are at least attacking the subject matter from a comparable level of analysis.

In what follows we will utilize the systemic and nation-state levels of analysis as methodological devices to assist us in organizing our enquiry into the underlying causes of US interventionism in Central America throughout the 1980s. This will help us in selecting not only relevant evidence but also those theories appropriate to the task of explaining it. Such an approach will also contribute enormously to ensuring that the evaluation of these explanations is approached in a logical and rigorous manner.

US HEGEMONY AND INTERVENTIONISM IN CENTRAL AMERICA

Since 1823, when President Monroe proclaimed the Monroe Doctrine, successive US administrations have sought (and fought) quite successfully to maintain Latin America within the US sphere of influence (see figure 4.1). Like the Soviets in their post-war relations with Eastern Europe, the US has been assiduous in its attempts to prevent the penetration of the region by foreign powers (specifically but not exclusively the Soviet Union) as well as by alien ideologies. Whilst it has never been completely successful in this task it still remains, without doubt, the dominant power on the continent.

Politically, economically and militarily the US exercises hegemonic power over its southern neighbours. Politically, only Cuba today stands outside the US sphere of influence, having become progressively allied to the Soviets since the revolution in 1959. Economically, the US remains the dominant trading partner and primary source of foreign capital investment throughout Latin America, despite growing economic penetration by European and Japanese capital. Militarily, the US too is also the primary supplier of arms and military hardware to the region's armed forces. Alongside this the Pentagon has cultivated extremely close contacts with the military throughout Latin and Central America. Effectively then, despite some erosion of its global hegemony (as Halliday 1987 notes), the US still remains the dominant external reality shaping the economic and political development of all Latin American states. Indeed, this is more so the case with respect to the Central American states than to most others in the hemisphere.

The Background to US Policy in the 1980s

Since the early days of this century the US has maintained a close interest in political developments throughout Central America. The completion of the Panama Canal, together with the region's proximity to the US, has made it strategically important (see figure 4.1). This, compounded by the endemic political instability which has afflicted many Central American states, has led inescapably to the US adopting, at various times, a strongly interventionist role in the region. During the 1920s for instance, in what is now referred to as dollar diplomacy, the US went so far as to send in the Marines to restore public order in Nicaragua. Even during the period of the 'good neighbours' policy, under Franklin Roosevelt, the US continued, in a less visible way, to exercise a largely controlling influence in the region. To paraphrase Roosevelt's quip about the undemocratic nature of most of the political regimes in the region: 'They may be sons of bitches but at least they're our sons of bitches.'

With the onset of the First Cold War it became even more important to ensure these states remained firmly within the US sphere of influence, with the consequence that the region was caught up directly in the battle to contain the spread of communism. Through the Rio Treaty of 1948, and the US Military Security Act of 1951, all states in the hemisphere were incorporated more closely than ever before under the US wing.

Throughout the 1950s and 1960s US policy towards Central America appeared to be predicated entirely upon containing the potential for communist inspired revolution. This policy took two distinct forms. Firstly, there was a willingness to intervene militarily or covertly, as in the case of the Dominican Republic in 1965 and Guatemala in 1954, to ensure the maintenance of regimes sympathetic to US interests. Secondly, there was extensive provision of economic and military aid to contain or eradicate the host of revolutionary movements which had emerged in many countries during the early 1960s, following the success of the Cuban revolution.

Whilst US policy was geared to buttressing the internal political stability of states within the region, it did not ignore entirely the question of social and political reform. There was a clear recognition in Washington, particularly within the State Department, that the political violence, repression and insurgency which generated so much instability throughout the region were products of oligarchical and dictatorial patterns of rule, combined with the profound inequalities of income and wealth found in most of the states. In a move to pre-empt growing political instability in the whole hemisphere, the Kennedy administration introduced the Alliance for Progress in 1960. Designed to provide economic and financial aid in return for domestic socioeconomic reforms throughout Latin America, the project failed rather dismally. Despite the Alliance for Progress the oligarchs, military juntas and dictators continued to rule in Guatemala, Honduras, Nicaragua and El Salvador. Only in Costa Rica was there any semblance of democratic government. US policy towards Central America appeared increasingly paradoxical: in the fight against communist totalitarianism it was engaged in alliances with highly undemocratic regimes.

However, the 1970s witnessed a transformation in US policy towards the region. Under the Nixon and Ford administrations the region was demoted in terms of overall foreign policy priorities. Economic and military aid was increased but the emphasis was upon maintaining the existing regimes in power as opposed to assisting socioeconomic reform. Nevertheless, in Nicaragua and El Salvador the domestic pressures for reform became uncontainable.

The Sandinista Front for the Liberation of Nicaragua (FSLN) became increasingly successful on both the military and political fronts in its campaign to overthrow the Somoza dictatorship. By 1979 the political crisis in the country was such that the Somoza regime, which had ruled the country for over 40 years, could no longer govern effectively since it had lost even the support of the military. Accordingly in July 1979 the Sandinistas took control of the levers of power in Managua. This was a historic development in many senses. But from the US perspective, it immediately threatened to undermine the political stability of the whole region. For it signalled to other revolutionary movements in neighbouring El Salvador and Guatemala that victory was within their grasp (see figure 4.2). Subsequently, partly in order to undermine popular support for the 'freedom fighters' in El Salvador, the Salvadorean military staged a coup in October 1979, bringing into power a visibly reformist military-civilian junta. However, this did not prevent the outbreak of a virtual civil war between revolutionary and right-wing forces. By the late 1970s, apart from Costa Rica and Panama, the whole region was engrossed in political turmoil.

Initially the US adopted a relatively accommodating stance to the forces of revolution and political reform. Under the Carter administration, which sought to extend democracy and human rights in the region, the US had alienated its traditional allies by halting military aid to Guatemala, El Salvador and Nicaragua (before the revolution).

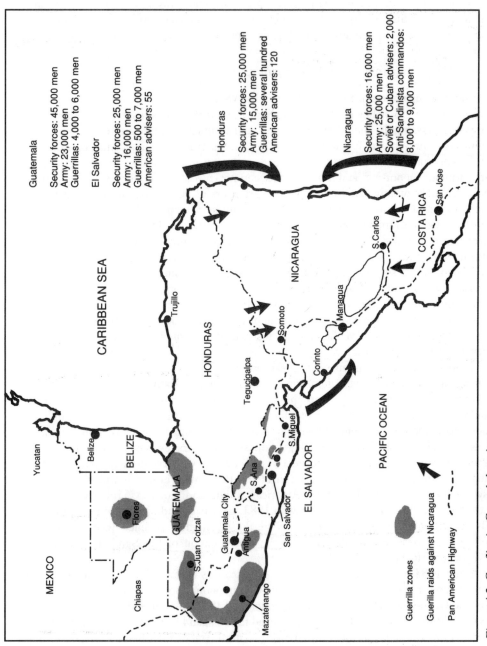

Guatemala

Security forces: 45,000 men
Army: 23,000 men
Guerrillas: 4,000 to 6,000 men

El Salvador

Security forces: 25,000 men
Army: 16,000 men
Guerrillas: 500 to 7,000 men
American advisers: 55

Honduras

Security forces: 25,000 men
Army: 15,000 men
Guerrillas: several hundred
American advisers: 120

Nicaragua

Security forces: 16,000 men
Army: 25,000 men
Soviet or Cuban advisers: 2,000
Anti-Sandinista commandos:
8,000 to 9,000 men

MEXICO

Yucatan

Chiapas

CARIBBEAN SEA

BELIZE

Belize

GUATEMALA

Flores

S.Juan Cotzal

Guatemala City

Antigua

Mazatenango

San Salvador

S. Ana

S.Miguel

EL SALVADOR

HONDURAS

Trujillo

Tegucigalpa

Somoto

Corinto

PACIFIC OCEAN

NICARAGUA

Managua

S.Carlos

COSTA RICA

San Jose

Guerrilla zones

Guerrilla raids against Nicaragua

Pan American Highway

Figure 4.2 Conflict in Central America

This was an attempt to promote domestic political and social reform. In effect the US intervened to undermine the harshest dictatorships and oligarchies by cultivating those centrist political forces in each country which sought moderate social and political reform. One of the most visible gestures in this direction was an official State Department public statement, just a year before the Sandinista revolution, opposing the continued rule of the Somoza family in Nicaragua.

US Policy in the 1980s and Early 1990s

With the inauguration of President Reagan in 1981, surprisingly few immediate changes were made in US policy towards the region. Rather, there was a substantial continuity in policy. Essentially, the administration sought to utilize military and economic aid as a means to prevent the further spread of revolution. However, one significant development was that the administration launched a covert war against the Nicaraguan regime by arming, supporting and training the counter-revolutionary forces – the Contra rebels. Subsequently, an increasing militarization of the region occurred with the deployment of US military forces and military advisers, combined with a strengthening of the indigenous military and security forces in El Salvador, Honduras and Guatemala (see figure 4.2). But alongside this coercion the US also initiated a diplomatic offensive against Nicaragua, cutting off loan and aid facilities in the hope that this might force it to abandon its socialist development strategy, its deepening links with Cuba and the Soviet Union, and crucially its assistance to all revolutionary forces in El Salvador. Moreover, through the Caribbean Basin Initiative it sought to provide economic assistance to the other states in the region in order to alleviate the consequences of the economic recession of the early 1980s and thus to prevent the further spread of revolutionary tendencies.

Despite the coercive nature of the Reagan policy towards Nicaragua, it brought little change in the Sandinistas' domestic or foreign policy. Rather it drifted into much closer alignment with Cuba and the USSR, both of whom supplied it with arms, military assistance and limited economic aid. In response the US increased its military and security assistance to neighbouring countries, including the construction of military bases in Honduras and the holding of massive military exercises involving tens of thousands of US troops. The prospect of direct military intervention appeared increasingly possible, but the extreme caution of the Pentagon, combined with the Vietnam syndrome which still affected the American public and Congress, ruled it out. As a result, following a major policy review in 1983, the Reagan administration concentrated its efforts on the covert war to destabilize the Nicaraguan regime. According to one official, the objective was to 'prevent the consolidation of the Sandinista regime in Nicaragua' (Rubin 1985, p. 227).

From 1983 to the late 1980s Central America was elevated into a fundamental test of US power in the world. A Bipartisan Commission, appointed by the President to review US policy towards the region, concluded that 'Central America's crisis is our crisis'. Subsequently, the President espoused the Reagan Doctrine as the basic blueprint for US foreign policy in the Third World; Central America became its primary testing ground.

By invading Grenada in 1983 to restore political order, the US signalled that direct military intervention to achieve its objectives in Central America could not be dismissed.

More importantly it also acted as a symbol to the American public and to the Soviets that the US remained willing to utilize its massive military power where its vital interests were deemed to be at stake. However, on the mainland of Central America, apart from increased troop deployments and military aid to its allies, the emphasis remained upon the expansion of the covert war against Nicaragua. The latter's harbours were mined by the CIA in 1984 and, in the wake of Congressional refusals to vote direct aid to the Contra rebels, there was even an illicit privatization of the war which became public with the Senate investigations into the Irangate affair commencing in 1987. What emerged from these investigations was that in a rather bizarre series of secret operations, directed by members of the President's national security staff, arms were traded with Iran (in complete contravention of established policy) for American hostages whilst the financial proceeds from these sales were channelled to the Nicaraguan Contra rebels in defiance of Congressional disapprovals of executive requests to grant them military aid. Whilst the legalities of this Irangate operation (as it became widely known) were in doubt, it demonstrated clearly the fervour with which elements of the US government pursued the Reagan Doctrine in Central America.

Combined with this covert campaign to subvert what by 1986 had become a democratically elected government in Nicaragua, the Reagan administration also stepped up its diplomatic offensive. A virtual economic blockade was imposed on Nicaragua. The US Agency for Internal Development (AID) refused economic assistance to Nicaragua and the US used its political leverage inside the World Bank and the Inter-American Development Bank to prevent the granting of further loans. Finally, in 1985 the President outlawed (by executive order) any US trade with the country. By the late 1980s, and the second term of the Reagan presidency, the US had become more deeply entangled in Central American politics than at any time since the 1920s.

Although attempts were made by a group of Latin American states, through what become known as the Contadora process, to obtain a negotiated settlement to the political turmoil in the region, these proved initially unsuccessful. This was partly because of US and Nicaraguan intransigence but also partly because there was no effective machinery to police any political settlement. Despite this, some agreement was reached on a peace plan (the Arias Plan) in November 1987, although without wholehearted US support. However, in the wake of the Iran-Contra scandal, Congress refused to grant the President any further military aid to supply the Contra rebel forces. By the autumn of 1988, despite valiant attempts to sustain the military pressure upon Nicaragua, President Reagan was forced to acknowledge that, during the remaining tenure of his office, no further requests to Congress for military aid for the Contras would be approved (Maidment and McGrew 1991, chapter 8). Coupled with the dramatic changes in US–Soviet relations, which involved joint agreement on resolving the situation in Central America, the US began to de-escalate its low-intensity war against Nicaragua.

The newly incumbent Bush administration did much to avoid a deepening entanglement in the Central American imbroglio. Following its much criticized military intervention in Panama in December 1989, when it acted to replace General Noriega's dictatorship, the new administration became less sanguine about further involvement in the region. In Nicaragua the invasion of Panama was perceived as a further warning that the Sandinistas' policies had to change. Peace talks between the Sandinistas and the Contra forces were held in New York. However, in a completely surprise development the Sandinista government was defeated in national elections in early 1990, helping to resolve the Bush administration's dilemma of how to deal with socialism in its back yard without a further recourse to military force.

EXPLAINING US INTERVENTIONISM

How are we to explain the resurgence of US interventionism in Central America throughout the 1980s? Clearly this is a big question, and one which disguises a more fundamental question about how we explain US behaviour as a global superpower. How do we begin to answer this big question? One way is to utilize what we know already about levels of analysis and the theoretical paradigms which have been introduced in this chapter and in chapter 1. This seems a sensible starting point for constructing even a rudimentary explanation of US interventionism in Central America.

Systemic Explanations: Realism and Neo-Marxism

Returning to our discussion of levels of analysis, we might begin our enquiry by investigating the systemic forces which condition superpower behaviour, particularly towards subordinate states. This brings into play one obvious difference between the superpowers: the US is not just a military superpower but, unlike the Soviet Union, is also an economic superpower. To explain the behaviour of the US in the global system we therefore need to examine how this is shaped by its distinctive hegemonic roles in both the interstate system and the world capitalist system. In doing so we will be introducing into the discussion both the realist and the neo-Marxist paradigms; this is the second dimension of our approach to explaining US actions in Central America.

Realism: the primacy of the international system

Realism stresses how the structure of the international system (whether it is bipolar or multipolar, i.e. whether there are two great powers or more than two) and a state's location in the hierarchy of power in that system almost predetermine its behaviour. It also posits that the anarchical character of the international system and the ever present threat of war have a profound influence upon the actions of all states regardless of their differing ideologies or domestic economic and political arrangements. Quite simply, the international system is regarded as having its own imperatives which induce all states, irrespective of their particular motives or ideological preferences, to behave similarly. Thus all states seek to maintain and to expand their power since only the acquisition of power guarantees the ability to promote and protect the state's core interests in a dangerous and uncertain world. But how does realism help us explain US actions in Central America?

In realist terms, the key to US interventionism in Central America is to be found in the bipolar structure of the international system and the consequent rivalry between the two superpowers. Because of this rivalry, each is forced to protect its interests anywhere on the globe where these are, or appear to be, threatened by the other. Should one side fail to do so, the other might take advantage of this failure and thereby expand its influence in the world. Accordingly, it is not ideology which drives superpower rivalry but a struggle for power, since with power comes the ability to defend one's global interests. What prevents this struggle from degenerating into open conflict, however, is a recognition that peace is best preserved through a balance of power. In this sense US interventionism in Central America can be explained as an attempt to preserve the global balance of power, and so is a function of the dynamics of superpower competition.

A realist explanation of the underlying causes of US intervention in Central America therefore gives primacy to the global struggle for power and influence between the two superpowers. Extending this systemic logic a little further would lead us into the realms of more contemporary realist thinking, namely neo-realism. Whilst neo-realists would accept the broad thrust of what has been argued so far, they would give much greater stress to the structure of the international system as the primary determinant of superpower behaviour. As Waltz, a leading neo-realist theoretician, has argued:

> In a bipolar world there are no peripheries. With only two powers capable of acting on a world scale, anything that happens anywhere is potentially of concern to both of them. Bipolarity extends the geographic scope of both powers' concern . . . Competition becomes more comprehensive as well as more widely extended.
>
> Waltz (1979, p. 171)

Accordingly, the sources of US interventionism in Central America can be traced not simply to US–Soviet rivalry but to the underlying fact that the bipolar structure of power in the international system turns the whole globe into one unified strategic arena, one giant chessboard on which the superpowers watch carefully the movement of every pawn. Regardless of how intense the desire to moderate their competition, the fact is that a bipolar division of the world ensures that almost every major political development anywhere round the globe comes to be defined in zero-sum terms – as a gain or a loss for either side. In this sense US policy towards Central America can be viewed as structurally induced, a function of the post-war bipolar international system. The readiness of the US, by the early 1990s, to de-escalate its military involvement in the region can also be traced to the reduced Soviet threat and the demise of the Cold War. The instabilities in the region could no longer be conceived in strictly East–West terms.

Neo-Marxism: the primacy of the world system

In contrast to the realist explanation, a neo-Marxist analysis of US interventionism in Central America commences with the role of the US as the world's dominant capitalist power. The focus is upon economic, as opposed to strategic and power-political, imperatives and the functions which the US, as the capitalist hegemon, has to perform to maintain the global capitalist order. At a systemic level then, neo-Marxists give primacy to the hegemonic functions of the US in the world system and the underlying rationale for what, in their terms, is considered US *imperialism* (not simply interventionism) in Central America.

A neo-Marxist analysis, as chapter 1 sketched out, offers a holistic conception of the world capitalist system in which all states perform certain functions in order to ensure the continued reproduction of the world capitalist order. The roles that states perform are determined by their position in the overall structure of the world economy. As the hegemonic capitalist power, the US has crucial functions to play in managing and ensuring the continued vitality of world capitalism. One of these functions, it is argued, is ensuring that states on the periphery are kept within the global capitalist order because they are essential to the continued expansion and stability of Western capitalism since they provide new markets, vital raw materials or opportunities for very profitable investment. Another function is ensuring that no vital areas of the world capitalist economy are closed off either by internal revolution or by external interference; vital areas being those which are essential to Western raw material requirements, foreign investment opportunities or trade. From this systemic perspective the US operates in the interests of managing and maintaining the world capitalist order and not in the parochial interests of US capital. An explanation of US interventionism in Central America therefore revolves almost exclusively around its hegemonic functions in the world capitalist order. In simple terms, the US resorts to interventionism in order both to ensure the states in the region are kept within the global capitalist order and to prevent the success of the socialist economic experiments, which could act as a spur to other states in the Third World to pursue more independent strategies of economic development.

State-Level Explanations: the National Security State versus the Capitalist State

Having explored two quite different outside-in explanations of US behaviour in the previous section, here we will concentrate upon the comparable inside-out explanations.

The national security state

To complement the realist explanation at the systemic level, we now turn to a realist explanation at the level of the state. In the language of realism, states act to further their own national interests and to promote national security. Foreign policy, and the external behaviour of states, can therefore be explained in terms of the pursuit of national goals. To understand why in the 1980s US policy became increasingly interventionist, we need to demonstrate how the American state (which in realist analysis is conceived as a unitary body which can rationally calculate and articulate a set of national policy objectives) defined the national interest and its political objectives in Central America. Once that is done we then need to demonstrate that there was some rational correspondence between the actions it took and the policy goals it sought to achieve. As Allison has pointed out, in realist interpretations of foreign policy at the nation-state level of analysis a valid explanation 'consists of showing what goal the government was pursuing when it acted and how that action was a reasonable choice, given the nation's objective' (1971, p. 13).

To explain US intervention in Central America we therefore have to show a correspondence between how the problem was defined by the key decision makers, what the US goals were and how the national interest was conceived, and how US actions related to the achievement of those goals and the prosecution of the national interest.

Schoultz, in his study of US policy towards Latin America, notes that: 'During the Reagan administration, Central America's reality was defined in terms of the East–West struggle. One country was on "their" side [Nicaragua], and the remaining four were on "ours"' (1987, p. 272).

The capitalist state

We will conclude our enquiry by explicating a neo-Marxist explanation at the state level of analysis to complement the earlier systemic focus. Such a new-Marxist explanation concentrates upon the underlying economic imperatives which propel the American state into an expansionary and imperialist foreign policy. Put simply, the argument is that global expansion of American capital can only succeed if supported by the power of the American state, which acts to protect and promote the interests of American capital abroad, particularly in Latin America. Because of huge US corporate investments throughout Latin and Central America, the unprecedented levels of debt owed to US banks by these states, and the need to ensure secure supplies of strategic raw materials, the US government had few options other than to adopt a highly interventionary policy in its dealings with its neighbours. Its policy towards Central America can therefore be explained as a consequence of the capitalist nature of the American state. The US intervened directly in the region not only to protect the immediate interests of American business there but also to ensure the maintenance of a hospitable climate for US corporate expansion throughout Latin America as a whole. Administration policy was thus shaped by the requirements of corporate capital as well as by the general needs of the American capitalist system.

In a study of US interventionism in Latin America, Krasner (1978) discusses two versions of neo-Marxism relevant to understanding the logic behind US policy. In the instrumental version of neo-Marxism, stress is placed upon the personal and class ties between US policy makers and leading corporations. Structural Marxists, on the other hand, suggest that US policy is driven by the requirement to sustain capitalism at home and reproduce it abroad. This is an important distinction since it relates to the issue of how far the US state is conceived as acting in the direct interests of big business with significant investments in Central America, as opposed to acting quite autonomously from such interests because it is motivated by a more fundamental logic which is to guarantee the successful conditions abroad for US investment.

It should be evident from this brief discussion that a neo-Marxist account of US interventionism in Central America revolves around the capitalist nature of the US state. In order to protect US corporate interests, investment opportunities, raw material supplies and financial interests, the US government sought to inject stability into the region through economic, military and political support for its allies whilst simultaneously attempting to neutralize its opponents. In this view it is not the national interest that is at stake in the region but rather the interests of US corporate capital and capitalism. Accordingly, US actions in the region are to be explained by the economic and material imperatives which shape the preferences of the dominant groups in American society and the needs of its economic system.

WHY HEGEMONY AND INTERVENTIONISM? AN EVALUATION OF COMPETING EXPLANATIONS

It is now time to consolidate what we have examined so far. In this section, we will attempt to assess critically the utility of the different theories introduced above as explanations of US interventionism in Central America. This will involve making some academic judgement about which is the most convincing, appropriate and substantial account of the underlying determinants of US behaviour towards Central America in the 1980s and early 1990s.

Competing or Complementary Explanations?

So far in this chapter we have simply explicated realist and neo-Marxist explanations of US foreign policy behaviour. Although we have indicated how these account for US interventionism in Central America, we have in no sense critically evaluated their relative explanatory utility. This is partly because we have first to be clear about what each account offers before we can begin to assess their relative capacity to explain events. Here we shall build upon that understanding to evaluate how far these different accounts should be considered contradictory or complementary explanations.

On the surface it would appear that realist and neo-Marxist accounts of US interventionism in Central America have little in common. Indeed they appear very much to be contradictory explanations, since in accounting for US foreign policy behaviour one focuses upon *strategic* imperatives whilst the other concentrates upon *economic* imperatives. Since we cannot hold both to be correct simultaneously, we are thus forced into making judgements about which is the better account. However, if we can demonstrate that there is some overlap and complementarity between the explanations, then it might be possible to argue that we should opt for a more eclectic explanation if neither by itself appears satisfactory. The important question is therefore: in what sense are realism and neo-Marxism competing or complementary paradigms of enquiry?

As table 4.1 indicates, there are major differences between the two paradigms in terms of their respective accounts of US interventionism in Central America. Realist explanations of US foreign policy, whether at the system or the state level of analysis, have much more in common with each other than with their neo-Marxist counterparts. The other point which arises from this brief exercise is just how extensively, within realism and neo-Marxism, the different levels of analysis intersect and complement one another. Realist accounts of US behaviour in Central America, whether focusing on systemic factors or state imperatives, share common assumptions about the world and offer overlapping accounts of what determines state behaviour. Such accounts are

Table 4.1

| Level of analysis | Theoretical paradigms | |
	Realism	Neo-Marxism
System	Balance of power Bipolar structure of power No peripheries	Structure of world capitalist system Functions of capitalist hegemon
Nation-state	National interest Goals State as rational, unitary actor	Capitalist state Protect/promote interests of capital and capitalist system

by definition therefore mutually reinforcing. A similar argument can be made for the neo-Marxist accounts we have identified. Accordingly, in the remainder of this discussion we shall simplify our task somewhat by concentrating upon the comparative utility of realist and neo-Marxist explanations of US interventionism in Central America, differentiating between explanations at different levels of analysis only where this is significant to the evaluation in hand.

There are two reasons why realist and neo-Marxist explanations of US foreign policy behaviour cannot be reconciled. Firstly, each conceives of the underlying determinants of US *behaviour* in radically different terms. Thus realists conceive of US interventionism as a phenomenon which is essentially politically driven; it is a product of the bipolar structure of the international political system, strategic imperatives and the pursuit of national interests. By comparison, neo-Marxist analyses consider US expansionism to be economically determined: a structurally induced consequence of its hegemonic role in the world capitalist system or (and not incompatible) a consequence of the requirements of US corporate capital.

Secondly, each conceives of the US *state* in quite distinctive ways. For a realist the state is a monolithic entity which is capable of articulating a coherent national interest; the national interest is defined in terms of the collective interests of the nation. The state is therefore conceived as above domestic politics; in other words it is able to act quite autonomously from societal influences in its articulation and prosecution of the national interest. Compare this view with the instrumental and structural versions of neo-Marxism, discussed earlier, which argue that the state is deeply enmeshed in the contradictions and constraints of capitalist society. As a result it is impossible to regard it as in any sense an autonomous entity pursuing the national interest, since there can be no national interest; the state can only function in the interests of the capitalist or of capitalism. The notion of the national interest is thereby regarded as an element of false consciousness.

Taken together, these two major points of comparison indicate that both paradigms have little in common; nor are the explanations they produce compatible. There would not appear to be any sense in which they can be combined into some overarching explanation, since they make contradictory claims about what determines US foreign policy behaviour. However, it would be wrong to exaggerate their incompatibility by overlooking completely some common ground.

Three points of convergence between realist and neo-Marxist explanations of US foreign policy behaviour do stand out. Although the logic by which each paradigm reaches similar conclusions may be different, it is nonetheless significant that the conclusions arrived at are similar. Firstly, both realism and neo-Marxism give particular weight to *structural* determinants of US foreign policy behaviour. Whether primacy is given to the structure of power in the international system or the structure of the world capitalist system, both paradigms stress the significance of structural constraints upon state behaviour. Associated with this is a tendency to argue that the state, as an agent or actor in the global system, has only limited scope for autonomous action. In other words it does not make its own history completely free from external constraints but moves with the tide of history.

Secondly, both paradigms regard *ideology* as an essentially secondary influence upon US behaviour. Compare these two quotations, the first written by a neo-realist and the second representing a neo-Marxist position:

According to the rhetoric of the Cold War, the root cleavage in the world was between capitalist democracy and godless communism. But by the size of the stakes and the force of the struggle, ideology was subordinated to interest in the policies of America and Russia, who behaved more like traditional great powers than like leaders of messianic movements.

(Waltz 1979, p. 172)

For Marxism, imperialism is not a political or ideological phenomenon but expresses the imperative necessities of advanced capitalism.

(T. Kemp quoted in Krasner 1978, p. 25)

Such statements contrast markedly with Halliday's (1987) view that ideology is a crucial determinant of superpower behaviour, particularly that of the US. This is an issue which has been explored already in chapter 2.

Thirdly and finally, both paradigms emphasize the significance of *military power* as a key instrument in US attempts to manage its client states within its regional sphere of influence.

There are then some areas in which the two paradigms complement and reinforce one another. However, on the fundamental questions of the sources of US behaviour and the conception of the US state, both paradigms offer conflicting answers. Which then offers the best explanation of US policy towards Central America?

Some Basic Criteria for Evaluation

The notion of 'best' implies that there is an objective standard of measurement against which it is possible to gauge the utility of competing explanations. This is far from being the case. Evaluation of competing explanations is a problematic exercise in which critical judgement is paramount. Of course this is not to suggest that theory evaluation is a process of merely confirming initial prejudices or accepting what fits comfortably with our own value system. Rather, there are general criteria which can assist us in making these evaluative judgements in a more systematic and less subjective way than simply accepting uncritically our own informed prejudices.

There is a mass of literature on the question of explanation in the social sciences. Moreover, a whole branch of philosophical enquiry – epistemology – is devoted to the study of what counts as valid knowledge and explanation. Thus in the limited space available here we can only afford a somewhat schematic and instrumental approach, although as the volume progresses we will build upon its intellectual foundations. The object here is to specify some general criteria with which to compare competing theories.

In a textbok on international relations, Charles Reynolds (1974) argues that there are two primary criteria for evaluating competing explanations of any phenomenon: coherence and consistency. *Coherence* refers to the extent to which any interpretation or account of a social or political phenomenon provides a clearly argued and reasoned narrative. *Consistency*, on the other hand, refers to the internal logic of a theory and its external connection to the facts of the particular case being explained. Thus to have any intellectual credibility, a theory not only must be internally consistent but also must be able to account for the facts of the case itself. To these two criteria a further two can be added: comprehensiveness and parsimony. *Comprehensiveness* concerns the degree to which a theory accounts for all the available evidence and how much evidence remains to be explained. The more comprehensive a theory, the less evidence remains unaccounted for. Finally, *parsimony* can be defined as the extent to which a theory provides an economical, selective, but accurate account of the subject matter under the analyst's microscope.

What is noticeable about all these criteria is that they involve making judgements of a relative rather than an absolute kind; in other words, each can be satisfied only to varying degrees. Accordingly, we are required to judge the degree to which an account is coherent rather than simply whether it is or is not coherent; and so on. In the discussion which follows, we shall attempt to make a judgement about the explanatory utility of realist and neo-Marxist accounts of the underlying causes of US inter-ventionism in Central America. However, you should note that what is on offer are my own evaluative judgements, ones with which you may well disagree entirely.

Overall I am more convinced by the realist explanation of US interventionary behaviour in Central America than with the neo-Marxist. Whilst both accounts can offer relatively *coherent* explanations, in that both provide reasoned arguments in which the conclusions follow from the premises and available evidence underlines these conclusions, it is with regard to the other three criteria that the realist account, in my judgement, comes out stronger. One difficulty with the neo-Marxist account is the issue of which take primacy in shaping behaviour: the interests of US capital, or the requirements of its hegemonic role in the world capitalist order. This tension is replicated in a similar way in the discussion of instrumental and structural versions of neo-Marxism. It is therefore far from clear what is the driving force behind US intervention. Now this may simply be a product of the fact that there is sufficient evidence for us to make a proper judgement about how far US corporate interests and the requirements of being a hegemonic capitalist power reinforced one another in this particular case. This generates a certain unease in my own mind about the *consistency* of the neo-Marxist explanation relative to its realist counterpart. For, as the chapter has amply demonstrated, US decision makers actually defined the national interest in terms of preserving the global balance of power and the rationale for interventionary action in terms of fulfilling this objective. Realism thus appears, relatively speaking, a more consistent account of the underlying causes of US actions.

Alongside this we can ask which offers the more *comprehensive* explanation. Again, my own judgement is that realism provides a more rounded account since it is able to explain why the US was so concerned by developments in Central America despite the region having very limited economic significance for the US. The evidence indicates that neither in trade and investment nor indebtedness was the region as economically critical to the US as were other Latin American states. Moreover, it accounts well for the declining interest in Central America in the wake of improved relations between Moscow and Washington in the early 1990s.

Of course this could be countered by the view that it was essential for the US government to act in order to protect US corporate interests in the region, lest this communicate the wrong signals to all Latin American states concerning its readiness to protect US economic interests in the hemisphere. The issue of Central America's economic significance to the US thus raises some doubts about the comprehensiveness of the neo-Marxist account relative to the realist one.

Finally, whilst the neo-Marxist explanation is *parismonious* it cannot compare with the elegant simplicity of the realist explanation, which revolves almost totally around the workings of the balance of power mechanism and the state's pursuit of the national interest. Overall then, in my judgement, realism provides a relatively more comprehensive, consistent and parismonious explanation of US interventionism in Central America than does neo-Marxism. For all these reasons I would argue therefore that realism is, on this occasion, the more convincing of the two explanations. But you may rightly disagree. Certainly to confirm my view or come to more meaningful conclusions, we need a more comprehensive examination of the whole evidence, particularly US economic interests in Central America.

HEGEMONY AND INTERVENTIONISM: THE ROLE OF THE MILITARY INSTRUMENT

So far we have been concerned with explaining the underlying sources of US behaviour in relation to its client states in Central America. In the concluding section of this chapter we shift the focus to the instruments of superpower intervention – how they intervene – which leads nicely into a comparison of Soviet and US hegemonic behaviour. This involves us directly in a consideration of the significance of military power in relationships between a superpower and a subordinate state. In particular, it raises questions about how far their preponderant military power gives the superpowers a controlling influence over the foreign and domestic politics of subordinate states.

One of the most curious aspects of US relations with Central America is that, despite its massive military power, the US appears to be somewhat impotent to control the direction of events in its own back yard. Another curious feature of the relationship is that even though the Reagan administration considered Nicaragua a serious threat to American interests in the region, it did not seek to invade and overthrow the Sandinista regime. This is particularly interesting given the willingness to go to war over Kuwait in 1991. But such caution about the exercise of force is not confined to the US. Throughout 1989 and 1990 the Soviets held back from overt military intervention in Eastern Europe to restore proletarian order. This suggests an important question about the significance of military power in superpower relations with subordinate states. It is an important question for it opens up the issue of how far the superpowers can translate their preponderant military power into real political power or influence in the world.

There are two popular misconceptions about the nature of military power and particularly its relationship to political power. The first is that the apparent reluctance of both superpowers to use military force overtly in order to control the affairs of subordinate states is indicative of the limited utility of military power in the contemporary period. The second is that the exercise of military power brings with it political control. Neither of these assertions has much intellectual credibility.

Whilst in comparison with the early Cold War period the US, apart from the invasion of Grenada in 1983 and Panama in 1989, has in the 1980s avoided direct military intervention in Central America, this suggests very little about the utility of military power. For there is a very crucial distinction to be made between the exercise of *military force* and the exercise of *military power* in interstate relations. Garnett makes this point graphically:

> Military power may depend to a large extent on the availability of military force, but conceptually it is quite different; it emphasizes a political relationship between potential adversaries rather than a catalogue of military capabilities. In a nutshell,

the difference between the exercise of military force and military power is the difference between taking what you want and persuading someone to give it to you. In a sense, therefore, the use of military force represents the breakdown of military power.

(1981, p. 71)

There is, therefore, a certain paradoxical relationship between military power and military force. The more a superpower has to resort to military force to control its clients, the more this represents a sign of its impotence rather than an advertisement for its military strength. For the use of force demonstrates unambiguously its failure to convert its massive military power into political influence. As Waltz argues:

Power maintains an order, the use of force signals a possible breakdown ... In international politics states supreme in their power have to use force less often. 'Non-recourse to force' – as both Eisenhower and Khrushchev seem to have realized – is a doctrine of powerful states. Powerful states need to use force less often than their weaker neighbours because the strong can more often protect their interests or work their wills in other ways ... Possession of power should not be identified with the use of force ... To introduce such confusions into the analysis of power is comparable with saying that the police force that seldom if ever employs violence is weak or that a police force is strong only when policemen are shooting their guns.

(1979, p. 185)

Thus the very fact that the US may not need to resort to the exercise of military force in its attempt to achieve its objectives in Central America is evidence of its successful use of military power rather than evidence of the limited utility or inappropriateness of the military instrument.

Although there is a general tendency to regard the exercise of military power and military force as instruments through which the superpowers can exert control over subordinate states, this also is a profound oversimplification. Moreover, it can lead to all kinds of dangerous prescriptions, including the view that a failure to control clients is a sign of military weakness which can only be rectified by enhancing one's military capabilities, and the view that force brings with it political control. Underlying such misconceptions is a rather crude notion of the relationship between military power and political power. There is a tendency to view the relationship in directly proportional terms: this much military capability equals this much political power or influence in the world. However, as Garnett suggests:

The relationship between military strength and political influence is certainly not the proportional one implied by Mao Tse-tung's famous dictum that 'political power grows out of the barrel of a gun'; but although it is not a straightforward connection, few would dispute that in general terms there is a relationship between military strength and political power.

(1981, p. 67)

The connection between military power and political power is a complex one. Military power may bring with it the ability to exercise political influence over subordinate states, but it does not deliver control over them. As Waltz states: 'Military power no longer brings political control, but then it never did . . . Military force, used internationally, is a means of establishing control over a territory, not of exercising control within it . . . Conquering and governing are different processes' (1979, p. 191). This conclusion is aptly demonstrated by the history of US relations with its Central American client states.

References

Allison, G. (1971) *Essence of Decision*. Boston: Little Brown.

Garnett, J. (1981) The utility of military power. In M. Smith (ed.), *Perspectives on World Politics*, London: Croom Helm.

Halliday, F. (1987) *The Making of the Second Cold War*. London: Verso.

Krasner, S. (1978) *Defending the National Interest*. Princeton: Princeton University Press.

Maidment, R. and McGrew, A. (1991) *The American Political Process*. London: Sage.

Reynolds, C. (1974) *Theory and Explanation in International Politics*. London: Martin Robertson.

Rubin, B. (1985) *Secrets of State*. New York: Oxford University Press.

Schoultz, L. (1987) *National Security and United States Policy toward Latin America*. Princeton: Princeton University Press.

Singer, J. (1969) The level of analysis problem in international relations. In J. Rosenau (ed.), *International Politics and Foreign Policy*, New York: Free Press.

Waltz, K.N. (1979) *Theory of International Politics*. New York: Addison-Wesley.

Part II

Technology
and
Global Political Integration

5

Military Technology and the Dynamics of Global Militarization

ANTHONY G. McGREW

Introduction

Reflecting upon the atomic bombing of Hiroshima and Nagasaki, the distinguished American strategist Bernard Brodie concluded in 1946 that:

> Thus far the chief purpose of our military establishment has been to win wars. From now on its chief purpose must be to avert them. It can have almost no other useful purpose.
>
> (p. 76)

These much quoted words capture the essence of the nuclear revolution which many would argue has transformed the traditional relationship between war and politics in the modern age. Nuclear weapons have made hegemonic war purposeless quite simply because their use would bring about the mutual annihilation of the warring parties. As President Truman observed, not long after his decision to use nuclear weapons against Japan, the 'bomb' required that: 'Man must abolish war before war abolishes man.' Technology, it appeared, not only had made war between the great powers obsolescent but also had transformed the assumptions upon which international politics was based. Constant preparation for war, rather than war itself, has thereby become one of the most visible realities shaping politics between and within the two great powers.

Industrialized warfare has altered the character of both international and domestic politics. It has made war a less rational means for all states to achieve their political objectives. And, as Pearton notes, it is the advent of nuclear weapons which now challenges the very utility of military force: 'Present policy makers, in contrast to their nineteenth-century predecessors, have to pursue their interests without relying on their main weapon' (1982, p. 255). Moreover, the permanent preparation for war, most evident in the contemporary superpower military relationship, demands a very close partnership between industry, science and the state in order to harness technology for military purposes. The domestic political ramifications of modern military technology thus have been far-reaching.

Equally, the diffusion of military technology throughout the world, combined with the rapid industrialization of peripheral states, has contributed to a *globalization* of military innovation and to the emergence of a highly interdependent world military order. Although this is a hierarchical order, with the superpowers at the top, the ramifications of innovations in weapons technology have a truly global dimension. As the superpowers, at the leading edge of military technology, develop and deploy new weapons systems, new military standards are established which all other states must strive to initiate in order to maintain their relative position in the global military pecking order. As Buzan notes:

> Because the leading edge of technological advance sets the standard for the international system, its continuous forward movement exerts pressure on the whole process of spread. As the leading edge creates ever higher standards of military capability, followers have either to upgrade the quality of their weapons or else to decline in capability relative to those who do.
>
> (1987, p. 38)

The technological dynamic of the superpower arms race thus imposes itself on all states in the global system. It is in this sense that technology acts as a globalizing force – a force which not only structures the political relations between states but penetrates national societies across the globe.

In this chapter we shall investigate the role and significance of technology in determining the dynamics of superpower arms competition (nuclear and conventional) as well as the character of the associated world military order. Essentially, the chapter sets out to explore how far technology is the major driving force behind the superpower arms dynamic and is an underlying cause of what has been referred to as the process of 'global militarization', a process which is manifest in the world-wide diffusion of military capabilities, the increasing destructive capacity of weapons, burgeoning world military expenditure and the militarization of societies across the world.

An examination of the superpower arms race also offers some very special insights into how technology has shaped, and may be continuing to reshape, politics within and between states in the global system. Even before the advent of nuclear weapons, modern military technology had altered considerably the parameters of international and domestic politics. Industrial war not only changed the conditions under which force could be successfully utilized but also contributed to more intensive state intervention in domestic society. Extending this line of argument, liberal-pluralists would argue that the advent of atomic weapons has not simply altered but has transformed the fundamental character of modern international politics. War, it is argued, is now so destructive that it is no longer a rational tool of state policy. Consequently, states have had to find alternative means of achieving their objectives in the global system without relying on military force. Politics between states has thereby become more complex and been transformed in the process.

THE SUPERPOWER ARMS DYNAMIC: TECHNOLOGY OUT OF CONTROL?

Just outside the city of Grand Forks, in North Dakota, USA, lies a rather unusual man-made construction very much like an ancient Egyptian pyramid. This peculiar edifice, however, was not a project dreamt up by a local firm of morticians as a prestige burial chamber for the rich farmers of the nearby valley of the Red River of the North. Rather it was part of a much more ambitious defence project, devised by the nation's nuclear priesthood in Washington, to defend the country's land-based nuclear deterrent force against a possible Soviet attack. Today, however, Grand Forks is a monument to the 'ancient' (1960s) technologies of nuclear defence, for in 1976 the site was mothballed, essentially because the technology proved unworkable; technically speaking the whole anti-ballistic missile (ABM) defence project was far too ambitious for the then current state of knowledge. For almost a decade defence against nuclear attack disappeared from public view except for the scars on the North Dakotan landscape. Yet, by the early 1980s, tremendous advances in a whole range of interrelated military and civilian technologies put defence against Soviet nuclear attack back on the political agenda.

On 23 March 1983, President Reagan announced the Strategic Defense Initiative (SDI), a programme which aimed to devise ways of defending the US against a Soviet missile attack. The President offered Americans the vision of a world in which nuclear weapons might become obsolete:

> Let me share with you the vision of a future which offers hope. It is that we embark upon a program to counter the awesome Soviet missile threat with measures that are defensive ... What if free people could live secure in the knowledge that their security did not rest upon the threat of instant retaliation to deter a Soviet attack, that we could intercept and destroy strategic ballistic missiles before they reached our own soil or that of our allies? I know that this is a formidable, technical task ... Yet current technology has attained a level of sophistication where it's reasonable for us to begin this effort ... My fellow Americans, tonight we're launching an effort which holds the promise of changing the course of human history.

For many the President's message appeared to confirm that yet again technology had come to prevail over politics, if not military common sense, whilst to others it suggested quite the reverse: here for the first time was a case of politics driving military technology. Only one thing seemed certain, namely that SDI was internally generated; it was not triggered by a similar Soviet programme.

Both the case of the ABM and that of SDI raise interesting questions about how far technological innovation is the major driving force behind the superpower arms race. Nor are these two cases atypical, for it would be possible to list scores of major weapons procurement programmes, both nuclear and conventional, which appear to have come about largely as a product of technological advances. Indeed in the military sphere technology seems to prevail over bureaucratic, doctrinal and political inertia. Nor is this a phenomenon confined to the US; it appears to apply just as much to weapons procurement in the Soviet Union and elsewhere. It is this *autonomous* character to technological innovation, with each new weapon almost becoming obsolete as it is deployed (Grand Forks being a good example), that leads to the view that the arms race is somehow beyond human and political control.

The question here is not whether technology may determine the choices about what weapons systems the military and politicians on both sides buy. That would seem logical enough. The issue is much more profound. It is that, in the post-war years, the requirements of technological innovation in the military sector seem to have led to a permanent restructuring of Soviet and American societies and economies in order for each to sustain their position at the leading edge of military technology. In this sense the arms race has been internalized and institutionalized, with the consequence that it reaches deep into the internal organization and functioning of their respective socioeconomic orders. Technology therefore prevails not because it determines what decisions the politicians and the military take but rather because it has redefined and become a substitute for traditional politics and diplomacy. As Winner suggests:

> The rule of technological circumstances in the modern era does in fact supplant other ways of building, maintaining, choosing, acting, and enforcing, which are more commonly considered political ... Political reality becomes a set of institutions and practices shaped by the domination of technical requirements. The order which evolves is marked by stringent norms of performance, rigid structural limitations, and a tendency to alter subtly the human master's relationship to the technological slave.
>
> (1977, p. 237)

Technological politics does not imply that there are no political choices to be made. The crucial point is that the vast military technostructures upon which national defence in both the Soviet Union and the US depends have reshaped the political arena to support their ends. The politics of weapons procurement now largely involves second-order choices about whether it is possible to afford or desirable to deploy the latest weapons systems, but rarely ever engages with first-order choices about whether or not it is rational or desirable to keep up with the leading edge of technological innovation across the military spectrum. Thus, despite the ending of the Cold War, military innovation continues apace on both sides. Defence politics is thus not about what ends should be pursued and how; on the contrary, it is about how the military's established missions and objectives might be carried out more efficiently and more effectively. According to Greenwood:

> To the military ... unlike most technologically-oriented organizations, the important question is not whether to introduce technological innovations but how to choose from a wide assortment of possibilities, what the costs will be, and how fast to proceed.
>
> (1975, p. 13)

There is then a very strong theme in the arms race literature that the superpower arms competition reflects a technological imperative which in some senses might be quite independent of political direction and control. But this is not by any means the only explanation of the superpower arms race. There are others which concentrate upon the interaction between the superpowers and the characteristics of their respective domestic political and economic structures. To develop a more robust account of what determines the arms race (and connected with this a greater understanding of how it shapes the contours of contemporary politics both East and West) we need to explore a range of possible explanations. We will then be in a stronger intellectual position to arrive at our own judgements about the role of technology in sustaining the contemporary military competition between the two great powers. But before proceeding it seems appropriate to raise the question: is there a superpower arms race?

Is There a Superpower Arms Race?

The term 'arms race' is now so closely identified with superpower military competition that its original meaning has been largely lost. When we talk of the arms race we are referring to the military rivalry between the Soviets and the US, which appears to drive both in the same direction of developing increasingly sophisticated weapons and expanding military capabilities. However, after a moment's reflection you would probably realize that equating superpower military rivalry with an arms race is somewhat problematical, particularly since the end of the Cold War. For instance, at some point all weapons systems become obsolete and have to be replaced. Does replacing obsolete equipment with new and perhaps more advanced equipment, incorporating state-of-the-art technology, imply arms racing behaviour? Or is this simply maintaining the status quo? A similar point may be made about defence expenditures, another commonly used measure of superpower military rivalry. Does, for instance, increasing defence expenditure on both sides betray an arms race, or is it simply a product of the growing expense of maintaining the present level of forces each country already deploys? These questions are vitally important, for if we fail to distinguish conceptually between an arms race and the normal pattern of rearming then clearly the concept of an arms race will become entirely meaningless. We are therefore badly in need of some conceptual clarification as to what constitutes an arms race.

One solution to this conceptual puzzle is to attempt to make some distinctions between the normal and the abnormal state of affairs. Buzan comes to our aid here by offering very helpful distinctions between three terms: the arms dynamic; arms racing; and the military status quo.

> In order to capture the full range of what needs to be discussed here, some new terms need to be adopted and used systematically. There is an especially strong need to find a term for the normal condition of military relations in an anarchic system, because it is the absence of such a term that has facilitated the overextended use of arms racing. If we find a term for the normal condition of military relations, then we also need a term to describe the whole phenomenon including both normal behaviour and arms racing. In what follows, the term *arms dynamic*, which has some currency in the literature ... is used to refer to the whole set of pressures that make states both acquire armed forces and change the quantity and quality of the armed forces they already possess. The term is used not only to refer to a general global process, but also to enquire into the circumstances of particular states or sets of states. One can refer, therefore, to the arms dynamic between the superpowers, or one can ask how the arms dynamic affects a single state like Sweden. The term *arms racing* is reserved for the most extreme manifestations of the arms dynamic, when the pressures are such as to lead states into major competitive expansions of military capability. The term *maintenance of the military status quo* is used to express the normal operation of the arms dynamic. Maintenance of the military status quo and arms racing can be used to describe either the activity of a single state, or the character of a relationship between two or more states.

Arms racing and maintenance of the military status quo relate to each other as extremes of a spectrum. Maintenance of the military status quo can escalate into arms racing, and arms racing can subside into maintenance of the military status quo. Between the two lies a grey area in which the direction of change may be a more appropriate guide to events than any attempt to locate a given case on one side or the other of some strict but arbitrary dividing line. Occasionally, one can find instances where one state increases its military strength without attracting a response, such as when the United States began to build up its navy during the late nineteenth century . . . Such cases of arms buildup depend on unusual geographical or political conditions, and are therefore rare. If sustained, they eventually lead to arms racing. If they taper off, they lead to maintenance of the military status quo.

(1987, pp. 73–4)

Table 5.1   Soviet and US strategic nuclear forces, 1960–1987

| | Soviet | | US | |
	Delivery vehicles	Nuclear warheads	Delivery vehicles	Nuclear warheads
1960	149	294	1,038	—
1965	434	381	2,126	2,056
1970	1,456	1,403	2,111	4,000
1975	1,652	1,875	2,097	8,500
1980	1,696	6,156	2,048	9,200
1987	2,475	11,248	2,001	13,012
1990	2,497	11,641	1,930	13,398

Sources: IISS (1987, 1990), Behrman and Baker (1982)

Table 5.2   Soviet and US armed forces (thousands)

	Soviet	US
1945	11,300	12,123
1950	2,800	—
1955	—	2,806
1960	3,027	—
1965	4,000	2,687
1970	—	—
1975	4,745	2,162
1980	5,132	2,063
1987	5,226	2,158
1990	3,988	2,117

Sources: Miller (1988), IISS (1987)

The distinctions Buzan has identified are very important since even a cursory overview of the history of superpower military competition would confirm that it has been punctuated by phases of greater or lesser intensity in which the relative military capabilities of each side may have expanded, stabilized or even declined. In no sense has this military competition been distinguished by a continuous, sustained expansion of military capabilities on both sides (see tables 5.1 and 5.2, and figure 5.1). It is therefore inaccurate to refer to it as an arms race. Accordingly, throughout the remainder of this chapter it will be described as the *superpower arms dynamic.*

Regardless of how the military balance between the superpowers is measured, these figures conceal more than they reveal. In particular this evidence provides no indication of the pace and the impact of technological innovations in weapons systems upon military capabilities. In other words the qualitative dimension is missing. Yet, as noted earlier, it is the process of technological improvement in weapons which may hold the key to the superpower arms dynamic. The problem is that there are few indices by which to measure such qualitative change.

This brief overview of some of the more significant trends in the military balance between the superpowers raises some very intriguing questions about precisely what forces sustain the arms dynamic in which both sides are entangled. Is it power politics, their respective military-industrial complexes, technology or economic necessity? In subsequent sections we shall explore three largely complementary accounts of the superpower *arms dynamic*: power politics; domestic imperatives; and the technological imperative (Buzan 1987, p. 74).

Understanding the Superpower Arms Dynamic: Power Politics and the Action–Reaction Thesis

In 1967 the then Secretary of Defense, Robert McNamara, announced the deployment of a partial ABM system to defend US missile sites against a nuclear strike. At the time he held deep personal reservations about the project, reservations which later

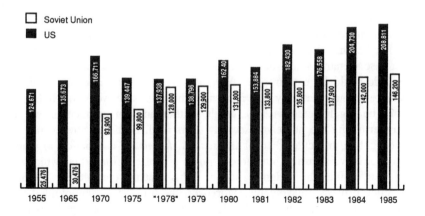

Figure 5.1 Soviet and US military expenditure since 1955 (US$ million at 1980 prices) (IISS 1987; SIPRI *Yearbooks* 1981, 1986)

proved to be correct for, as noted earlier, the Grand Forks ABM site was decommissioned in less than a decade. Specifically, McNamara believed that if the US went ahead with deployment of a full ABM system this would provoke a reaction from the Soviets and stimulate a new round in the strategic arms competition. The result would be to undermine the stability of the strategic balance and increase the risks of war. By articulating the obvious, McNamara systematized a conception of the superpower arms dynamic which still dominates much of our thinking about Soviet–US military competition. For he stated quite unambiguously that from where he sat the arms dynamic appeared to have a simple cause:

> What is essential to understand here is that the Soviet Union and the United States mutually influence one another's strategic plans. Whatever their intentions or our intentions, actions – or even realistically potential actions – on either side relating to the buildup of nuclear forces necessarily trigger reactions on the other side. It is precisely this action–reaction phenomenon that fuels the arms race.
>
> (quoted in Freedman 1981, p. 254)

This was a modern restatement of the classical realist view of the arms dynamic.

Underlying this action–reaction model is a rather simple logic, but one grounded in a whole set of unspoken assumptions about superpower behaviour. At a superficial level it seems fairly obvious that, given their deep-seated mistrust and rivalry, both superpowers plan their military capabilities in relation to one another. Who is in danger from whom is quite clear. Accordingly, when one side tests or deploys a new weapons system it is logical to assume that this is likely to provoke a similar response from the other side to counter the perceived new threat. Thus, for example, within four years of the US acquiring nuclear weapons the Soviets exploded their first nuclear device. And when the Soviets launched Sputnik 1 in 1957, the US rapidly developed its own strategic missile force. The action–reaction account of the superpower arms dynamic therefore appears convincing. It also has an appeal because of its simplicity and the fact that the same logic seems to be at work in a whole host of day-to-day social situations and interactions. Anyone who has young children prone to sibling rivalry will know all about the action–reaction cycle. However, as an explanation of the superpower arms dynamic the action–reaction cycle can only be properly understood as a product of deeper structural determinants in the international system.

As we have noted, both the US and the Soviets plan their military forces in relation to each other because they are rivals. To ensure their security, each plans on the basis of a worst case scenario since the consequences of underestimating the capabilities of the other side could be catastrophic. Any measures taken by one side to defend its interests therefore automatically pose a threat to the other side even though the former's motives may be largely defensive. As a result, neither side can enhance its own security without undermining the perceived security of its rival. Both the Soviets and the US are thus caught in an acute form of the *security dilemma* – a situation in which one side arms to achieve security, but thereby poses a threat to the other, which arms in response, reinforcing the original action. This makes competitive arming, the action–reaction process, unavoidable. Moreover, the process is compounded by ideological and political rivalry, since each side is striving to sustain or expand its influence in the global system. Because military power is perceived as the currency of political power, military competition simply becomes a further expression of this global power struggle. As a consequence, the superpower arms dynamic can be conceived as a product of an underlying power struggle and not, as many believe, a process which is driven simply by technological innovation or a military-industrial complex. Realist and neo-realist analyses of the superpower arms dynamic would agree with this view.

Looked at in this way, the arms dynamic between the superpowers becomes explicable only in terms of the structure of their whole relationship: each is arming not for the sake of arming but because the process is driven by the logic of the security dilemma and a power struggle. This is perhaps best illustrated by the decade of expansion in US military capabilities which began under the Carter administration in 1979. What is significant about this period is the apparent connection between the rapid expansion in US capabilities and the steady expansion of Soviet capabilities. As Halliday (1987) implies, what provoked the US desire to regain military superiority was the massive growth in Soviet conventional and nuclear forces throughout the 1970s. Whether measured in terms of defence expenditures, manpower figures, the strategic or the conventional military balances, the evidence can be explained in terms of an action–reaction process. Moreover, at the level of major weapons procurement pro-grammes the action–reaction logic offers insights into why, for instance, in the face of growing Soviet naval power, the US committed itself to a 600 warship navy. In the strategic arena too, the perceived window of vulnerability led not only to a massive strategic modernization programme but also to the deployment, in 1986, of Peace-keeper, the Strategic Air Command's new land-based missile system. The evidence thus can sustain an interpretation based upon the action–reaction thesis, although this is not the one which Halliday offers.

Turning the tables, one can also see evidence of the action–reaction process at work in shaping Soviet force levels and deployments. This is most evident for the 1960s, when the US began deploying its massive intercontinental ballistic missile (ICBM) force. The Soviet reaction was to begin deployment, from the late 1960s to the mid 1970s, of its own huge ICBM force. At one point, Soviet ICBM construction and deployment rates were frenetic, with some 300 missile sites being constructed in one year alone in the drive to establish parity with the US. Parity became the primary objective of Soviet strategic policy in the 1960s in order to ensure that the US could never again impose its will on the Soviets, as it had done over Cuba in 1962. Again, in the late 1970s the Soviets began deployment of multiple independently targeted re-entry vehicle (MIRV) strategic missiles in response to the US deployment of MIRVs in the early 1970s. Indeed in the strategic sector, since the earliest days of the nuclear age, the Soviets appear to have largely reacted to US developments and deployments. In fact, it would be possible to catalogue many other important examples of Soviet reactions to US weapons developments. The action–reaction process appears to account for Soviet behaviour too.

There is a further dimension to the action–reaction process: it has a cumulative momentum. Each sequence of action–reaction gives rise to a further sequence of action–reaction, and so on *ad infinitum*. At each point, decisions about what weapons to buy are framed by the previous round of action–reaction and, once implemented, set the agenda for a further sequence of weapons procurement decisions. A good illustration of this is the pattern of ICBM procurement on both sides over the last two decades.

In the late 1950s the US perceived a growing missile gap in which the US was being left behind. As a consequence it embarked upon a massive ICBM deployment programme which in turn stimulated a reciprocal response from the Soviets. The consequence of this Soviet buildup was to provoke fears in the US strategic community of a window of vulnerability opening up in the late 1970s. As a result, the US took the decision to deploy a new mobile ICBM in 1979 and to initiate a major strategic modernization programme in 1981. This in turn has set the agenda for Soviet procurement decisions into the 1990s. The sequence of action–reaction thus generates a powerful progressive momentum which pulls along behind it the military planning of both sides.

Whilst very plausible in its own terms, the action–reaction thesis does not stand up to much critical scrutiny. There are four significant areas of criticism which together suggest that, at best, it can only ever be a partial and simplistic explanation of the arms dynamic. The four criticisms are that: it concentrates upon motivation as opposed to processes of arming; it ignores military planning; it neglects the problem of timing; and it de-emphasizes mechanisms of control and restraint. Let us examine each of these failings in turn.

Firstly, the action–reaction process is a systemic explanation of the arms dynamic. It focuses upon the pattern of sequential interaction between the superpowers, and explains their arming behaviour in terms of their mutual responses to external threat. Thus it tells us a great deal about why the superpowers procure the level and type of military forces that they do, but says very little about how these decisions come about and are implemented. As an explanation then it is more concerned with motives than with the processes which give rise to certain patterns of behaviour – the question of how the arms dynamic comes to take the course that it does. This domestic dimension, as we shall discover, cannot be ignored.

Secondly, even the most superficial account of defence policy making in both the US and the Soviet Union demonstrates that, except perhaps in times of crisis, the military do not react; they plan. One of the great revolutions in military affairs has been the institutionalization of planning within the defence apparatus. Planning involves a series of highly complex stages.

Crucially it also involves anticipating the other side's behaviour and decisions, in every sector from weapons procurement to what might transpire on the battlefield. Therefore, in engaging in military planning both the Soviets and the Americans are constantly anticipating, rather than reacting to, the weapons procurement and force level decisions of their rival. To describe the arms dynamic in terms of a basic action–reaction process is therefore somewhat of an oversimplification.

The third criticism relates to the fact that, for most modern weapons systems, it takes on average eight to ten years between the initial design stage and actual deployment. To give a good example, the MX Peacekeeper missile, at the time of writing the most advanced in the US strategic arsenal, was originally conceived in the late 1960s with initial deployment commencing in 1986. On the Soviet side, design of the SS-19 ICBM began in 1965 yet it was not deployed until 1975. In both cases three US Presidents and numerous Secretaries of Defense had been and gone. Given such long lead times the original rationale, requirement and desirability of procuring any modern weapon system may change dramatically over the procurement cycle. Indeed as time passes it becomes increasingly difficult to cancel any major weapons programme because of the powerful momentum which builds up behind it. Thus obsolete weapons may be deployed or, as is more often the case, new missions may be found simply to justify a decision to deploy a new weapons system. The extended nature of the weapons procurement cycle undermines the credibility of the action–reaction thesis.

Fourthly and finally, the superpower arms dynamic is not completely autonomous but is actually consciously managed by the Soviets and the Americans. Such management may not be very effective or pursued with vigour, but it is the case that both sides recognize the dangers of falling into an uncontrolled arms race. Accordingly, the pressures on both sides to engage in arms control are overwhelming. Equally, there are economic constraints upon both sides which restrict the scope for an open-ended action–reaction competition. At various times too both superpowers have recognized that certain weapons developments or force postures should not be pursued. This was the case with the ABM in the 1960s, and exists today with respect to their tacit agreements about anti-satellite (ASAT) weapons. In the context of the demise of the Cold War and the signing of the START agreement in July 1991, a builddown rather than a buildup may be a better description of the superpower arms dynamic.

Taken together, these four criticisms suggest that we cannot accept without severe qualifications the action–reaction explanation of the superpower arms dynamic. By itself this account is much simplistic and ignores vital factors. As Buzan comments:

> Although its basic logic has force, its specific ideas are frequently difficult to apply to particular cases. In addition there are many cases where the model does not seem to provide anything like a complete explanation for the observed behaviour. Frustration with the model, especially amongst those concerned to understand the arms dynamic of the superpowers, has therefore driven enquiry away from interaction factors between states, and towards domestic ones within them.
>
> (1987, p. 93)

Accordingly in the next section we shall examine some of the domestic imperatives which determine the character of the superpower arms dynamic.

Understanding the Superpower Arms Dynamic: Domestic Imperatives

Over the years since 1945, huge permanent defence establishments have grown up in the US and the Soviet Union. The arms dynamic has thus been internalized and institutionalized, penetrating deep into the very functioning and lifeblood of both societies with profound consequences for the nature of their domestic polities. On both sides enormous interlocking sets of bureaucratic, industrial, political and scientific constituencies exist not only which swallow up vast amounts of scarce resources but also whose livelihood and interests depend vitally upon the vigilant maintenance, continuous improvement and even expansion of national military capabilities. A good case can therefore be made that the superpower arms dynamic is driven more by domestic imperatives than a reaction to external threats.

In terms of sheer resources, the military establishments on both sides pre-empt a considerable proportion of national budgets, scarce scientific talent and industrial capacity. Whether this is a wise or economically beneficial use of scarce resources is not at issue here; that is a quite separate debate in itself. What is relevant is the sheer magnitude, as well as the nature, of the resources devoted to defence and how this

Table 5.3 Western estimates of Soviet defence expenditure as percentage of GNP

	1955	1960	1965	1970	1975	1980	1990
Bergson							
(current rouble factor cost)	10.3						
(1950 rouble factor cost)	10.7						
Lee (1970 roubles)	11.5	9	10	12	14–15	18	
CIA (1970 roubles)				11–13	11–13	12–14	
IISS							>15%

Source: Holloway (1983, p. 118)

Table 5.4 US defence expenditure as percentage of GDP

Year	$ GDP
1955	10
1965	7.4
1970	7.7
1975	5.8
1980	6.9
1990	5.9

Table 5.5 Military manpower resources and defence employment of US and Soviet Union

	US	Soviet Union
Total armed forces 1987 (inc. reserves)	3,310,700	11,433,600
% of population	1.4	4.0
Defence related employment 1978	1,775,000	—

Source: IISS (1987), Mosley (1985, p. 91)

conditions the arms dynamic. Tables 5.3, 5.4 and 5.5 provide a general picture of just how far in both states the defence economy penetrates the civilian economy. But the picture becomes even clearer if we examine the most advanced sectors of the economy. Taking the US economy first, it is salutary to note that defence production and defence requirements account for a significant proportion of the output of the most advanced industrial sectors. A similar situation can be found in the Soviet Union, where the defence industry not only is 'the highest priority sector in Soviet industry' but also 'has been given its own supply industries' to protect it from the 'shortcomings in the rest of the economy' (Holloway 1983, p. 119). In both states, defence production and defence requirements sustain the existence and expansion of some of the most strategic industries in the national economy. This, combined with the fact that there are literally millions employed in the defence sector in both states, creates very strong industrial and economic pressures for the maintenance and expansion of defence spending. Thus even with the demise of the Cold War there remains a compelling logic for sustaining certain types and minimum levels of defence expenditure. But these factors cannot be isolated from other equally significant domestic imperatives, as becomes evident if we examine the weapons procurement process.

The processes by which advanced weapons systems are developed and finally come to be deployed in both the US and the Soviet Union share a number of common features. Weapons procurement follows a number of stages, commencing with the identification of a military need, conceptualization of the weapons project, research and development (R and D), prototype construction and testing, production, and finally deployment. At each of these points in the procurement process, decisions are taken about whether or not to proceed in relation to technical, budgetary, strategic and political criteria. However, the actual procurement process is much less rational and more indeterminate than this sketch suggests. For decisions about major defence programmes are highly politically charged, since they involve the vested interests of very powerful groups within the state and outside it: the military; the defence bureaucracy; defence related industry; and the defence related scientific community.

As we noted earlier, both superpowers engage in complex processes of military planning; each attempts to anticipate, with the assistance of the intelligence services, the weapons programmes and developments of the other. However, in many instances much of the initiative for developing new weapons systems arises domestically out of the process of R and D. The institutionalization of military R and D in the form of weapons laboratories and design bureaux leads to a process of perpetual technological innovation, since the primary objective of such agencies is to develop ever more sophisticated and advanced weapons systems. Moreover, since in both the Soviet Union and the US the various R and D establishments often compete with each other to push the boundaries of military technology to its limit, the whole process of weapons development can become solely internally generated. As Greenwood remarks, in an excellent study of US MIRV development:

> This process of continual replacement is to some extent self-perpetuating. Large organizations have been created that owe their existence solely to their ability to invent or design new weapons and sell them to the political decision makers.
>
> (1975, p. 13)

Holloway confirms that, despite its more bureaucratized weapons acquisition process, similar pressures exist in the Soviet Union:

> If the military R and D effort is rooted historically in international rivalry and strongly influenced by that rivalry, it is also true that the large military effort has created institutions that occupy a powerful position in the Soviet system and provide a dynamic and pattern of their own to weapons development and production.
>
> (1983, p. 150)

What this suggests is that the weapons R and D process in both states generates its own imperatives which are largely autonomous and only tenuously connected to a rational evaluation of either the external threat or military requirements. This is certainly much more so the case in the US, where a greater premium is placed upon maintaining technological supremacy in the defence sector. Recent studies of major US strategic programmes, such as MIRV and MX, confirm how the imperatives of military R and D push new weapons systems on to the military agenda well before any identifiable military need has arisen. In the case of MIRV, for instance, a whole series of quite unconnected technical innovations came together in the early 1960s. Once the engineers and scientists recognized that MIRV was technically feasible, this justified further development work, so that by 1964 the programme had developed a powerful technological and bureaucratic momentum. Yet the decision to develop the system was taken in the absence of either any defined threat to which it could be legitimately regarded as a response or any identification of its precise military mission. According to Greenwood:

> In 1964 ... the Mark 12 Task Group realized that the MIRV system it was developing could not be justified by any existing mission requirement. *Its members made a conscious effort to find a strategic rationale.* Counterforce targeting and growth of Soviet missile forces provided the solution. MIRV could be justified by the need for greater target coverage. Later that year ... BSD (Ballistic Systems Division of the Air Force) formed a series of panels to prepare arguments to sell the MIRV programme.
>
> (1975, p. 53; italics added)

In lay terms MIRV was originally a weapon in search of a mission. Moreover, at the same time as the USAF was developing MIRV the Pentagon was also busily engaged in a battle to obtain approval for the deployment of an ABM system. Yet MIRV technology was justified publicly as a counter-measure to Soviet ABM deployments. Paradoxically, the military was busily engaged in building one system (MIRV) which made another of their own cherished programmes (ABM) obsolete; this is further evidence of the autonomy of domestic imperatives in shaping weapons procurement programmes.

SDI is perhaps an even more obvious example of the imperatives of military R and D. Since the late 1960s the US weapons laboratories have been working on third-generation nuclear weapons, which involve state-of-the-art laser and particle beam technology. Developments in this sector, combined with massive advances in computer and information processing technology, made it possible for scientists to visualize the technical possibility of strategic defence. However, strategic defence only became a major R and D programme following its adoption by the Reagan administration in 1983. This underlines the significance of other domestic factors in the weapons procurement process.

It would be absurd to argue that the technological and institutional imperatives of the R and D establishments in the US and the Soviet Union solely determine the superpower arms dynamic. There are also other significant domestic pressures aside from those emanating from the R and D community. Any major weapons programme has its bureaucratic protagonists and opponents within the state machine. In the US this means the Pentagon, the Joint Chiefs of Staff (JCS), the separate armed services and the President's own executive office; and in the Soviet Union, the Defence Council, the Defence Ministry, the armed services and the Politburo. Interservice rivalry and bureaucratic self-interests also play an important role in shaping the outcomes of the defence procurement process.

Each service presses for its own priorities and the weapons systems to fulfil established and newly defined missions. But in both the US and the Soviet Union, this occurs in the context of a highly bureaucratized policy process in which organizational rules, procedures and planning impact directly upon procurement decisions. As a result, there is a great deal of bureaucratic politics involved in procurement decisions. Interservice rivalry is commonplace on most major procurement programmes since each service has many other uses to which defence resources could be put. For a long time the USAF opposed the Navy's Polaris programme, and in the Soviet Union sections of the military have opposed the diversion of resources from conventional to nuclear forces. However, many studies suggest that once a bureaucratic consensus has crystallized in the military and defence apparatus over the desirability of a particular weapons programme, this tends to make cancellation impossible. Since bureaucracies tend to operate upon an incremental logic, the normal strategy is for the services to obtain agreement to their programmes by stealth, making it increasingly difficult over time for decisions to be reversed. Indeed, once a weapons system gets to the stage of engineering development it is highly unlikely that it will be cancelled. Thus within the weapons procurement process there are bureaucratic imperatives at work which operate largely in favour of the development of new and ever more sophisticated weapons.

Again the case of MIRV is instructive in this regard. Once the decision to go ahead with engineering design work on the MIRV was made in 1964, a bureaucratic consensus emerged within the Pentagon to support further development of the programme. According to Greenwood, MIRV

> was rapidly accepted within both the military and civilian sides of the Defense Department with only a brief and scattered resistance. All concerned increasingly saw MIRV as a solution to their own particular problems. The consensus in favour of proceeding solidified rapidly. By 1965 it was fully formed.
>
> (1975, p. 13)

One of the consequences of this was that MIRV proceeded smoothly through the remaining stages of the procurement process – until, that is, the Arms Control and Disarmament Agency (ACDA) and a number of Congressional politicians opposed a favourable decision on its deployment. But as many studies have indicated, by this stage the programme was so far advanced and so many other strategic modernization programmes depended upon its fulfilment that it was inconceivable that there be any delay, let alone cancellation. Bureaucratic and organizational imperatives thus triumphed over MIRV's opponents.

Alongside bureaucratic factors there are also considerable industrial interests at stake in any significant weapons programme. Kurth (1973) suggests that there is a powerful follow-on imperative which puts enormous pressure on the state to keep the military production lines busy most of the time. The logic of this is simple: once a programme has been fulfilled, the need to maintain military production capabilities intact leads either to further new contracts being issued or to production runs being expanded. This occurs in both the US and the Soviet Union, except that in the case of the US there are also additional pressures arising from the need to maintain employment and industrial profitability. Indeed, neo-Marxists would argue that in the US there are strong economic imperatives at work, encouraging the maintenance and growth of military procurement programmes, arising from the capitalist nature of economic production. This is perhaps well illustrated by the case of the B-1 bomber.

Originally proposed in the early 1970s, the B-1 was cancelled by the Carter administration in 1977. However, Rockwell and the other major contractors were kept busy with the prototype programme and, along with the Air Force, continued to press Congress and the President to reinstate it. In 1981 the programme was reinstated under the strategic modernization programme initiated by the Reagan administration – largely, according to some experts, in order to keep intact a militarily crucial sector of the aircraft construction industry. Since it has been reprieved, Rockwell and the other major contractors have continued to press for a longer production run in order to keep them fully employed until the next major procurement programme is realized.

Although the follow-on and economic imperatives of arms production may offer convincing accounts of the weapons procurement process, we need to avoid the danger of lapsing into a crude economic determinism. Politics also matters considerably. In the US the role of Presidents and Congress can be crucial in determining the fate of weapons programmes. Since many Congressional politicians, particularly those from the sunbelt states of the south and west, represent constituencies which depend significantly upon defence contracts, there exists very strong political interests in favour of maintaining or increasing defence spending. Equally, Presidents determined to proceed with a particular weapons programme, such as President Reagan with SDI, can normally achieve their objective. Alternatively, political intervention by Congress or by Presidents, as with the case of the B-1 referred to above, can lead to the cancellation of a programme or, as more often occurs, its scaling down or alteration. A rather dramatic illustration of this occurred in the case of the MX missile (mentioned earlier), whose deployment was radically altered by an alliance between environmentalists and the arms control lobby in Congress. Political intervention in the procurement process is even more evident in the Soviet Union where the Party apparatus vigorously monitors all major defence programmes. According to Holloway:

> The ICBM program is closely directed by the Party leaders, since ICBM development remains central to Soviet policy. The history of the ICBM program shows how the Party leadership has brought designers, industrial managers and soldiers together to create an effective strategic force.
>
> (1983, p. 154)

Putting all these factors together, a picture gradually emerges of a series of convergent domestic pressures generating the momentum behind the superpower arms dynamic. This suggests the existence of a powerful military-industrial technocomplex in both the Soviet Union and the US. And this is a conclusion with which both liberal-pluralist and neo-Marxist accounts of the superpower arms dynamic would concur.

In Halliday's neo-Marxist view, the military industrial complex or the 'iron triangle' is driven by the requirements of capital, binding 'Congress, the Pentagon and the arms industry together in an unchallenged process of military expansion' (1987, p. 122). Similarly, Holloway's (1983) largely liberal-pluralist account of Soviet weapons procurement concludes that the Soviet Union does not have 'a military-industrial complex' because it 'is a military-industrial complex'. However, we need to be extremely careful about employing uncritically the notion of the military-industrial complex. We therefore need to qualify the term and demonstrate how it reflects the many domestic imperatives discussed above.

Domestic imperatives do not so much determine the arms dynamic as structure the choices which face the organizations, groups and individuals involved. Although the word 'imperatives' implies a command, commands do not always have to be obeyed. Indeed, whilst domestic imperatives tend to create convergent pressures towards ever increasing defence expenditure and the procurement of increasingly sophisticated weapons, there are also countervailing and contradictory forces at work. It has been noted already that there exist intense interservice rivalries which accompany virtually every major weapons project. Often these can sabotage a particular weapons procurement programme in its early stages of development, well before any bureaucratic momentum has gathered behind it. A case in point is the American Project Vista (1952), which 'argued for the tactical use of nuclear weapons as initially a more effective way to stop the Soviet armies than strategic bombing. With this recommendation it thus challenged directly the [present] ideas of the Strategic Air Command. The Air Force sought to modify and then to suppress the report' (Elliot 1986). And it was successful. Interservice rivalry and the conflict of service interests complicate the procurement process with quite unpredictable consequences.

Large organizations, as theorists of bureaucracy constantly remind us, tend to be inherently conservative; this is perhaps more true of the military and defence bureaucracy in both the US and the Soviet Union than of any other sectors of the state apparatus. Resistance to change produces a bias towards incremental rather than radical change in weapons systems, military doctrines and strategic policy. As a result, although the weapon labs may propose new weapons concepts these can be neglected because of the inherent conservatism of the military and defence bureaucracy. Holloway suggests that in the Soviet Union:

> The role of the MOD in weapons acquisition seems to reinforce the tendency towards conservative and evolutionary technological change: the complex committee structure for approving a new development program is likely to inhibit innovation while the different services might be expected to press for follow-on systems – pressure that may be welcome to the design bureaus, since it will keep them occupied with designs that are not too challenging.
>
> (1983, p. 144)

Many innovations may thus be killed off well before they reach the production phase. There are many examples of this from the US, where the most fanciful weapons systems, such as nuclear propelled bombers, shipborne nuclear ballistic missiles, space-based orbital nuclear bombing devices, 100 megaton bombs and a host of other nasties, never got beyond the concept stage. The conservative instincts of the military thus do not always lend themselves to rapid technological innovation. As Lord Melville remarked to the British Colonial Secretary in 1828:

> Their Lordships (the Admiralty) felt it their bounden duty to discourage to the utmost of their ability the use of steam vessels, as they consider that the introduction of steam was calculated to strike a fatal blow at the naval supremacy of the Empire.
>
> (quoted in Pearton 1982, p. 52)

Things may not have changed so dramatically in the subsequent century!

Finally, weapons procurement decisions have to be paid for and legitimized as a necessary addition to the nation's military capabilities. Both these requirements can impose important political constraints upon the procurement process. In both the US and the Soviet Union there are very strong countervailing pressures, within the state and outside it, against devoting ever increasing resources, both financial and otherwise, to defence. In the US the problem of a huge budgetary deficit has imposed its own limits upon the growth of defence programmes. And in the Soviet Union the desire to switch resources to other uses also sets limits to the expansion of the defence sector. Indeed in both cases the economic burdens of defence spending create a strong imperative for arms control measures which impact upon the arms dynamic. This in part was the impetus behind the 1972 SALT agreement which limited ABM systems on both sides.

To explain the superpower arms dynamic as if it were simply the unencumbered operation of a military-industrial complex and associated domestic imperatives would be to ignore many of the subtleties and countervailing influences mentioned above. In using the term 'military-industrial complex' as shorthand for the interlocking institutional structures and domestic imperatives which underlie the superpower arms dynamic, we acknowledge that, in both the Soviet Union and the US, it is far from being the monolithic, conspiratorial and autonomous organism portrayed by its many critics. Rather it is highly fragmented, open to countervailing and contradictory pressures, and a much more highly politicized decision-making arena than is widely assumed. Moreover, there are considerable differences, as well as strong similarities, between the mode of operation of the military-industrial complex in the US and that in the Soviet Union. Despite this the significance of domestic imperatives in shaping the pattern and the pace of the superpower arms dynamic is undeniable.

Understanding the Superpower Arms Dynamic: the Technological Imperative

'Nuclear weapons are no less the products of the industrial revolution than indoor plumbing, automobiles, refrigerators, and the equipment in modern hospitals' (Mandelbaum 1983, p. 40). This perceptive observation echoes the argument of some that technological progress in general has been responsible for the transformation of war in the twentieth century. In addition, the industrialization of war has made it impossible to draw boundaries between civil and military technology. Advances in one stimulate innovation in the other; they are inseparable. Thus to argue that the superpower arms dynamic is driven solely by technological innovation in the military sector is to miss out completely the pervasive impact of technological advance which is the life-force of all industrial societies. Accordingly the arms dynamic can be conceived as driven by the process of technological change in industrial society as a whole – a process which has its own independent momentum.

Innovation in military technology is inseparable from technological progress in general. President Reagan's proposed SDI programme would have been unthinkable without the rapid advances which have been made in computer and information processing technologies and which have revolutionized industry and commerce. Equally, our ability to receive direct broadcast television is a result of the enormous advances made in satellite and communications technology, both of which were originally developed for military purposes. But it is not the *purpose* to which technology can be put which is relevant to the discussion here so much as the origins and consequences of technological change. What is pertinent is to identify how far technology itself can be regarded as an autonomous and self-generating force fashioning the military competition between the two superpowers.

A rather simple proposition would be that technology sets the defence agenda such that the military and political decision makers are effectively led into adapting their forces and strategies to take advantage of each new technological innovation. Rather than making real political choices, the state and its agents are thus engaged largely in a process of adaptive responses. Most of us probably have experienced, in a whole host of settings from the home to the workplace, the process of adapting our behaviour to meet the requirements of new technology. For instance, just think of how television and video recorders have affected the dynamics of behaviour within the household. Technology then, according to some accounts, determines the whole pace and character of social and political change. This technological determinist position, is difficult to sustain as an explanation of the superpower arms dynamic since, as we observed earlier, technology does not always prevail. As an explanation it is also somewhat suspect since it sweeps aside any notion of human agency and choice.

Returning to the case of MIRV, which was introduced earlier, Greenwood notes that:

> MIRV was clearly a technology whose time had come. It was firmly grounded in the technological developments of the 1950s and was primarily an extrapolation of concepts of the same period. It is therefore not surprising that MIRV was 'invented' almost simultaneously in several places within the technological community.
>
> (1975, p. 13)

This statement suggests that technological innovation has its own momentum which is deeply rooted in the process of scientific enquiry and the drive to translate knowledge into artefacts. The fact that the same innovation came about simultaneously in different parts of the scientific community demonstrates just how autonomous technological progress can be. But there is also an unpredictable element to technological innovation. Advances in one area may impinge quite unintentionally on other areas, with dramatic consequences. The result is that innovation may arise less by conscious planning and purposive enquiry than by a process of technological drift. A good illustration of this is the MX Peacekeeper missile, referred to earlier, which emerged from advances in many different areas of technology: missile guidance technologies, computer technology, missile engine technology, warhead miniaturization technology and so on (Holland Hoover 1985). A further example is the cruise missile, which became feasible only after a series of advances in turbofan technology, warhead miniaturization and guidance technologies – advances which were all made quite independently of each other (Huisken 1981, chapter 1).

To talk of a technological imperative shaping the superpower arms dynamic involves rejecting the crude notion of technological determinism and accepting that the process of technological innovation is more indeterminate than we may like to believe. However, this does not imply that military technologies are merely tools to be selected off the shelf to fulfil particular strategic purposes and therefore that technology is subservient to political direction and human control. On the contrary, technology thrives only by restructuring its environment; for any technology to operate effectively certain requirements must be met. As Winner has argued:

> If you desire X and if you have chosen the appropriate means to X, then you must supply all of the conditions for the means to operate. To put it differently, one must provide not only the means but also the entire set of means to the means. A failure to follow the correct line of reasoning in formal logic brings an unhappy outcome: absurd conclusions. Failure to follow the dictates of the technological imperative has an equally severe outcome: a device produces no results (or the wrong ones). For this reason, once the original choice has been made, the action must continue until the whole system of means has reached its proper alignment . . . One need only think of the thousands of requirements that must be met before the automobile can be a functional part of social life – manufacture, repair, fuel supply, highways, to name just a few.
>
> (1977, pp. 101–2)

Winner's point is a profound one, for what he is arguing is that once a decision is taken to develop and exploit a technology it necessarily involves ensuring that all the requirements to operate that technology efficiently are in place, even if many of those requirements were originally unforeseen. As Winner poetically describes it, 'Technology legislates the conditions of its own existence'; that is, technology creates a form of order which is essential to its continued and proper functioning. It is in this sense that technology can be regarded as having its own imperatives and as being *relatively autonomous*. But Winner goes further and argues that, once in place, sophisticated technologies lead to a process of 'reverse adaptation'. What he means by this is simply that the original ends or purposes for which a technology is devised are gradually transformed to suit the available means. A good illustration of this was ABM technology. Originally developed to protect cities against a Soviet nuclear attack, the system was finally deployed to defend missile sites against a Chinese nuclear threat. Since ABM technology could not at the time fulfil the original purpose for which it was developed, new goals were established which the system could just about meet. These new goals made little strategic or military sense, but that did not really seem to matter to the defence decision makers.

   A rather different illustration of the same point is provided by MacKenzie in his study of the evolution of nuclear missile guidance technology. He argues that technology and politics are inseparable:

> The missile revolution did not occur because a President or Secretary of Defense decided that the United States needed strategic ballistic missiles. It was engine-ered largely (though not exclusively) from below, and the missiles proponents had to reshape not just technology but also organizational structures and eventu-ally national strategy. They were assisted by developments in other technologies, particularly the hydrogen bomb, and by a growing sense of a missile race with the Soviet Union. In part the latter reflected external events, most dramatically the launch by the Soviet Union of the first artificial earth satellite, Sputnik, on October 4, 1957. But in part it was the result of the ballistic missiles proponents

own efforts in changing ... US 'insider' perceptions of the path of technical development followed in the USSR ...

No single person or organization decided what the American nuclear arsenal should look like. The 1961–1963 Kennedy administration ... might seem to have done so ... But the position of Kennedy and McNamara at the head of the government by no means translated into the capacity simply to make the choices that they thought best reflected the national interest, and, even had that been the case, those choices were between options that had largely been shaped before they came to power ... Nor did the actions of the Soviet Union determine in any detail the course of the missile revolution ... More generally, it can be concluded that the United States built its missile arsenal without any agreed understanding – even within elite circles, much less among the general population – of why it was doing so ... With political leaders by no means simply in command, the Soviet Union a shadowy mirror reflecting American fears ..., and nuclear strategy often rationalization after the fact rather than a genuine guiding principle, the initiative for new missile systems came largely from below.

(1990, pp. 96, 161–2)

Winner's notion of reverse adaptation implies that technologies can prevail not because they remove the moment of political choice, in the sense of politicians or the military determining what choices are made, but because they largely restrict political choice to the question of how best to sustain the systems that have been created. Technology therefore does not supplant politics so much as create a distinctive form of politics. As he explains:

Decisions made in the context of technological politics ... carry an aura of indelible pragmatic necessity. Any refusal to support much needed growth of crucial systems can bring disaster. The alternatives range from utterly bad service, at a minimum, to a lower standard of living, social chaos, and, at the far extreme, the prospect of lapsing into a more primitive form of civilized life. For this reason, technological systems that provide essential goods and services – electricity, gas, water, waste disposal, consumer goods, defense, air, rail, and automobile transportation, mass communications, and so on – are able to make tremendous demands on society as a whole. To ignore these demands, or to leave them insufficiently fulfilled, is to attack the very foundations on which modern social order rests.

(1977, p. 259)

The relevance of this to explaining the underlying causes of the superpower arms dynamic should be apparent. It suggests that the harnessing of technology for military purposes has required the ordering of society and the economy to ensure this can be acheived with maximum efficiency. In the process, society and the economy become reliant upon servicing the needs of a vast, complex and sophisticated defence apparatus. As a consequence, defence is transformed from simply a means to protect and promote national security into an end in itself. Defence becomes synonymous with building, maintaining, stockpiling and constantly improving a whole array of increasingly destructive technologies. Permanent preparation for war, which touches every aspect of the functioning of modern society, is viewed as a natural and irreversible state of affairs. As Pearton comments:

Preparation for war is no longer a matter of keeping the barracks manned and the powder dry. It is a continuous activity, reaching deep into all aspects of society and eroding, even nullifying, conventional distinctions about the 'civil' and 'military' spheres of life. The reasons are mainly to be found in men's response to the opportunities offered by technology in the industrial age.

(1982, p. 11)

To talk in terms of the superpower arms dynamic being a product of a technological imperative is therefore to recognize just how deeply the military competition of the superpowers is embedded in their respective industrial systems. The arms dynamic is conditioned by the general process of technological advance in both societies and the requirements of industrial systems which have become geared to permanent preparation for war. In this view the military-industrial complex is largely an institutional expression of an underlying technological imperative, and as such is an essentially secondary influence upon the arms dynamic. As Buzan concludes:

A large percentage of the behaviour that is commonly identified as arms racing stems directly from the underlying process of technological advance. When countries compete with each other in armaments, they must also compete with a standard of technological quality that is moving forward by an independent process of its own. When they institutionalize military R and D, countries are seeking to exploit, and not be left behind by, a process that is already under way in society as a whole. They may be able to steer the process to some extent, and influence its pace, but they are basically riders, and not the horse itself.

(1987, p. 107).

THE TECHNOLOGICAL IMPERATIVE AND GLOBAL MILITARIZATION

In 1945 only the US possessed nuclear weapons. Two decades later another four states (the Soviet Union, the UK, France and the People's Republic of China) had acquired a nuclear capability. At the start of the 1990s the nuclear weapons club had at least six more states on the verge of membership, and perhaps as many as ten with the technological capacity to join if they so desired. The problem of *horizontal proliferation* – the spread of nuclear weapons capability to more and more countries – is a vivid reminder that technology is a global force which recognizes no national boundaries. Both the diffusion of knowledge and the unrelenting march of industrialization across the globe have bequeathed to an increasing number of states the capability to develop, or to acquire, extremely sophisticated and incredibly powerful military technologies on a hitherto historically unprecedented scale. Indeed, technology has contributed directly to the creation of a highly interdependent world military order with its own global arms dynamic.

In the preceding sections of this chapter we investigated the underlying causes of the superpower arms dynamic but refrained from exploring its global consequences. Yet one of the most politically (and historically) significant ramifications of the super-power arms dynamic is the fact that it has come to impose itself on every other state in the international system; its consequences then are global in scope. This is simply because the technological imperatives which condition the pace and direction of superpower military competition come to shape the global strategic environment in which all states have to operate. Pearton explains this well:

> Their possession of the means of nuclear manufacture on the scale they command makes them 'superpowers' but, in producing weapons related to threats from each other, they have defined the problems of policy and technology which other states have to face. So the qualitative change does not only affect the superpowers *vis-à-vis* each other: all states electing to stay in the international competition, at some level or other, have been compelled continuously to organize and exploit their scientific and industrial resources to the greatest possible extent.
>
> (1982, p. 246)

Britain's attempts to maintain some sort of technological parity, in both nuclear and conventional forces, with the superpowers confirms Pearton's basic point.

One consequence of this is that the post-war period has witnessed the emergence of a closely interconnected world military order. Although hierarchical, with the superpowers at the top, and displaying enormous disparities in military capabilities, it is nonetheless a highly interdependent order with its own arms dynamic. The existence of this world military order, in part, accounts for the fact that the military plan and operate in very similar ways across the globe. It is often said, for example, that the US military and the Soviet military have more in common with each other than with their respective political leaderships.

Three factors underpin the nature and the dynamics of the current world military order. The first has been alluded to already, namely the impact of the superpower arms dynamic in setting global standards for military technology. The second relates to the impact of technological innovation in globalizing the superpower competition, and the third to the global trade in armaments.

One of the most significant consequences of the advance in military technology since 1945 is that, as far as the superpowers are concerned, it has turned the globe into one single strategic arena. The modern world is now a global battlefield. In any superpower, military confrontation strategy, military deployments and the use of force will be planned on a global scale. Because of the greater mobility of military forces, the existence of global intelligence and communications networks, and the ability to direct nuclear as well as conventional attacks to any geographic location of military significance, the world has become a unified strategic arena. The revolution in military technology contributed directly to the globalization of superpower military rivalry and encouraged both powers to take a great interest in local and regional military balances. That interest is transformed into intervention through the mechanism of arms sales.

World arms sales now stand at well over $21 (billion) per year. Most of the export trade in weapons is accounted for by the US and the Soviet Union but the major Western European states are now significant arms suppliers (See Table 5.6). The largest slice of arms exports, some two-thirds or more, goes to those developing and industrializing countries whose indigenous defence production facilities are in most cases negligible or non-existent (See tables 5.7, 5.8 and figure 5.2).

Whilst the arms trade has certainly led to a greater global spread of weapons technology, its impact upon recipients is felt even more deeply than simply dependence upon foreign military suppliers. For it plugs importing states into the permanent

Table 5.6 The leading major-weapon exporting countries: values and percentage shares, 1982–1986 (values in US $ million at 1985 prices)

Country	1982	1983	1984	1985	1986	1982–6	% of total exports to Third World, 1982–6
USA	12,707	12,011	10,276	9,104	10,462	54,562	51.6
	37.8	37.3	31.3	30.1	33.3	34.0	
USSR	9,552	8,850	9,433	11,134	9,881	48,850	76.1
	28.4	27.5	28.7	36.8	31.4	30.5	
France	3,472	3,380	4,170	4,170	4,196	19,387	86.1
	10.3	10.5	12.7	13.8	13.3	12.1	
UK	2,065	1,077	1,925	1,777	1,947	8,791	66.5
	6.1	3.3	5.9	5.9	6.2	5.5	
FR Germany	861	1,822	2,432	942	870	6,928	62.9
	2.6	5.7	7.4	3.1	2.8	4.4	
Third World	1,165	1,462	1,081	740	772	5,220	95.3
	3.5	4.5	3.3	2.4	2.4	3.3	
China	748	890	1,194	863	1,208	4,902	97.1
	2.2	2.8	3.6	2.9	3.8	3.1	
Italy	1,357	973	865	551	327	4,073	98.0
	4.0	3.0	2.6	1.8	1.0	2.5	
Others	1,673	1,720	1,456	938	1,797	7,586	61.0
	5.0	5.3	4.4	3.1	5.7	4.7	
Total	33,600	32,185	32,833	30,219	31,460	160,298	69.0

Source: SIPRI *Yearbook* 1987

competition for qualitative improvement in weapons systems in which all the leading exporters are engaged. Moreover, with imported weapons comes a whole approach to warfare: military doctrines, tactics, planning and so on. Thus importing states are easily tied to the military doctrines and strategies of their suppliers. As a consequence the arms trade binds states together into a global military order which is dominated by the most militarily advanced nations.

However, there is also a quite autonomous force at work which is leading to a growing diffusion of military capabilities: industrialization. We have already noted earlier in the chapter how industrialization and the technological imperatives it unleashes profoundly influence the nature of modern military competition. With the growing industrialization and technological advancement of many more countries in the Third World has come the greater diffusion of the technical ability and industrial capacity to produce many types of modern weapons systems. For instance, Brazil is now one of the leading arms exporting nations, yet only two decades ago it was still regarded as a less developed nation. Its pace of industrial and technological advance has been so rapid that it is now capable of constructing ballistic missiles, and with some technical effort it could probably manufacture nuclear weapons within the space of a couple of years. As table 5.9 illustrates, since 1950 the military-industrial capabilities of the

Table 5.7 The top ten Third World suppliers of major weapons, 1982–1986

Supplier	% share in total TW exports of major weapons 1982–6	Production of major weapons 1980–4		Number of recipients		Major recipient			
		% share in total TW	Rank	TW	IC	Region	% share	Country	% share
Israel	23.9	24.4	1	15	2	FE	38.8	Taiwan	38.0
Brazil	23.3	10.3	3	24	4	ME	48.3	Iraq	36.7
Egypt	14.1	2.9	9	9	0	ME	89.2	Iraq	89.2
Jordan	7.3	0	—	2	1	ME	91.4	Iraq	88.0
Libya	7.3	0	—	8	0	ME	80.8	Syria	47.4
S. Korea	7.2	6.3	7	6	0	FE	43.4	Malaysia	31.6
N. Korea	5.5	4.8	8	5	0	ME	95.8	Iran	95.8
Syria	3.3	0.	—	2	1	ME	98.9	Iran	88.5
Singapore	2.1	1.0	10	6	0	FE	50.9	Taiwan	40.7
Indonesia	1.6	0.5	12	3	0	ME	64.3	Saudi Arabia	64.3
Others	4.4	49.8							

TW = Third World; IC = industrialized countries; FE = Far East; ME = Middle East.
Sources: SIPRI *Yearbook* 1987 (p. 198).

Table 5.8 Rank order of the 20 largest Third World major-weapon importing countries, 1982–1986 (rank 1981–1985 in parentheses)

Importing country	% of total Third World imports	Importing country	% of total Third World imports
1 Iraq (1)	12.1	11 Jordan (9)	2.0
2 Egypt (2)	9.8	12 Iran (20)	2.0
3 India (4)	9.5	13 Algeria (14)	1.8
4 Syria (3)	8.5	14 Angola (17)	1.7
5 Saudi Arabia (6)	7.2	15 Cuba (12)	1.6
6 Libya (5)	4.5	16 Nigeria (13)	1.5
7 Argentina (8)	3.3	17 Kuwait (19)	1.5
8 Pakistan (11)	2.9	18 Venezuela (15)	1.3
9 Israel (7)	2.4	19 North Korea (—)	1.3
10 Taiwan (10)	2.4	20 Thailand (—)	1.2
		Others	21.5

Total value (constant 1985 prices)   US $110,571 million

Source: SIPRI *Yearbook* 1987 (p. 201)

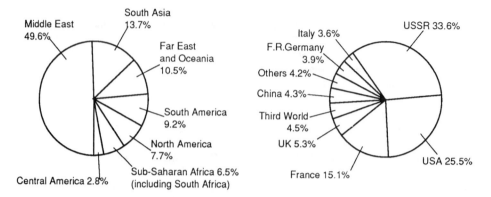

Figure 5.2 Percentage shares of trade in major weapons with the Third World, 1982–1986 (SIPRI *Yearbook* 1987)

Third World have expanded enormously. Industrialization has established a global arms dynamic which in part operates quite autonomously from the superpower arms dynamic since it is driven by the diffusion of largely civil technology. This is quite evident in two sectors: nuclear energy and the chemicals industry.

Horizontal proliferation has become a major global problem because the diffusion of civil nuclear technology has given an increasing number of states the capability to manufacture nuclear weapons. Despite international controls to prevent the spread of the most militarily sensitive aspects of civil nuclear power technology, the growing scientific and industrial sophistication of many Third World states eventually may undermine the effectiveness of these controls simply because they will be able to develop the necessary technology themselves. Argentina and Pakistan are cases in point. Both states were unable to purchase uranium enrichment technology (a technique which can be used to produce reactor fuel and also nuclear weapons material) from the leading nuclear suppliers, yet each now has operating small prototype or experimental enrichment facilities. As the technological and industrial capabilities of states develop, so too does their potential ability to produce even the most awesome of weapons.

During the Gulf War of 1991 the allied forces constantly feared and prepared for Iraqi missile attacks using chemical warheads. This demonstrates how relatively easy it is for moderately industrialized states like Iraq to manufacture fairly sophisticated weapons of mass destruction by using existing civil industrial techniques and facilities. With the global spread of the chemical industry and missile technology many states in the Third World now have the latent capabilities to produce weaons of mass destruction.

What both these examples show is just how far the spread of industrial technology underpins the growing global diffusion of military capabilities. It is also a process which is beyond the control not only of the two superpowers but also of any individual state, even the most powerful. For the dynamic of technological innovation 'is based globally rather than within single states' (Buzan 1987, p. 108).

One of the consequences of the global spread of military technology is that it is often associated with the process of global militarization. Militarization has been defined as 'a steady growth in the military potential of states. Such growth is usually accompanied by an increasing role for the military institutions both in national affairs, including the economic, social and political spheres, and in international affairs' (quoted

Table 5.9 Number of Third World producers of at least one major weapon system, 1950–1980 (examples of types of major weapons produced)

1950	1959–60	1969–70	1979–80
Argentina (ships, light plane)	Argentina (light plane)	Argentina (trainer, sub)	Argentina (all types)
Brazil (ships, light plane)	Brazil (light plane, trainers)	Bangladesh (PB)	Brazil (all types)
Colombia (CPB)	Burma (corvette)	Brazil (trainer/COIN, transports)	Chile (tanker)
India (trainer)	Chile (light trainer)	Burma (gunboat)	China (all types)
China (PB)	China (all types)	Chile (ships)	Colombia (light plane)
	Colombia (LC)	China (all types)	Dominican R. (LC)
Total = 5	Egypt (trainer)	Colombia (light plane, sub)	Ecuador (corvette)
	India (trainers and engines, transport planes)	Dominican R. (LC, PB)	Egypt (ATM, PB, helicopters)
	Indonesia (trainer)	India (all types, aeroengines)	Fiji (survey ship)
	Israel (trainer)	Indonesia (light plane)	India (all types)Indonesia (trainer, helicopter, LC)
	Korea, N. (PB)	Iran (MBT rebuild)	Israel (all types)
	Mexico (CPB)	Israel (all types, inc. missiles)	Korea, N. (PB, sub)
	Peru (tanker)	Korea, N. (PB, subs)	Korea, S. (fighter, APC)
		Korea, S. (CPB)	Malaysia (PB)
	Total = 13	Pakistan (ATM)	Mexico (CPB)
		Peru (PB, tanker)	Nigeria (helicopter)
		S.Africa (fighter, armoured car)	Pakistan (helicopter, trainer, ATM)
		S. Vietnam (trainer)	Peru (frigate, survey ship, tanker)
		Sri Lanka (PB)	Philippines (CPB, light transport, helicopter)
		Thailand (PB)	Singapore (PB)
		Taiwan (trainer)	S.Africa (all types)
			Sri Lanka (PB)
		Total = 21	Taiwan (fighter, AAM, ShShM, helicopter, PB, frigate)
			Thailand (PB)
			Venezuela (PB)
			Total = 26

AAM	air-to-air missile
APC	armoured personnel carrier
ATM	antitank missile
COIN	counterinsurgency
CPB	coastal patrol boat
LC	light craft
MTB	main battle tank
PB	patrol boat
ShShM	ship-to-ship missile
	submarine

Source: Newman (1984)

Table 5.10 Arms imports average annual growth rates, 1973–1983 (per cent)

	1973–83	1980–83
All developing countries[a]	7.0	0.0
Africa	18.1	−9.4
East Asia[b]	1.9	−11.9
Latin America	12.8	5.5
Middle East	9.2	8.6
South Asia	11.6	−6.2

[a] As determined by the US Arms Control and Disarmament Agency.
[b] The ACDA's data for East Asia, unfortunately, include one advanced industrial country – Japan.
Source: US Arms Control and Disarmament Agency, *World Military Expenditures and Arms Transfers 1985* (Washington, DC: ACDA publication 123, August 1985), p. 8

Table 5.11 Armed forces average annual growth rates, 1963–1983 (per cent)

	1963–73	1973–83	1980–83
All developing countries[a]	3.8	1.3	0.3
Africa	9.0	5.5	−1.4
East Asia[b]	3.8	0.8	−2.7
Latin America	2.2	3.5	3.6
Middle East	6.7	4.6	−0.4
South Asia	4.0	2.6	12.8

[a] As determined by the US Arms Control and Disarmament Agency.
[b] The ACDA's data for East Asia, unfortunately, include one advanced industrial country – Japan.
Sources: US Arms Control and Disarmament Agency, *World Military Expenditures and Arms Transfers 1963–73* (Washington, DC: ACDA publication 74, 1975), pp. 14–19; ACDA, *World Military Expenditures and Arms Transfers 1985* (Washington, DC: ACDA publication 123, August 1985), p. 6

Table 5.12 Military expenditure growth rates, 1963–1983 (per cent)

	1963–73	1973–83	1980–83
All developing countries[a]	7.2	4.7	2.1
Africa	6.5	7.3	3.2
East Asia[b]	7.5	11.8	2.1
Latin America	3.9	3.4	−0.7
Middle East	14.7	7.6	3.7
South Asia	2.9	5.3	9.5

[a] As determined by the US Arms Control and Disarmament Agency.
[b] The ACDA's data for East Asia, unfortunately, include one advanced industrial country – Japan.
Sources: as table 5.11: ACDA (1975, pp. 14–19); ACDA (1985, p. 4)

in Ross 1987). If this were the case, then clearly it has enormous ramifications for our understanding of the nature of contemporary politics between and within states. However, the evidence of growing militarization on a global scale is hotly disputed (see tables 5.10, 5.11 and 5.12).

Whilst the evidence of increasing global militarization is somewhat questionable, the impact of modern military technology on the character of contemporary politics, both within and between states, has been profound. Indeed, many respected academics would argue that the post-war revolution in military technology has *transformed* politics both at the international level and at the domestic level. In the final section of the chapter we return to the theme with which we began: the relationship between the globalization of military innovation and the character of contemporary global politics.

MILITARY TECHNOLOGY AND THE TRANSFORMATION OF GLOBAL POLITICS

When asked about his role in making the atom bomb feasible, Einstein replied 'If only I had known, I should have become a watchmaker'. Yet his deep pessimism about the arrival of the nuclear age was countered by the views of those, amongst whom was President Truman, who believed that the bomb would revolutionize international politics. Mandelbaum describes this optimistic vision succinctly: 'The industrial revolution, Marx believed, would transform politics within states. At the dawn of the nuclear age it was similarly believed that nuclear weapons would transform politics among states ... the familiar international institutions and practices, the old ways of doing business among nations, seemed suddenly and completely obsolete' (1981, pp. 1–2). Given the absence of war between the superpowers, this belief in the revolutionary impact of nuclear weapons has gained widespread adherence. Technology appears to have transformed the nature of contemporary international politics. But is this so?

In this concluding section of the chapter we shall review some of the arguments about how far, and in what ways, the nuclear revolution has transformed politics both within and amongst states. By concentrating upon the nuclear revolution we shall be able to illustrate more vividly the impact of military technology upon the character of contemporary politics. But the focus is not exclusively upon nuclear weapons as such, since many of the most militarily and politically significant technological developments have concerned the means of delivering the bomb. For instance, the fact that submarine launched ballistic missiles can reach their targets in 15 minutes or less has altered fundamentally the relationship between war, strategy and diplomacy as well as that between the military and the political decision makers. Moreover the rapidly blurring boundaries between conventional and nuclear weapons technology, combined with the global diffusion of very advanced delivery systems, now imposes dilemmas similar to those experienced by the superpowers on a growing number of militarily advanced states. War, even before the advent of nuclear weapons, was already becoming 'obsolete'. The enormous advances in, together with the world-wide spread of, military technology have undoubtedly had a global political impact. Using the intellectual device of levels of analysis, which was introduced in chapter 4, the discussion here will explore the impact of military technology upon the international system and then upon the state.

War, Strategy and International Politics in the Nuclear Age

Nuclear weapons and the ability to deliver them to their targets almost instantaneously, according to a large body of contemporary liberal-pluralist analyses, has transformed the nature of international politics. The destructiveness of atomic weapons, alongside the catastrophic global consequences which would flow from their use anywhere in the world, have fundamentally altered the nature of war. Military force, at least between the two superpowers, is now regarded as an inconceivable instrument through which to challenge the status quo. And for the lesser states, new and external constraints have been placed on the use of force where it might lead unintentionally to superpower confrontation. The political consequences of the nuclear revolution thus have been enormous.

Whereas in the past war and the exercise of military force were used to achieve political ends, that connection has now been broken. Since the use of force by the superpowers could readily escalate into a nuclear conflagration, there are no political objectives worth attaining given the costs involved. Even realists such as Northedge acknowledge that: 'Perhaps the most important effect of nuclear weapons . . . is finally to break the link, which once served so clear, between the actual use of force and the political objectives which force . . . is supposed to achieve' (1976, p. 292). The point is not that nuclear weapons have made war impossible but that they have made it an increasingly irrational instrument of state policy – if by 'rational' we mean the use of military might to successfully achieve given political objectives. Since neither side can possibly win, and nothing but total devastation of both camps is likely to result from war, the political logic of war and the use of military force have been seriously brought into question. This is confirmed by Mandelbaum:

> Nations went to war in the past because they believed that they could win. A large scale nuclear war would so damage the two sides engaged in it as to call into question the very idea of victory. This is a revolutionary feature of nuclear weapons for which there is no precedent . . . The destruction from nuclear exchange would be so great that it is questionable whether the conflict would deserve to be described as war. War implies the use of force for some political purpose. It is difficult to imagine a political purpose that would be served by the slaughter and devastation that even a handful of nuclear weapons would bring to societies at which they were aimed.
>
> (1983, pp. 24–5)

Accordingly, the primary purpose of military force has now become to deter war rather than to fight it.

Despite the fact that nuclear war may serve no political purpose, this does not mean that military power and military force are no longer useful. Far from it, for force may be used, as it was in Korea, Vietnam, Afghanistan and the Gulf, to achieve limited political purposes. Thus whilst the notion of *general war* or *hegemonic war* is unthinkable, the nuclear age has brought to the fore the prospect of *limited war*. One of the consequences of nuclear weapons therefore is to so increase the risks and dangers arising from even limited military conflict between the superpowers, or their allies, that the use of force to achieve political objectives in most circumstances has been severely called into question. This in turn has altered fundamentally the relationship between military power and the exercise of political power in the world. Nuclear weapons, by limiting the utility of military force as an instrument of state policy, thereby may have contributed, as many liberal-pluralist analyses suggest, to the increasing importance of new sources and instruments of state power in the global arena.

If modern military technology has made war less rational, it has also had a salutary influence upon great power behaviour. The ever present threat of nuclear annihilation has made cooperation between the superpowers to manage international affairs a very visible feature of international politics in recent years. During the Gulf War of 1991 the superpowers supported each other and were in constant communication with one another. The Soviets even tacitly approved the US use of force to eject Iraq from Kuwait. Here we have evidence of both superpowers managing the world if not, by joint action, attempting to govern it. The permanent threat of nuclear war has thus contributed to a quite historically unprecedented attempt by the great powers to manage international politics to maintain stability and order.

Although the nuclear revolution has brought with it the threat of global catastrophe, the development of missile technology too has, in the words of Thompson, 'annihilated the very moment of "politics"' (1982, p. 8). Flight times of 30 to 40 minutes, even with the sophisticated global intelligence and early warning systems deployed by both superpowers, collapse the political decisions about war or peace into hours rather than days or weeks. As Morgenthau observed:

> To compress a catastrophic war within the span of time that a man can stay awake drastically changes the politics of war, the process of decision, the possibility of central control and restraint, the motivations of the people in charge, and the capacity to think and reflect while war is in progress.
>
> (quoted in Mandelbaum 1981, p. 4)

Shrinking decision times have abolished the traditional distinction between peace and war, since permanent preparation for war is now an accepted feature of everyday life in the US and the Soviet Union, even since the end of the Cold War. As there is relatively little time to mobilize for war, permanent preparation is essential to national security. In this context, what we regard as peace is only a hair-trigger away from global conflagration. It also means that there is increasing reliance on military planning and the organization of society along lines which are conducive to a permanent condition of military readiness. In the process the distinction between civil and military affairs is lost and strategy reaches deep into the functioning of domestic society.

Limited decision times too considerably reduce the scope and the relevance of traditional diplomacy and its integration with military strategy. Diplomacy has been replaced by crisis management and direct communication between the political leaderships of both superpowers and their allies. Whilst in theory this provides politicians with greater control over the direction which events take, the pressure of time, combined with the ever present fear in a crisis that the other side may strike the first blow, makes it extraordinarily difficult to resist the powerful logic of pre-existing military plans and strategy. Transcripts of recently discovered tapes of the deliberations within President Kennedy's crisis management team during the Cuban missile crisis tend to confirm this. At one point, at the height of the crisis on the afternoon of 27 October 1962, the following exchange was recorded:

General Maxwell Taylor: Mr President the Chiefs have been in session . . . the recommendation they give is as follows: that the big strike – OP Plan 3-12 – will be executed no later than Monday morning the 29th unless there is irrefutable evidence in the meantime that offensive weapons are being dismantled and rendered inoperable; that the execution of the Strike Plan be part of the execution of 3-16, the Invasion Plan . . . days later.
(pause)
Robert Kennedy: That was a surprise.
(laughter)
Taylor: It does look now from a military point of view . . . They just feel that the longer we wait now . . .

(Bundy 1987, p. 63)

Given the constraints of time and the political need to be seen to be acting under conditions of dire threat, the pressures to pre-empt during a crisis are deeply ingrained in the situational logic. Military planning and strategy thereby become a substitute for politics and diplomacy.

Whilst nuclear crises may not differ so fundamentally from crises in the past, the broader relationship between military strategy and international politics has altered in the nuclear age. Strategy now revolves around the art of using military power to deter war and to promote or protect the national interest wherever possible without recourse to war. This is largely at odds with the traditional role of the military, which has been to fight and to win.

The Military, the State and Domestic Politics in the Nuclear Age

So far we have concentrated almost solely upon how nuclear weapons technology has altered the nature of politics between states. In this section we shall broaden the discussion to examine how far the requirements of modern military technology shape the nature of the modern state across the globe. Obviously in attempting to develop some general observations we will be focusing upon tendencies rather than suggesting that there is some natural process of convergence at work. In this regard the existing literature points to two significant aspects of political life which have been affected by modern military technology: civil–military relations; and the relationship between state and society.

Because of the destructiveness of modern military technology, both conventional and nuclear, and the shrinking time frame within which decisions about the use of force have to be made, politicians in most advanced states have taken a great interest in military matters. The desire to exercise political control over the military is therefore perhaps stronger now in many states than in any previous historical period. Moreover, the nature of modern communications technology means that the political leadership can actually direct, if it so decides, the employment of military force. During the Falklands War, in 1982, the British war cabinet had a fuller picture of what was happening than did many on the ground. The Prime Minister was also able to participate directly in taking certain military decisions, like the sinking of the *Belgrano*, which in previous times would have been taken solely by the military. The Gulf War of 1991 also demonstrated the revolutionary impact of modern communications technology in terms of both the conduct and the outcome of the conflict. However, the capacity as well as the technical ability to exert greater political control is somewhat undermined by other developments.

The fact that a considerable amount of military effort now goes into strategic and operational planning has important consequences for the degree to which effective political control over the military can be exercised in modern societies. To take the case of the US, about whose war planning a great deal is known, many recent studies have argued that the complexity of the military apparatus and of military planning leaves little scope for purposive political direction. It is no accident that in the Gulf War the US President frequently emphasized that the military would not be subject to political interference in carrying out their plans. It is not that the military deliberately usurp political authority but rather that the technology of modern warfare requires increasing specialization, professionalization and integrated military planning of the highest order. The consequences of this are to remove the possibility of effective civilian control over the military in time of conflict. As Bracken argues, this is particularly acute in respect of political control over nuclear weapons:

> The introduction of nuclear weapons into civil–military relations has the potential for upsetting the equilibrium of civilian control of the military. This potential, whether actual or threatened, forces compromises on the subordination of the military to political control . . . National leaders are vulnerable to destruction, as are the communication circuits that connect them to the forces of retaliation. This simple fact inevitably makes delegation of nuclear launch authority a serious possibility . . . Instead of a military engine governed at all times by a political hand that directs it to meet the objectives of statecraft, in the nuclear age an enormously stupid and complex organism has come into being . . . Because of the vulnerability to paralysing attack, the nuclear organism is designed to kill even while being cut to pieces, and war is transformed into a continuation of grand tactics bereft of political control . . . I am concerned not with the usurpation of political power by the military, but rather with the arrangements devised to manage a strategy of deterrence, and with how these may lead to a 'provincialization' of strategy that removes the possibility of political understanding, let alone control, of military operations.
>
> (1987, pp. 352–3)

Here is a rather chilling illustration of Winner's notion of reverse adaptation.

What Bracken says also applies in some degree to most militarily advanced states, whose military planning and operations are becoming increasingly dependent on sophisticated command and control mechanisms. But there is also an additional barrier to the exercise of political control: operational planning may bear little relationship to stated political objectives. As studies of US nuclear war planning since 1948 have demonstrated, the national security and strategic objectives set by the politicians have only a tenuous connection with the actual operational plans of the military (Rosenberg 1983; Ball 1983). The problem of political control is thus compounded by the uncertain connection between stated political objectives and the requirements of efficient military planning. This became apparent at several critical junctures during the Gulf War.

Whilst civil authorities have always faced difficulties exercising political control over the military, particularly before modern communications systems existed, the contemporary situation is somewhat different precisely because it does not arise out of the lack of technical means or motivation to exercise such control. On the contrary, it results from the interrelated effects of the industrialization and bureaucratization of warfare combined with the professionalization of the military.

Besides influencing the pattern of civil–military relations, the requirements of modern military technology have also contributed to greater state intervention in domestic society. This in turn has had important consequences for the nature of domestic politics. Both the permanent preparation for war and the need to harness science and industry to military purposes have had a profound impact upon the role of the state in society. In the post-war period the ability of a nation to defend itself has depended not just on its wealth or its military prowess but also on its ability to organize and exploit industry and science. Those states that have not been able to do this have to depend on those that can to procure the military capabilities to defend them against their rivals. This has forced states to intervene more closely in the management of domestic affairs, since the security of the whole nation is at stake. The post-war drift towards what Galbraith calls the 'new industrial state' thus has to be understood as being driven by the demands of *warfare* as well as *welfare*.

If the requirements of a modern defence capability have contributed to greater state intervention in domestic affairs, equally they have assisted in eroding the distinctions between the civil and the military, the foreign and the domestic. Pearton has explained this very cogently:

> Government is . . . central and has to assess and implement priorities for the security of the nation. For these reasons, foreign and defency policy is not a separate activity but one which ramifies into society as a whole. What we are accustomed to consider as purely domestic, such as education or welfare, is directly related to the options open to the makers of external policy. It is no use embarking on a supersonic jet fighter or complex electronic devices if the educational system fails to produce the right kind of engineers at the highest level of professional competence . . . The curriculum need not be tailored to meet the needs of defence policy but governments have to be aware of its relationship to the future security of their society.
>
> In the contemporary world, strategy is a question of managing resources and taking explicit decisions about technology. It reaches into the society as a whole and can no longer be confined to the military aspects of it. 'Civil' and 'military' have become two sides of the same coin.
>
> (1982, pp. 254, 246–7)

Some argue that we are witnessing a growing militarization of society, and on a global scale. What seems incontrovertible is that the pattern of domestic politics in almost all modern states is now at least partially shaped by the imperatives of producing, maintaining or simply utilizing modern military technology.

References

Ball, D. (1983) *Targeting for Strategic Deterrence*. Adelphi Paper 185, London: IISS.

Behrman, R. and Baker, J.C. (1982) *Soviet Strategic Forces*. Washington DC: Brookings Institution.

Bracken, P. (1987) Delegation of nuclear command authority. In A.B. Carter et al., *Managing Nuclear Operations*, Washington DC: Brookings Institution, 352–73.

Brodie, B. (1946) *The Absolute Weapon*. New York: Harcourt Brace.

Bundy, M. (1987) October 27 1962: transcripts of the meetings of Excomm. *International Security*, 12 (3), 30–93.

Buzan, B. (1987) *Strategic Studies – Military Technology and International Relations*, London: Macmillan.

Elliot, D. (1986) Project Vista and nuclear weapons in Europe. *International Security*, 11 (1), 163.

Freedman, L. (1981) *The Evolution of Nuclear Strategy*. London: Macmillan.

Greenwood, T. (1975) *Making the MIRV*. Boston: Ballinger.

Halliday, F. (1987) *The Making of the Second Cold War*; London: Verso.

Holland, L.H. and Hoover, R.A. (1985) *The MX Decision*. London: Westview Press.

Holloway, D. (1983) *The Soviet Union and the Arms Race*. New Haven: Yale University Press.

Huisken, R. (1981) *The Origin of the Strategic Cruise Missile*. London: Praeger.

IISS (1987, 1991) *The Military Balance*. London: International Institute for Strategic Studies.

Kurth, J. (1973) Aerospace production lines and American defense spending. In S. Rosen (ed.), *Testing the Theory of the Military Industrial Complex*, Lexington, MA: Lexington Books.

MacKenzie, D. (1990) *Inventing Accuracy – A Historical Sociology of Nuclear Missile Guidance*. London: MIT Press.

Mandelbaum, M. (1981) *The Nuclear Revolution*. Cambridge: Cambridge University Press.

Mandelbaum, M. (1983) *The Nuclear Future*. New York: Columbia University Press.

Miller, J.H. (1988) The geographical disposition of the Soviet armed forces. *Soviet Studies*, XL (3), 406–33.

Mosley, H. (1985) *The Arms Race*. Lexington, MA: Lexington Books.

Newman, S.G. (1984) International stratification and Third World military industries. *International Organization*, 38 (1), 167–98.

Northedge, F.S. (1976) *The International Political System*. London: Faber.

Pearton, M. (1982) *The Knowledgeable State*. London: Burnett.

Rosenberg, D. (1983) The origins of overkill: nuclear weapons and American strategy 1945–1960. *International Security*, 7, spring, 3–71.

Ross, A.L. (1987) Dimensions of militarization in the Third World. *Armed Forces and Society*, 13 (4), 561–78.

Thompson, E. (1982) Notes on exterminism. In *Exterminism and Cold War*, London: NLR Verso.

Winner, L. (1977) *Autonomous Technology*. Boston: MIT Press.

6

Regimes and the Global Commons: Space, Atmosphere and Oceans

JOHN VOGLER

This chapter is about political responses to technological change on a global scale. Specifically, the concern is with the so-called global commons. These are areas such as the oceans, the deep seabed, the atmosphere and outer space which for one reason or another cannot be parcelled up and placed under the sovereign control of nation-states. Apart from the oceans it is only in the last few decades that the commons have been politicized, because it is only relatively recently that humankind has possessed the technological capability both to exploit and to degrade them. An awareness of the general problem posed by unconstrained exploitation, particularly of the environmental commons, is now widespread, as is the related understanding that some form of cooperative management is urgently required. However, this immediately raises the classic problem in international relations of how a political system fragmented into over 160 sovereign units can cope with the consequences of interdependence. This is perhaps most graphically illustrated by the problem of global warming. It seems to be the case that the very high levels of interdependence and vulnerability stimulated by technological change now necessitate new forms of global political authority and even governance. Presumably these forms lie somewhere between the anarchy of competing sovereign states and the idealist vision of a world government; but how can they be described, what functions do they fulfil, and how do they come about? This chapter will attempt to deal with these questions through the use of regime analysis and its application to the specific problems of international cooperation in the management of the commons.

THE GLOBAL COMMONS

The oceans were the first area to be recognized as a global commons. Seaborne commerce, warfare and fishing have engendered a long history of international conflict and attempts at rule making. Traditionally, national jurisdiction extended to the three-mile limit, and beyond that the oceans were open to free use. The relationship between rights and rules and the prevailing technology is well illustrated by the observation that three miles was considered to be the extreme range of a cannon shot. In the twentieth century new technologies in offshore oil drilling and factory fishing, along with the discovery of rich mineral deposits on the seabed (manganese nodules) and an awareness of increasing maritime pollution, have stimulated extensive political and legal consideration of the ocean commons. It was indeed in this context that Arvid Parvo, then foreign minister of Malta, first introduced the concept of the oceans as 'common heritage of mankind' in 1967. This did not prevent the United Nations Conference on the Law of the Sea (UNCLOS) from presiding over a major expansion of sovereign territorial control involving the extension of the limit of the territorial sea to 12 miles and the creation of a much more extensive exclusive economic zone (EEZ) based upon the continental shelf. Much the most controversial issue emerging from the Third UNCLOS, concluded in 1982, has been the management and exploitation of the deep seabed and its mineral resources. Defined as the common heritage of mankind they were, in the Third LOS Convention, made subject to an International Seabed Authority. The provisions under which the Authority and its related Enterprise would license mining, transfer technology and preside over the equitable redistribution of revenues were both complex and highly controversial. Their rejection by the United States and the United Kingdom, along with the failure of a large number of states to ratify the Convention, explains why this attempt at managing the commons remains at an embryonic stage.

The exploitation of outer space for both military and commercial purposes dates from the first successful attempt to orbit a spacecraft in 1957. Since then, space activities have become a vital component of military operations (communications, command, control and intelligence gathering) as well as proposed weapons systems, for example the American Strategic Defense Initiative (SDI). In the civilian sector, which has a sometimes symbiotic relationship with the military, world telephone and data networks are interconnected by satellite, notably through the Intelsat system set up in 1972. Direct broadcasting by satellite (DBS) is now commonplace. Major capital investments are being made in dedicated communications systems, which allow corporations to bypass established national telephone systems, and in mobile communications, where Inmarsat has established maritime communications links and is now extending coverage to aircraft and even long-distance trucks. Satellites are also used for the civilian equivalent of military intelligence, which involves the remote sensing of the earth's resources.

Space questions have moved rapidly into the political domain. Three areas of controversy may be highlighted. First, there are the peaceful uses of outer space. Here the concern has been with the avoidance of the stationing of weapons of mass destruction in orbit and the inherent dangers of the development of anti-satellite (ASAT) weapons, which threaten to destabilize strategic relationships by placing intelligence and communications assets at risk. Second, it is a fundamental characteristic of DBS, dedicated satellite data networks and remote sensing that such systems are no respecters of terrestrial sovereign boundaries. Many national governments, especially but not only in the Third World, have become alarmed at the implications for their sovereignty and have sought to regulate such activities by instituting a requirement for national prior consent to boundary crossing transmissions. The third major area of controversy is fundamental to most space-based communications. The latter rely on one particular satellite orbit, geostationary orbit (GSO), sometimes known as the Clarke Belt. (Arthur C. Clarke of science fiction fame was the first to suggest the use of GSO in the mid 1940s.) The GSO, which is an equatorial orbit 36,000 km out from the earth's surface, has the unique property that a spacecraft travelling in the same direction as the earth's rotation will be held stationary in relation to points on the earth's surface. Hence use of this orbit is indispensable to DBS television and cost effective telephone and data communications links. There are now in excess of 150 commercial satellites in GSO providing such services. Most of them are owned and operated by the developed countries or by international organizations such as Intelsat and Inmarsat, and GSO positions are increasingly in short supply. This shortage arises not from any risk of physical collision, but from the need for adequate spacing to avoid interference between the radio frequencies used for the up and down links to earth. The business of managing the problem is in the hands of an international organization, the International Telecommunication Union (ITU), which has long been concerned with the technical problems arising from the international use of the radio frequency spectrum. (Satellites tend to use superhigh frequencies in the gigahertz bands, notably the C band (4–8 GHz) and the Ku band (12.5–18 Ghz) which are themselves in short supply.) Developing countries, for whom satellites represent a particularly attractive and cost effective means of building national communications networks, have been understandably aggrieved that many of the most useful GSO positions and related frequencies have been appropriated by the advanced countries. Their claim has been that the GSO represents a global resource that must be used on an equitable basis. It gave rise to a decade of debate and technological diplomacy within the ITU which culminated in agreement in 1988 (Final Act of World Administrative Radio Conference (WARC) on Geostationary Orbit) to a plan which ensured that every state member was allocated its own national orbital position and frequencies.

The most recent commons to achieve high political salience has been the earth's atmosphere. Environmental issues had been on the agenda since the United Nations Stockholm Conference of 1972. However, the dramatic discovery of depletion of the earth's stratospheric ozone layer during the 1980s led to uncharacteristically rapid international action in the negotiation of limits to the use of ozone depleting gases, notably chlorofluorocarbons (CFCs) and halons, in the Montreal Protocol of 1987. This agreement, which itself emerged from the Vienna Convention of 1985, has been subject to continuous review and revision, leading to much more stringent limitations at the London Conference of June 1990. At the same time growing scientific disquiet and public alarm at the projected rate of global warming, associated with emissions of greenhouse gases, has stimulated an ambitious programme of international climate conferences guided by scientific studies within the Intergovernmental Panel on Climatic Change (IPCC). These are scheduled to result in a convention governing the emission of carbon dioxide and other gases, to be concluded in 1992.

What Have the Commons in Common?

As Krasner (1985, p. 227) has pointed out, the resources briefly mentioned above may have very little in common apart from a shared legal history. Some would be seen by economists as exhibiting the characteristics of a collective good, while others might, theoretically at least, become private property. Some, like deep seabed manganese nodules, clearly represent a resource that can be depleted; others, as environmentalists remind us, require sustainable development if they are not to be destroyed with catastrophic consequences. Yet others, like the GSO and the radio frequency spectrum, are not depletable but require high levels of coordination amongst users if their benefits are to be enjoyed.

The first point to make in a work about global politics is that all have to a greater or lesser extent been politicized. That is to say, human technological capabilities have turned what often used to be areas of purely scientific interest into valued resources which can be exploited for commercial or military advantage. This is obviously the case for outer space or the seabed, but it is also true for the atmosphere or the oceans in the sense that industrial development exploits them as a free waste disposal system. As the recognition dawns that these resources are limited and that the costs and benefits of their exploitation are, under existing arrangements, very unevenly distributed both amongst current users and of course between present and future generations, they are inevitably drawn into the nexus of global politics. The classic concern of the latter has been national security, and it comes as little surprise that all the areas under consideration have security implications. This is self-evidently so in the case of the oceans and space, but it is also receiving recognition in discussions of environmental diplomacy. Another way of making the same point is to use the distinction between high and low politics. High politics traditionally involves the classic issues of war, peace and national interest – the items that one might expect to find on the agenda of summit meetings. Low politics, by contrast, denotes the workaday issues of international relations involving airline timetables, vaccination certificates, frequency registration etc., which are the domain of technical experts and seem to have little political content. This would have described the work of the ITU quite adequately until the 1970s, when to the horror of many observers (and in common with a number of other functional organizations) it appeared to become politicized. The politicization of environmental issues, their emergence as the stuff of high politics, has been even more dramatic. Having languished for decades as the province of the technical and scientific expert, suddenly in the late 1980s they began to appear on the agenda of Group of Seven summit meetings.

One way of generalizing about the political and economic problem of the commons is to assert that it arises from their rapid exploitation (made possible through the agency of technological change) and overuse. A classic statement was provided by Hardin's (1968) 'tragedy of the commons', in which short-sighted individualistic exploitation results in depletion of the resource and general harm. In Hardin's example of medieval grazing rights, the problem is solved by enclosure – the allocation of individual property rights to what used to be a collective resource. The incentive to overgraze the common land was replaced by the incentive to husband one's individual plot. A defining characteristic of the commons under consideration here is that such a solution is for technical or political reasons *not* available. In the case of the oceans the enclosure solution was clearly adopted in the form of extended territorial waters and EEZs, but this has not been so for the deep seabed. Similarly, an attempt was made by a group of equatorial states to lay claim to sovereignty over the GSO in the Bogotá Declaration of 1976. Needless to say, both the insecure scientific basis and the sheer political impossibility of such a claim made it little more than a curiosity. It is equally obvious that problems related to the earth's stratospheric ozone layer or the global climate system do not admit of solutions through enclosure. If this is so, and the result of continued individualistic exploitation will not exhibit that general harmony of interests beloved of classical liberal economic theorists, some form of international cooperation is necessary. This is essentially Keohane's (1984) point when he writes that it is the absence of harmony that is the spur to cooperation.

Cooperation is not easy. As Mancur Olson (1965) argued, there are no incentives for individuals or groups to pay for the provision of public goods such as a pollution-free environment. A particular problem with the global commons is that measures for their collective regulation and management are predicated upon the consequences of inaction over future decades and for succeeding generations, whereas the time horizons of business of political decision makers tend to be obsessively restricted to the next year's profit and loss account or the forthcoming election. This is compounded by scientific uncertainty as to the scale or even the existence of commons problems. Recent argument as to the rate and impact of global warming is very much a case in point, and provides decision makers with a plausible excuse for inaction. In the case of GSO congestion, the point has often been made by spokesmen for the developed countries that no problem really exists because predicted technological advances will ensure that more orbital slots and frequency space will become available. Even if a problem is generally acknowledged to exist, its solution will probably entail unwelcome costs and raise intensely political questions as to the distribution of burdens and benefits. Negotiations on global commons issues exhibit inevitable clashes of interest between developed countries with differing stakes in say the exploitation of maritime resources, satellite use or the emission of greenhouse gases. A common thread running through all the negotiations is that they have been marked by North–South disagreements. It was the less developed countries (LDCs) who pressed for an international authority to control and allocate the resources of the seabed, for the equitable distribution of satellite orbits and frequencies, and for the costs of substituting CFCs to be borne by the developed countries.

Finally, it goes without saying that the problem of the commons is an international problem. Whereas within one domestic political system there is a sovereign power which has the capacity to enforce compliance, to regulate business and to levy taxation, management on a global scale encounters the problem of cooperation under anarchy. In the examples considered above and elsewhere, technological advance has brought about high levels of interdependence and mutual vulnerability within a political system that is ill-equipped to cope.

INTERNATIONAL COOPERATION AND REGIMES

Recently, and particularly in the United States, the problem of the basis and extent of international cooperation has been dealt with by developing the concept of international regimes. However, as Strange (1983) has pointed out, academic debate about their nature and significance is very much a continuation of classic disputes between realist and liberal-idealist conceptions of world politics.

The concept of an international regime first saw the light of day around 1975 and has been defined as follows: 'principles, norms, rules and decision-making procedures around which actor expectations converge in a given issue area' (Krasner 1983, p. 1). The date is significant, for most academic theorizing in international relations tends to reflect contemporary political problems and policy debates. The clash between realism and idealism in the inter-war period was, for example, very much a commentary on the rise of the European dictators and the trials and tribulations of the League of

Nations system. As noted elsewhere in this book, the early 1970s was a period of turbulent change for the United States, so much so that American commentators began to agonize about the consequences of the collapse of US hegemony. The apparent growth of interdependence and vulnerability, alongside the recession of American leadership, prompted speculation as to the future basis of international order in its absence. Alongside these particularly American concerns there was also an awareness of the global problems posed by rapid technological and economic development. It is thus significant that the article by Ruggie (1975), which is often cited as having introduced the concept of regime, was entitled 'International responses to technology'. In it he argued that there was now political recognition of a collective problem of management and coordination brought about through technological change and the sense in which policy choices by different nations were interdependent.

This must by now be a familiar theme, and describes some of the developments that have been traced in the global commons. What is less clear is why a new theoretical apparatus was required to understand policy coordination under conditions of interdependence. In Ruggie's view the concept of regime was required because the existing literature relating technological trends to international cooperation had focused not on 'institutionalization but on institutions and organizations' (p. 568). What was needed was a wider view that would include not just international law and organization but also the often implicit understandings between a whole range of actors, some of which were not states, which served to structure their cooperation in the face of common problems.

Thus proponents of regime analysis hold that regimes comprehend collaborative principles and arrangements that include but also transcend international organizations. They have a greater degree of permanence than specific agreements in that they carry a sense of general obligation. They allow us to understand how global activity is coodinated in the absence of management by a central government, and may be 'conceptualized as intervening variables between causal factors and outcomes and behaviour' (Krasner 1983, p. 1). The definition of regimes given above, in terms of principles, norms, rules and decision-making procedures, was very much a compromise amongst a number of scholars. Some like Young (1989) would go further and argue that regimes are essentially one type of social institution and like other social institutions have a major significance for the determination of behaviour. On the other hand many realists and Marxists would dismiss regimes as epiphenomena, and Strange (1983, p. 354) has argued that a proper understanding of 'who gets what' in the international economy 'is more likely to be captured by looking not at the regime that emerges on the surface but underneath, at the bargains on which it is based.' Leaving this controversy aside for the moment, we may proceed by considering whether the concept of regime can be used to describe and analyse the arrangements which exist for the international management or governance of the commons.

DEFINING AND ANALYSING REGIMES

When it comes to the business of actually analysing and comparing regimes, it may be argued that Krasner's (1983) fourfold definition is deficient in at least two respects. First, while the distinction between some form of rule or principle and the decision-making procedures used to implement and adjudicate them is clear, the distinction between principles, norms and rules is very much one of degree and could involve us in endless hairsplitting. (Keohane 1984, pp. 57–9 recognizes this without proposing a clear alternative). Essentially the three categories range from the general to the very specific, and while this may be of interest it is not central to our investigation. Second, what is central is the extent of international collaboration over the various global commons. As they stand, Krasner's categories cannot really cope with this. The requirement is for a framework which will allow us to determine whether commons issues are treated through individualistic national action or through some form of authoritative international regime.

Useful guidance is provided by Donnelly (1986), who has tried to deal with the same problems in the field of human rights. In order to determine the strength of a regime, Donnelly provides a classificatory scheme as outlined in figure 6.1. A glance at the diagram reveals that regimes are classified in terms of two dimensions: *norms* on the vertical axis and *decision-making procedures* on the horizontal axis. It is possible to use the categories which lie along these axes to define the absence of a regime – purely national standards and decision-making procedures – and a range of possible regime types:

1 Declaratory, weak or strong
2 Promotional, weak or strong
3 Implementation, weak or strong
4 Enforcement, weak or strong.

Essentially the strength and scope of a regime increases as we move from the bottom left-hand corner of the diagram to the top right-hand corner. In other words these points represent the ideal types of full national sovereignty (or perhaps corporate freedom) and something approaching world government. We are probably unlikely to encounter an example of the first and we will certainly not encounter the second, but between them we have a scale with which to measure regimes.

Before any such exercise in classification, an even more basic task is the identification of where regimes are likely to exist. The answer to this question is not as self-evident as it may seem. An initial approach to the global commons would no doubt be

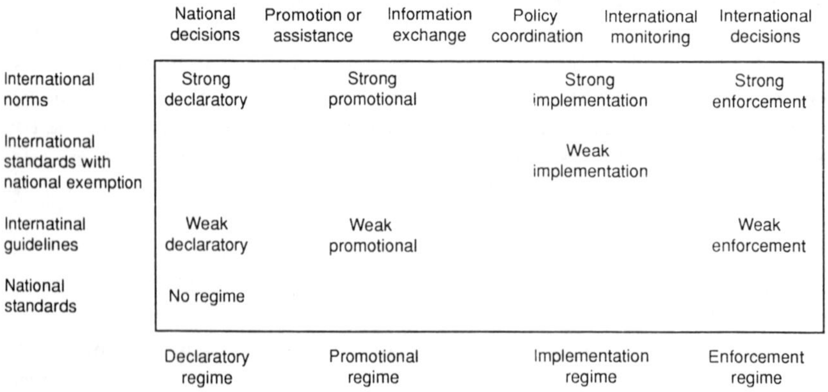

	National decisions	Promotion or assistance	Information exchange	Policy coordination	International monitoring	International decisions
International norms	Strong declaratory		Strong promotional		Strong implementation	Strong enforcement
International standards with national exemption					Weak implementation	
International guidelines	Weak declaratory		Weak promotional			Weak enforcement
National standards	No regime					
	Declaratory regime		Promotional regime		Implementation regime	Enforcement regime

Figure 6.1 Regime classification
Source: Donnelly 1986

predicated on the existence of oceans, space and atmospheric regimes. However, there is a clear difference here between what might be logically desirable or even ecologically necessary and what may be observed. (There is a long-standing debate over whether a holistic approach to global environmental problems is to be preferred to a more piecemeal one; as Haas 1975 put it, 'Is there a hole in the whole?') In surveying the rules that guide international activity related to the commons, it soon becomes clear that only in the most notional sense is there an overarching oceans, space or atmosphere regime. In reality there is a set of rules for territorial seas tenuously linked to an entirely different and stillborn regime for the deep seabed. Although there may be a general space treaty (Outer Space Treaty 1967) it enshrines general declarations rather than specific rules. As one commentator, Ploman (1984, p. 155), aptly observes, 'this concept of international regimes is helpful in revealing the absence of any single overall regime' when applied to the field of satellite communications.

Keohane (1984, p. 61) makes the important point that regimes should be defined in terms of issue areas. These are 'sets of issues that are in fact dealt with in common negotiations and by the same, or closely coordinated bureaucracies'. Thus for present purposes (although most definitely not for others) the *a priori* attempt to analyse general regimes for each of the commons may be abandoned. Instead, the identification of regimes should be guided by the actual perceptions and behaviour of actors who have an interest in the utilization of the commons.

Using this definition, it is possible to determine a whole set of issue areas and potential regimes relating to the utilization of the commons. As far as the oceans are concerned, the determination of the boundaries between the high seas and the territorial seas and of the rights and rules relating to each has always been the main issue area. Separate, but linked within the LOS framework, has been the issue of the ownership and exploitation of the deep seabed. In outer space, international activity tends to define at least three clusters of issues. There is the question of satellite communications and information flows across boundaries; the question of the military uses of space, which may be seen as a branch of the general arms control enterprise; and, basic to most space activities, the question of the ownership and allocation of orbital slots and the frequency spectrum. Until now the new diplomacy of the global atmosphere has tended to focus upon two major issue areas: stratospheric ozone depletion, the subject of the Vienna Convention of 1985 and Montreal Protocol of 1987; and the problem of global warming, as represented in the IPCC meetings and the Climate Conference 1992. Two important reservations should accompany this list. First, it is hardly exclusive and it would be very easy to determine a large number of additional issue areas according to the interests of the observer. Second, the issue areas themselves will change over time and have very fluid boundaries. For example, the issue area relating to information flows and sovereignty contains not only space-based communications but terrestrial ones as well, and will be debated not only at specialized forums such as the UN Committee on the Peaceful Uses of Outer Space (COPUOS) but also within, say, GATT deliberations on the trade in services.

A Classification of Commons Related Regimes

Using Donnelly's (1986) scheme it is possible to arrive at the following classification of the regimes governing the issue areas outlined above.

Oceans

High seas

The ancient rights and customs of navigation have been codified in the LOS Conventions to provide a strong declaratory regime. Within the agreed limits of territorial seas and EEZs, national decisions hold sway.

Seabed

Here there was an attempt to create a strong implementation regime, providing for authoritative allocation of common heritage seabed mineral resources by an international decision-making authority. The refusal of major maritime powers to accept such limitations on their freedom of action means, that as yet, there is no regime.

Space

Information flow

Attempts have been made within COPUOS and UNESCO to regulate transborder data flow and broadcasting and to establish a right of national prior consent. They have not met with general acceptance. The 1977 ITU Conference on Direct Satellite Broadcasting in Europe did provide a scheme under which national DBS frequencies and coverage areas were allocated, but the technical definitions were soon outmoded, to the effect that, while the failed BSB TV had to operate within the plan, Sky TV does not. There are various national attempts to regulate, but one might say that there is either no regime or a *de facto* free-flow regime.

Military

The military use of space has been very much the preserve of the US and the USSR, although the international community has supported the declaratory principle of demilitarization in the 1967 Space Treaty. There is an, as yet uncodified, assumption between the two main space powers that space should be a sanctuary and that ASAT weapons should not be deployed. In the absence of any international monitoring or implementation, this may be regarded as a weak declaratory regime.

Orbit and spectrum

A strong implementation regime exists under the auspices of ITU. Allocation of orbit and spectrum involves extensive decision making at the international level, and there is a complex system of registration with the International Frequency Registration Board

(IFRB). Although most frequency use is on a first-come, first-served basis, the 1988 Orbit Conference agreed a plan under which each nation is granted an orbital slot for a fixed communication satellite. There is no provision for enforcement within the regime, and IFRB relies on national monitoring of frequency use.

Atmosphere

Ozone

In this area there has been a rapid shift from the promotional regime sponsored by the 1985 Vienna Convention to the implementation regime embodied in the 1987 Montreal Protocol. This committeed signatories to specified reductions in CFC and halon manufacture and was inspired by more far-reaching national decisions. At the 1990 London Conference the regime was tightened such as to commit developed country signatories to a complete phasing out by 2000. The regime enshrines an international monitoring and review process and even envisages possible economic sanctions in cases of non-compliance. It is partial, with 59 signatories as of 1990 excluding many LDCs, and attention has been directed to securing Chinese and Indian acceptance through a compensatory fund.

Climate carbon dioxide

As yet there is only a weak promotional regime involving conferences, declarations and scientific information exchange and consensus building in the IPCC. The much more difficult business of limiting carbon dioxide emissions may be regarded as having reached the same stage as the ozone regime in the mid 1980s.

ACCOUNTING FOR REGIMES

The preceding sketch of the regime arrangements for the oceans, space and the atmosphere reveals great variation in the degree to which there may be said to be a form of international governance – in terms of strong implementation regimes with well-developed decision-making and monitoring procedures. How can this be explained? Why in some issue areas are there strong regimes, while in others it is arguable as to whether anything describable as a regime exists at all? The question is of particular importance if we are concerned with building new institutions and if we accept the argument that existing spontaneous *laissez-faire* arrangements will, if allowed to persist, bring about a 'tragedy of the commons'. International Relations scholars have advanced a number of potential answers. These theories about regimes frequently owe their genesis to classic debates between realism and liberal-idealism.

Traditionally, the academic debate on the scope and potential of international cooperation has developed in terms of the clash between realist and liberal-idealist conceptions. Realism, it will be recalled, posits a world of competing national interests in which only a minimal order established on the basis of considerations of power is achievable. National economic and political interests and the desire to maximize status tend to predominate over common global interests – the existence of which is often denied. International organizations are seen not as actors in their own right, but rather as collections of sovereign states. Any common arrangements that may be arrived at constitute a reflection of underlying power realities and accommodations between competing state interests. (Recent writers in the realist tradition have tended to adopt the confusing labels 'structuralist' and 'neo-mercantilist', and even 'neo-realist' and 'modified structuralist'. These have meaning for close students of the debate about regimes, in so far as they indicate nuances of interpretation within realism, but they will as far as possible be avoided in the discussion that follows.)

Realism and Hegemonic Stability

The distinctive contribution of realism to the debate about regimes has been a power structural explanation – the hegemonic stability thesis. The argument is that under realist assumptions regimes have to be created and led by a hegemonic actor capable of imposing rules on an anarchic system. The most recent such actor has of course been the United States, which as the dominant power in the 1940s was able to construct the Bretton Woods regime and the open world trade regime centred around the GATT. As we have seen, much of the interest in regimes may be understood as a reaction to the supposed loss of US hegemony in the early 1970s, notably in the world monetary regime.

Attempting to apply the hegemonic stability thesis to the regimes under consideration runs the risk of entering the debate as to whether the US remains a hegemon. Whatever may be the conclusion on this, there is little doubt that only the US is a candidate for this role by virtue of the enormous size of its economy, the global reach of its business corporations and its very susbtantial scientific and technical base. Attempts to test the hegemonic stability thesis empirically have at best proved inconclusive (Webb and Krasner 1989 provide a review). In terms of the cases under consideration here, there is little or no evidence to suggest that the US has played an active role as regime creator. However, it has probably been the dominant force in sustaining some existing arrangements and in blocking proposals for institutional change. The latter role emerges most clearly in the issue areas of the seabed and information flow. It was above all American refusal to ratify the 1982 LOS Convention that ensured that a new regime for the seabed has not been implemented. In terms of both ideology and perceptions of corporate interest the United States has been a fervent defender of the notion of free flow, and has used its undoubted muscle to block the development of global communications regulation and to emasculate UNESCO. At the same time the US government seems to have been a somewhat tardy convert to the Montreal Protocol and has not been in the vanguard of those urging a new convention on carbon dioxide emissions. Profligate energy use in the vast US economy is generally reckoned to be responsible for about 20–25 per cent of the problem and the acceptance of restrictions would be costly. Indeed the American government irritated many of its partners by a display of scepticism as to the scale and implications of global warming. At a 1990 meeting on the IPCC report the US delegation is said to have introduced 46 pages of amendments to a proposed executive summary only 31 pages long (*The Guardian*, 31 August 1990).

The pattern that emerges is of the pursuit of national interest, which appears to be very well served by the absence of strong regulatory regimes and which is most definitely opposed to attempts to create international authorities that will divide up common resources in line with some conception of equity. Thus over the seabed negotiations, the COPUOS and UNESCO discussions on information, and the campaign for equity in orbit in the ITU, the US could be relied upon to be the leading opponent of schemes for planning and redistribution. This might validate hegemonic stability arguments in the somewhat negative sense that the hegemon is able to prevent regime formation or to maintain regimes which are essentially weak and permissive.

It is perhaps unfortunate that so much time has been spent debating the question of hegemonic stability at the expense of other realist insights. As Young (1989) notes, realist thought implies a model of behaviour based on status maximization, and this has provided quite a powerful critique of the activities of the Third World coalition in global negotiations. According to Krasner (1985), Third World sponsorship of the 'new international economic order' (NIEO) and a movement from market oriented to 'authoritative allocation' regimes reflect, not economic welfare demands, by LDCs, but rather the requirement of inadequately legitimized political systems for enhanced status. Thus for Krasner, the most important consequence of the UNCLOS negotiation 'was the legitimation of the extension of sovereignty of littoral states over vast areas of the seabed, a conclusion that is congruent with the fundamental NIEO objective' (p. 263). To this one might add that in the case of the 1988 ITU plan for satellite services, the great majority of states allocated orbital positions, had neither the intention nor the capability to use them, but nevertheless were vigilant in ensuring that individual national slots had technical parameters which were just as good as those of other states.

Undoubtedly the most significant realist contribution to any debate on the bargaining that must surround regime creation is the concern with relative power capabilities. Once again it is important to note that a power distribution that can be described in terms of hegemony is something of a historical rarity. During the period of the Second Cold War, the implicit regime concerning the military use of space involved the accommodation of the mutual interests of the two superpowers and reflected the military balance between them. A fairly standard instance of cooperation within conflict was observable, because both were vulnerable to ASAT development and had good reason to adhere to rules that maintained space as a sanctuary. Elsewhere, realists who are not overly wedded to the traditional indices of military might will be able to ascertain various different power distributions. The power resources that states use to determine the outcome of bargaining over the rules of a regime will, as Keohane and Nye (1977) have argued, be increasingly issue specific as the level of global interdependence increases. Market share, technological expertise, energy resources, conservation programmes etc. will be significant power resources in so far as they have a bearing on the production of workable international rules in a particular issue area.

A realist answer to our original question regarding the strength and weakness of regimes will thus be simple and robust. Regime arrangements will reflect bargains struck between the national interests of those possessing power in a particular issue area and will be sustained by just those power capabilities. Hence, as Krasner (1985, p. 263) asserts in relation to the ill-fated seabed regime, 'stability is not likely. There is too much incongruence between underlying power capabilities and decision making within the regime.' Universal membership regimes are likely to be stillborn, and 'efforts to create and maintain rules of the game should be restricted to states that have the power to disrupt them' (p. 264); the case cited with approbation is the limited Antarctic Treaty system. However, some intriguing anomalies remain which suggest that the connection between national power resources and regime formation is not quite so clear cut. Why in particular have the US and other developed countries, dominant in terms of market share and technical expertise, been prepared to compromise over planning for satellite services? The American position (usually mirrored by other advanced countries) had been one of resolute opposition to an *a priori* planning regime for GSO communications satellites in line with its stance elsewhere. However, first in 1979 it acquiesced in the calling of two special ITU conferences (WARC ORB 1985 and 1988) to establish equity in orbit, and then it was prepared to be party to a final agreement which, however limited, introduced the principle of planning a fixed satellite services system which allows each nation its own orbital position. Equally, why was the US prepared after initial scepticism to sign the Montreal Protocol and in 1990 to accept a foreshortened timetable for the phasing out of ozone depleting gases and the establishment of a compensatory fund? This suggests at least a partial need for some alternative form of explanation.

Liberal-Pluralism and Interdependence

Modern realist thought arose as a reaction to liberal idealism, and the debate between the two schools centred upon the question of the meaning and potential of international organization and notably the League of Nations. The orthodox liberal view of political economy has its roots in the writings of Adam Smith and others, who argued that, left to themselves, economic actors in the market-place pursuing their own interests would realize the best interests of all. There was a natural harmony of interests, and a hidden hand at work. However, increasing interference by nation-state governments in pursuit of security and narrowly defined national interest was seen by many liberals to militate against such natural harmony, bringing about armed conflict, protectionism and destructive trade wars, which conspired to reduce the general level of welfare. Thus liberal idealists (or sometimes rationalists) sought the construction of a new rationally organized world order which would, through the development of international law and cooperative activity, allow the full realization of common interests. Liberal idealists stressed the importance of international organization as a means of overcoming the damaging short-sightedness inherent in a world dominated by sovereign nation-states. For them, international organizations exist in their own right and exemplify common interests. International cooperative activity is particularly likely to bear fruit in so-called functional areas where technical specialists can agree rational solutions to common problems untrammelled by the animosities of high politics. In summary, whereas realism assumes behaviour to be based upon the pursuit of power and status, the liberal tradition assumes a world of actors pre-eminently concerned with the individualistic and rational pursuit of economic utility.

The influence of the latter assumptions can be seen in one of the most significant books in the field, Keohane's *After Hegemony* (1984). As the title suggests, the author grapples with the problem of how regimes may persist in the absence of a hegemonic actor. Those unimpressed by the hegemonic stability thesis may well feel that the effort was misplaced; but Keohane's answers do illustrate how liberal thought can provide an explanation of regimes which is based not upon dominance, but upon a conjunction of enlightened self-interest amongst the parties. Keohane's approach is very much indebted to the tradition of liberal political economy, which has attempted to provide a theory of political action and the state based upon the assumptions of neo-classical economics. Normally it is 'assumed that in a free market exchanges between individuals will lead to an efficient or optimal allocation of resources' (Barry 1989, pp. 68–9) and there is no justification for the state to interfere. However, there are two areas of market failure where this will not be so. The first concerns externalities of production like pollution, where it may be in the interest of individuals to impose costs on the rest of the community. The second is in the provision of public goods, which are necessary but will not be provided by individuals interested in profit maximization; clean air and defence may be cited as examples. In such cases state action on behalf of the community is justifiable.

At the global level, Keohane argues, the same problems exist and need to be resolved in the interests of all parties; yet there is of course no world government to enforce rules, tax pollution and finance public goods. Regimes provide a substitute. Without the set of stable expectations that they can provide, for example, the transaction costs of engaging in international commerce are excessively high. The fundamental problem of cooperation in the absence of government in this area is often illustrated by the game of the prisoner's dilemma (figure 6.2). The dilemma is that encountered by two prisoners arrested for the same crime and held separately in police cells, while detectives offer each inducements to confess. The police need a confession to ensure a conviction, and both prisoners can avoid this if they cooperate by staying silent, although in this instance some penalty could be imposed in terms of lesser charges. However, each knows that the other has an incentive to turn Queen's evidence, and in the absence of trust this is exactly what rational players can be expected to do. As the matrix indicates, when both players do this they experience a worse outcome than would have been available through a cooperative decision to remain silent.

However, as many studies have indicated, if the game is played over and over again (iterated prisoner's dilemma) then cooperative behaviour frequently emerges. The key to this is the expectation that one will have to deal with the other player in the future and that defections will only be met by counter-defections, leaving everybody worse off in the long run. Thus according to Axelrod (1984, p. 182) 'the foundation of cooperation is really not trust but the durability of a relationship', and for cooperation to be stable 'the future must cast a sufficiently long shadow' (p. 174). The temptation to make short-run gains at the expense of the other party will be checked by the certainty that he or she will reciprocate. Cooperation, which is entirely self-interested, can develop spontaneously and even tacitly between parties. This, according to Axelrod,

Column player

	Cooperate	Defect
Cooperate	$R = 3, R = 3$ Reward for mutual cooperation	$S = 0, T = 5$ Sucker's payoff, and temptation to defect
Defect	$T = 5, S = 0$ Temptation to defect, and sucker's payoff	$P = 1, P = 1$ Punishment for mutual defection

Figure 6.2 The prisoner's dilemma: payoffs to the row chooser are listed first
Source: Axelrod 1984

appears to have been the case in the reciprocal interaction between soldiers facing each other across no man's land in 1914–18, who evolved rules of behaviour which served a mutual interest in staying alive.

In global politics such understandings and rules of behaviour would constitute a regime. The findings of Axelrod and other theorists of the prisoner's dilemma are highly significant because they demonstrate the falsity of the common view (often attributed to idealist thinkers) that international cooperation must necessarily require national self-abnegation or a fit of sustained altruism. It can just as readily be grounded upon mutual self-interest. This would be one way of understanding the tacit understanding on space as a sanctuary that existed between competing space powers during the Second Cold War. A crucial function of more developed regimes, according to Keohane (1984), is that they assist such cooperation by improving the quality of information available, reducing uncertainty as to the actions of others and promoting ways of monitoring compliance. 'Such regimes are important not because they constitute quasi governments, but because they can facilitate agreements and decentralized enforcement of agreements between governments' (p. 244). The regime for the management of orbit and spectrum constitutes a case in point. Rules are required if users are to be able to communicate and broadcast effectively without signal interference, and attempts to evade them would prove counter-productive in the long term as other users retaliated.

The basis of such cooperation is thus interdependence – in the sense of an awareness of mutual vulnerability. The ozone regime may be understood in this way. Major chemical industry corporations such as Dupont and ICI had for some time prior to the Montreal Protocol been aware that environmentalist pressure in the developed countries would require that they developed CFC alternatives. 'These would be costly to develop and higher priced than CFCs. So the makers had an interest in an early, clear framework of regulation applying to as many potential competitors as possible' (*The Economist*, 16 June 1990, p. 22). Sustaining a regime that gave such a stable business framework was important because guarantees were required that the new alternatives (with an estimated market of $100 billion) would not be undercut by the continuing manufacture of cheap CFC-based products. Thus corporations and their governments had a clear stake in elaborating and supporting the rules. At a more general political level, there was also an awareness of real mutual vulnerability in terms of skin cancers etc., if nothing were done to arrest the depletion of the stratospheric ozone layer. Such consequences could be conceived of as a shared global problem. Although often bracketed together, the ozone and global warming problems are really rather different in this regard. The latter is infinitely more complex because it is not readily apparent that all the potential signatories of a global climate convention would have a shared conception of vulnerability to the projected rise in temperatures. As Skolnikoff (1990, p. 81) notes, 'not all the effects will necessarily be damaging: some activities will be enhanced and some localities and nations may benefit by changes, at least in relation to others.' This is to say, not that an effective climate regime is impossible, but that it will be much more difficult to achieve than the ozone regime. There are highly complex asymmetries between the parties in their assessments of the costs and benefits of global warming and the measures proposed for its curtailment. These are very much more extensive than in the ozone case, where specific chemicals and a relatively small number of manufacturers are involved. Instead the range of greenhouse gases (notably carbon dioxide) is wide, and they are produced by human activities which are essential to economic well-being and day-to-day survival. Thus even without examining the detail, it is clear that a broad spectrum of relative vulnerability exists across nations and different economic sectors. Even though the textbooks may often seem to suggest that interdependence implies equal vulnerability, this is rarely if ever the case. Instead, different levels of vulnerability lie at the heart of the politics of regimes and the bargains that will have to be struck if a climate regime is to be achieved.

The conclusion that interdependence will determine the success of regime building is supported by evidence from the other cases. Whereas strong regimes have emerged in areas of manifestly high interdependence, such as orbit, frequency spectrum and ozone, elsewhere a lack of shared vulnerability has meant that significant actors have had little incentive to support any restrictive regulation of their activities. This is certainly true for the absence of any rules for prior consent in space-based communications and for the ill-fated seabed mining regime.

The concept of interdependence can also illuminate the mechanisms whereby regimes are created and changed. It provides one explanation of why realist expectations that the strong will always hold sway may not always be fulfilled. It may be recalled that this was observed in the context of discussion of the two strong regimes mentioned above. During the last 20 years the ITU's frequency and orbit regime, based as it was on a first-come, first-served rule which operated to the benefit of advanced countries, was challenged by a loose coalition of less developed countries. Because the LDCs lack both technological and economic weight, the most significant political card available to them in the ITU, as in other UN organizations, was that they constituted a majority in plenary sessions of an organization which had a one-state, one-vote rule. This enabled them to place the campaign for equity in orbit on the agenda from 1979 onwards and implicitly to threaten the smooth running of the organization and its associated regime. The fact that by 1988, much against their better judgement, the US and other developed countries had come to a compromise involving the planning of part of the frequency spectrum and the GSO on the basis of equity, is a testimony to the value of the regime. In the interdependent world of satellite and radio communications the developed countries had very much more to lose and were significantly more vulnerable to a disruption of the rules than the LDCs. An American communications specialist put the point cogently: 'Economically, US dependence on telecommunications discourages ignoring ITU because of the destructive economic chaos that would ensue. More important, US leadership in telecommunications technology promises substantial economic benefits from a global expansion of communication' (Branscomb 1979, pp. 142–3). It is instructive to recall that a closely linked campaign for a new world information and communication order, which included the demand for prior consent, was also being sponsored by the LDCs within UNESCO at the same time. Whatever the rights and wrongs of this and the behaviour of the organization's director, it remains true that the UK and the USA simply left UNESCO. In comparison with the ITU case, there was little or no perceived vulnerability to the possible stunting of the organization's activities and little need to sustain a national presence.

The need to make compromises because of vulnerability to the collapse or absence of regime arrangements is also evident in the developed nations' approach to strengthening the Montreal Protocol. Here, it has already been noted that massive investments in ozone-friendly technology and the ozone layer itself were vulnerable to potential non-participants in the regime. India and China, who were not original signatories, argued at the June 1990 review conference that they could hardly be expected to adhere to the rules if it meant that their nascent CFC-based industries would be disadvantaged and the costs of national development raised by the need to buy the new Western produced technologies. Thus the cost for developed countries of a regime including India and China would be special treatment on the phasing out of CFCs, compensatory funding and technology transfers. As Indian delegate Maneka Ghandi said, 'The West has caused the problem and must help us clean it up' (*Financial Times*, 28 June 1990). As a consequence of the London meeting, the US and other countries were persuaded to contribute to a compensatory fund of $240 million, and Indian and Chinese delegates promised to recommend signature of the Montreal Protocol to their governments, on the clear understanding that technology transfers would also be forthcoming. In the future, attempts to create a regime to limit the greenhouse effect will be inordinately complex. As a recent study observes:

> No one nation or group of nations can make a substantial impact on emissions and future concentrations without the cooperation of other nations. Yet the countries from which the bulk of future emissions growth is likely to come – China, India, Brazil – are unlikely to curb that growth without international assistance on an unprecedented scale (Nitze 1990, pp. 1–2)

Cognitive Approaches

Whereas realist and liberal approaches proceed from fixed assumptions as to the motivation of actors, whether in terms of the pursuit of power and status or of economic welfare, proponents of cognitive explanations lay emphasis on shifts in perception and knowledge. According to Haas (1980, p. 360), 'institutionalized cooperation can be explored in terms of the interaction between changing knowledge and changing social goals.' This significant, yet relatively underdeveloped, perspective may help us to explain not only those shifts in the understanding and evaluation of interests that lie behind the creation of regimes, but also the ways in which those institutions themselves generate allegiance and channel behaviour.

A cognitive perspective highlights the role of technical experts whose shared interests and professional lives transcend national boundaries, and who may constitute epistemic communities united by a common understanding of particular problems. They are likely to be very influential in so far as only they possess the necessary expertise, upon which governments must be reliant, to comprehend the intricacies of subjects such as the management of the frequency spectrum or global climate modelling. The ITU constitutes a classic example. It is dominated by an engineering subculture and a belief in a rational, technical and apolitical approach. This assists cooperation (although it may also stifle radical change) and ensures that national administrations run by engineers and space and telecommunications specialists operate according to well-established ITU rules. Similar points might be made about international maritime lawyers and the LOS; arms control specialists and the military space regime; and the epistemic community of environmental scientists whose activities have been articulated by the United Nations Environment Programme (UNEP). Perceptions within international organizations and amongst wider publics are also shaped by a very large number of international non-governmental organizations (INGOs). They frequently have a special status within UN organizations and are invited to submit testimony and advice (UNEP, for example, recognizes some 500). The activities of Greenpeace in raising awareness of environ-mental issues immediately spring to mind, and the role of such organizations as global pressure groups has been a very much neglected aspect of regime analysis, preoccupied as it still is with the activities of nation-states.

Perhaps the major problem faced by those concerned with the management of the commons is how to translate an uncertain but potentially doom-laden scientific estimate of the consequences of inaction into a workable programme of regime creation. Many regimes have evolved almost spontaneously out of the habitual practices of states and other actors (for example the high seas regime); but virtually all assessments of global environmental change necessitate a much more proactive approach. This will depend upon what Greenpeace has described as 'paradigm shifts in human behaviour – particularly in the field of cooperation between nation-states – which have no precedents in human history' (Leggett 1990, p. 457). Such shifts require first the generation of international scientific consensus as to the scale of environmental problems, their impacts and their solutions, and secondly the kind of public awareness that will occasion a re-ordering of governmental priorities. Although this may seem utopian, there are some grounds for optimism in the way in which the UNEP system has approached the cognitive aspects of regime creation.

UNEP was the creation of the UN's first environmental conference in Stockholm in 1972. It was to be a 'small coordinating body to lead and direct environmental initiatives at the international level and coordinate and stimulate action, serving as a catalyst rather than an executing agency' (United Nations 1979, p. 168). In this the organization has had significant success. Many commentators have pointed out the importance of the discovery of the Antarctic ozone hole in the mid 1980s as the shock which provided the political impetus for negotiation of the Montreal Protocol. Behind this lay a decade of UNEP inspired scientific work on ozone trends, and very specifically the World Meteorological Organization's decision to sponsor a reactivation of the British Antarctic Survey's study which revealed the existence of the hole. The methods employed by UNEP and other interested agencies in building the ozone regime are often seen as the blueprint for future environmental cooperation. They involved the negotiation of an initial framework convention which acknowledged the problem, followed by an assessment and review process which generated scientific and then policy consensus leading to the 1987 Protocol and its extension at the 1990 London meeting. A similar procedure has been adopted for global warming. Progress towards a convention and measures to limit carbon emissions etc. is critically dependent upon achieving a consensus of scientific opinion within the IPCC on the projected dimensions and implications of global warming. This is, of course, particularly difficult because by the time the effects of global warming become obvious they will have become irrevers-ible. Effective action will require substantial and sustained cognitive changes at the expert, governmental and above all public levels, entailing a recognition of the extent of interdependence and mutual vulnerability, which in turn may provide the foundation of international cooperation and a climate regime.

CONCLUSIONS

This has not been a comprehensive treatment of the regime literature, which is both diverse and voluminous. Many important issues have been neglected: the ethnocentric character of regime thinking, its obsession with order as opposed to justice, and its unfortunate tendency to neglect the activities of non-state actors and movements. These and other issues have been critically surveyed by Strange (1983), Haggard and Simmons (1987) and Tooze (1990).

Within the limited compass of the present chapter, the regime concept as modified by Donnelly (1986) has been shown to have some use in classifying forms of international collaboration relating to the global commons. In fact this method displays the great variation in the extent and strength of rules existing within the various issue areas. There is no question that technological change has thrown up problems of interdependence that desperately require more effective means of international management. However, it may be concluded that the regimes surveyed at best allow for policy coordination between states and do not represent a decisive shift to new global authority structures.

Analysis of the variation between the regimes demonstrate that both realist and liberal approaches have some explanatory utility. If a generalization is to be attempted it might tentatively run as follows. Technological change leads to extensive cooperation in terms of the creation of a strong and valued regime in so far as it creates conditions of interdependence defined in terms of mutual vulnerability. This in turn provides opportunities for the exercise of a type of power which may be based, not on structure or issue, but on a potential ability to disrupt regime arrangements. However, even a brief acquaintance with the pressing issues of the global environmental commons indicates that such a conclusion is inadequate. It begs the crucial question of how perceptions of mutual vulnerability and interdependence are to be created and sustained, and it is perhaps to the cognitive aspects of regime creation that attention should be most urgently directed.

References

Axelrod, R. (1984) *The Evolution of Co-operation*. New York: Basic Books.

Barry, N.P. (1989) *An Introduction to Modern Political Theory*. London: Macmillan.

Branscomb, A. (1979) Waves of the future: making WARC work. *Foreign Policy*, 34, 139–48.

Donnelly, J. (1986) International human rights: a regime analysis. *International Organization*, 40 (3), 599–642.

Haas, E.B. (1975) Is there a hole in the whole? Knowledge, technology, interdependence and the construction of international regimes. *International Organization*, 29 (3), 827–876.

Haggard, S. and Simmons, B. (1987) Theories of international regimes. *International Organization*, 41 (3), 491–517.

Hardin, G. (1968) The tragedy of the commons. *Science*, 162.

Keohane, R.O. (1984) *After Hegemony: Cooperation and Discord in the World Political Economy*. Princeton: Princeton University Press.

Keohane, R.O. and Nye, J.S. (1977) *Power and Interdependence*. Boston: Little Brown.

Krasner, S.D. (ed.) (1983) *International Regimes*. Ithaca: Cornell University Press.

Krasner, S.D. (1985) *Structural Conflict: the Third World against Global Liberalism*. Berkeley: University of California Press.

Leggett, J. (ed.) (1990) *Global Warming: the Greenpeace Report*. Oxford: Oxford University Press.

Nitze, W.A. (1990) *The Greenhouse Effect: Formulating a Convention*. London: Royal Institute of International Affairs.

Olson, M. (1965) *The Logic of Collective Action*. Cambridge, MA: Harvard University Press.

Ploman, E. (1984) *Space, Earth and Communication*. London: Pinter.

Ruggie, J.G. (1975) International responses to technology: concepts and trends. *International Organization*, 29 (1), 557–83.

Skolnikoff, E.B. (1990) The policy gridlock on global warming. *Foreign Policy*, 79, 77–93.

Strange, S. (1983) Cave! hic dragones: a critique of regime analysis. In S.D. Krasner (ed.), *International Regimes*, Ithaca: Cornell University Press, 337–54.

Tooze, R. (1990) Regimes and international co-operation. In A.J.R. Groom and P. Taylor (eds), *Frameworks for International Co-operation*, London: Pinter, 201–16.

United Nations (1979) *Everyone's United Nations: a Handbook of the United Nations, its Structure and Activities*. New York: United Nations.

Webb, M.C. and Krasner, S.D. (1989) Hegemonic stability theory: an empirical assessment. *Review of International Studies*, 15 (2), 183–98.

Young, O.R. (1989) *International Cooperation: Building Regimes for Natural Resources and the Environment*. Ithaca: Cornell University Press.

7

Global Technologies and Political Change in Eastern Europe

NIGEL SWAIN

INTRODUCTION

1989 was the year of revolution in Eastern Europe. One by one the socialist satellite states of the Soviet Union fell, to be replaced by multiparty liberal-democratic systems. The process in fact started in Poland and Hungary before 1989, but by the end of the year a non-communist government was in power in Poland, and all the Eastern European countries (with the exception of Albania) were operating *de facto* multiparty systems in anticipation of elections in 1990. This chapter examines the role of technological change and its globalization in this process. It considers whether there is any sense in which this dramatic political transformation can be said to have been the consequence of global technological change.

There is a media illusion which suggests that technology has indeed influenced political events. When satellite technology brings us a television reporter describing the end of the Berlin Wall while actually standing on top of it, the impression is given that technology must have influenced the political events that led up to it. But this is no more than an illusion. The more closely events are examined, the less clear it is that technology plays an independent role in them.

Two general varieties of theory postulate a link of some sort between technology and political reform of the kind witnessed in Eastern Europe. The first is of the view that there is something inherently democratic about the quantity of information flows that have been made possible by new global technologies. Closed, totalitarian, single-party political systems are seen as unworkable when the mass of the population has the facility not only to receive information from alternative sources but also to produce and disseminate it itself. The problem with this theory is not that it is implausible, but that it is unspecific as to the agency and the mechanism by which this process operates. It also ignores entirely another feature of the information flows produced by the new technologies, namely their high degree of centralization; and this can operate directly counter to increased democracy.

A second approach is more specific in stipulating the mechanisms by which technology exerts an influence on politics, but it is empirically refutable. The argument runs as follows. New technologies (of any kind, but especially developments in information technology) can only be developed and successfully applied in a market economy, and competitive market economies require a competitive, pluralist political system. The first link in this chain holds, but the second does not. The existence of a market economy, especially one with a dynamic small-scale sector, does indeed appear to be a requirement for rapid technological innovation. But the link between market economies and political pluralism is much more tenuous. The fastest growing economies of East Asia are not models of political pluralism, and even democratic Japan has effectively been a one-party state since the Second World War. The problem with this theory is that it presumes a symmetry between the political and economic market-places which does not hold. They differ radically in essence, and use of the market analogy in politics holds only when examining the struggle for votes in an already competitive system. On the economic market a multitude of actors compete for the same clearly defined goal: profit, or at least increased market share. On the political market, a much smaller number of actors compete for a multitude of goals. There is no single goal, no single definition of national interest, because the very essence of politics is to contest such goals. But contested political goals can produce uncertainty, and, faced with too much uncertainty, economic actors have historically shown an inclination for non-competitive political systems.

A third view of the link between global technologies and political change in Eastern Europe might take a much narrower focus, concentrating on the role of new technologies in influencing the pace of change rather than the fact of change itself. It would suggest that the very speed with which information about East German refugees occupying embassies in Budapest and Prague was received influenced the future course of events in East Germany, Czechoslovakia, Bulgaria and ultimately Romania. It is true that there was a significant knock-on effect in the political events in Eastern Europe in 1989, but it is difficult to argue that near-instantaneous transmission of information in itself was a significant independent determinant of change. The fact that news in 1989 could travel in seconds compared with the days that had been the case in 1848, an earlier year of European revolution, did little more than intensify the knock-on effect of consecutive revolutions. The interval between each revolution in 1989 was not so short as to have required instantaneous global communication.

The approach to be adopted in this chapter takes elements of the first two theories presented above, but endeavours to be more specific about agency and the mechanism by which technology can act as an independent factor influencing politics. In order to achieve this, it examines first the ways in which technological advance can be said to have an independent effect at all, before considering how this effect can take place in the arena of politics. Having set the scene in this way, and discussed what is to be understood by phrases such as 'global politics', it turns to the question in hand: the impact of global politics on political change in Eastern Europe. In Eastern Europe there certainly was a technological imperative behind moves towards market reform. This was most explicitly the case in Hungary, but even the GDR was contemplating reforms to stimulate the small-business sector before the collapse of the regime. But market reforms did not require multiparty politics, or rather the former only required the latter in the sense that a fully functioning market reform required the total overthrow of the old regime, and this was only conceivable in the context of a demand for political pluralism. The degree to which political democracy will remain once the economies have been reformed depends on the strnegth of democratic institutions and the nature of the political culture rather than on a market induced imperative for them. Although this chapter focuses on global technologies and their role in the fall of the old regimes, it should be noted that global information technology at least will have an important role to play in the new politics of Eastern Europe. Despite the rhetoric of 'getting back to Europe' shared by many of the reformers in Eastern Europe, political traditions in these countries are largely undemocratic. A key factor in the new politics will be a struggle between non-democratic political traditions and the new European values – and the new European values will be disseminated by Europe's global technologies.

GLOBAL TECHNOLOGY AND POLITICS

The Origins of Technological Change

There is considerable unanimity about the origins of technological change. Writers from backgrounds as diverse as Raymond Williams (Marxist literary theorist and student of television) and Rothwell and Zegveld (students of science and technology policy) reject single-factor explanations and point rather to the importance of two factors: the interdependence of a variety of influences over the lifetime of a given technology, and the paramount importance of prospects for commercialization in its conversion from idea to reality. In the terms of the different intellectual milieux in which they operate, Williams (1974) rejects the 'straw men' argument between economic determinism and technological determinism; and Rothwell and Zegveld (1985) reject as simplistic the technology-push and needs-pull theories of technological change.

Williams (1974) is concerned with placing technology inside society and considering it in the context of human intention. He thus rejects both economic and technological determinism, together with what he terms 'symptomatic technology' theories where technologies exist in a separate sphere, not creating new societies but waiting to be taken up by society if and when they become appropriate. Technological forms must be seen as being 'looked for and developed with certain purposes and practices already in mind' (p. 14). Although these purposes and practices originate in a technical context, they are developed by economic and social imperatives. Radio, for example, was developed originally as an improved form of telegraphy between 1885 and 1911. Only after the First World War, in the context of the mass production of consumer durables such as cars and electrical appliances, did it transform itself into a form of entertainment which required the mass production of radio receivers and their placement in every home in the Western world.

Rothwell and Zegveld (1985) place similar emphasis on the importance of commercialization to the process of innovation. For them, an invention is the 'creation of an idea and its reduction to practice', a rough laboratory test suitable for patenting, not even a pre-production prototype (p. 47). Industrial innovation, on the other hand, is a much larger process involving 'the commercialization of technological change'. Crude technology-push theories, which postulate a unilinear process of discoveries of basic science leading through applied science and engineering to manufacturing and finally marketing, are rejected, as are the equally unilinear needs-pull theories which progress from market need through development and manufacturing to sales. After an extensive review of the available literature, Rothwell and Zegveld conclude that technological innovation is a dynamic, iterative process and point to the importance of the 'confluence of technological capabilities and market needs within the framework of the innovating firm' (p. 50).

Whether the writers' primary concern is to reincorporate intentional activity into the Marxist dialectic, as is the case with Raymond Williams, or to convince policy makers that science policy is an altogether more complex process than simply directing funds towards research and development, as is the case with Rothwell and Zegveld, there is considerable unanimity about the context in which new technologies develop. Inventions are only transformed through industrial innovation to become a new technology when societies perceive an expressed need for them. They are by definition goal-driven.

The Intended Consequences of Technological Change

Since technologies are goal-driven, they necessarily have intended consequences. In modern market societies, the overriding goals are either a profitable market, the commercialization of technological change that Rothwell and Zegveld emphasize, or military priorities considered necessary to defend the free-market system. The importance and interaction of military imperatives and possibilities for commercial exploitation can be illustrated in the history of the computing industry. Initial interest in computing began in the Second World War and the early Cold War period, and was entirely military in nature. Computers were introduced to help with the development of radar, cryptography and ballistics (Flamm 1987, pp. 29–79). In the late 1940s and very early 1950s even IBM saw no commercial market for computers (p. 63). From the mid 1950s IBM recognized the commercial potential of computers and responded aggressively to the commercial possibilities, switching its product line increasingly to the requirements of the commercial rather than the scientific and military market. But the importance of government support for military objectives did not disappear. All of the principal areas of computer hardware innovation from the mid 1950s through the 1960s benefited from such support, although the first microprocessor, designed by Intel in 1971, had no detectable roots in government funded research projects, and software development generally was developed much more closely with commercial markets (pp. 8–28). Computers were invented as part of the defence of the Western world from first fascism and then perceived communist aggression. They were developed in order to extend this defensive posture and further the commercial interests of IBM and its competitors.

Technologies, then, are goal-driven; and, in modern market societies, this goal is inevitably the pursuit of directly commercial goals such as increased profit or increased market share, or such military goals as political leaders consider necessary to defend the free-market system. In this sense, technologies can never be neutral, and will always be imperialist. IBM sells computers because it makes money selling them. Commercial companies buy them because they are seen as a way of increasing profits or market share by cutting costs or, less often, improving the level of service. Public sector institutions buy them in order to offer better value for money for their budget controllers. Technologies are introduced with a goal in mind, and that goal is determined by the market context. If they also have the effect of deskilling labour or reducing wages it is because this is what the market demands. Technologies cannot escape the context in which they were developed or applied.

Similarly, there is a sense in which technologies will always be imperialist when technological leaders are asked to transfer their technology to less developed parts of the world. The seller or licenser of technologies will do so in pursuit of its commercial goals. These cannot be identical to those of technology purchasers since the latter are in a position to become potential competitors. The company selling or leasing technology will inevitably do so on its own terms. All the purchaser can hope to do is to improve rapidly on the bought-in know-how and steal a march on the developer of the technology. This is essentially what Japan and to some extent West Germany have done. Both countries are net importers of technology (Rothwell and Zegveld 1985, p. 12). But it is a less easy proposition for Second and Third World nations which lack the necessary competitive industrial base and technological infrastructure to further develop imported technologies.

The Unintended Consequences of Technological Change

Although technologies are goal-driven, they have two sorts of effect that are independent of their goal-driven origins. First, they can be further developed in ways that are unrelated to their original purpose. This is especially the case the closer a technology comes to constituting a new techno-economic paradigm (see below) and develops a mass consumer market. Second, technological developments transform the world in which they operate and, in doing so, amend all economic, social and political agendas. All subsequent economic, social and political development takes each stage of technological advance as given.

In a paper arguing what he sees as the case for technological determinism, Freeman isolates four categories of innovation: incremental innovation; radical innovation; changes of technology system; and changes in techno-economic paradigms or technological revolutions (1987, pp. 12–14). The last of these is most significant for Freeman's interpretation of technological determinism, since the consequences of developments of this kind, such as the computer, are so all-pervasive that they affect the structure and the conditions of production and distribution for almost every branch of the economy. When a technology pervades all areas of economic and social life in this way, its consequences need bear little relation to the goals that stimulated its initial development. This is especially the case when the technology develops to the stage of permitting large-scale manufacture of consumer products. Computers were developed first to make possible complex calculations for the military, and second to allow large companies to automate clerical procedures and reduce costs. But with the development of personal computers, which cost no more than a month or two's salary, they can be used by a variety of organizations for purposes as diverse as the tracking by trade union research bodies of company donations to the UK Conservative Party, graphic design, and the writing of music by means of computer controlled synthesizers.

Technology and Politics

There are therefore altogether three areas that should be considered in order to address the political consequences of technological change. These are the political dimensions of: (1) the intended, goal-driven consequences of technological development; (2) the unintended, goal-neutral consequences of technological applications; and (3) amendments to the political agenda that technological developments permit. Most technologies have rather few directly political consequences, if this is understood to mean altering the shape of politics rather than becoming another subject of political regulation. The internal combustion engine, for example, has not altered the shape of politics radically, although it is the subject of political regulation.

Clearer political issues relating to the personal freedoms are raised by the issue of the use of centralized computer data bases. The facility to store digitally vast quantities of information and retrieve it virtually instantaneously has qualitatively changed the nature of all filing systems. Information can be used much more actively; it no longer resides relatively passively in the file. Two dangers flow from such mechanization of information storage. First, some information is inevitably wrong. This did not matter so much when stores were used passively, but with the possibility of their more active use new issues of civil liberties arise. Although in computer terms this is just another manifestation of garbage in, garbage out (GIGO), if the garbage concerns credit references or political affiliations it is of considerable social significance. Second, the increasing mechanization of information storage can result in the centralization of control. Even if data are not actually stored centrally (that is, distributed systems are in use), access to data is controlled centrally. Any host system will always restrict the access of outsiders by passwords or encryption, and the only way around such central control is by illegal hacking. Because computer held information is necessarily centrally controlled, and because mainframe computers are expensive, it will inevitably be the power brokers in any society who retain legal access to them. These civil liberty issues are clearly political consequences of technological developments in computing. Whether they are interpreted as intended or unintended consequences of the technology is likely to depend on how benign commentators consider the state to be.

The example of the internal combustion engine, on the other hand, illustrates how technological developments which lead to the production of mass consumer goods can transform the political agenda. On the one hand, it has increased the significance of ministers of transport in political discussion; on the other, it has profoundly influenced the nature of transport policy debates. However much the proponents of rational, ecologically sound transport policies might want to control the private motor car, it cannot be wished away. Limitations on car usage would inevitably have profound political consequences for the political party that introduced them.

Global Technology and Politics

The concept of global technology is a rather imprecise one. For the purposes of this chapter, a global technology will be seen to be one of two things: a technology which, by virtue of its intrinsic properties, facilitates and accelerates the global exchange of people, material and ideas; or a technology which encourages the global dispersal of the production process and of phases within the production process. As technological developments take on global dimensions, their political consequences have wider implications and extend to the classical unit of political analysis since the nineteenth century: the nation-state.

The centralization of information that has accompanied developments in information technology, for example, has international ramifications. The new information technologies are inevitably spread unevenly around the globe, and this can result in a potential loss of sovereignty or at least increased dependency. Because of the ever decreasing cost of communications, it is becoming cheaper even for Third World companies to send their design problems, their research and their routine data processing abroad where data processing can be done more economically. Data centres in the developed world contain expertise not available locally, and data bases in the developed world contain information not obtainable in the Third World. When, to use an example cited by Lenk (1982, p. 297), this is merely a question of a French journalist being able to obtain only an American account of French history by accessing the *New York Times* news data bank, then the threat is to cultural identity rather than to national sovereignty. But if a Third World query to the First World data bank were of economic or scientific significance, then issues of sovereignty might arise. Transnational companies tend to make little systematic effort to encourage local research and development in the Third World (Rada, 1982, p. 225). If these same companies control the data banks, Third World countries could be denied access to such information altogether.

GLOBAL TECHNOLOGIES AND POLITICAL CHANGE IN EASTERN EUROPE

The preceding discussion suggests that consideration of the consequences for the politics of Eastern Europe of the growth of global technologies requires the following: an examination of the ways in which technologies which facilitate the global exchange of people, materials and ideas, and the global dispersal of processes and phases within the production process, have had political consequences in terms of their intended and unintended effects and their influence on the political agenda in Eastern Europe. The remainder of the chapter will argue that, although there is no way of quantifying them, it is likely that both intended and unintended consequences of global technologies have had the effect of reinforcing the crisis of legitimation that was developing in Eastern Europe, because of economic stagnation, in the 1980s. They also structured the political agenda such that a return to the economics and politics of the 1950s was impossible.

The Intended Political Consequences for Eastern Europe of the Growth of Global Technologies

The clearest example of a global technology with direct political intent in relation to Eastern Europe is broadcasting. This includes both the self-consciously political radio broadcasting which has been directed at Eastern Europe since the Cold War, and television, which can be received in much of Eastern Europe but is not transmitted with direct political intent. Both overtly political radio broadcasting and non-political television broadcasting have been widely received throughout Eastern Europe. They have had no discernible direct political effect, but have permitted contrasting interpretations of economic and social reality to be presented.

Ever since the end of the Second World War the Western governments have been broadcasting directly to the Eastern bloc. Such broadcasts have, of course, been regularly jammed by Eastern European governments, a process which in the Soviet Union alone is estimated to cost $150 million a year, involve 3,000 transmitters and employ 15,000 people. Broadcasts to the Soviet Union were jammed between 1948 and 1963, between 1969 and 1973, and from 1980 onwards. Broadcasts to Hungary, as well as Albania, Czechoslovakia and Romania, are not jammed.

While those involved in broadcasting to Eastern Europe would deny that they produce propaganda, they readily accept a political motivation to their work; Evolution not revolution seems to be the hope. Nationalism and religion are stressed because these are areas where Eastern European governments are politically weak. Germany's Deutsche Welle sees its role as the rectification of historical truth distorted by the Soviet media. Editorials from the Voice of America 'crisply but firmly' reflect the positions of the US government. On the other hand, the sell has become softer since the 1960s, with a greater degree of professionalism. The BBC's broadcasts have traditionally been non-political. Its brief has been to broadcast 'in the national interest', but it considers veracity and credibility to be in the national interest. The aim is to demonstrate democracy (warts and all) rather than preach its advantages. However, this does not relieve even the BBC of the charge of bias. As media watchers such as the Glasgow Media Group have demonstrated, bias can be built into even the most 'objective' broadcasts.

It is hard to quantify the degree of success this form of direct cultural attack has had. The broadcasters themselves are convinced of its significant contribution. Both Solidarity leaders and the Polish government have stated that the Solidarity underground would not exist but for Radio Free Europe. But these may be merely politically inspired statements, the one side aiming to get further Western support, the other blaming an internal crisis on outside intervention. A more realistic view of the consequence of radio broadcasting to Eastern Europe is that it provides Eastern European citizens who were already sceptical with an alternative interpretation of such events as the Soviet shooting down of the Korean Airlines airliner. It is less able to convince people of ideas for which a germ is not already present. Audience research has shown, for example, that only one in seven of the adult urban Soviet population is receptive to basic Western ideals of civil liberties, and that 'Western radio is less able to influence the Soviet population than the domestic media when the direct interests of the average Soviet citizen are made to appear threatened' (Parta 1986, p. 242).

Work by both Western and East European researchers has revealed an audience for Western radio broadcasts already predisposed to questioning the views of the official media, whether it was the natural questioning of youth, personal familiarity with the West and its news, or both. The Voice of America's researchers give the following figures for the percentage of the adult population who listen to Voice of America: 12 per cent in the Soviet Union, 40 per cent in Poland, 30 per cent in Czechoslovakia, and 20 per cent in Bulgaria, Romania and Hungary. Other researchers give slightly higher figures: 14–18 per cent of the Soviet population listening to Voice of America, 8–12 per cent listening to Radio Liberty and 7–10 per cent listening to the BBC. Voice of America researchers also found that Hungarian Voice of America listeners tended to be younger than the audience of the BBC or Radio Free Europe, although the general profile of the Western broadcasts listener is an educated urban male aged 30–49. Radio Free Europe claimed the following percentages of the Eastern European population as an audience: Czechoslovakia 37 per cent, Poland 68 per cent, Hungary 58 per cent, Romania 64 per cent and Bulgaria 33 per cent. Again, women and younger people under 25 are less highly represented, although so too are university educated people (McIntosh 1986, p. 245). These figures are clearly open to some suspicion, since they are produced by the broadcasters themselves, but are not incredible since they referred to doing no more than occasionally turning the dial and tuning in to, say, a news broadcast. Hungarian researchers, not surprisingly, found a much smaller audience for Radio Free Europe in 1965, but it was distributed in an interesting way: 18 per cent of Budapest workers, 23 per cent of Budapest doctors, but 48 per cent of the Budapest population with a technical education, admitted listening to Radio Free Europe. Developments in television technology have made domestic foreign programmes easily receivable in much of Eastern Europe. Almost all of the German Democratic Republic, with the exception of the region around Dresden and north-east Mecklenburg, was able to receive West German television, and could watch it openly after Honecker lifted the proscription on listening to Western radio and television in 1973. A survey of 205 emigrants from the GDR found that only 10 per cent were regular watchers of GDR television, compared with 82 per cent, of those able to receive it, who watched West German television almost every day. A survey of TV viewers in Hungary in 1972 found that 28 per cent of the adult population (42 per cent of TV owners) had seen foreign TV. Of these, 600,000 had watched Austrian TV, 735,000 Slovakian TV, 435,000 Romanian TV and 563,000 Yugoslavian TV. TV broadcasts have never been jammed because, unlike radio, they have not been directly political. The only barrier between Eastern and Western TV is the colour system, all Eastern nations having chosen the French SECAM system in preference to PAL. Modern Hungarian TV sets however, like modern sets in Western Europe, have a built-in adaptor and receive both PAL and SECAM systems; hence they receive Soviet, Hungarian and Austrian colour broadcasts equally well. Satellite stations, such as Super Channel, Rupert Murdoch's Sky Channel and the French TV5, could also be received by the 1980s, and by the mid 1980s Hungary operated 13 cable television stations broadcasting to an estimated 110,000 households.

There was no directly political content to these broadcasts as far as Eastern European viewers were concerned, although again many would see a political dimension to their domestic programming strategy. Nevertheless, the existence of an alternative view, any alternative view, is of political significance in Eastern European societies that do not encourage the formation of alternative views. When normal television provides the Hungarian viewer with American soap operas, Western European thrillers, Austrian news bulletins and teletext, and satellite television provides such goodies as 'Jim'll Fix It', 'Dr Who' and 'The Muppets' together with international, European and business news, then it is difficult to keep the population in ignorance of what is happening in the outside world. As with the less propagandistic radio broadcasts, however, it must be noted that the picture that is being received is still incomplete. Western TV news and teletext reflects the selection criteria of what is considered newsworthy by the Western establishment, while soap operas and detective serials scarcely present a fully rounded picture of Western life.

Although it is correct to view the spread of radio and television ownership as an intended consequence of technological change, it had one (perhaps uniquely totalitarian) unintended consequence. Television, and to a lesser extent radio, was perhaps the most important consumer technology of the 1960s and 1970s. The number of TV and radio licence holders in Hungary, for example, increased as follows:

TV		Radio	
1958	16,038	1950	619,505
1960	103,658	1955	1,421,620
1965	831,182	1960	2,223,741
1970	1,768,561	1965	2,484,248
1975	2,390,000	1970	2,530,262

1980	2,766,000	1975	2,537,000
1985	2,930,000	1979	2,608,000

But if the intended consequence of developing radio and television as a consumer good was a mixture of satisfying a demand that had been stimulated by comparison with the West and pursuing their educational and propaganda possibilities, it had one unintended consequence. Audiences could listen or watch whatever channel they wanted; gone were the days of piped radio, centrally received and transmitted via a network of loudspeakers, or communal radio listening in the fields.

Clearly, these broadcasts had little direct effect on the events of 1989. It is probable that news coverage of the occupations by East Germans of West German embassies in Budapest and Prague encouraged more to try their luck, and the East German events also had an impact on revolution in Czechoslovakia. But the broadcasts have beamed towards Eastern Europe for years. They could not possibly have been the spark which set the 1989 revolutions in motion; and they manifestly failed in China where, despite political broadcasts, the revolution was suppressed. Yet it seems plausible that, in the long term, the breakdown of the cultural and political monopoly that these broadcasts represented – a monopoly which the regimes had progressively given up defending in the 1970s and 1980 – reinforced doubts about the legitimacy and success of the regime that were being generated by domestic economic and social failure.

The Unintended Political Consequences for Eastern Europe of the Growth of Global Technologies

When one considers the unintended consequences of global technologies, the focus shifts from broadcasting to communications technologies. Partly as a component of the general globalization of production discussed elsewhere in this volume, but more particularly as a consequence of an economic imperative to catch up technologically with the West, Eastern European governments increasingly developed their contacts with Western European companies. Somewhat belatedly, Eastern European governments acknowledged that this required, in addition to better knowledge of Western markets and practices, better communications. This has had certain political consequences, of significant though not radical benefit to the political opposition; but it has further extended the breakdown of cultural monopoly. The very people who were sent abroad on business were the people who were, as has been noted, the most prone to listen to foreign radio broadcasts.

By the 1960s and 1970s it was clear that the Soviet Union and Eastern Europe were technologically many years behind the West. According to a variety of sources, Soviet agriculture in 1962 was 32 years behind the United States; Soviet computers in 1972 were 10–16 years behind the US; the Soviet chemical industry in 1973 was on a par with the West for basic chemicals, but was dependent on the West for advanced chemicals; and by the 1980s the Soviet Union was some years behind the US in transport and communications, and lagged behind the US in numerically controlled machine tools because of the lack of suitable computers (Brada 1985, pp. 10–12). In order to get over this technology lag, in 1975–6 the Soviet Union had 11 industrial cooperation agreements with Western Europe and 214 with the US. The rest of

Eastern Europe had 187 such agreements with Western Europe and 222 with the United States (p. 21).

Clearly improved telecommunications were of fundamental importance for economies which were decentralizing and integrating themselves to an increasing extent with the outside world. Both subscriber trunk dialling and international direct dialling became necessary if contact was to be maintained with suppliers and customers. In Hungary, this trend was even more pronounced. Economic decentralization associated with its New Economic Mechanism, and the right later granted to form subsidiary enterprises, increased the demand in enterprises for improved telecommunications, as did the pattern of subcontracting to the industrial affiliates of cooperative farms. The USSR, Hungary, Romania, Poland and Cuba had a number of banking outlets in the West which dealt in Eurocurrency and required good international telecommunications, as did those commercial enterprises, such as Hungary's Vidoeton, which had foreign subsidiaries in both West Germany and the UK. But the need for better communications with customers was even more pressing. One commentator noted: 'It is often unbelievable but true that we have failed to make deal after deal because we could not telephone or could not get the necessary information in time' (Figyelo, no. 24, 12 June 1986, p. 7).

But this demand was met only slowly and belatedly. Even at the end of the 1980s the Hungarian telephone system remained antiquated by any standards. In 1986 the Hungarian network extended to only 13.9 per cent of the population, compared with 20 per cent in Bulgaria, 22 per cent in Czechoslovakia, 45 per cent in Austria and 85 per cent in Sweden. Waiting lists for private phones in Eastern Europe, especially outside the capitals, were unbelievably long; most trunk calls had to be put through by the operator, for whose services there was a long wait. More critically, the lines were not sufficiently reliable to form the basis of a computer network. Plans to computerize the services of the newly decentralized insurance sector in Hungary in the mid 1980s required the physical despatch of floppy disks from 200 local offices to Budapest, partly because the telephone system would not handle a fully networked system, and partly because the sector did not have a computer big enough to handle such a network. The only online element to the system was a link between the Budapest office and the software services company's IBM mainframe computer. Similarly the computer system introduced to handle the new personal income and value added tax systems – using computers paid for by World Bank loans – was planned to provide information to local offices on microfiche only, because the telephone system did not support an online network. Hungary's only link with the outside world of satellite computer communications was via Radio Austria's computer and a single telephone link to Budapest. Hungary had no domestic packet-switching network, but facsimile transmission links with West Germany started in 1986 (30 additional terminals were purchased from Canon of Japan as part of the World Bank loan). A public videotext service was planned for 1987, with the Ministry of Industry, the Meteorological Institute, the Trade Union Holiday Bureau and other information institutes taking part. The system, IPCOM, which was developed by the Ministry of Industry and the Electrical Energy Research Institute, began operations in February 1988; 150 terminals nationally were expected by the end of the year. Non-interactive teletext began in 1984 with a system based initially on 200 pages of information, and a national system for telephone paging bleepers was planned for 1986.

In the mid 1980s debates took place in Hungary as to how best to finance much needed investment. Telephone bonds were introduced, the holders of which gained accelerated access to telephone equipment. In the summer of 1987 the government received a World Bank loan of $70 million specifically to improve the telephone service. In addition, the seventh five-year plan (1986–90) projected double the expenditure of the previous plan on telecommunications in an attempt to catch up the 10–15 years that Hungary felt it was behind the West in this field.

Despite this communications technology lag over the last decade or so, the number of places which can be contacted by direct dialling has increased; it is of significance for the breakdown of cultural autarchy that it is now possible to call the West direct from public call boxes in provincial towns as well as Budapest. Nor is it possible in the era of international direct dialling for dissidents to disappear. They can inform foreign journalists of harassment, and foreign journalists can interview offending bureaucrats by phone.

If the political opposition benefited to some extent from the unintended consequences of developments in international communications technology, the same cannot be said for the personal computer. In Western Europe personal computers were widely used for non-intended purposes and by politically oppositional groups. In Eastern Europe in the socialist era, personal computers did not become a consumer good, and even in Hungary, where a dynamic personal-computer-based small-scale sector did develop, personal computers did not become a significant tool of the political opposition.

The unofficial opposition in Hungary produced its journals and books using conventional publishing technology, exploiting the technological neutrality of printers working in the second economy. Word processors were a luxury for Hungarian researchers, academics and dissidents alike. Data base technology had not been harnessed to help monitor political and economic events. Video cameras were available in Hungary in the final years of the socialist system, on the other hand, as were some 60,000 video recorders in mid 1985 (produced in Hungary under licence from Matsushita of Japan). It takes only a little imagination to convert the holiday video into a privately produced documentary. Groups on the left in the United Kingdom have for many years produced videos to promote various causes and to challenge the media monopoly. In Hungary, samizdat video was in its infancy when the changed nature of politics made it redundant.

Global Technologies and the Political Agenda in Eastern Europe

This final section will argue that the intended and unintended consequences of technological development modified the political agenda in Eastern Europe in two ways. First, they fed into and reinforced the crisis of legitimation that was developing throughout the region in the 1980s. Second, they helped close off the option of a return to the Stalinist past.

In retrospect it is clear that the depth of the legitimation crisis throughout Eastern Europe was profound. The ease with which the regimes, except that in Romania, fell; the exceptionally poor showing of the communist parties under whatever new names (and excepting Romania and Bulgaria) in the first free elections; the huge numbers of East Germans who were prepared to abandon all for a new life in the Federal Republic; all are indicators of regimes that had lost legitimacy. This loss of legitimacy is well documented in Hungary, and the experience of Hungary is pivotal to the revolutions of 1989. It was Hungary's decision in the midst of its peaceful revolution to let East

Germans leave for West Germany via Austria that triggered the events in East Germany which led to the fall of the Berlin Wall; and with the fall of the Wall a change of regime in Czechoslovakia was only a matter of time.

The period from 1985 onwards in Hungary witnessed several signs that the legitimacy of the regime was coming increasingly into question. From the mid 1970s, and more clearly from the early 1980s, the twin characteristics of Hungary's economic situation were stagnation in the socialist sector, supplemented by an increasingly encouraged and institutionalized dualism to counter the former's worst effects. The second economy, present but not acknowledged throughout Eastern Europe, had been openly encouraged in Hungary via the institutions of the economic work partnerships and enterprise economic work partnerships, by which workers supplemented their incomes on a private subcontracting basis, making use of enterprise machinery and resources. The consequences of this were twofold: a decline in social morale, and the gradual birth of extensive if not mass opposition. After more than a decade of the government obliging Hungarians to lead a double life, forcing them to take on a second job simply to survive, and tacitly encouraging them to adopt one set of values when working for themselves in the partnership and another, much more instrumentalist, set when working for the state, it is not surprising that a decline in both altruism and a sense of social solidarity became apparent.

Since the late 1970s, Hankiss (1989) has produced a series of articles documenting, in an ever more precise fashion, the social pathology of Hungary's failure to create new community values. Having successfully destroyed all institutions of the old world's civil society, Hungary's socialism failed to create new ones, a telling failure in a society dominated by shortage and where petty corruption became inevitable. Hankiss's vast output, which moves from noting an imbalance between economic growth and the value system to discovering a second society to mirror the second economy, is based on rather little empirical evidence. Its significance is twofold, however. On the one hand, he provides some concrete evidence for a decline in social morale over the socialist period. This is reflected in the results of an international survey on social values to which he refers on a number of occasions. This survey shows, for example, that:

> To the question ... 'Is there anything you could sacrifice yourself for, outside your family?' 50 to 60 per cent of the Englishmen, Frenchmen, Germans, Spaniards and Italians answered: 'No, I would not sacrifice myself for anything outside my family.' In Hungary the corresponding figure is 85 per cent. To the question 'Would you raise your children to have respect for other people?' the European average of 'Yes' answers was between 40 and 60 per cent, while the Hungarian figure was 31 per cent. (pp. 56–8)

The second significance of Hankiss's work is simply the popularity it achieved. His models of first and second society work in skeletal, oversimplistic dichotomies: first society is homogeneous, diffuse and atomized, second society is differentiated and integrated; first society is organized vertically, second society is organized horizontally; first society is dominated by politics, second society by social and economic concerns; first society is strongly ideological, second society is non-ideological or allows many ideologies (p. 119). His statement that 'the evolution of the second society was the most significant movement of the 1960s and 1970s in Hungary' (p. 142) hardly takes our understanding of the period beyond the standard account of Kadarism, namely that it was characterized by a social compact between economic opportunity and political obedience, and by the slogan 'he who is not against us is with us.' The popularity of Hankiss's work has to be explained rather by the idea of second society itself, by the fact that in their daily lives people were experiencing the schizophrenia of the institutionalized dualism of first and second economies. The idea of second society struck a chord with everyday social experience.

Public opinion poll findings over the period also reveal a dramatic decline in the population's faith in the government's ability to solve the economy's problems and put socialist goals into practice. An analysis of the responses to public opinion surveys carried out by the Hungarian Public Opinion Research Institute over the ten years or so preceding 1988 found significant changes in attitude in 1982 and again in 1986. In 1982, unspecified dissatisfaction became focused on the economy and day-to-day economic problems. In 1986, a more dramatic shift of opinion took place and the general public seemed to lose faith in the leadership's ability altogether, expressing the view not only that they were worse off than before, but that the economy in general was in decline. The Institute constructed two indices, one reflecting evaluations of the national economic situation, and the other evaluations of individuals' personal economic situation, both indices ranging from +100 to −100. In 1982, the personal index fell from −38.0 to −63.0, and the national index from +26.25 to +3.0. Both then recovered marginally until 1986, when a very marked decline took place. The personal index fell from −57.5 at the beginning of 1986 to −74.66 at the end of 1987. The fall in the national index was even more marked, from +17.0 in early 1986 to −39.75 at the end of 1987 (*Figyelo*, no. 46, 17 November 1988, pp. 1–4).

This decline in the population's faith in the ability of the government to solve the economic crisis was mirrored by a general decline in the view that the government was meeting what might be considered socialist objectives. Table 7.1 shows responses to the question 'In what ways is Hungary better than the West?', and reveals a catastrophic

Table 7.1 What is better in Hungary when compared with the West? (per cent)

	1981	1986	1988	1988 Party	1988 Intellectuals
Possibility of bringing children up satisfactorily	98	87	42	46	27
Right to work	96	93	80	88	80
Level of health supply	90	66	47	45	23
Level of social morality	88	81	50	59	38
Balanced family life	86	73	36	40	24
Material welfare	46	29	10	9	1
Equal opportunities	78	69	38	49	29
Freedom to express views	74	67	43	50	29
Money keeps its value	66	41	6	6	2
Chances of getting flat	63	39	16	19	5
Amount of free time	58	46	27	26	17

Source: Nagy (1989, p. 55)

decline in belief in the regime's ability to provide the basic welfare measures that had previously constituted the superiority of Eastern European countries for commentators from East and West alike. The belief that Hungary's education system was better at providing a satisfactory education for its children fell from 98 per cent in 1981 to 87 per cent in 1986, and then in 1988 plummeted to 46 per cent on a national basis and only 27 per cent amongst intellectuals. The belief in Hungary's superiority in providing material well-being fell equally dramatically, from 46 to 29 to 10 per cent, with only 1 per cent of intellectuals by 1988 believing that material well-being was better in Hungary than in the West.

This loss of faith in the regime's ability to guarantee basic socialist values was complemented, in 1988, by a high degree of cynicism (or realism) concerning the motives of the party. As table 7.2 indicates, even party members believed that the party represented the interests of its own upper leadership, *apparatchiks* or enterprise management before that of the workers.

Nevertheless, there remained a high national commitment to welfare principles, reflected partly in the fact that all Hungary's new political parties consider the state should have a role in guaranteeing minimum standards in health care, even if all also call for the development of private, insurance-based schemes. These high popular welfare expectations can be seen in the results of an international survey on attitudes to inequality and welfare. Public support for welfare was highest in Hungary in a survey which covered Italy, West Germany, Britain and the Netherlands in Europe, together with Australia and the USA. Some 78 per cent of Hungarians strongly agreed that the state should provide everyone with a guaranteed basic income, compared with 67 per cent in Italy, 51 per cent in West Germany and 20 per cent in the USA (Smith 1989, pp. 61–2).

The survey evidence appears to suggest that Hungarians retained a commitment to socialist values of public welfare, but that over the 1980s there was a growing belief that Hungary's socialist economy was failing to produce the wealth necessary to support it. Into these growing doubts about the viability of the socialist system were fed the

Table 7.2 Whose interests does the party represent? (ranking of answers)

	Population as a whole	Party members	Intellectuals
Top party leadership	1	1	1
Workers in party apparatus	2	2	2
Enterprise managers	3	3	3
Party members	4	5	4
Intellectuals	5	6	7
Workers	6	4	5
The young	7	8	8
Peasants	8	7	6
The old	9	10/11	11
Small entrepreneurs	10/11	10/11	9
Non-party members	10/11	9	10

Source: Nagy (1989, p. 56)

alternative world views presented by foreign radio and television and by increased personal communications with the West. There is a tenuous causal chain between the increased communication with the West, made possible and to an extent even stimulated by intended and unintended consequences of the application of global technologies, and moves towards political reform. As was noted earlier, it was those with technical educational qualifications who listened most to foreign radio broadcasts to Hungary. This was also the group most likely to have business or academic contacts with the West, and it was the group least satisfied with the regime's legitimacy by the late 1980s. And it was the group most active in the reform movement, especially in the early months in Hungary as elsewhere in Eastern Europe. The early activists in the Hungarian Democratic Forum consisted of writers, teachers and the provincial intelligentsia; those in the Alliance of Free Democrats were Budapest-based economists, sociologists and lawyers.

Global technological developments have also amended the political agenda; they have restricted the political choices a Hungarian government has available. The political openness which allowed in foreign television and global communications technology was a necessary concomitant of Hungary's pursual of a strategy of economic change in Eastern Europe. But once these concessions had been made, a reversal to cultural and economic autarchy was impossible. After all, an important contributing factor to the revolution in Hungary in 1956 was the combination of a relaxation of political control in 1953 and 1954 and a tightening in 1955 and 1956. This created a delegitimation amongst the elite and a crisis of rising expectations which were then frustrated. And in Hungary 1956, the reimposition of control was scarcely more than a year after the initial relaxation. In Eastern Europe in the 1980s, for all the essential Stalinism of the regimes, all countries (with the exception of Romania) had been undergoing a process of some degree of liberalization in terms of the constraints on everyday life, albeit rather slight in Czechoslovakia and the GDR, for one and a half decades.

More pragmatically, international telecommunication links and the availability of satellite television antennas could not easily have been severed by direct political decision without there being severe political repercussions. But much more significantly, such a strategy would have incurred significant economic costs. An already acute economic situation would have been further worsened if telecommunication links had been withdrawn. As has been stressed in earlier sections, modern economic relations require modern telecommunication systems; and modern telecommunication systems do not differentiate between politically acceptable business and politically suspect private callers.

CONCLUSIONS

This chapter has examined the significance of global technologies in explaining political change in Eastern Europe. It has sought to avoid oversimplification either as to agency and mechanisms, or in terms of symmetry between economic and political market models, by working from a more or less generally accepted understanding of technology's relationship to the economic and social world and then considering how it can have political effects. Finally, it has attempted to use as much empirical evidence as can be obtained in addressing areas where, for understandable political reasons, reliable evidence is hard to find. Its conclusion is suitably modest.

There is no sense in which developments in global techniques have been the determining factor in the political revolutions of Eastern Europe. Nevertheless, an increasing amount of evidence is becoming available concerning the crisis of legitimacy of the regimes that accompanied the relative economic stagnation of the 1980s, and this crisis was certainly exacerbated by the intended and unintended consequences of global technologies, introduced in the 1970s and 1980s, which challenged the political and cultural monopoly of the parties. It is difficult to assess the significance of these factors in modifying the political agenda. The different scale and course of the 1989 revolutions in Romania and to some extent Bulgaria, when compared with those in Czechoslovakia, Poland, the GDR and Hungary, are the results of many cultural and historical factors. Nevertheless, one element must have been the rather intangible proximity to the West; and it is precisely this proximity that was created by the development of global technologies.

References

Brada, J.C. (1985) Soviet–Western trade and technology transfer: an economic overview. In B. Parrott (ed.), *Trade, Technology and Soviet–American Relations*, Bloomington: Indiana University Press.

Flamm, K. (1987) *Targetting the Computer*. Washington DC: Brookings Institution.

Freeman, C. (1987). The case for technological determinism. In R. Finnegan, G. Salaman and K. Thompson (eds), *Information Technology: Social Issues*, Sevenoaks: Hodder and Stoughton.

Hankiss, E. (1989) Kelet-európai Alternatívák. Budapest: Közgazdaságiés Jogi Könyvkiadó.

Lenk, K. (1982) Information technology and society. In G. Friedrichs and A. Schaff (eds), *Microelectronics and Society: for Better or for Worse*, Oxford: Pergamon.

McIntosh, M. (1986) Public opinion assessment and Radio Free Europe's effectiveness in Eastern Europe. In K.R.M. Short (ed.) *Western Broadcasting over the Iron Curtain*, London: Croom Helm.

Nagy, G.L. (1989) A Ketteszakadt tarsadalom. *Jelkep*, X(4).

Parta, R.E. (1986) Soviet area audience and opinion research (SAAOR) at Radio Free Europe/Radio Liberty. In K.R.M. Short (ed.), *Western Broadcasting over the Iron Curtain*, London: Croom Helm.

Rada, J.F. (1982) A third world perspective. In G. Friedrichs and A. Schaff (eds), *Microelectronics and Society: for Better or for Worse*, Oxford: Pergamon.

Rothwell, R. and Zegveld, W. (1985) *Reindustrialization and Technology*. Longman: Harlow.

Smith, T.W. (1989) In quality and welfare. In. R. Jowell et al. (eds), *British Social Attitudes: Special International Report*, Aldershot: Gower, 59–86.

Williams, R. (1974) *Television Technology and Cultural Form*. Glasgow: Fontana.

Part III

A Global Economy?

8

The International Economic Order between the Wars

RICHARD BESSEL

THE FIRST WORLD WAR AND THE INTERNATIONAL ECONOMY

During the late nineteenth century and until 1914 there existed a relatively well-functioning international economic and financial system, characterized by stable currencies based on the gold standard and with Britain at its centre. Britain, the first industrial nation and the world's chief creditor, occupied a crucial position, able both to invest substantially abroad and to absorb the imports of other industrial nations (notably Germany). Of course, the pre-1914 system was not without its strains and stresses – as evidenced during the Great Depression, which was characterized by a downturn in investment in many countries after 1873 (Glismann et al. 1981, table A.2, pp. 95–8). Nor could it have been maintained unchanged but for the unfortunate accident of the First World War; sooner or later the rapid growth of the industrial economies of the United States, Germany and Russia and the relative economic decline of Britain would have caused a restructuring of a financial system with London at its centre. But, with hindsight, it appears that the pre-1914 global system functioned comparatively smoothly and provided a framework for quite remarkable economic growth around the world, especially during the period 1895–1913 (Milward 1981, pp. 45–6).

The First World War changed all that. Almost immediately after the outbreak of war the combatant powers suspended the convertibility of their currencies into gold, that is they discontinued the gold standard system, which was too inflexible to allow for the unprecedented levels of expenditure required to fight the war. International trade links were cut; terms of trade were altered to the benefit of countries producing primary goods, the prices of which soared; state budgets grew tremendously and governments borrowed massively to finance the war effort; state controls were put into place to regulate raw materials and labour; and investment in productive capacity was throttled in the effort to devote as much human and material resources as possible to war production. Many of the world's leading industrial economies emerged from the war economically exhausted, plagued by massive debts, inflation, run-down plant and machinery and, in the case of France and Russia, by the physical destruction of a significant proportion of their economic assets.

There also were beneficiaries. For Spain, which remained neutral, the war presented considerable economic opportunities. Spanish agricultural products found a ready market at high prices; the disappearance of Welsh coal from the market led to a boom in the coalfield of Asturias; clothing mills in Catalonia were kept busy supplying the French army. As a result, Spain was able to eliminate her chronic trade deficit and repatriate the national debt (Carr 1982, pp. 497–8). Much of Latin America also profited. Latin American agricultural exporters (such as Argentina and Uruguay) received higher prices for meat and grain; Venezuela's oil reserves were first tapped during the war; the fact that European industrial exports were curtailed encouraged import substitution and thus stimulated domestic industries; and many Latin American countries generated considerable foreign trade surpluses as a result of reduced imports and buoyant demand for their exports (at high prices) (Hardach 1977, pp. 266–74). Another country which profited from the war was Japan, whose involvement as a combatant was only peripheral. Japan's engineering, shipbuilding, chemical and iron and steel industries expanded considerably; the number of Japanese factory workers grew from 1.2 million in 1914 to 2 million in 1919. Japan's young export industries benefited from the withdrawal of European competition from Asian markets, as well as from the wartime boom which occurred in the United States; and during the war Japan registered large balance of payments surpluses, leaving her in the position of a net international creditor at the war's end (pp. 258–61). Canada profited too, at least in the short term, as the war proved a stimulus to domestic industries, particularly those processing natural resources for export, and Canada benefited as a major grain exporter.

The most important beneficiary of the war was the United States, however. Unlike the other major combatants, the United States entered the conflict rather late, in 1917. While the economies of Britain, Russia, France and Germany were weakened substantially by the war, the United States emerged stronger industrially and financially. While the US remained neutral she experienced an export-led boom. The belligerents needed food, raw materials and armaments, and the United States supplied them (Hardach 1977, pp. 254–8). Soon after the outbreak of war the British government placed large contracts with the American steel industry, as subsequently did the French and Italians. When the British found their own industries unable to satisfy the army's insatiable demand for munitions, they turned to America and thus helped to build up an American armaments industry which had been tiny in 1914. American wheat flowed to France; American bacon replaced Danish bacon (the export of which almost came to a halt owing to the blockade); American farm prices rose substantially and American industrial profits soared. And, perhaps most important, the European Allies drew upon American money. From the middle of the war the British had become dependent not only on American industry to supply armaments, but also on the American government and American banks for the money needed to pay for those armaments (Burk 1982, pp. 91–2). American private investment abroad more than doubled between 1914 and 1919, while foreign investment in the US declined sharply. As a result, whereas before the war the United States was a net debtor nation to the tune of some $3,700 million, in 1919 she was a net creditor by about the same amount (Aldcroft 1987, p. 37). Thus the United States emerged from the war in a uniquely powerful position: the US was a major supplier of raw materials and of agricultural and industrial goods, had generated large export surpluses, and had been transformed into a major creditor nation (Hardach 1977, p. 257).

These developments signified a fundamental shift in the world economy. The relative position of Europe declined, and the economies of many countries hitherto on the periphery of the world economy grew remarkably. For example, Japanese manufacturing output increased by nearly four-fifths during the course of the war, and the production of steel and cement and the generation of electricity each more than doubled; South African industrial activity increased by 200 per cent (Aldcroft 1987, pp. 34–9; Allen 1962, p. 113). Some European economies were deeply damaged. Chief among these was Russia, which had possessed one of the world's fastest growing industrial economies before 1914 but which all but dropped out of the world economy after the First World War and whose industrial output in 1920 was barely one-eighth what it had been in 1913 (Aldcroft 1987, p. 34). Germany was adversely affected as well. After the post-war political upheavals, territorial losses and sharp drops in productivity, in 1919 German industrial production fell to less than two-fifths what it had been in 1913 (Holtfrerich 1986, p. 204; Wagenfuhr 1933, p. 64) and real national income (net social product) was only two-thirds of the 1913 figure (Witt 1974, p. 424; Holtfrerich 1986, p. 224).

The United States, on the other hand, emerged to occupy a disproportionately large role in the international economic system. The dominant position of the United States and its emergence as a major creditor put it, and its currency, at the centre of world financial affairs. The dollar became the world's strongest and most important currency; in fact, it became the only really stable major currency. This meant that the health and stability of the international economic and financial system, as well as of particular currencies and economies within it, was dependent upon the actions of the Americans. However, after the First World War the American government declined to take an active role in shaping the post-war order commensurate with the economic power of the country it governed. The isolationist reaction after the war led the United States to turn its back on the League of Nations and active political participation in shaping the post-war European order (the Versailles system). (The US took a somewhat more active role in the Far East.) Nevertheless, American concern to avoid becoming entangled in foreign (and particularly European) affairs did not prevent American economic policy, and the actions of American financial institutions, from having a major impact upon the economic and political health of the rest of the world.

THE POST-WAR DEPRESSION

The 1914–18 war unleashed world-wide inflation. This continued into the immediate post-war period and was fuelled further by the lifting of wartime economic controls and by the post-war boom of 1919–20. The boom came to an abrupt halt in late 1920 and 1921; prices and output in most major industrial countries fell, and unemployment rose steeply. (In both the UK and the US industrial unemployment trebled between 1920 and 1921, and in mid 1921 – at the trough of the slump – 22 per cent of all insured persons in Britain were registered as unemployed.) Between 1920 and 1921 industrial production slumped by 20 per cent in the US, 18.6 per cent in Britain and 11 per cent in France (Holtfrerich 1986, p. 209). In some countries, such as Sweden and the United Kingdom, the declines in production and income during the depression at the beginning of the 1920s were greater than the declines during the depression which started at the end of the decade (Aldcroft 1987, p. 68). In others – Germany, Austria, Poland, all countries which suffered severe inflation during the 1920s – industrial production went up. The depression affected not only the industrialized world; it also had severe repercussions for raw materials exporters. Commodity prices plunged, leaving countries such as South Africa that were dependent upon the export of primary products in a bad way as demand for their exports fell and the prices they received for what they still could sell plummeted.

To some extent, the contraction of 1920–1 reflected the business cycle, and probably was an inevitable reaction to the boom which had followed the war. The world's economies had overheated, and the high government spending during and immediately after the war could not continue indefinitely. The post-war boom had rested in part upon inflationary monetary policies and speculative investment, which had to come to an end sooner (as in the US and the UK) or later (as in Germany). However, the financial policies of the British and, particularly, the Americans also contributed to the downturn. In the United Kingdom the authorities first fuelled the boom with easy credit and then restricted economic activity with dear money by raising interest rates in 1920, at just the time when the boom was coming to an end anyway. In the United States the downturn reduced demand for other countries' exports, and American fiscal policy reduced the outflow of financial assistance to Europe. Indeed, Milton Friedman and Anna Jacobson Schwartz see inappropriate American monetary policies as the major reason for the post-war slump; they claim that the American Federal Reserve failed to raise interest rates in order to reduce inflationary pressure during 1919 and then raised rates too much in 1920 when the economy was already going into reverse (Friedman and Schwartz 1963, pp. 237–8, 360). The importance of the United States in the world economic and financial system meant that, in effect, the Americans dragged much of the rest of the world down with them.

The end of America's post-war boom in 1920 and the reduction of imports into the United States resulted in an acute shortage of dollars in Europe, and the depression radiated out from America. The fact that the world's most important creditor was running substantial trade surpluses created problems all round; for how were the debtors to repay their debts unless they ran a trade surplus themselves? What is more, the substantial drop in American price levels during 1921 made debt problems worse, since debt which had been contracted at inflated prices had to be paid back in dearer money. This combination – of a reduction in American imports, falls in prices around the world, and a dollar shortage – spelled tremendous difficulties for countries seeking to stabilize their economies and currencies in the wake of the First World War.

Further difficulties arose from the complex network of international debts and financial obligations which the war left behind. Most of the belligerents had borrowed heavily in order to finance their war effort. After the war inter-Allied debts stood at $26,500 million, and in 1921 Germany's reparations bill was fixed at $33,000 million (or 132,000 million gold marks). France, which had been a major creditor before 1914, emerged as the principal debtor among the Allies; Britain remained a creditor, but owed huge sums to the Americans; and the United States was the main inter-Allied creditor. Thus the French owed money to the British, who in turn owed money to the Americans; the French (and, to a lesser extent, the British) needed to extract reparations from the Germans to pay the money they owed either directly or indirectly to the Americans; and in order to maintain levels of economic activity which would enable them to pay reparations, the Germans became dependent upon loans from the United States.

Does this mean that America occupied a hegemonic position with regard to the global economy after the First World War? Certainly the United States occupied a position of immense importance: its currency was the strongest in the world; its industrial economy was by a considerable margin the largest in the world; its financial and trading policies had world-wide ramifications. But shifts in American policy after the First World War also were part of general world-wide trends. Throughout the industrialized world (with the important exception of Soviet Russia, which had quite different criteria for economic policy) governments, spurred on by financial and industrial interests, were eager to abolish wartime controls. Throughout the world the inflationary pressures aroused alarm, and in 1920 governments from Sweden to the United States, from Japan to the United Kingdom, turned to restrictive credit policies to reduce inflationary pressure. They did not do this because the Americans did it; they did it for reasons similar to those which led the Americans to do it.

The Stabilization of the Post-War Monetary System

The history of the international economy during the 1920s was in large measure the history of a search for stabilization, and the cornerstone of post-war stabilization was the stabilization of currencies. Because of the strength of the American dollar, currency stabilization after the First World War essentially meant stabilization vis-à-vis the dollar. In 1919 the United States had been the first country to return its currency to the gold standard, and the Americans pressured other countries to return to the gold standard as well (Ziebura 1984, p. 37). While such a move posed few difficulties for the United States, it involved considerable problems for other countries, many of which had large international debts and for which returning to pre-war gold parity was difficult if not impossible. Nevertheless, it was a belief commonly held among central bankers and treasury ministers that a return to the gold standard should be a major objective of financial policy, and most major industrial countries managed to fix a gold parity for their currencies during the 1920s. However, unlike before 1914, when London had functioned as the centre of a stable international financial network, after the First World War long-term or even medium-term currency stability proved impossible to maintain.

The most important attempt to resurrect pre-war currency arrangements was that by the United Kingdom. Much has been written about the British decision in 1925 to return sterling to the gold standard at the pre-war parity of $4.86 (see especially Moggridge 1972). This is not the place to enter into the debate about whether Britain should have returned to the gold standard or whether reimposing pre-war parity harmed the British economy by overvaluing sterling. No doubt an expensive pound did not help British industry on world markets, although it probably aided City interests by, in effect, revaluing their capital assets (and one of the goals of the return to gold was to re-establish the position of the City of London). But, whatever the merits or otherwise of the return to the gold standard, heavy dependence upon foreign trade and the continuing importance of London as a world financial centre meant that the decision to peg sterling at $4.86 left Britain very exposed.

British decisions had to be coordinated closely with the Americans. As the dollar was *the* gold-based currency, the 1925 sterling exchange rate rested on the relationship with the dollar and thus depended upon the level of American prices: if American prices did not rise sufficiently to help compensate for the revaluation of sterling, the new arrangement would be threatened. Furthermore, Britain needed substantial credit facilities from the Americans (both from the Federal Reserve system and from merchant bankers J. P. Morgan and Co) for use as a cushion once sterling was again convertible into gold (Moggridge 1972, p. 60). To a very considerable degree, Britain's attempt to return to gold and to strengthen the City as a world financial centre was dependent upon American financial policy.

Paris was the third major world financial centre after London and New York, although the French position was fundamentally weaker than that of Britain or the United States. A major creditor before the war, France emerged with a devastated industrial base in the north, substantial internal and international debt and a chronically weak currency. In the event, reparations from Germany were not sufficient for France to pay off her war debts and make good the devastation in the north. Government borrowing continued at high levels after the war, and the French national debt increased by nearly two and a half times between 1918 and 1924 (Jackson 1985, p. 10). Inflation continued as well (except during the depression of 1921–2), and the French currency depreciated on the foreign exchanges. The resulting loss of confidence in the currency made matters worse, stimulating the flight of capital from the country and periodic speculation against the franc. And government instability, with ministries following one another in rapid succession, did not help matters. (Between September 1924 and July 1926 France had ten different finance ministers.)

The problem of the depreciating currency came to a head in July 1926, when the franc plunged on the foreign exchanges and a right-wing government led by Raymond Poincaré took office in a panic atmosphere. Poincaré's government immediately instituted a rigorous programme of reductions in spending, increases in taxation and a restructuring of France's debt; in August the Bank of France announced that it would buy pounds at a fixed rate. The measures worked; confidence in the French currency was restored, and capital started to flow back into France. In June 1928 this *de facto* currency stabilization was given a formal underpinning when the franc was placed formally on a gold standard – but at a parity one-fifth that of the pre-war *franc germinal*. In contrast to what had happened in Britain, France emerged with an undervalued currency, which provided a welcome boost for French exporters and the French tourist industry (Kemp 1971, pp. 85–6). The way the franc was stabilized – as an undervalued currency – was one reason why, initially, France was relatively little affected by the depression sparked by the 1929 stock market crash. This changed in 1931, when the devaluation of sterling wiped out France's competitive advantages on world markets and turned the franc into an overvalued currency almost overnight. The determination of French governments during the 1930s to defend and maintain the *franc Poincaré* – which necessarily involved deflationary policies – depressed economic activity and contributed to France's economic stagnation and rising unemployment between 1932 and 1936 (when unemployment in other major industrial countries was diminishing).

The stabilization of the Italian lira provides a contrast with the stabilization of the French franc. Whereas before 1926 in France a succession of weak governments and lack of control over state expenditure had played a major role in undermining the currency, in Italy in the mid 1920s neither of these conditions existed. After being formed in 1922, the Mussolini government rapidly brought down the budget deficit:

in 1920–1 the level of state expenditure was almost double that of receipts, but by 1924–5 the Italian budget was in surplus and expenditure had been slashed (table in Rafalski 1984, p. 41). The lira's problems lay elsewhere. For one thing, Italy still owed large debts to the Allies; thus until agreement was reached in November 1925 with the US and in January 1926 with the UK over repayments, Italy 'was unable to pursue an active and independent stabilization policy' (Cohen 1972, p. 647). For another, a rapid expansion of domestic credit during the first four years of Fascist rule, designed to promote industrial development, weakened the lira. And, perhaps most important, Mussolini made the 'battle of the lira' a major political issue and a symbol of Italy's virility and international standing. The trigger for action was a substantial drop from May 1926 in the value of the lira (which from late summer 1925 the Italian Treasury had supported, with the aid of informal exchange controls, at a rate of about 25 to the dollar). Against the background of the General Strike in Britain and the collapse of the French and Belgian currencies, the lira came under speculative attack, and in August Mussolini announced his intention to defend its value. In the attempt to raise and stabilize the international value of the lira the Italian government pushed through deflationary measures, and the rate at which the lira was fixed in December 1927 – at 19 to the dollar and 92.46 to the pound (the *quota novanta*), or at slightly less than one-quarter of its pre-war value (and considerably higher than the levels at which it had been trading during the previous two years) – left the currency considerably overvalued. This depressed industrial growth, exports and domestic price levels, and increased unemployment.

The problems involved in Germany's stabilization were of a different order. The German inflation, which peaked in 1923, was the worst ever suffered by a major industrial power. Its roots lay in the way in which imperial Germany had financed the war: largely by borrowing. However, instead of being able to force the French to pay for the war, as they had hoped, the defeated Germans faced huge Allied reparations demands. In a Germany already impoverished – suffering from coal shortages, drastic declines in labour productivity, territorial losses and a huge war bill of its own – this was a tremendous burden. For a government whose grasp on power was tenuous and whose legitimacy was not accepted by a large proportion of the population, inflationary social and financial policies probably were less dangerous than a tough policy of stabilization, which necessarily would have led to a substantial rise in unemployment. As Charles Kindelberger has written, 'The German inflation rested at basis on the incapacity of organized and powerful groups to agree how to share among them the burdens of reconstruction and reparations (1984, p. 31).

The problems of currency stabilization were bound up closely with reparations. It was not until April 1921, with the London Payments Plan, that Germany's reparations bill was agreed; faced with an Allied ultimatum, the Germans accepted the plan. However, arrangements soon broke down; unwilling or unable to generate the necessary budget surpluses to pay reparations, the Germans failed to make the required payments in 1922. The French responded harshly: after France claimed that the Germans had failed to make required shipments of wood and coal, French and Belgian troops occupied the Ruhr. The German government proclaimed a policy of passive resistance which, with Germany's largest industrial area at a standstill, virtually bankrupted the state and completely undermined the currency. Whereas until 1922 the inflation had provided considerable benefits to the Germans – who enjoyed the foreign trade benefits of a depreciating currency, and experienced very low rates of unemployment while joblessness in other major industrial countries shot up in 1921 – in 1923 things had got completely out of hand. Prices changed daily, production and living standards plummeted, the paper mark was supplanted by foreign currencies or by barter as a medium of exchange, and farmers refused to sell food for paper money. At this point the inflation consensus finally crumbled, and the German government and Reichsbank finally opted for stabilization.

In the autumn of 1923 a new currency, the Rentenmark, was introduced. Valued at one gold mark, the Rentenmark was backed by a mortgage on agricultural and industrial property – which, since no one could redeem the currency for agricultural land as one could redeem a currency for gold, meant in effect that the Rentenmark was backed by nothing. Thus the Rentenmark was a confidence trick, in every sense. However, because the amount of the new currency and the credit available to the Reich government were limited, the confidence trick worked and the new currency held its value. In August 1924 it was replaced by the Reichsmark, which was worth 1 million million old marks and which remained the German currency through the Second World War (until superseded by the Deutschmark in 1948). As in France and Italy, currency stability in Germany required that government control its expenditure and end vast budget deficits – which in turn meant economic contraction and substantial unemployment.

The stability of the new currency also depended upon a settlement of the reparations issue. In November 1923 the Reparations Commission set up committees to draft a plan, and under the chairmanship of Charles Dawes (a prominent American banker, and future Vice-President under Calvin Coolidge) a provisional schedule was drawn up in April 1924 for reparations payments related to Germany's ability to pay. The Dawes Plan not only outlined a schedule for repayment; it also prescribed the sources (customs duties, taxes etc.) from which the money was to come, and the establishment of an office in Berlin – run by an American financial expert, S. Parker Gilbert – to supervise and administer the financial transfers. This settlement provided a framework within which American capital again could flow into Germany. In a country where, after the inflation, capital was very short, this helped to provide funds for the investment which would help Germany generate the money to make reparations payments. The Dawes Plan was followed in 1929 by the Young Plan, drafted by a commission under the chairmanship of Owen Young, who had been Vice-Chairman of the Dawes Commission. The new settlement provided for somewhat lower initial payments than Dawes, and effectively restored German sovereignty by abolishing the Reparations Agency and foreign controls on German finances. However, the plan aroused a political storm in Germany – with the Nazis and their conservative allies in the German National People's Party organizing a noisy but unsuccessful referendum campaign against acceptance – and fell apart during the depression, when German reparations payments ceased altogether. Once the reparations plan was in place, large sums of American money found their way into Germany. Germany became dependent upon foreign capital, which in turn was needed to generate the economic activity necessary for reparations payments. When the sources of short-term American money dried up after 1929, the German economy was hard hit. However, it would be mistaken to assume that the Germans were totally at the mercy of the all-powerful Americans. Recently Stephen Schuker has argued that when all the reparations payments, American lending, lost investments in Germany during the inflation and defaults are added up, Germany came out ahead by some $3,500 million (Schuker 1985, p. 371; Schuker 1988).

Other countries which suffered hyperinflation in the wake of the First World War – Austria, Hungary, Poland – also needed international intervention to stabilize their currencies and economies. Like Germany, they initially had profited from inflation, which had helped industrial capacity to expand and offered a measure of protection against imports from countries with stronger currencies. But, as in Germany, when inflation spun out of control and threatened economic stability, permitting it to continue became more painful than the alternative. In Austria (1922) and Hungary (1924), currency stabilization was carried out through the League of Nations, which oversaw budget reform, arranged international loans and supervised these countries' finances until 1926 (Aldcroft 1987, p. 139; Spigler 1986, p. 121). Thus, in order to achieve currency stability, Austria and Hungary essentially had to abdicate control over their own economies for a period. In Poland repeated domestic attempts were made to impose fiscal controls and bring about currency stability, but not until 1926–7 was monetary stability really imposed as budgetary equilibrium was achieved, an international loan was arranged by the League, and a new currency (the zloty) replaced the old Polish mark (Aldcroft 1987, p. 141; Spigler 1986, pp. 121–3). The economic history of Poland in the mid 1920s is in large measure a story of attempts to cut public expenditure and increase taxes, economic warfare with her western neighbour, and a scramble (largely in New York) to gain foreign loans. The scramble resulted in modest success, the culmination of which was a $62 million and £2 million loan concluded in October 1927 – arranged by American and European banks represented by Bankers' Trust, the Chase National Bank and Lazard Brothers, with the active involvement of the Governors of the American Federal Reserve and the Bank of England (Polonsky 1972, p. 206; Pease 1986, pp. 59–104) – which succeeded finally in stabilizing the Polish currency.

It would be wrong to conclude that European countries could stabilize their currencies during the 1920s only with the aid of American financial institutions and the meddling of British and American central bankers. Latvia managed to stabilize her currency without foreign aid in 1921, as did Czechoslovakia soon thereafter, by imposing rigorous fiscal and monetary measures (Aldcroft 1987, pp. 137–8). However, the problem was a global one: how to impose economic and currency stability after the upheavals of war and inflation, and how, in effect, to distribute the economic losses occasioned by the First World War. And the solutions bore remarkable similarities across national boundaries: bringing state budgets into balance by cutting public expenditure and raising taxes, applying deflationary pressure on the economy, and creating a climate which promoted the confidence of a conservative banking community centred in New York and London – policies which almost invariably involved increasing unemployment. But this stabilization proved quite fragile, in both its economic and its political dimensions. On the political side, many democratic governments failed to withstand the pressures of the inter-war years; on the economic side, no discussion of the stabilization efforts of the 1920s can ignore that they soon were to smash against the rocks of the world economic crisis of the 1930s.

THE ECONOMIC CRISIS OF THE 1930S

The beginning of the world-wide depression of the 1930s is popularly regarded as the New York Stock Market crash of 1929. Yet despite the drama of the crash, the depression which followed had deeper causes, which predated October 1929. Neither the world's agricultural economy, nor general levels of business activity, nor the state of financial markets, pointed to a smooth road ahead even before the world's stock markets went into a tailspin. The problems were not just a product of speculation on Wall Street.

Of all the difficulties already apparent by autumn 1929, those facing agricultural producers had been looming the longest. Their difficulties stemmed from world-wide overproduction arising from the global expansion of agricultural production during the First World War. After the war, as European production recovered in the mid 1920s (and grain exports from the Soviet Union resumed at the end of the decade) there was downward pressure on prices and a growth of agricultural stockpiles; world agricultural prices were about 30 per cent lower in the summer and autumn of 1929 than they had been over the period 1923–5, and stockpiles were 75 per cent higher. The slide in agricultural prices accelerated thereafter, so that by August 1930 they were a mere 45.5 per cent of the 1923–5 figure; at the end of 1932 world agricultural prices were less than a quarter of the 1923–5 levels, and stocks were more than two and a half times as high (Kindelberger 1987, pp. 73–4). Heavily indebted farmers, from Nebraska to Schleswig-Holstein to New South Wales, faced bankruptcy as their costs and borrowings remained high and their incomes declined. The decline in farm prices also caused serious problems for national economies dependent upon sales of agricultural goods. For example, a collapse in coffee prices caused severe financial difficulties for Brazil. Declining wool prices during the late 1920s, deteriorating rapidly after August 1929, and falling demand in the industrialized countries greatly hurt the Australian economy, where wool exports accounted for more than two-fifths of exports and 14 per cent of national income. Depressed world sugar prices, caused partly by rapid increases in European sugar-beet production, led to riots in Cuba in 1928. And Soviet grain exports in the early 1930s, made while millions of peasants starved during the brutal collectivization campaigns, helped to depress world grain prices, deepen the agricultural depression and undermine political stability in other countries.

It is also clear, with the benefit of hindsight, that business around the world was already beginning to decline well before October 1929. In the United States building activity was falling, and car production dropped substantially from its March 1929 peak. In Germany unemployment remained alarmingly high in the late 1920s and there were clear signs that the economy was going into recession before autumn 1929. In the UK, the US, Germany, Canada, South Africa and Belgium, business cycles appear to have peaked in the spring and summer of 1929 (Kindelberger 1987, p. 103). In other words, whatever would have happened on the world's stock markets, it appears that the global economy was headed for recession during the early 1930s. Further signs of impending trouble were developments on financial markets. During the summer of 1927 the American Federal Reserve, worried about possible recession and sagging world commodity prices, lowered interest rates – a decision which Friedman and Schwartz have argued contributed to the speculative boom on the New York Stock Market in 1928 and 1929 (Friedman and Schwartz 1963, pp. 291–2. Galbraith, on the other hand, has argued that this was not the case. See Galbraith 1955, p. 16). Then in the spring and summer of 1929 American interest rates were pushed upwards, as the Federal Reserve became worried about an overheated stock market. Together with concern about the acrimonious nature of the negotiations over the Young Plan and the effects of French gold conversions, this led to substantial interest rate increases around the world which served to accelerate a downturn which was already beginning. In addition, in mid 1928 there had been a sharp drop in American lending abroad, especially to Europe (particularly Germany), Asia and Oceania. In fact, there was a substantial net inflow of funds to the United States, as money was diverted towards the booming stock market – which led to a rise in the level of interest rates in the US, which in turn 'produced a cut-off of capital lending to Germany and the periphery' (Kindelberger 1987, p. 61).

Another problem was protectionist tariffs. The 1920s were a period of high tariff barriers. This was due in part to the post-war settlement, as new states erected tariff walls to protect their industries, and in part to the political pressure of agricultural producers hoping to be shielded from slumping world prices. There had been periodic calls for a lowering of tariffs, but to little avail. Britain effectively abandoned her former policy of free trade with the McKenna duties of 1916 and the Safeguarding of Industries Act of 1921; other members of the Commonwealth pushed for tariff increases and preference for Dominion goods; the United States passed the Fordney-McCumber tariff in 1922, and in 1930 – as a consequence of political pressure from both industrial and hard-pressed agricultural interests – passed the Smoot-Hawley Tariff Act; and the Germans imposed duties on foreign goods as soon as they were free to do so. Although there is doubt about the extent to which these tariffs actually played a major role in contracting world trade, they certainly did not help.

The scale of the depression of the early 1930s was unprecedented. It has been calculated that world industrial production in 1932 (excluding the Soviet Union) stood at 65.1 per cent of what it had been in 1928. (These and the following figures on industrial production are calculated from the table in *Statistisches Jahrbuch 1935*, 'Internationale Übersichten', pp. 50–1.) The two major industrial economies hit hardest were Germany and the United States: in Germany, industrial production in 1932 was a mere 58.7 per cent of the 1928 figure; in the United States the comparable figure was 57.7 per cent. In other countries industrial production also declined by more than a third during this period: in Canada, the comparable figure was 62.8 per cent; in Poland 53.7 per cent; in Belgium 63.0 per cent; in Czechoslovakia 66.2 per cent; and in Austria 66.3 per cent. Other countries suffered substantial declines, although not so steep as those given above: in Great Britain, which got off relatively lightly, industrial production in 1932 stood at 88.4 per cent of the 1928 figure; in Fascist Italy the comparable figure was 73.0 per cent; in Sweden 83.7 per cent; in France 75.6 per cent. Of the major capitalist economies, only Japan appears to have registered a modest rise in industrial production in the early 1930s.

Employment statistics present an equally dismal picture. In the United States, the number of industrial workers declined by 26.2 per cent between 1929 and 1931 (calculated from the table in *Statistisches Jahrbuch 1935*, 'Internationale Übersichten', p. 52). In Germany, there were only 63.9 per cent as many people employed in January 1932 as there had been in June 1929, while the number of people recorded as unemployed shot up to over 6 million (Institut für Konjunkturforschung 1933, pp. 13, 15) and the real figure may have been in the vicinity of 9 million (Overy 1987, pp. 233–5). In the UK 22.4 per cent of people with unemployment insurance were unemployed in January 1932; in Belgium the figure was 20.0 per cent and in the Netherlands 33.7 per cent (*Statistisches Jahrbuch 1933*, 'Internationale Übersichten', p. 170). Those people who were lucky enough to remain in work had to contend with wage and salary cuts and short-time working. World trade also declined sharply. By

1932 British exports had declined to 36.2 per cent of their 1929 levels in terms of current prices. By 1932 German exports had fallen to 42.5 per cent, French exports to 39.5 per cent, and American exports to a mere 30.9 per cent of their 1929 levels (*Statistisches Jahrbuch 1933*, 'Internationale Übersichten', p. 109). Wherever one looked, with the exceptions of Japan and the Soviet Union, economic activity was going into reverse.

The transformation of a severe, but nonetheless not completely exceptional, economic contraction into the worst depression in modern history came with the financial crisis of 1931. The difficulties started in the United States, where large parts of the banking system had come under severe strain owing first to the agricultural slump and then to the general downturn in business activity. During the 1920s American bank failures had become alarmingly frequent, particularly in rural areas in the Midwest and the South, but in late 1930 the problem assumed a new dimension with a fully fledged banking crisis. Whereas in 1929 a total of 642 banks suspended payments, in 1930 there were 1,345 bank failures. Of these, 256 failed in November 1930 and another 352 in December; the most important was the New York based Bank of the United States, which closed its doors on 11 December. This was the largest bank that, up to that time, had ever failed in the US. In early 1931 another banking crisis hit the American system, as depositors – increasingly distrustful of banks – sought to convert their savings into currency or put it into postal savings schemes. Altogether in 1931 there were 2,298 failures; in 1932 there were 1,456 failures (Hicks 1963, pp. 232, 277; Friedman and Schwartz 1963, pp. 308–15). Nine million American savings accounts were wiped out (Leuchtenberg 1963, p. 18). However, in mid 1931 the spotlight of financial collapse switched to Europe.

During late 1930 some important bank failures occurred in Paris, and in the ensuing nervousness large amounts of French funds were withdrawn from London. Then in May 1931 Austria's largest bank, the Creditanstalt, collapsed. The run on the Creditanstalt not only sank that bank; as a consequence the Austrian National Bank also ran into foreign exchange difficulties and had to seek international loans. The French apparently used the opportunity to link financial help with pressure to drop the customs union idea (i.e. to use economic pressure to further political goals), while Austria's financial difficulties deepened; finally the Bank of England stepped in, a move which may have led to the Bank of France's destabilizing withdrawals of gold from London a few months later. Soon after the Creditanstalt disaster, Germany's banking system was in trouble. The reverberations of the Austrian crisis, the speculative expansion of some German banks, the difficulties facing some of Germany's major companies, and political insecurity put severe pressure on the German banking system. In May 1931 German bank deposits fell; in June gold started flowing out of the country in large amounts, and the large Danat-Bank (the Darmstädter- und Nationalbank, which had expanded rapidly in the late 1920s) was in deep trouble. By July the entire German banking system was teetering towards collapse, and Reichsbank President Hans Luther frantically toured London, Paris and Basle seeking foreign help. The British could not help; the French were willing to do so only if the Germans were prepared to make political concessions. On 13 July German banks were closed for three days; the government and the Reichsbank stepped in to block foreign withdrawals and drastically raised interest rates in an effort to keep money in the country. Against this background President Hoover proposed a temporary moratorium on intergovernmental debt payments – which, as things turned out, proved to be a permanent moratorium on German reparations payments. Germany's financial system emerged badly shaken, and the substantially raised interest rates further depressed business activity and sent an already ailing economy into a nosedive.

The next target for speculative attack was the one-time linchpin of the world financial system: sterling. British budget deficits, pressure against sterling (as European banks sold sterling to increase gold reserves to make up for losses in the German crisis) and French hostility pushed Britain's reserves downwards during late July despite foreign loans and repeated rises in the Bank of England discount rate. Faced with the apparent need to cut spending and the budget deficit and to attract further foreign money, the Labour government fell on 24 August. Less than one month later, on 21 September, Britain left the gold standard, and sterling began a free fall, dropping from \$4.86 in August to \$3.25 in December. Many of the world's currencies followed sterling off gold – in effect allowing their currencies to depreciate against the dollar (Kindelberger 1987, pp. 154–9). Altogether, 25 other countries, those most dependent upon trade with Britain, followed the British lead and cut their currencies loose from gold. Only the dollar remained untouched, but that too was soon to change. When Franklin Roosevelt became American President in March 1933, the United States faced a terrible financial crisis. The banking system was in disarray, gold was leaving the country and there was speculation that America soon would leave the gold standard. Roosevelt's first move on 4 March, the day he took power, was to declare a bank holiday, temporarily closing all the banks in the country and prohibiting the export of gold. Then, in April, the dollar was taken off the gold standard, and it quickly depreciated from \$3.24 to the pound in the first half of April to \$3.85 at the end of April and \$4.00 at the end of May (Kindelberger 1987, pp. 195–212). The entire system so painfully pieced together in the 1920s had collapsed.

It was against this background that a world economic conference, the International Conference on Monetary and Economic Questions of June 1933, was held in London. Called formally by the League of Nations, the conference was to cover both financial and economic questions: monetary policy, international credit, exchange stabilization and capital movements on the one hand, and trade and tariff policies, restrictive trade practices and conditions of production on the other. Prime ministers, foreign ministers, finance ministers and central bankers assembled in London; the US sent Secretary of State Cordell Hull. The conference was a failure, however. Roosevelt and Hull made it clear that the Americans' first concern was American domestic policy, not the coordination of world economic policy, and that the latter would have to take a back seat to the former. There were arguments between the Americans and the French, who stuck to the gold standard. The British insisted on bringing up war debts, to the displeasure of the Americans. The Germans, whose new Nazi-led government was represented incompetently by Economics Minster Alfred Hugenberg, declined to play a constructive role. And a stabilization agreement to halt the slide of the dollar was rejected – in effect torpedoed – by Roosevelt, who stated from America that 'the world will not long be lulled by the specious fallacy of achieving a temporary and probably artificial stability in foreign exchange on the part of a few large countries only' and that 'the sound internal economic situation of a nation is a greater factor in its well-being than the price of its currency' (quoted in Kindelberger 1987, p. 216).

That may have been true for a country whose massive internal resources left it less dependent upon foreign trade than other nations, but it hardly suggested a way to settle international economic problems. Roosevelt essentially announced that he intended to revive the American economy and was not too bothered about how his policies might affect the international economy, and his outburst effectively broke up the conference. In its wake, the Germans went their own way, towards more restrictive trade and currency controls and the promotion of autarky; the members of the British Empire formed the sterling area; a 'gold bloc' was formed of those countries (principally France, which saw the advantages of its formerly undervalued currency eroded as other countries devalued) which still adhered to the gold standard; and the dollar plunged to $4.86 to the pound in mid July, when the Federal Reserve finally intervened to support it, and once its value again was fixed against gold in October it had been devalued substantially. The world essentially was divided into three monetary blocs: the sterling area; the dollar area; and those countries which maintained the gold standard. Some countries – Nazi Germany, the Soviet Union – maintained controls and restrictions which in effect suspended currency convertibility; others, most notably (and successfully) Japan, engaged in competitive depreciations (Foreman-Peck 1983, pp. 249–51). International economic management had failed.

SOME CONCLUDING REMARKS

Any attempt to explain the catastrophic failure of international economic management during the inter-war period must grapple with the central role played by the United States. The United States possessed the most powerful and productive economy in the world, and responsibility for the severity of the world depression of the 1930s is frequently placed at the door of American policy makers. Two important explanations of what went wrong are those put forward by monetarist economists Milton Friedman and Anna Schwartz on the one hand, and by economic historian Charles Kindelberger on the other. When, in the view of Friedman and Schwartz, the Americans – or, more specifically, the American Federal Reserve – pursued ill-advised, badly timed and overly restrictive monetary policies, they effectively generated world-wide depression (Friedman and Schwartz 1963, p. 229). Kindelberger, however, sees the problem stemming not simply from flawed American monetary policy but from a broader shift in the centre of gravity of the world economic system – from Britain to the United States – and the need for a stabilizer to regulate and coordinate the world economy. According to Kindelberger, before the First World War Britain had acted as stabilizer (maintaining an open market, providing stable long-term lending and providing liquidity in financial crisis) 'with the enormous help of gold standard mythology, which internalized both stable exchange rates and coordinated macroeconomic policies'; however, during the inter-war economic crisis 'Britain could not act as a stabilizer, and the United States would not' and 'when every country turned to protect its private interest, the world public interest went down the drain, and with it the private interests of all' (Kindelberger 1987, pp. 289–91).

Such explanations are useful tools with which to examine the international political economy between the wars. However, they are tools and no more; and their use should not preclude a critical examination of the role of the United States in the inter-war world economy. It is undeniable that the United States played a central and damaging role in the international economic order, and that without the United States no international regulatory system or meaningful coordination of economic policy could have been formulated. But does this mean that effective coordination of international economic policy necessarily would have been possible *with* American involvement? Were the structural problems so global in nature that they were beyond the power of any potential stabilizer – even of a United States with an enlightened government concerned about the world beyond America's shores – to solve?

Perceptions of failure reflect perceptions of success. The economic history of the inter-war years is used repeatedly to provide examples of disastrously misinformed economic policy: of the dangers of unrestrained stock market speculation, of the follies of protectionism and economic nationalism, of the stupidity of attempting to revive the gold standard, of the chaos created by the failure of the dominant economic power to exercise responsible leadership, of the need for functioning international regulatory organizations in the economic as well as the political spheres. Until recently, one could triumphantly assert that the world had learned the lessons of the inter-war period. During the decades after the Second World War, with the phenomenal record of economic growth and apparently successful management of the global economy, it was possible to believe that the 1920s and 1930s had been an unpleasant aberration. However, it is no longer easy to be so smug. Perhaps the decades after the Second World War, in which the United States assumed a unique role which could not be sustained over a longer period, formed the aberration. Perhaps the inter-war period was more normal than many people care to think.

During the 1920s, in the attempt to achieve stabilization, financial orthodoxy was imposed by foreign bankers and advisers upon European economies ravaged by war, inflation and economic mismanagement. No doubt they were right, at least in the short term, to demand fiscal and economic responsibility; and no doubt they provided a convenient alibi for politicians in various countries who were unwilling to take responsibility for imposing harsh but unavoidable measures themselves. No doubt today's Western bankers and advisers prescribing policies for the emerging democracies of Eastern Europe – which have also been damaged profoundly by inflation and economic mismanagement – are equally justified in insisting that financial orthodoxy is necessary for the establishment of stable currencies and robust market economies. But we should not forget that earlier in this century attempts to impose financial orthodoxy upon the states of Eastern and Central Europe, while they may have been economically necessary, were followed not only by the worst depression the world has yet seen but also by the collapse of democratic systems and political instability which plunged the world into the Second World War.

References

Aldcroft, D.H. (1987) *From Versailles to Wall Street 1919–1929*. Harmondsworth: Penguin.

Allen, G.C. (1962) *A Short Economic History of Modern Japan* (2nd edn). London: Allen and Unwin.

Burk, K. (1982) The Treasury: from impotence to power. In K. Burk (ed.), *War and the State: the Transformation of British Government, 1914–1919*, London: Allen and Unwin.

Carr, R. (1982) *Spain 1808–1975* (2nd edn). Oxford: Oxford University Press.

Cohen, J.S. (1972) The revaluation of the lira: a study in political economy. *Economic History Review*, xxv, 642–57.

Foreman-Peck, J. (1983) *A History of the World Economy: International Economic Relations since 1860*. New York: Barnes and Noble.

Friedman, M. and Schwartz, A.J. (1963) *A Monetary History of the United States 1867–1960*. Princeton: Princeton University Press.

Galbraith, J.K. (1955) *The Great Crash, 1929*. Boston: Houghton Mifflin.

Glismann, H.H., Rodemer, H. and Wolter, F. (1981) Lange Wellen wirtschaftlicher Wachstums. In D. Petzina and G. van Roon (eds), *Konjunktur, Krise, Gesellschaft: Wirtschaftliche Wechsellagen und soziale Entwicklung im 19. und 20. Jahrhundert*, Stuttgart: Klett-Cotta.

Hardach, G. (1977) *The First World War 1914–1918*. London: Allen Lane.

Hicks, J.D. (1963) *American Ascendancy 1921–1933*. New York: Harper and Row.

Holtfrerich, C.L. (1986) *The German Inflation 1914–1923: Causes and Effects in International Perspective*. Berlin and New York: Walter de Gruyter.

Institut für Konjunkturforschung (1933) *Konjunkturstatistisches Handbuch 1933*. Berlin: Verlag von Reimar Hobbing.

Jackson, J. (1985) *The Politics of Depression in France 1932–1936*. Cambridge: Cambridge University Press.

Kemp, T. (1971) The French economy under the franc Poincaré. *Economic History Review*, xxiv, 82–99.

Kindelberger, C.P. (1984) A structural view of the German inflation. In G.D. Feldman, C.-L. Holtfrerich, G.A. Ritter and P.-C. Witt (eds), *The Experience of Inflation: International and Comparative Studies*, Berlin and New York: Walter de Gruyter.

Kindelberger, C.P. (1987) *The World in Depression 1929–1939*. Harmondsworth: Penguin.

Leuchtenberg, W.E. (1963) *Franklin D. Roosevelt and the New Deal 1932–1940*. New York: Harper and Row.

Milward, A. (1981) Cyclical fluctuations and economic growth in developed Europe, 1870–1913. In D. Petzina and G. van Roon (eds), *Konjunktur, Krise, Gesellschaft: Wirtschaftliche Wechsellagen und soziale Entwicklung im 19. und 20. Jahrhundert*, Stuttgart: Klett-Cotta.

Moggridge, D.E. (1972) *British Monetary Policy 1924–1931: the Norman Conquest of $4.86*. Cambridge: Cambridge University Press.

Overy, R. (1987) Unemployment in the Third Reich. *Business History*, xxix (3), 253–81.

Pease, N. (1986) *Poland, the United States and the Stabilization of Europe, 1919–1933*. New York and Oxford: Oxford University Press.

Polonsky, A. (1972) *Politics in Independent Poland 1921–1939: the Crisis of Constitutional Government*. Oxford: Oxford University Press.

Rafalski, T. (1984) *Italienischer Faschismus in der Weltwirtschaftskrise (1925–1936): Wirtschaft, Gesellschaft und Politik auf der Schwelle der Moderne*. Opladen: Westdeutscher.

Schuker, S.A. (1985) American 'Reparations' to Germany, 1919–1933. In G.D. Feldman, C.-L. Holtfrerich, G. A. Ritter and P.-C. Witt (eds), *Die Nachwirkungen der Inflation auf die deutsche Geschichte 1924–1933*, Berlin and New York: Walter de Gruyter.

Schuker, S.A. (1988) *American 'Reparations' to Germany, 1919–1933: Implications for the Third-World Debt Crisis*. Princeton Studies in International Finance no. 61, Department of Economics, Princeton University.

Spigler, I. (1986) Public finance. In M.C. Kaser and E.A. Radice (eds), *The Economic History of Eastern Europe 1919–1975. Vol. II: Interwar Policy, the War and Reconstruction*, Oxford: Clarendon Press.

Statistisches Jahrbuch für das Deutsche Reich 1933 (ed. Statistisches Reichsamt). Berlin: Verlag von Reimar Hobbing.

Statistisches Jahrbuch für das Deutsche Reich 1935 (ed. Statistisches Reichsamt). Berlin: Verlag für Sozialpolitik, Wirtschaft und Statistik.

Wagenfuhr, R. (1933) *Die Industriewirtschaft: Entwicklungstendenzen der deutschen und internationalen Industrieproduktion 1860 bis 1932 (Vierteljahrshefte zur Konjunkturforschung, Sonderheft 31)*. Berlin.

Witt, P.-C. (1974) Finanzpolitik und sozialer Wandel in Krieg und Inflation 1918–1924. In H. Mommsen, D. Petzina and B. Weisbrod (eds), *Industrielles System und politische Entwicklung in der Weimarer Republik*, Düsseldorf: Droste.

Ziebura, G. (1984) *Weltwirtschaft und Weltpolitik 1922/24–1931: Zwischen Rekonstruktion und Zusammenbruch*. Frankfurt am Main: Sukrkamp.

9

The Nature and Government of the Global Economy

JEREMY MITCHELL

By 1918 British hegemony in the international economy was declining, although the pound sterling was still important in the international monetary regime. The leading economy was now the United States but, in the inter-war period, and the 1930s in particular, the US was much more concerned with internal domestic economics. This had a number of systemic consequences. The US provided no leadership for the coordinated regulation of the global economy and, because they put primacy on domestic economic objectives, the policies of the US had highly undesirable consequences for the domestic economic management of other economies. This followed from the dominant role of the US in world trade and in financial markets, and one result was the competitive devaluations and general economic instability of the late 1930s. However, after 1945 and the disruption caused by the Second World War the United States acted differently. One of the implicit policy assumptions of those actors who tried to shape the post-1945 international economic environment was that the failure of the inter-war system was a major cause of the war itself; economic disorder was seen as linked to political disorder and conflict. Global economic coordination beyond that provided by market forces was needed to avoid a recurrence of such conflict in the future. So in planning for post-war reconstruction the United States took a major role in trying to establish a set of institutions which would make a similar failure less likely to recur.

Here we come to a major theoretical problem. After 1945 a bipolar system of international power developed which also provided elements of stability within the global system. Simultaneously a new economic order, different from that of the inter-war period but with some elements of continuity, was created. But was there a connection between the new international economic order (IEO) and the bipolar Cold War political system, between the global patterns of economics and politics? The answer that emerges here is basically neo-realist, but in discussing the post-1945 economic world we need to consider both the institutions themselves and the subsequent development of the global economy within – and in part outside – this framework. The history of the post-war international economy is, however, not just a history of the industrialized economies, of the relations between them and their relative success or failure in absolute terms; it is also a history of international economic institutions and international economic management. Behind these institutions lie sets of theoretical assumptions which need examining too. And beyond the industrialized countries, and increasingly part of the international economic order, are the less developed countries outside the capitalist core – countries that are linked to this core by ties of trade, finance, policy and politics. So one needs at least to consider the position of areas such as Eastern Europe and the emergent economies of South East Asia.

The story of the world economy since 1945 is a story of reconstruction, recovery and growth, followed by a slowdown in growth and the emergence of severe problems in many of the constituent national economies in the late 1970s and early 1980s. But the story is not just a study of development and change in terms of trade and finance over the post-war period. The institutional structure has changed too. These developments are covered separately in the first two sections of this chapter: the structure of institutions, in particular the World Bank, the International Monetary Fund and the General Agreement on Tariffs and Trade; and then the overall performance of the world economy in the post-war period.

What was the origin and nature of the modern world economy? It is usual to date its existence to the emergence of Britain as the dominant industrial and commercial power in the third quarter of the nineteenth century. Much world trade was centred in London, and many commodity markets were located there; the pound sterling became the major international currency; and British liberal economic policies such as free trade played a role in determining the world pattern of trade. However, by the end of the nineteenth century Britain's relative economic decline had begun, and by 1918 the United States had developed into the dominant world economy. This was still the case in 1945. But in what way was the global economy of the last 100 years different from the international economy that preceded it? What is it that has been globalized? After all, there had been very extensive international networks of trade which predate the modern state system. Briefly the assumptions made here about the nature of a global economy are as follows. The progress of industrialization, first in Britain and then later in other countries within the capitalist core and outside it, brought a major change in the scale of economic activity and economic power. This in turn stimulated economic trade and brought increased international specialization and a new international division of labour, based in part on differential factor endowments and comparative advantage. The end result is a set of linked, interdependent economies with a global reach. The linkage is not just laterally between states and regions but vertically within subsystems in a hierarchy of markets. It is economic activity itself that is globalized, and in the contemporary world system this is overlaid by technological and military interdependence.

For much of the post-war period the United States' dominance remained, and a later section looks at its role within the global system. At the end of the war the US was in a pre-eminent position; it was by far the largest and strongest of the mature industrialized economies, and its economic infrastructure had been relatively undamaged by the ravages of the war. Its major pre-war competitors – Britain, Germany etc. – had all suffered extensive loss and were in need of major economic reconstruction, so the war had increased the relative economic strength of the US. Partly because of this, the US view of the future management of the IEO was a major influence on the international economic regime that was established. So this order reflects American economic (and ideological) assumptions, such as the primacy of economic liberalism and free trade. But economic power is linked to political power – albeit in a diffuse, sometimes indirect and complex manner. So one could argue that this American hegemony in 1945 had political consequences and that the new IEO was used to further American political objectives. Since 1945 this relative dominance has changed as the pattern of the global economy has changed, and so we need to look at the nature of this change and its consequences.

The current structural problems of the world economy and especially those associated with the relative decline of US economic dominance will also be discussed. The US debt crisis is a major problem for the future stability of the world economy, because the US is still the leading economy – if not as dominant as it was 40 years ago – and because its economic position is linked to other aspects of global order, politically, militarily, technologically and even perhaps culturally. The problems here are not just external for the IEO but *internal* for US domestic politics too. But this should also suggest questions about the realist view of the global system: are the economic policies of the United States driven by domestic concerns? So we examine the political as well as the economic consequences of the current crisis. The final section looks briefly at the other consequences of recent changes in the global system.

THE NEW INTERNATIONAL ECONOMIC ORDER: THE MANAGEMENT OF THE GLOBAL ECONOMY AFTER 1945

A truly global economy is a relatively new phenomenon. At the outbreak of the Second World War it was probably less than a century old and had originated with the growth and dominance of British trade and finance in the mid nineteenth century. But between 1918 and 1939 the international economy had failed, with individual countries retreating from free trade and economic liberalism to economic nationalism and protectionist policies. One major contributory factor to this failure of the international economy was the lack of explicit institutional management; there was an implicit rather than an explicit international economic regime. But one consequence of globalization was that all the major economies were affected by the economic policies of the dominant economy. The policies of the hegemonic economic power contributed to the instability of the system. Before 1914 Britain had acted as the systemic stabilizer, but the relative decline in size and importance of the British economy had left a gap which in the 1930s the United States, as the world's largest economy, was unwilling or unable to fill:

> What does this failure tell us? The obvious conclusion is that the attempt at the international management of the world economy failed because the Americans wrecked it: Roosevelt essentially announced that he intended to revive the American economy and was not bothered about how his policies might affect the international economy. But the United States still remained the lynchpin of the world economy, and the international regulatory system or meaningful coordination of economic policy could not be formulated without her involvement.
>
> (Bessell 1989, p. 59)

By 1941 the increased demand resulting from war production had completed the recovery in the US economy which was initiated by the New Deal. The US entered the war on the side of the Allies, and to some the economic dislocation of the 1930s was seen as one contributory factor to the war itself. This, together with the new theories of economists such as Keynes, made it possible for the two leading allied powers – the UK and the US – to plan the reconstruction of the international economic order in a way that had not been possible before. So the post-war economic world represents something of a fresh start in international economic relations. In addition, as suggested earlier, there is the nature of the post-war political settlement. In the divided and politicized world order that came into being, the USA felt obliged to support its Allies in economic terms. US–UK negotiation on the post-war economy started in 1941–2, proceeded over the remainder of the war and led to the Bretton Woods agreement of 1944. Despite this agreement the two major parties operated with different sets of assumptions, and indeed expected the institutions created to operate in different ways (on the background to Bretton Woods see Gardner 1980). However, both sides were committed to free trade and agreed that the future IEO should be regulated in a way that the inter-war economy had not been. Such regulation in their view implied at a minimum three things:

1 That there should be full currency convertibility both between leading trading currencies and between these and gold
2 That there should be some regularized adjustment mechanism between individually traded national currencies
3 That there should be some coordination from the centre of the international system.

Taken together these imply mechanisms for the creation of international liquidity and for multilateral clearing, and powers to act to restore international equilibrium through an intervention agency. Beyond these constraints, countries would enjoy internal autonomy in economic policy making. (But as Gilpin and others have pointed out, the principle of autonomy of national policies, fixed exchange rates and currency convertibility were not necessarily consistent; see Gilpin 1987b, p. 132.) They also institutionalized a link between domestic policy and the international economy. The adjustment of individual economies was to be carried out by use of demand management and other *internal* policy measures. But this was to be within an institutionalized framework of fixed exchange rates which constrained domestic policy making by ruling out the use of currency devaluation to increase international competitiveness.

The institutional expression of these aims was achieved by the establishment of the International Monetary Fund (IMF) and the International Bank for Reconstruction and Development (IBRD) – the World Bank. Both of these institutions were planned and located in the United States whilst the war was still in progress, with the result that international economic policies, later critics would say, were dominated by the US. The purpose of the institutional arrangements was to prevent the competitive realignment of currencies and large capital flows which had been destabilizing elements of the pre-war system.

Both institutions were in place by the end of the war. A third element, an international trade organization (ITO) to regulate world trade, reduce tariffs etc., was not. The proposal for an ITO eventually failed and it was partially replaced by the General Agreement on Tariffs and Trade (GATT). The overall effect of the new institutions of the IEO can be summarized as follows:

1 They reflected the dominant role of the US and the assumptions of Liberalism, such as free trade. (Some critics have maintained that this framework was designed to maintain the dominance of the United States within the global economy.)
2 For the major Western European liberal democracies the new IEO went in parallel with a commitment to domestic economic planning and the development of a welfare state as a mechanism for avoiding the mass unemployment and social crisis of the 1930s. There is here a convergence between domestic and international economic concerns.
3 The IMF has a clearly political role through the conditionality of loans and the power given to it to intervene in the domestic economic policy making of borrowing countries.
4 The largest economies have a dominant role in the governing institutions.
5 GATT is slightly different in both origin and form; it was not part of the original grand design, and is based more on mutual bargaining and reciprocity rather than on central direction. The larger economies have less of a dominant or decisive role – at least as compared with the IMF or the World Bank.

Many of these assumptions are political ones, both about the nature of the global system (points 1 and 4) and about domestic politics (points 2 and 3). So perhaps the world economic order created after 1945 is fundamentally a political solution to the problem of managing a global economy.

But politics intrudes in other ways. The original negotiations were conducted by a group of two – the United Kingdom and the United States. Informal economic summit meetings between the leaders of the major economies have been added to the formal institutions of global economic management in the post-war period.

In this global system, economic stability was maintained through the institutional order established after 1945 – by international negotation via GATT, by economic summits, by ideological, technological and military interdependence. But stability was only contingent. There was a tension between national economic objectives and supra-national ones. For example, the adjustments envisioned by the Bretton Woods system may conflict with national welfare state objectives; the conditions attached to a loan from the IMF may increase domestic unemployment. So the system may be dynamically unstable. One way of inducing stability in such a system was through the use of side payments, whether economic, military or political. Again we come back to the funda-mental point that, in the post-war Bretton Woods system, economic and other objectives are inextricably linked.

THE GROWTH OF THE GLOBAL ECONOMY

The story of the post-war economic order is not straightforward. Some of the important institutions had been established soon after 1945, but their operation was overshadowed by the problems of economic reconstruction and recovery once the war had ended. The changing balance of power within the world economy also delayed the implementation of the Bretton Woods system. The failure of the projected international trade organization (ITO) and the emergence of GATT brought further changes to the original proposals. As the war had a disruptive effect on all of the leading pre-war economies but one – the US – the latter became the major source of capital goods for reconstruction, and the dollar became the major source of international liquidity in the immediate post-war period. This reinforced the dominant position of the US economy. This economic dominance in turn was a major factor in producing the political consequences suggested earlier. The problems that this caused for other countries (and particularly for the other international currency, sterling), the shortage of liquidity, and the so-called dollar gap, can be found discussed elsewhere.

Post-war reconstruction in Europe was eventually helped by the Marshall Plan (1948–52) through which American aid was channelled to Europe. Note that the recipients of Marshall aid were decided by political criteria. A summary of the subsequent growth of the world economy, or at least the Organization for Economic Cooperation and Development (OECD) countries, after 1950 is given in table 9.1. The distribution of world exports for 1960–70 is shown in table 9.2. The overall picture is one of fairly rapid economic recovery after 1945, followed by a period of sustained economic growth between 1950 and 1970. But within this overall pattern there are pronounced differences between countries; for example, compare the UK and Germany or Japan on any set of indicators of economic activity. There are also differences between areas in the global system; compare the industrialized and less developed countries (LDCs) in table 9.2. There were inqualities in *national* economic performance which changed the balance of economic power within the group of developed countries, and between this group and the LDCs. Such changes had political implications for the functioning of the IEO.

Indeed, the tables show the following features of the world economy since 1950:

1 The remarkable economic growth of the industrialized core countries after 1945 and particularly in the period 1950–73

Table 9.1 Growth of output, OECD countries, 1950–1985 (average annual percentage growth rates)

	1950–60	1960–70	1970–80	1980–85
Belgium	2.9	4.9	3.2	0.7
Canada	3.9	5.0	4.0	2.4
Denmark	3.3	4.8	2.3	2.4
France	4.4	5.8	3.6	1.1
Germany (West)	7.6	4.8	2.9	1.3
Italy	5.9	5.7	3.1	0.8
Japan	n.a.	11.0	4.9	3.8
Netherlands	4.9	5.1	3.4	0.7
Norway	3.5	5.0	4.6	3.3
Sweden	3.3	4.4	1.9	2.0
Switzerland	5.1	4.6	1.2	1.2
United Kingdom	2.6	2.8	1.9	2.0
United States	3.2	4.0	3.0	2.5

Sources: 1950–60, Scammell (1983, p. 52); 1960–70, *EEC: Basic Statistics of the Community, 1971*, table 11; 1970–80 as 1960–70 plus *EEC: Basic Statistics, 1981–82*; 1980–85, World Bank, *World Development Report, 1987*, table 2

Table 9.2 Growth of world exports, 1960–70 (value of trade in current US$ million)

Year	World exports	% increase on previous year	Industrial countries	% increase on previous year	Less developed countries	% increase on previous year
1960	113,100	—	73,168	—	28,572	—
1961	118,200	4.5	77,022	5.2	29,567	3.4
1962	124,400	5.2	82,184	6.7	29,284	−0.95
1963	135,500	8.9	90,581	10.2	30,649	4.7
1964	151,900	12.1	99,128	9.4	31,430	2.5
1965	164,700	8.4	107,620	8.6	33,329	6.0
1966	181,023	9.9	119,059	10.6	36,157	8.5
1967	190,261	5.1	126,188	6.0	36,767	1.7
1968	212,885	11.9	143,433	13.6	40,670	11.1
1969	244,059	14.6	171,150	19.3	49,150	20.8
1970	279,721	14.6	197,342	15.3	55,041	12.0

Source: OECD, *The Growth of Output, 1960–1970* (Paris: OECD, 1976)

2 Their relative slowdown after 1973
3 The position of the LDCs within the global economy
4 The changing position of the US economy within the world economy

We could add more points of detail, for example on the extent to which the post-1945 IEO is primarily a *political* settlement. Note the allocation of Marshall aid and its effects on domestic economies; in France, West Germany and Italy it helped the introduction of planning and structural intervention by central government (see Holland 1987). Here again we find a political/economic linkage across the levels of the global system. What appears to be an economic decision is determined by US political objectives and in turn reinforces individual *national* political objectives. But is this the end of the story? There were two other significant developments within the global system after 1950: the growth of regional economic subsystems, and the growth of multinational corporations (MNCs) which operate across national boundaries. MNCs increase globalization but can also be seen as posing a threat to national economic autonomy.

Table 9.2 identified industrialized countries and LDCs. However, within the industrialized core, patterns of regional economic activity have emerged: a West European economy, a North Atlantic economy, and one developing around the Pacific and South East Asia. Some of these subsystems overlap and, as with countries, some regions develop at faster rates than others. The emergence of a financial and securities market centred on New York, Tokyo and London is a symptom of regionalization and globalization through interregional linkage. Developments in telecommunications and information technology also play a major role. The growth of MNCs is both cause and consequence of globalization. The emergence of world markets, an international division of labour and a stable international economic regime provided an environment favourable to the growth of transnational firms. The initial tendency after 1945 was for such companies to be predominantly US based; the dominance of the US economy and the need for investment capital for post-war reconstruction, which could only come in the immediate post-war period from the US were both factors which helped. In extreme form it led to one firm dominating a particular sector of the global economy and imposing standards upon it. The classic example is IBM, which at one time accounted for more than 80 per cent of the world market in computers and was able to use this dominant position to define standards within this sector to maintain or increase its market share and/or competitive advantage. But one should not exaggerate the *newness* of MNCs. General Motors has existed since the 1920s, and the major oil companies from about the same period. What is different with the development of the global economy after 1945 is the number, range and diversity of MNCs and the changing balance between them – in banking, oil, car manufacture and so on. The growth in the number of MNCs, whilst (possibly) producing further complex inter-dependence in the global economy, posed difficult problems for national economies in areas of investment, capital movement and control of technology. It also produced a new class of corporate manager who moved between companies, economic sectors and countries in a way that was wholly new.

One criticism of the spread of US capital and US-based MNCs suggests that it is just a more indirect means to maintain US economic and political dominance of the global system. The nature of US hegemony or dominance will be discussed later in terms of the role of the US within the world economy, and of the relationship between the institutional structure of the world economy – particularly the regulatory agencies established at Bretton Woods – and the problems of the international system.

But can we say anything more about the structure of the world economy? Table 9.3 shows the flow of trade in percentage terms between the developed, the less developed and the centrally planned economies in 1960. Table 9.4 shows the trade shares of some leading industrial countries over the period 1938–83. First, an obvious difference is that between developed and less developed countries (tables 9.2 and 9.3). The economic growth that occurred after 1945 has affected economies differentially, and the LDC share of world exports declined in the period 1960–70. The gap between rich and poor nations is, if anything, widening. Table 9.3 also shows a balance of trade between developed and less developed countries changing in favour of the former. Secondly, table 9.3 shows the relative isolation of the centrally planned economies, in terms of both their share of world trade and their interaction with the core industrialized countries. After World War II these economies did not receive Marshall aid, and with the emergence of the bipolar Cold War international system their links with the industrialized core countries became relatively few. This isolation was therefore primarily *political* in origin. The very recent signs of economic liberalization together with the need to import capital and technology from the capitalist core may reintegrate them into the global economy, but again this would be the result of political rather than economic decisions. Thirdly, even within the industrialized countries there are differences in economic performance between national economies. Table 9.1 shows the relative growth performance of a group of core systems. There are high-growth countries such as Japan and West Germany; the UK economy grows at a lower rate. This is supplemented by table 9.4, which illustrates the export performance of a group of

Table 9.3 Matrix of world exports, 1960 (per cent)

	Industrial countries	Other developed areas	Exports from Less developed countries	Centrally planned economies	Total
Exports to					
Industrial countries[a]	37	5	16	2	60
Other developed areas[b]	4	e	1	1	6
Less developed countries[c]	14	1	5	1	21
Centrally planned economies[d]	2	e	1	8	12
Total	57	6	23	12	100

[a] EC countries, Austria, Canada, Denmark, Japan, Norway, Sweden, Switzerland, United Kingdom, United States of America.
[b] Other Europe, Australia, New Zealand, South Africa.
[c] Underdeveloped countries which were members of IMF.
[d] Europe and Asia.
e Negligible.
Discrepancies in totals due to rounding.

Source: IMF, *Direction of Trade*, vol. 2, 1960–4

Table 9.4 Geographic distribution of world trade shares of some leading industrial countries, 1938–1983 (% global product)

	1938	1950	1966	1973	1979	1983
UK	13	10.0	7.8	5.3	5.5	5.7
Germany, France, EC	20	15.4	27.1	30.0	28.1	30.4
US	10	16.7	15.0	12.2	10.8	9.3
Japan	4	1.4	4.5	6.4	6.3	8.7
Other AICs	18	17.9	16.3	16.4	14.5	15.9
CPEs	8	6.1	9.7	10.1	9.3	10.1
USSR	1	3.0	4.2	3.7	3.9	4.2
Other	7	3.1	7.4	6.4	5.4	5.9
Latin America	7	12.4	6.5	6.0	5.2	5.4
NICs	3	5.0	2.2	2.0	1.9	2.9
Asia	11	11.7	5.7	5.2	6.1	8.2
NICs	—	2.8	1.5	2.1	2.3	3.4
Other LDCs	6	6.0	4.3	4.4	4.5	2.3
Middle East	2	1.4	2.9	4.2	8.7	4.6

AICs advanced industrialized countries
CPEs centrally planned economies
NICs newly industrialized countries
LDCs less developed countries
Source: adapted from Gordon (1988)

leading countries. Note again the performance of the UK over time, the very strong recovery of the rest of Europe in the post-war era, and the downturn in the position of the US by 1960.

The changing relative performance of national economies becomes particularly important if we conceive of political and economic power as linked. Any change in economic power should produce a lagged change in the intrasystem distribution of power between national political systems. For much of the post-war period the United States was the dominant economic power within the global system. The next two sections look at this hegemony in more detail, and the consequence of any relative decline in this pattern of economic dominance and political power.

THE UNITED STATES AND THE WORLD ECONOMY

The ground rules for regulation of the new IEO after 1945 were laid in the bilateral US–UK negotiations which culminated in the Bretton Woods agreement of 1944. But the balance of power between the two Atlantic partners had changed by the end of the negotiations. The UK economy declined both relatively and absolutely, and the strength of the US together with its position as the major source of goods and capital ensured that it became the dominant economy in the post-war period. This position was reinforced by the Marshall aid programme, and US dominance was extended to the newly established international agencies such as the IMF and the World Bank. This process ran parallel with the establishment of military alliances in which the US again played a key role. Deriving in part from both of these factors the US became a major source of technology, a point which raised questions of technology transfer and the regulation of economic activity with military or security implications. One example of this US dominance can be seen in the field of computers. As mentioned earlier, at one time in the 1960s IBM controlled over 80 per cent of the world market in computers. It used this dominance to set price levels to maximize its own revenue, to define standards in machine performance and to tie its customers firmly to IBM (by not allowing the connection of non-IBM peripherals etc.). By the late 1980s IBM was still the dominant force in this sector, but its position had been cut back by changes in world manufacturing capacity, by competition from other producers, and by techno-logical changes within the industry. But IBM still accounted for over 35 per cent of world turnover in this sector (Strange 1987).

But the evidence also shows that as the world economy recovered and grew, the *relative* position of the US declined in terms of its share of the global economy. It was still the leading economy but was no longer as dominant as before. At the same time the dollar had become the *de facto* world currency, which imposed additional constraints on the US. Immediately after 1945 there was a strong demand for dollars, both to finance trade and for investment in capital goods etc. By the late 1960s this had changed; there was no dollar shortage. In addition the growth of other effective international currency instruments, such as the Eurodollar, had raised problems of international monetary control, although the exchange system was still tied to the dollar and indirectly to gold, as in the Bretton Woods system. In 1971 the US responded to these problems by effectively suspending fixed dollar convertibility to gold, and as a result world trade and finance moved to a system of flexible exchange rates rather than the fixed parities and regulated adjustment mechanisms that had been planned originally.

The move to flexible exchange rates could have created instability in the monetary system. The price (exchange rate) of currencies could have fluctuated rapidly in a pure market system, so the larger economies agreed to a system of coordinated managed floating. The central banks of the major economies, sometimes acting in a concerted fashion, intervened in the money markets to keep the fluctuations within constrained limits and reintroduce some stability into the international system. Two consequences follow from this change. One is the importance of cooperation between the larger economies to coordinate action on exchange rates, and this developed gradually. Secondly, this change reinforced the linkage with national politics. One of the major mechanisms for influencing exchange rates is the central bank base rate, but interest rates themselves have usually been seen as one of the major instruments of domestic economic management.

Despite these changes, much of the Bretton Woods framework remained. Bretton Woods had created two regimes – a monetary one and a trade one. Both were characterized by international decisions, norms etc. But there was a difference between the two, as the monetary regime was stronger than the trade regime. GATT was based upon multilateral negotiation and decision making and, as the Uruguay round has shown, this may not produce an agreed outcome. The monetary regime was dominated by the larger economies, and the global institutions (IMF, World Bank) could act to impose constraints on client nations through such devices as the conditionality of loans.

So the two regimes differ, and one explanation for the stability of the monetary regime suggests that this resulted from the dominance of the US economy and the transformation of this economic power into political power. This is in marked contrast to the instability of the inter-war international economy. Then the US played no role; after 1945 it did. Some would suggest that it was essentially the willingness of the US to assume a dominant role that produced both the institutions and the stability of the international economic order. This, at least in a simple form, is the theory of hegemonic stability. Hegemony here refers to the relative share of global GDP of the hegemonic nation to the rest of the world (Conybeare 1987).

In its simplest form the theory asserts that there is a clear tendency for instability in the international economic system. This instability can be avoided if the largest or dominant economy acts as a hegemon and creates and maintains or enforces a system of rules and institutions. Note that I have deliberately been a little imprecise here; there are several versions of the theory, and this outline is meant only to be a general description of it. The word 'hegemony' is derived from the Greek and means leadership or predominance. So the hegemon is the predominant system actor providing leadership. In this form the theory can be seen as a variant of the concept of an international regime, but the theory of hegemonic stability goes further than the suggestion of regime existence: within the regime there is a dominant actor who stabilizes the system.

In the post-1945 global economy the hegemonic actor, the dominant economy, was initially the United States.The US had played a key role in establishing the institutions of the post-war economic order – the IMF, the World Bank and GATT. The US economy played a central role in the operation of the Bretton Woods system because the dollar – linked to gold – acted as *numéraire* in the system of fixed exchange rates, as well as being a major source of international liquidity. And the US was in a political position to achieve its aims in relation to the nature of the post-war order because of its dominant economic position; its Allies and partners had been weakened and exhausted economically by the effects of the Second World War.

One can see the role of the US in creating the post-war IEO, but how was such an order governed subsequently? In part this was through international institutions, but the theory of hegemonic stability stresses the role of the US in dominating the system or, put another way, the dependence of the global economy upon the US economy. So the maintenance of order in the system is derived from the actions of the US both in economic and in political terms. We have seen that the global economy has changed over time; how does the theory of hegemonic stability account for this? One answer is that the system gradually adapts. But one could ask a more fundamental question: once it is established, does the system need a hegemon? In an interdependent system of states, do you need one state to act as a guarantor of the system?

Again a variety of answers have been given to this question. One is political. In 1945 the US was able to impose its view of the world. The later actions of the US provided ideological and moral leadership in a divided world. But a second argument is more general. The United States wished to create a stable international monetary and trading system, but the existence of such a regime provides a public good for the world community (if we define a public good as one which is available collectively and from whose consumption no individual can be excluded, even if he has not contributed to its provision). All countries would share in the benefits of stability and none could effectively be excluded from them. However, there is no way of allocating the cost of organizing and operating such a system, so the theory suggests that such public goods tend to be chronically underprovided. In addition, there are incentives for individual countries not to contribute to the cost of maintaining the system since they can opt out and still enjoy the benefits – the so-called free-rider problem. The role of the hegemon is first to create the system that provides the public good, and then to allocate and impose costs on the (reluctant) beneficiaries and to police the system. It is generally assumed that the hegemon bears a large share of the costs of the system when necessary. So the public goods argument for the theory of hegemonic stability is that the US created and maintained a stable institutional and monetary regime which would not otherwise have come into existence or survived. The US was committed to a stable system of free trade and it used its dominant position to realize this commitment.

The key idea of the theory is that order within a multistate system, in this case economic order, depends upon the existence of a dominant state. So international economic stability since say 1950 has been dependent upon US economic dominance within the IEO. But can economic power alone explain systemic order? Is the relationship between economic power and other forms of power either as simple or as unidirectional as a straightforward reading of the theory of hegemonic stability might imply?

Over the last 20 years the dominance of the US within the world economy has declined (although there are problems about the dimensions of dominance), but many of the institutions of the IEO have survived and the US remains committed both to such institutions and to multilateralism and trade liberalism. The dollar has retained its role as the principal international currency for the funding and settlement of transactions, and this has helped to keep the US at the centre of both monetary and trade regimes. But the world has changed too, with the emergence of Western Europe

– particularly West Germany – and Japan as major economic powers. The new distribution of economic power is illustrated by Keohane (1984), who comments: 'The distribution of world trade power is no longer hegemonic in any sense; unlike the situation in money (and oil) Europe has at least as much potential bargaining power in trade as the United States does' (p. 211). The fact that Germany and Japan do not use this power overtly for political purposes during much of the period up to the mid 1980s should raise further questions about the relationship of economic to political power within the present global system.

However, Europe is not a unified actor and has its own internal problems of policy coordination, although this may be changing in both the monetary and the trade fields. The internal market will operate after 1992 and there are also moves towards a single currency and the formation of a European central bank independent of political control. Other recent changes in economic and non-economic relations within the global system have raised further problems. The European response to the change in political regimes in Eastern Europe has been both bilateral and multilateral; it has involved the creation of new institutions such as the European Bank for Reconstruction and Development. The reunification of Germany has both short-term and long-term implications for the position of Germany within the economic system. Finally, one effect of the Gulf crisis of 1990–1 has been to reassert the *political-military* role of the US within the global system despite its continuing relative economic decline.

How will the existing IEO change as the decline in the position and leading role of the US continues? Underpinning the institutions of world trade and finance are certain sets of ideas: the US is still committed to multilateralism, to free trade, to an open world. But can this 'embedded liberalism' (Ruggie 1982) survive when US hegemony does not exist or is implicit rather than explicit? To put this question in context one should remember that the development of a truly global economy is a fairly recent phenomenon. Since the mid nineteenth century there have been only two dominant or hegemonic economies: Britain, which was still the world's leading trading nation in 1938, and the United States (see table 9.5). But share of world trade is only one measure of the economic performance of a particular system, and so only one dimension of hegemony. (For a further discussion of this point see below.) The relation between

Table 9.5 *Britain and the US as hegemons: share of world trade (per cent)*

Britain 1870	24.0
Britain 1890	18.5
Britain 1913	14.1
Britain 1938	14.0
United States 1950	18.4
United States 1960	15.3
United States 1970	14.4
United States 1980	13.4

There are differences and similarities between this table and table 9.4; they are drawn from slightly different data sources.
Source: Keohane (1984, p. 36)

economic performance and political hegemony for both these nations can be neatly summarized as in figure 9.1. One dimension shows economic growth from terrible to extraordinary; the other shows political hegemony from none to strong. In the period 1853–73 Britain was at the zenith of its global power; its economy was still growing fast and it had strong political influence. Since this period Britain's economic performance has declined both relatively and absolutely, and at the same time its global political role has diminished. Note how this schematic analysis links with much else that has been said. The US did not use its economic predominance in the inter-war period and so the system was unstable and non-hegemonic. Britain may still have been the leading trading nation in 1938 (table 9.5) but it was no longer in a strong enough position to be able to stabilize the world monetary or trade systems. But note too what figure 9.1 does *not* say. Both the Pax Britannica and the Pax Americana are dated from the time of their undoubted existence; there is no indication of how each of these systems was created, although for the Pax Americana the post-war Bretton Woods system has been extensively discussed.

Such an analysis assumes that extraordinary economic growth, and therefore presumably relative economic hegemony or even absolute economic dominance in the global system, translates into strong political hegemony. But there is no indication of how the one is transformed into the other.

The decline of Britain's hegemony was followed by regime collapse, but in the present IEO the existing trade and money regimes may be both relatively independent of each other and relatively self-perpetuating. Could such regimes continue to exist in a global economy without a single hegemonic power? Or in a system with two or three relatively large countries or trading blocks such as the US, Europe and Japan? Self-consciousness of decline in the US may have brought a growth of protectionist sentiment and economic nationalism together with a questioning of some of the basic regime assumptions, as in some recent reactions to Japanese investment. Where the

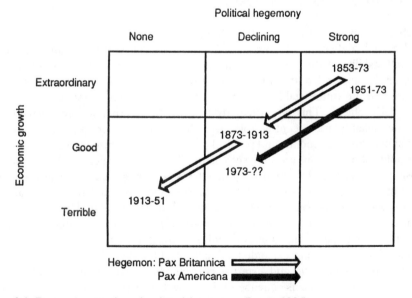

Figure 9.1 Economic growth and political hegemony (Lewis 1984)

two regimes dominated by the UK and the US differ significantly is in terms of the structure of international institutions within which they operated, and in this later period the overall growth and structure of the global economy.

The recession of the late 1970s coincided with the emergence of two other issues in the global economy: the rise of newly industrialized countries (NICs) such as Taiwan, Singapore and South Korea, and the problem of the US trade deficit. To some extent the problems of the countries outside the core of Western industrialized countries have been separated and discussed within other institutionalized frameworks such as the North–South dialogue. New problems have emerged: the changing relationship between East and West, the drive to integrate some of the countries from Comecon into the wider European economy, together with the wish to help the USSR modernize and transform its economy too. But the debt problem remains central to the future of the established IEO as the US dollar still plays a key role in both trade and monetary regimes.

Although the US may have declined in relative economic terms, the dollar has retained its global role. As a result of this and its continuing broad commitment to trade liberalism and through its military and defence commitments – which if anything have now expanded as the old bipolar alliance system has decayed – the US has become a major debtor nation, and this imposes structural strains on the global economy. Attempts to solve the problem have internal consequences for US politics, as well as for the global system. It raises fundamental questions about the relationship between economics and politics, the overall limits of system stability, and indeed the nature of hegemonic dominance. So the position of the US economy in the late 1980s, the problems of the trade debt and the future of the international financial regime all have implications for economic power and for political and strategic power as well.

THE US DEBT CRISIS AND THE FUTURE GOVERNANCE OF THE INTERNATIONAL ECONOMIC ORDER

The US economy is central to the IEO despite its relative decline. However, the scale of the US trade deficit and the nature of its external debt have raised questions about the overall stability of the IEO. Keohane, amongst others, has emphasized that much of the overall framework of the IEO remains from the period of unchallenged American hegemony. So the future stability of the international economic system is not just an institutional problem. This is particularly true of the international monetary system where the dollar plays a central role. But this raises further questions about the relationship between economic and political power: economic resources may be necessary for political power, but are they sufficient? (Refer back to figure 9.1 and the brief discussion of change in hegemonic regimes for some initial discussion of this point.) The counter-examples of Japan and West Germany are relevant here; both are now major *economic* powers, but this is not reflected in their *political* influence in the international system. The Gulf crisis of 1990–1 has re-emphasized this problem and has clearly demonstrated the domestic political constraints that affect the ability of both countries to assume any expanded military role. Obviously the post-war settlement, together with the domestic and external perceptions of their international role, are important here. But one consequence of the growth and success of the EC is that it does allow some political expression of German economic power. Japan has the additional problem that there is a constitutional limitation on military expenditure, and this may limit its ability to transform economic power into political power. But such analysis assumes that political power has a military/defence dimension; if it does, is the reverse true for a declining power such as the UK?

In discussing the relationship between economic and political power, most attention has been paid to *nation-state* actors. State cooperation may be important in stabilizing the global economy, but there are other systemic actors such as multinational companies. According to Holland (1987) the 200 largest multinationals account for almost a third of world GDP. Over 80 per cent of these companies are based in five large economies: the United States, West Germany, France, Britain and Japan. (Note the threefold division into the US, Japan and Western Europe.) MNCs certainly contribute to the stability of the international economic system; they certainly benefit from it too in terms of open multilateral trading, the availability of an international financial system and so on. But do they contribute to political stability? It is easy to assume that such developments as the spreading availability of Coca-Cola may further US political aims, but firms and states may have conflicting aims. In the case of MNCs there is no simple connection between economic power (some) and political power (notionally non-existent). Finally, it is notable too that Japan has been extending its economic position through globalization in some sectors of activity, e.g. the acquisition by Sony of CBS, and there have been parallel developments by German corporations too.

An important element of US economic dominance derived from the performance of its manufacturing base and its ability to gain and maintain a large segment of world trade. Industry and exports have continued to grow but in recent years they have been overtaken by imports, giving the US a negative trade balance. The recent position on the US deficit is shown in table 9.6. It has been suggested that in the post-1945 period US political power and economic power were interdependent and were reinforced by a US trade surplus and economic growth for much of this period. What are the political and economic implications of the reverse situation: weak economic growth, a declining share of world trade, an overall negative trade balance and a dependence on overseas finance to fund a continuing government deficit? Does this mark a new phase in the relative decline of US economic power within the IEO? The decline itself is not new,

Table 9.6 The US trade balance (current US$ billion)

	Total			Manufactured goods		
	US exports	US imports	Net imports	US exports	US imports	Net exports
1976	114.7	124.1	−9.3	67.3	64.6	2.7
1977	120.8	151.7	−30.9	69.6	76.9	−7.3
1978	142.0	175.8	−33.8	81.9	100.1	−18.2
1979	184.5	211.8	−27.3	99.4	110.9	−11.6
1980	224.2	249.6	−25.3	123.2	122.4	0.8
1981	237.0	256.1	−28.1	133.1	139.1	−6.0
1982	211.2	247.6	−36.4	119.8	140.3	−20.6
1983	200.7	262.8	−62.1	112.7	159.3	−46.6
1984	220.3	328.6	−108.3	121.4	217.9	−96.5

Source: Gilpin (1987b)

but for much of the period – say since 1971 – it has not been accompanied by any parallel adjustment in US political power.

The outline of the IEO originated with negotiations between Britain and the United States before the end of the war. These negotiations did not initially foresee a world divided politically. The post-war East–West division led to the formation of the Western alliance based on an extended US military presence. So if the US is both central to the global economy and linked to the political-military structure of the Western alliance, then any major change either in the position of the US economy or in the internal priorities of US economic policy makers could have major effects at all levels – economic, political, military. The fundamental problems are *structural*; the crisis is one with long-term implications for the future of the IEO and the linkage between US economic power and the other global dimensions of this power. Note too that the short-term increase in US military power may actually exacerbate the situation, as it draws US domestic attention to the existing imbalance between military power and economic power by focusing on the contributions made by others to what is seen as essentially joint expenditure.

Commentators such as Gilpin (1987a) suggest that changes in the position of the US economy, particularly in response to the current debt problem, not only affect what he calls the 'American system' but are also linked to, and in part caused by, the extended US defence role. Gilpin describes the global economy in familiar geographic sectoral terms – the United States, Western Europe and Japan – and spells out the consequences of relative decline. First there is a shift of the US from a creditor to a debtor nation. After World War II the US was the major source of international liquidity; now the US budget deficit and the inflow of capital necessary to finance it threaten the stability of the IEO as modified since Bretton Woods. The budget deficit and the trade deficit are linked to falling US economic growth and the declining relative productivity of the American economy.

But, secondly, US domestic politics is linked to the world economy in a complex way. The linkages are partially macroeconomic through trade, but also indirectly from influence on the world economy. Despite current problems the US is still the most important economy in the IEO and the dollar is still the major medium of international finance. In the short term the other major Western economies, particularly West Germany and Japan, have an interest in financing the US deficit. The provision of Japanese capital derives from the continuing need for Japan to maintain economic growth. However, as was suggested earlier, some of the problems are clearly military and are caused by the extended defence role of the United States. This defence role may be made more acceptable by greater burden sharing, but will certainly be questioned more in the medium to long term.

Thirdly, and more fundamentally for the continuing existence of the IEO, Gilpin suggests that economic realities will bring an adjustment of the US political position and changes in the basis of the existing order. He suggests that there will be a retreat from multilateralism, in effect a reduced commitment to the tenets of economic liberalism and free trade, and a limited growth of protectionism and economic nationalism. He suggests too that the future success of GATT will be limited and that existing trading blocks (the EEC, Japan) are not committed to further liberalization. This analysis has been partially confirmed by the breakdown in the most recent GATT negotiations. The implication is that there is a limit to the globalization of the world economy and that the present system may develop into a series of linked regional economies with only limited integration between them.

Such analysis draws attention to the crucial importance of economic ideology and the domestic political-economic imperatives in the United States. A commitment by the US to free trade may have been important in establishing the IEO; it may have been domestically affordable when the US was the dominant economy. But as dominance declines and global competition increases, the US relative economic position will continue to be eroded. At some point domestic interests may force the US to reconsider its underlying commitment to an open economic order which, with some modifications, has been the basis of its international economic commitments since 1945.

These economic realities are linked not just to a possible adjustment of political position but also to the structure of defence alliances in which the US is engaged, and to military technology too: 'The nuclear, conventional, and political realms are intimately linked; they must not be separated' (Gilpin 1987a, p. 59). The question to ask is *how* these factors are linked to economic power. One might question the relative autonomy of both economic and political power, or the nature of the relationship between the two. Does political power derive in a direct way from economic power during a period of economic hegemony? Does this relationship still hold during a period of hegemonic decline, or in this situation does economic power (perhaps) derive in some part from political power?

The answers given to these questions will help in assessing the strategies that the US could adopt to reduce the costs of its defence commitments – and to recover from the constraints of the debt crisis. One option is to decrease reliance on nuclear weapons. Another is to transfer some defence costs on to other partners in the Western alliance, such as Germany or Japan. But the ability or willingness of these countries to carry such costs is limited.These two countries face severe international and domestic constraints on their ability to carry increased defence costs. In the case of Japan, one major domestic constraint derives from the post-war constitution and the limitation this placed on future military activity. In Germany there is internal questioning of increased military expenditure and defence commitments from new political forces such as the Greens. Any internationally perceived recurrence of militaristic nationalism would have political consequences for both countries. In both states too such limitations, whether willingly accepted or not, have been brought out by attempts to contribute to the international military action against Iraq in 1990–1. This suggests that there are limits to the extent that political power may derive from economic power, and particularly indicates the complex role of military or strategic power in this equation.

The problem for the United States is that, if nothing is done, a continuing deficit could seriously weaken its position within the global economy, and this would have political and military consequences. But to act to protect its economic position would also have political consequences and could damage the very economic position that such actions are designed to protect. Any action may bring a change in the US position – and have an effect upon the structure and stability of the IEO. What has changed is the nature of the military commitments that US policy makers may wish to preserve. The new, and fragile, relationship between the US and the USSR, and particularly the Soviet withdrawal in Eastern Europe, may allow for some reduction in US defence expenditure. While this may bring a decrease in US expenditure in Europe, it may help to increase US expenditure in other areas.

CONCLUSION

The global economy since 1945 can be characterized both as dynamic, with changes in structure over time, and as divided between the Western industrialized countries and other economies. Patterns of growth and change, and in particular the changing position of the United States, the dominant economy for much of the period, have also been discussed. Rather less was said about the *divisions* within the global system – between the industrialized core and the periphery of LDCs – and less still about the relative isolation of the centrally planned economies for much of this period. Beyond this, the internal divisions of the capitalist core (weak and strong economies) and geographic divisions into regional groupings were also mentioned. Finally, some attention was paid to the role of international agencies and agreements – the IMF, the World Bank, GATT and the EC. The point to be considered is the primacy of purely economic factors in creating, maintaining or changing this overall structure, or in determining the actions of states and institutions within it. Can we explain the global economy by purely internal economic factors? Surely the answer is no; there are political factors which helped both to establish and to maintain the new IEO after 1945. It was underpinned at first by a generalized ideological belief in the virtue of free trade on the part of the US. And at the time the US was broadly in a position to play a decisive role in the institutions that were established as part of this new economic system.

This links to a second problem: the governance of the global economy. Again we have examined some evidence on the IEO both direct and indirect, as in the theory of hegemonic stability. We can divide the post-war period into phases: up to the early 1950s, reconstruction; 1950–70, relative growth and stability in the IEO under US hegemony and the regular operation of the Bretton Woods agencies (IMF, IBRD); after 1970, declining American hegemony and uncertainty over global economic management. We might perhaps now add a fourth phase from 1990, in which there are a number of equally strong economic groups within the same framework of international institutions and in which the former centrally planned economies become linked to the capitalist core to a greater extent. But even after 1970 there is still a structure and a pattern of management within the IEO. It is still dominated by a small group of large economies which meet regularly at economic summits to coordinate the system. There is a difference between the financial regime and the trade regime. In the former the large economies continue to dominate system management. However, the key institution in the trade regime, GATT, is multilateral and involves bargaining between a larger number of actors. Partly as a result of this it cannot be dominated by the larger economies to the same extent.

But the global economy both shapes and is shaped by domestic and international politics. There is a link between the international economic order and the imperatives of domestic politics. In many Western capitalist societies, global economic management in the post-war period was predicated on the development and maintenance of a domestic welfare state; in addition the management of the US domestic economy became linked to the monetary regime of the IEO. For much of the period after 1945 the overall pattern has been one of US hegemony within an explicit framework of rules. This is in marked contrast to the period of British hegemony in the global economy before 1914, and the inter-war period of economic nationalism. What overall global pattern may emerge from the decline of US hegemony? Is the IEO entering a fourth phase as suggested earlier?

We can speculate on some of the possible futures for the global system by locating previous and current systems in a two-dimensional grid, defined by the presence or absence of global economic institutions and norms on one axis and the existence or non-existence of a hegemonic power within the system on the other, as in figure 9.2. This figure has much in common with figure 9.1. The path of the global economy over time is shown as the open arrows from system A to system B to system C. How might the system develop in the future? There are a number of possible alternative futures which are indicated by the numbered solid arrows in figure 9.2. In possibilities 1 and 2 there would be a breakdown of the existing IEO institutions, with the US remaining a hegemonic economy (case 2) or becoming a non-hegemonic economy within the subsequent system (case 1). Alternatively (case 3) the system could evolve into one which retains a framework of rules/norms/institutions – that is, it would still be a regime in the normal sense of the word – but without a single hegemonic power. In this case there might be a plurality of large economies or regional blocks. Or finally (case 4) one single system could replace the US within the existing framework; the suggestions put forward are Europe or Japan.

What has not been done is to question the overall framework of hegemonic stability theory itself, particularly as a way of understanding the future dynamics of the IEO. The previous brief discussion of hegemonic stability theory was in terms of both the theory of public goods and a definition that stressed the moral and ideological basis of hegemony. I also asked whether the global system needed a hegemon. The argument put forward by Keohane (1984) and Gilpin (1987b), amongst others, is that the dominant position of the United States is now declining, and both authors try to draw out the implications of this for the global economy. Keohane discusses trade, monetary

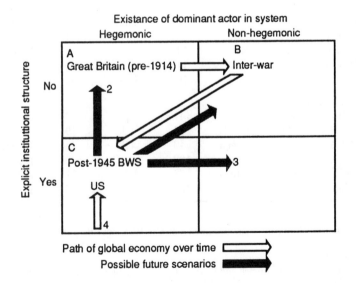

Figure 9.2 The future of the international economic order?

and other regimes. Gilpin considers the consequences of US trade and debt problems and their linkage to other issue areas. But we need to look at the concept of hegemonic stability in more detail too.

What do we mean by dominance in the global system, and how might it be measured? Much of the previous discussion has been in terms of trade and finance. (British hegemony in the late nineteenth century was defined essentially in terms of share of world trade.) The US share of world trade may have declined, but the implications that can be drawn from this are not obvious, because the decline in trade may tell us little about changes in the US economy in general. To say more we need to know the importance of foreign trade within the US economy. But aside from share of world trade, Russett (1985) has suggested that there are several other dimensions of hegemonic power which we could use. Table 9.7 (which is taken from his analysis) gives a historical dimension to three of these: GNP, military expenditure and manufacturing production. The four largest or most important systems on each of these dimensions are

Table 9.7 Four leading powers indexed to hegemon,[a] 1830–1983

Year	Largest		2nd largest		3rd largest		4th largest	
Gross national product								
1983	*USA*	100	USSR	41	Japan	35	W. Germany	20
1950	*USA*	100	USSR	29	UK	19	France	13
1938	USA	100	Germany	37	USSR	37	UK	27
1913	USA	306	Russia	123	Germany	113	*UK*	100
1870	USA	117	Russia	117	*UK*	100	France	86
1830	Russia	132	France	105	*UK*	100	A-H	87
Military expenditure								
1983	*USA*	100	USSR	100	China	19	UK	16
1950	USSR	106	*USA*	100	China	18	UK	16
1938[b]	Germany	657	USSR	481	UK	161	Japan	154
1913	German	129	Russia	125	*UK*	100	France	99
1872[c]	Russia	127	France	119	*UK*	100	Germany	68
1830	France	148	*UK*	100	Russia	92	A-H	54
Manufacturing production								
1980	*USA*	100	USSR	47	Japan	29	W. Germany	17
1953	*USA*	100	USSR	24	UK	19	W. Germany	13
1938	USA	100	Germany	40	UK	34	USSR	29
1913	USA	235	Germany	109	*UK*	100	Russia	26
1870	*UK*	100	China	75	USA	51	France	37
1830	China	319	India	185	*UK*	100	Russia	59

A-H   Austria-Hungary
[a] 'Hegemon' at the time is in italic; there was no hegemon in 1938, but I have arbitrarily used the US values as the base.
[b] USA ranked fifth.
[c] 1872 data used, as figures for French and German (Prussian) military spending were inflated in 1870 and 1871 by the Franco-Prussian War.
Source: Russett (1985)

indexed in relation to the chosen hegemon, so the table gives a different interpretation of dominance in the international system from the one derived from a consideration of foreign trade only.

On all three dimensions the United States continues to dominate the international system (with the exception of military expenditure in 1983). It also continues to have a considerable advantage over its nearest competitor in terms of GNP and manufacturing production. This should suggest a cautious approach to any idea of hegemonic decline. The table also brings out an interesting point about the other suggested hegemon in the modern international system – the United Kingdom in the late nineteenth century. Its power base was much more fragile than that of the United States after 1945 and was not based on any of Russett's three dimensions; foreign trade was more important to the British economy in the nineteenth century than it is to the economy of the United States today. If Britain did exercise hegemony it was perhaps based on political skills as much as on economic or military power (see Kennedy 1987).

Strange (1987) makes a related critical point about the theory of hegemonic stability. She suggests that structural power in the global system has four elements: security/defence; economic production; finance and credit; and production of knowledge and culture. In all four areas the United States is still pre-eminent. So if US hegemony appears to have declined, if the global system appears to lack leadership or governance, this may be because the United States is either unwilling or unable to provide it. We need not discuss the reasons for this (they could be related to US domestic politics), but this analysis is in agreement with the earlier criticism of hegemonic stability theory.

Perhaps the hegemon provides free trade for the international economy as a public good. But the economic theory of international trade suggests that a dominant economy will maximize its trading advantage and national revenue by imposing tariffs on small states. In such a situation, the small states are harmed more by tariff retaliation – exports are more important to them than to the hegemon – and so a rational hegemon should not favour free trade. One commentator concludes that the theory 'in its basic form is simply analytically wrong; free trade is not a public good' (Conybeare 1987, p. 72). If this is the case, then it may be that the hegemon aims to provide peace or stability for the international system, but it can be shown that these are not public goods either!

There are two implications of these criticisms. First, the concern with the decline of the United States in the global economy may be exaggerated. In the early 1990s it was still the dominant world economy. When it wishes it can still provide leadership and exercise hegemonic power. It could be argued that in the Gulf crisis of 1991 the US did indeed do just that: affirm certain moral and/or ideological values. The problem is the limited global acceptance of such values. The governance of the global economy is still largely dependent upon the United States. But, secondly, within the existing parameters, any future IEO will be a product of political power as much as of economic power, and a result of the interaction of both domestic and international factors. Such conclusions are at the heart of the neo-realist analysis of the global economy (such as by Keohane and Gilpin). These analyses suggest that the workings of the system result from self-interested actors operating under uncertainty within a set of broadly structural constraints – and as such this also sets limits to the degree of change in the current IEO that can occur in the short run.

196   Jeremy Mitchell

References

Bessel, R. (1989) The international economy in crisis: the inter-war years. Paper 14, *D312 Global Politics*, Milton Keynes: Open University.

Conybeare, J. (1987) *Trade Wars*. New York: Columbia University Press.

Gardner, R.N. (1980) *Sterling–Dollar Diplomacy in Current Perspective: the Origins and the Prospects of Our International Economic Order*. New York: Columbia University Press.

Gilpin, R. (1987a) American policy in the post-Reagan era. *Daedalus*, 116(3), 33–67.

Gilpin, R. (1987b) *The Political Economy of International Relations*. Princeton: Princeton University Press.

Gordon, D. (1988) The global economy: new edifice or crumbling foundations. *New Left Review*, 168, 24–64.

Holland, S. (1987) *The Global Economy*. London: Weidenfeld and Nicolson.

Kennedy, P. (1987) *The Rise and Fall of the Great Powers*. New York: Random House.

Keohane, R.O. (1984) *After Hegemony: Cooperation and Discord in the World Political Economy*. Princeton: Princeton University Press.

Lewis, W.A. (1984) *The Rate of Growth of the World Economy*. Taipei: Institute of Economics, Academia Sinica.

Ruggie, J.E. (1982) International regimes, transactions and change: embedded liberalism in the postwar economic order. *International Organization*, 36(2), 379–415.

Russett, B. (1985) The mysterious case of vanishing hegemony; or, is Mark Twain really dead? *International Organization* 39(2), 207–31.

Scammell, W.M. (1983) *The International Economy since 1945* (2nd edn). London and Basingstoke: Macmillan.

Strange, S. (1987) The persistent myth of lost hegemony. *International Organization*, 41(4), 551–74.

10

Economic Autonomy and the Advanced Industrial State

GRAHAME THOMPSON

Introduction

The issue of economic autonomy for the advanced industrialized economies discussed in this chapter centres around whether they can continue to manage their national economies effectively under the contemporary conditions of a globalizing economy. The question is discussed in relation to two different cases. These examples are designed to illustrate a set of problems that confront the analysis of international economic relations in the present era, and that are of vital importance to policy makers.

The main example concerns the United Kingdom economy and particularly its relationship to Europe. The growing interdependence of Europe, heralded by the completion of the single market in 1992 and the proposed moves towards monetary and possibly complete economic union thereafter, has served to raise afresh and in an acute manner the issue of the continued autonomy and sovereignty of the UK economy. Autonomy and sovereignty are not to be confused. Autonomy refers to the ability of a state to independently direct its economic policy, while sovereignty refers to the purely legal control a state has over a definite territory. Thus it is quite possible for a sovereign state to lose its autonomy while it maintains its sovereignty.

But increasingly these two aspects, involving economic relations in particular, are tending to become enmeshed with one another. The moves towards a globalizing economy imply a rapid growth in integration as well as of interdependency, and it is the possible implications of this growing integration and the forces that lie behind it which are focused upon here. In the case of Europe the UK has voluntarily entered a supranational organization which is increasingly taking responsibility for the political regulation of the economic affairs of its member countries. The original customs union character of the European Community (EC) has progressively given way to an institutional complex that now controls exchange rates (the European Monetary System, EMS), that has a separate budget, that will supervise the progressive integration of labour and capital markets and that could herald full monetary and economic union in the future.

Secondly, and in contrast to this, we look at the case of Canada, which in 1989 concluded a comprehensive free-trade agreement (FTA) with the United States of America. In this case those opposed to the agreement in Canada argued it would undermine Canada's wider economic and political sovereignty even though, ostensibly at least, it only explicitly dealt with trade matters. The Canada–US FTA is neither a customs union nor a supranational organization like the EC, though similar concerns arose with its possible consequences as with the case of the UK's relationship to the evolving EC programme.

These two cases are designed to raise some general problems and point to trends that typify the overall characterization of contemporary international economic relationships involving the advanced industrial countries. But before we move on to the detailed examination of each in turn it will be useful to outline the general framework in which the two examples will be discussed in the rest of this chapter.

Theoretical Issues: Autonomy versus Interdependence

The distinctive feature of an international economy in which individual nation-states continue to exist and operate is the contrast it throws up between their autonomy and their interdependence. On the one hand individual countries struggle for and enjoy an *autonomy* in the conduct of their economic policies, while on the other they are progressively drawn into patterns of *interdependence* by virtue of the interactions between them. From a historical point of view it will be useful to introduce a distinction between various stages in the evolution of the endemic, almost dialectical, relationship between national autonomy and economic interdependence. This will help clarify the particular stage in which the global order finds itself under present conditions and the problem this poses for policy makers.

The early origin of international economic relations can be traced to the emergence of so-called long-distance trade between the societies of pre-history. This enduring system of exchange continues in many parts of the world even today, if in a modified form. Comprising mainly the exchange of luxury and utility goods that typify craft production, this kind of trade represents the precursor of the more organized trade between genuine nation-states that began in earnest in the fourteenth and fifteenth centuries. Thus the features of such a pre-fourteenth-century *internationalized economy* involved occasional economic interactions, conducted on an essentially bilateral basis, between economies whose main business was still heavily oriented to the domestic sector and where the international activity only involved a very small section of the population and fraction of its economic output. For these reasons the societies involved remained highly autonomous in their international economic relations.

Around the fourteenth century, however, a different stage in international economic relations began to emerge. This eventually matured into what might be termed a *world-wide economy*. Such an economy was typified by a series of more systematic international interactions between economies, with a pattern of enduring trade and investment relations emerging that focused attention at the world level. A division of labour between the different economies arose under these circumstances, some tending to produce raw materials and agricultural products, say, while others specialized in the production of manufactured goods. In addition, as such a system matured, financial relationships progressively displaced trading relationships from the centre stage of economic interactions and the sources of investment became the predominant poles around which the system moved.

What would particularly mark this idea of a world-wide economy would be the gradual drawing together of an increasing number of countries into a set of enduring multilateral international economic relationships, involving the division of labour at the world level as just outlined. Under these circumstances, systematic interdependence between the different national economies and different types of economic agent arises, creating a new problem of coordination between them.

This period of history also saw the development of what subsequently came to be known as the multinational corporation (MNC). The distinctive feature of these organizational units is that, while they operate in a number of different countries, they continue to have a clear home base in one particular country. The home-base country serves as the organizing centre for an MNC's operations, and it is normally required to meet the regulatory obligations set by the government in the home-base country.

Perhaps we can now discern a further stage in this evolution of international economic relations, very much typifying certain tendencies observed in the contemporary world. This might be termed a *globalizing economy* to indicate its difference from the world-wide economy just outlined. To a large extent such a globalizing economy implies the dissolution of the features of the world-wide economy as at the same time it transforms them.

If the world-wide economy is an economy characterized by a *widening* of the range of countries and other agents involved in international economic relations, then the globalizing economy could be characterized by a *deepening* of these interactions. The globalizing economy represents a qualitative change rather than a quantitative one. Furthermore, the focus shifts to a global economy as an all-encompassing characteristic structure which exists independently of or in addition to purely national economies. Thus the global economy would encompass an economy whose principles of operation might *supplant* those of national economies and undermine the division of labour into which they had fallen. We would then be dealing not just with a number of interacting individual national economies or economic agents – whose fundamental attachment was still towards their domestic environments despite their coincidental further involve-ment in a structured set of international economic interactions – but rather with a different entity altogether: the global economy. It is the global economy that increasingly defines and structures the individual economies that form its parts, not the other way around. With a world-wide economy we still have national economies as dominant. With the globalizing economy it is the global economy that dominates the national economies existing within it. Once again, this poses a new set of problems for continued economic autonomy.

The characteristic international economic organizational unit in this kind of an economy is no longer the MNC of the world-wide economy but rather the transnational corporation (TNC). With this organizational form the home-base aspect tends to become significantly less important. A TNC represents the epitome of global capital; its base of operation would be the global arena rather than one particular country or even a small group of countries. It would probably source and manufacture in a wide variety of locations across the globe and have a global view of its market, without being committed to any single centre of operation. The developmental planning, manufacturing and marketing processes would form an integrated and interdependent whole in the global context. In addition, it would escape any easy regulation by a national authority because of these features of its operation. Thus instead of inter-national relations being typical of cross-border economic interactions, we would now be finally in an era of transnational relations, articulating an economy that no longer conforms to a national remit.

Each of these forms of international economy thus displays its own typical character-istic combination of economic autonomy and interdependency. Important for these is the increasing role of markets in breaking down barriers to international interdepen-dency. A wide range of economic agents come into play here which cut across divisions around nation to nation relationships. This creates the potential for tension between the sovereignty of the nation-state on the one hand and the activity of private economic agents who need not respect that sovereignty on the other.

However, this is not to suggest that the three stages are necessarily mutually exclusive. Just as we could think of the world-wide economy as enfolding that of the internationalized economy without completely destroying it, so we might think of the globalizing economy as enfolding the world-wide economy in its turn. Thus features of all these forms of international economy could continue to inform the analysis of contemporary international economic relations. We can find traces of all three forms within the complex articulation of the contemporary global economy.

Thus what has grown up within the more recent transition period, as world-wide economic interactions have progressively given way to those with a more globalizing character, is a complex structure formed by relations of interdependence between nations and equivalent links between them and private economic agents. Morse (1971) suggests three main forms of this complex pattern of interdependency: strategic interde-pendency between essentially separate national units; systemic interdependency charac-terizing the system as a whole; and, finally, public-good production within the system designed to regulate it in some way.

The first case – strategic interdependency – characterizes a continued relatively autonomous set of national interdependencies which leads to billiard-ball clashes between individualized nation-states, where the policy initiatives and economic activity of one country tend to simply bounce off the economy of the other.

With the second type – systemic interdependency – national borders are more permeable, so the foreign/domestic distinction within economic policy making can break down. This leads to a heightened politicization of the domestic economic policy-making process as the number of independent policy instruments available to individual governments for economic management decrease. Thus a more relatively interde-pendent network of interdependencies emerges here.

The final form of interdependence – public-good production – raises issues of how the system is to be governed and policed via the provision of the public goods necessary for its operation. While all members of the system benefit from public-good production, not all can be forced to pay for that production. Asymmetries of power between producers and consumers of public goods and differential incentives to supply them typify this issue.

One further consequence of a growing structure of interdependence can be a breakdown in both domestic and international mechanisms of control, with no guarantee of the development of new instruments to maintain political or economic order. That is, *integration* does not necessarily automatically follow interdependence; it must be deliberately fostered by explicitly cooperative effort. The destabilization of autonomy and order that a growing interdependency can stimulate may tend to equalize the relative power of any government *vis-à-vis* others. The larger powers may thus have to give up some of their influence while smaller powers gain an added influence and authority; all this takes place in the context of the collective desire to achieve order. If this is the case, it reduces the *power of positive inducements* to cooperate by the larger, possibly hegemonic power and increases the *power of denial* on the part of smaller nations just at a time when explicit cooperative effort is needed. Here is the site of a potential conflict between the hegemonic power and others in any regime as the character of that regime moves from one of relative autonomy between its members to growing interdependence amongst them – from an internationalized or world-wide economy to a globalized one.

Many of these insights have proved useful in the analysis of the evolving international economy over the post-war years. In a preliminary way this could be characterized as a transition from the internationalized or world-wide economy of the pre-war period to the globalizing economy of today. In such a transition, the relative autonomy of country interrelationships may have given way to a growing interdependency between them of the systemic kind. This is the hypothesis we shall be exploring in the following sections of this chapter, and I return to a fuller assessment and review of it in the concluding section.

The rest of this chapter proceeds as follows. The next section describes the way the UK economy is placed in a system of international economic relations and analyses the possible consequences of this in terms of the government's ability to manage the domestic economy. This is followed by a section on the UK's relationship with the EC, which discusses the emerging debate about sovereignty as the European economy began the 1992 single-market programme and the policy of economic and monetary union. As a contrast to the EC experience, the way the Canada–US FTA is likely to affect domestic political developments in Canada is analysed in the following section. Finally, the strategic position of the US economy in a globalizing context is raised in the concluding section.

THE UNITED KINGDOM AND ITS INTERNATIONAL SETTING

The UK economy is caught in a complex web of international economic relationships. Indeed, it is one of the most open economies in the world. The City of London hosts the largest concentration of international banking businesses, with over 800 companies operating in London at the end of 1987. The liabilities of these foreign-owned banks operating in London were greater than the combined liabilities of the UK's indigenous domestic banks, something unique to an advanced industrial economy. Of the estimated $5,000 billion (approximately) in world-wide outstanding international bank loans at the end of 1989, $1,000 billion (20 per cent) was booked in the UK. The UK was the largest single international banking centre for much of the 1970s and 1980s, though it was just eclipsed by Japan in 1988 (Thompson 1990, table 15, p. 185).

The story of the 1980s as far as international banking is concerned involved the dramatic rise of Japan as an international banking centre, from 9 per cent share of international banking in 1984 to 21 per cent just four years later in 1988. Japanese banks in London alone did more international business there in 1989 than did the combined UK and US banks.

All this international activity in financial assets has partly to do with raising short-term finance for trade and providing liquidity to non-bank institutions. It also has consequences for the foreign exchange markets. In large part the financial institutions operating in London are dealing in different currencies and therefore affect the exchange rates of those currencies. The banks buy and sell currencies in the foreign exchange markets in the light of their assessment of the underlying value of those currencies and on the expectation of how other agents and the national authorities will react to changes in economic and political circumstances. These private economic agents (banks) thus anticipate what governments might do and may also affect those decisions, sometimes quite dramatically. They articulate the market sentiment on currency valuations.

As well as short-term borrowing and lending of this type, the City of London is also involved in long-term investment business. This takes the form of overseas portfolio investment and direct investment. In fact the UK became a major net overseas long-term lender in the period after its remaining exchange controls were abandoned in 1979 (Thompson 1990, table 17, p. 189). In 1988 net overseas non-bank lending of this type amounted to £110.8 million (*Bank of England Quarterly Bulletin*, November 1989, table M, p. 544). Given that the UK had a significant balance of payments deficit on its current account (over £14.5 billion in 1988, rising to £20.5 billion in 1989), and that the net overseas long-term investment amounts to a deficit on the capital account, the only way the overall balance of payments could be balanced was through a resort to short-term borrowing via the banking sector just described. In 1988 this short-term borrowing amounted to £16 billion. Thus the position in 1988 (as well as in 1989, as it turned out) was one in which the UK economy ran a large deficit on both its long-term capital account and its current account and borrowed heavily in the short-term to finance the resulting deficit.

This position largely accounted for the historically high interest rates in the UK in 1988–9. To attract the necessary short-term finance to cover the deficits, high sterling interest rates were needed. By making sterling attractive to hold in this way the government was also tending to push up the price of sterling – at least while confidence in the government's determination and ability to maintain sterling's value remained in the markets. High interest rates are thus one way of maintaining confidence in a currency.

But short-term investment is a very fickle instrument. It is sometimes referred to as hot money, moving rapidly round the globe from one financial centre to another and from one currency to another at the touch of a button, looking for the highest and most secure return. Thus if governments are forced to rely on this to finance their balance of payment deficit they are playing against a highly sophisticated but volatile market system in their attempts to stabilize the value of their currencies. Perhaps there are other, better policies? We return to this question later.

In addition to this financial activity the UK economy is involved in a set of trading relationships. Here it is its membership of the EC that is of central importance in determining the contemporary character of trade relationships. Since the UK joined the EC in 1973 (the EC itself came into existence in 1958) its trade policy has been heavily constrained by the rules, regulations, tariffs and quotas of the EC. Amongst the EC members there are no formal tariff barriers. However, the EC is also a part of the more extensive General Agreement on Tariffs and Trade (GATT) regulatory mechanism, which over the post-war period has set international trade relations within a multilateral framework.

In 1989 the UK exported goods and services to the value of 24.7 per cent of gross domestic product (GDP) and imported the same to the value of 28.5 per cent of GDP. Thus nearly a third of UK GDP is internationally traded. The proportion of this UK trade with its EC partners increased significantly from 22 per cent in 1958 to 50 per cent in 1987. The EC thus now dominates in the pattern of UK trade. Amongst the 12 EC countries, 60 per cent of their trade was intra-Community trade in 1987.

These statistics point to the firm integration of the UK economy into the EC trading system and into the globalizing economy beyond. This gives the UK an economy highly interpenetrated in international terms. The UK both originates a high proportion of international economic activity and hosts a high proportion of it. What is more, this international interpenetration seems to be growing in importance. This may imply that the UK is a relatively soft state. Shocks emanating from outside its borders may have a more dramatic impact on its domestic activity than it would elsewhere, in economies not so highly integrated with international economic mechanisms (so called billiard-ball states or hard states, where shocks bounce off more easily).This could make it more difficult for any government on the one hand to cope with exogenous shocks, and on the other to develop an independent policy response to meet purely domestic needs. Once again we are faced with what Morse (1971) characterized as an erosion of the foreign/domestic distinction within economic policy making. Systemic interdependence undermines strict economic autonomy as the range of independent policy instruments shrinks.

Moreover the UK economy has to cope not only with a range of other nations and multilateral (official) institutions in its economic dealings on the international stage, but also with a very high-profile set of private economic agents. In addition to the range of multinational banks already mentioned, the UK economy originates and is penetrated by a range of multinational manufacturing enterprises. The position as far as these were concerned in the middle 1980s has been summarized as follows:

> The leading seventy or so British manufacturing multinationals had foreign output of about £100 billion in 1983, whereas their production at home was £70 billion: they were larger abroad than at home. Their exports of roughly £13 billion were 20 per cent of the national total ... At the same time, foreign multinationals had assets with book value of £35 billion invested in Britain, managed by approximately three thousand local companies. Here too extreme concentration is evident. The top twenty-five manufacturers and oil companies had local sales of nearly £40 billion, perhaps 75 per cent of the total foreign controlled output.
>
> (Stopford and Turner 1985, p. 3)

The estimated 1,400 British parent companies with overseas investments were increasing their employment abroad and reducing their employment in the parent (domestic) branches. The trend towards foreign investment meant British multinationals increased their opportunity to switch production overseas if they wished, one they seemed to be grasping in the 1980s (see Williams et al. 1990). The most important countries as far as multinational companies are concerned, Britain and Germany, each contributed 14 per cent to the world total of such companies in the middle 1980s; thus these two countries alone accounted for nearly a third of the multinationals between them.

The UK was thus interpenetrated by a range of private organizations to a higher degree than most other comparable countries in the 1980s. In this sense the UK is faced with a plurality of players – all of which may have objectives quite different from those of governments. Clearly this is likely to increase the difficulty of independently managing the UK economy.

But whilst Britain may have been particularly subject to these trends in the last 20 years or so, they represent a feature to which almost all highly industrialized economies are having to accommodate. As outlined in the earlier section, the maturing of the world-wide economy and its transition towards a globalizing one, where some of the multinationals mentioned above are surely becoming truly transnational corporations in their operation, results in the increasing interpenetration of all the national economies. In the UK case in particular, however, this would seem to have gone well beyond Morse's strategic interdependence category and to be more an example of his systemic interdependence.

The political impact of this highly systemic form of interdependence displays a number of what are by now well-recognized features of the domestic political environment in the UK. The political profile of the City of London for instance is well known, and many have argued that this has unduly determined domestic political considerations, largely to the detriment of domestic manufacturing interests whose confidence has been undermined and which are in decline as a result (though this may not be the only reason for such a decline). A concentration on financial activity and the enduring concern with maintaining the external value of the pound represent the domestic repercussions of the City's dominant impact on economic policy making. In addition, the control of the MNCs (and even more so of the TNCs) may escape the direct purchase of UK governments, yet decisions by these agents have important domestic ramifications, in terms of employment for instance, as we have seen. What is more, the integration of the UK economy into the EC presents UK governments with the necessity to formulate cooperative policies with their Community partners. It is this last point that we take up and develop in the next section.

THE UNITED KINGDOM AND THE EUROPEAN COMMUNITY

In October 1989 the West German Bundesbank raised German interest rates by 1 per cent; two days later the Bank of England was forced to raise UK interest rates by an equal amount. This small episode, unimportant by itself perhaps, is indicative of the growing interdependence of the UK economy with its European counterparts and particularly the dominant influence of the German economy within Europe; when Germany sneezes, there is now a strong possibility that the rest of Europe could catch a cold! Thus despite the City of London's pre-eminent position within international financial flows, the UK economy is still very much at the mercy of the stronger German economy when it comes to interest rate policy. Indeed, it may be because the UK economy remains at the centre of such financial flows whilst at the same time its industrial base has been eroded that makes it particularly vulnerable to the dictates of stronger economies with a continuing robust manufacturing sector.

By all accounts the UK's relationship to Europe has been and continues to be a stormy one. After much wrangling the UK finally joined the Community in 1973, some 14 years after it had been set up. Since then it could hardly be said that the relationship has been harmonious. When the EMS was created in 1979 the UK chose to remain outside its central feature, the exchange rate mechanism (ERM), though it participated in the other elements of the EMS. A long series of battles over the Common Agriculture Policy and the Community budget more generally in the early 1980s maintained the soured relationship. As of the early 1990s, programmes of monetary and economic union continue to threaten a united European front, with the UK government taking up minority and sceptical positions on many of the issues involved.

One policy the UK embraced with some enthusiasm, however, was the 1992 single-market programme. This represents an attempt to eliminate all the remaining non-tariff barriers between the Community members, to allow the free movement of capital and labour within the Community and eventually to create a truly common market in goods and services. It is around the issues of the moves toward a *common market* on the one hand and a *financial and economic union* on the other that the rest of the discussion in this section is focused.

Common Market or Monetary Union?

It is convenient to begin with the EMS and ERM when considering the contemporary integrationist developments within the EC. These mechanisms represent the first joint venture that had major institutional implications for the way the members conduct their economic management. The EMS arose in a period of disillusionment with the floating exchange rate regime that had been established after the demise of the Bretton Woods system in 1972–3. Floating rates were supposed to have given economies the chance of uncoupling their domestic monetary policies from the policy pursued (or economic outcome arising) in the USA. It was supposed to have increased the economic autonomy of individual governments in the conduct of their monetary policy, particularly in the context of their attempts to control domestic inflation rates (and thus the aggregate global inflation rate).

However, events never quite worked out like this in practice. The period of totally floating rates produced substantial and highly disruptive fluctuations in exchange rates, with significant over shooting of the nominal exchange rates in relation to real exchange rates (nominal exchange rates adjusted for domestic inflation) and equilibrium or fundamental exchange rates (the exchange rate commensurate with economic variables thought to underlie the real competitive conditions of any economy). A thoroughly disruptive international economic system thus emerged, fuelled by the deregulation and integration of international capital and money markets. Although inflationary pressures considerably eased in the late 1970s and early 1980s, this was thought to be more the consequence of the world-wide depression of that period than a result of the new floating rate regime.

It was as a reaction against the floating rate regime just described that the EMS was set up. This was to provide a system of stability within the EC, particularly with respect to the US dollar, so that further steps towards genuine integration of the European economies could begin. The currencies within the system were to be aligned within narrow bands against each other, with assistance given to prevent exchange rate realignments (though these are not ruled out and indeed have happened within the EMS on occasions).

The reasons put forward for sterling's failure to join the ERM in 1979 were partly economic and partly political. Originally, it was thought the international role of sterling – particularly its newly acquired petrocurrency status – and the City of London would suffer if the pound were tied into a closely banded system. This was related to the fear that UK domestic economic policy might become increasingly dominated by the stronger mainland economies, particularly the German economy, if the UK joined. In fact, the EMS has turned out to be very much a Deutschmark currency system in practice. Additionally, this was tied to the UK's deep ambiguity towards Europe and its strong continued commitment to the Atlanticist association with the US. This is an ambiguity ingrained deeply in the British political psyche, which has yet to be fully resolved.

The EMS provides a form of public good to the member countries involved – Morse's third type of interdependency mentioned above. In fact, this is exactly what the Bretton Woods system tried to do for a wider range of countries, and in that it led to exchange rate stability it fulfilled this task. But in that case, those critical of its other implications would charge it with providing the 'public bad' of inflation instead of an overall public good of economic stability and welfare gain. One problem confronting any interpretion of the EMS is to assess whether it has led to the public good of greater economic stability than would have emerged had the European exchange rates been allowed to float against each other; another is how to judge the overall inflationary consequences of the EMS. The British government in particular was highly suspicious of the extension of the EMS to an absolutely fixed exchange rate regime, as proposed by the Delors Committee (Committee for the Study of Economic and Monetary Union 1989), seeing it as inevitably leading to inflation.

Crucial to this assessment is the role of the German authorities since, in effect, it is they who are charged with policing the EMS system in terms of inflation and thus with securing its public-good characteristics. Some have argued that in the period of the late 1980s the UK was free-riding on the ERM and German leadership. The UK tried to shadow the Deutschmark in 1988 and in 1989 for a while, hoping to gain the deflationary advantages of this while at the same time not becoming a full member of the system and thereby not having to bear any of the political and economic costs of full membership either. The inflation rates of the mainland European Community economies had moved closer into line during the late 1980s, tending towards the lower German rate, while the UK inflation rate continued to fluctuate and remain at a much higher level. This implied a loss of competitiveness on the part of the UK in relation to its European partners. The traditional way the UK economy had adjusted to becoming internationally uncompetitive in these circumstances was to devalue its currency. By trying to fix the pound at the rate of DM3 the UK government hoped to break out of this currency devaluation cycle. Without the option of a depreciating currency the only way UK companies could remain competitive would be for them to become more efficient, resist excessive wage claims and so on. Shadowing the Deutschmark would thus put the downward pressure on the UK inflation rate that was needed. This discipline would result without the UK authorities having to pursue any other policies than maintaining the exchange rate against the Deutschmark.

In fact this policy failed as UK domestic circumstances (the consumer boom of the late 1980s) called for higher interest rates to head off a full-blown credit-led inflationary upsurge and to help finance the growing imbalance on the international payment accounts. But this episode is indicative of the way policy might be conducted when the UK became a full member of the ERM, as it did in October 1990.

The relative success of the EMS acted as something of an example for the growing attempts at cooperative coordination between the main world economies after 1985. A general disillusionment with the totally floating regime initiated in 1972–3 had set in by 1985 when the Group of Seven largest economies began a process of hesitant coordination of their economic policies to try and achieve a more steady and sustained growth of the world economy. While these policy initiatives were confined to exchange rate intervention and coordinative monetary policy, they threaten to increase in scope and extent as interdependency grows. Economic interdependence implies externalities; policy actions taken in one country affect welfare in others. Since politically sovereign policy makers are not responsible for welfare in countries other than their own, their behaviour may result in an outcome that is inefficient; the outcome of a cooperative regime might improve welfare in all countries. Thus uncooperative behaviour could result in a worse situation overall. But cooperation requires policy makers to give up at least some of their sovereignty. This can become invested in a supranational agency (like the IMF or the EC) or it could be shifted into a set of binding policy rules (as has happened with the EMS to some extent).

Coordination expressed in these terms, however, is not quite as strong as full cooperation. Coordination stresses the linked nature of outcomes (either through time or over issues), where *quid pro quo* arrangements might predominate. Coordination is a subclass of cooperation. It implies only a limited loss of sovereignty. Thus the exchange rate coordination of the G7 and G5 economies has neither undermined their sovereignty as such, nor led to binding rules. It has mainly meant intervention in the market to try to slow down movements or support particular currencies at times, and has been very much confined to crisis management.

The EMS/ERM, on the other hand, is a case of genuine (if so far limited) long-term cooperation. As Keohane (1984) expresses it, cooperation requires a change in domestic goals and policies and therefore a loss of individual country autonomy. With the push towards economic and monetary union amongst the Community members, cooperation and the loss of individual country sovereignty could accelerate. The 1992 programme of a genuine common market was seen by the British government of Mrs Thatcher as more a case of coordination, whereas the ERM and monetary union beyond is seen as a clear case of cooperation with loss of individual sovereignty. Since it is this issue of loss of sovereignty that has so exercised the debate about the future evolution of Europe, it will be worth exploring it at greater length now.

Sovereignty and the Evolution of European Unity

If the EC evolves as envisaged in the Delors Report the final outcome would be one in which the responsibility for the conduct of members' economic policy was shared between the Council of Ministers and the Commission, acting in the name of the European Parliament, and a new European federal central bank system which could be politically independent. On the monetary side it envisages a single currency for the whole of Europe, irrevocably fixed exchange rates (indeed no exchange rates) and a single interest rate, all under the immediate control of the federal bank. The precise constitution of the federal bank was one of the main points of contention in the debate during the early 1990s. Two main forms were suggested; they are slightly exaggerated in this account to bring out the differences between them.

The first sees the federal bank modelled on the Bundesbank, which is independent of political pressure in Germany (it is claimed) and which has a constitutional duty to prevent inflation written into its founding statutes. The second sees it as a politicized bank in which each of the countries has its representative; the representatives decide monetary policy on the basis of political bargaining between them. It was argued that each of these models could have quite different consequences in terms of inflationary objectives and outcomes; the first would be more likely to prevent inflation by maintaining a tight monetary stance, while the second would be more prone to embody inflationary tendencies as it bends to political pressures for a looser monetary policy.

As far as fiscal policy is concerned, the implications of Delors were less clear cut. The most likely outcome looked to be a centralization of this policy area in the Commission. There would be a single Community-wide budget, voted by the Parliament but administered by the Commission. As envisaged in the Delors Report and in the allied set of proposals emanating from the Commission in the late 1980s, fiscal policy would be buttressed by a social charter, embodying rights and responsibilities with respect to working conditions and social benefits, and an expanded regional fund, designed to help with restructuring the industrial base of the more disadvantaged parts of the Community as the single market and economic union progressed.

This package of measures represented a clear political initiative emanating from the Commission in its attempt to force the pace of political union and engineer a radical transformation of the institutional complex at the European level. It would create a truly superstate if it ever materialized in precisely this form. But like all visions, it is very unlikely to emerge in quite this way; the timescale involved is unclear, and unforeseen events would inevitably interrupt the process and force it to take different turns. Indeed, many saw the startling changes in Eastern Europe during 1989 as representing just such a new unanticipated series of events which would both delay (or which should delay) the Delors-type moves and require a dramatic rethink about the framework for European integration involving not just the EC.

The main problem expressed in regard to the Delors proposals was the accelerated loss of economic (and political) sovereignty implied by monetary and economic union. Clearly, this represented more of a problem for some countries than it did for others. The UK in particular objected to the further loss of the individual sovereignty it believed it possessed even after signing the Single European Act in 1985. It was the Single European Act that launched the move towards the genuine single market in 1992. But the issue here is whether continued sovereignty is compatible with a single market as embodied in the 1992 programme. The programme will eventually involve complete freedom of capital movement; an integrated financial services market; common merger, takeover and competition policy codes; tax harmonization; the free movement of labour; reciprocal recognition of professional and other standards; in short, no tariff or non-tariff barriers of any kind. It is difficult to see what would be left of traditional notions of national economic sovereignty within Europe after these changes were in place. If nothing else the way private economic agents would be allowed to operate relatively unrestrictedly in this environment would have a profound impact on national sovereignty, and certainly on national economic autonomy.

Indeed, the other European partners approached the issue of sovereignty somewhat differently. The French, in particular, looked to the development of monetary union as a way of *increasing* their sovereignty. They saw this as a way of pooling sovereignty and thereby regaining some of it lost to either private agents or stronger governmental authorities.

From this point of view, the transition from the EMS to a deeper monetary cooperation with tighter exchange rate controls, as envisaged by Delors, would strengthen the hand of the weaker Community economies against the vagaries of the international economic order beyond Europe on the one hand and with respect to the dominant position of Germany on the other. As the remaining French and Italian capital controls were being dismantled in 1989–90 in anticipation of the requirements of 1992, interest rate policy within these countries was likely to become more problematical and they saw themselves becoming more and more under the sway of the Bundesbank as a result. Politically this would become increasingly difficult to handle on the domestic front, they suggested. Without a movement forward to create new institutions, the EMS was in danger of collapse, it was argued. This these countries did not want, as it would make them even more vulnerable to outside pressures if it happened. Thus for them, the necessary response was the creation of a more pooled system of sovereignty, where the Bundesbank itself would eventually be replaced by the federal bank of Europe which would inevitably have to act in a more political manner and respond to quite legitimate political pressures. Even the Bundesbank itself was having to bend to this kind of political pressure as the conditions for monetary union between the two Germanies evolved during 1990.

The UK government also proposed a number of alternatives to the Delors Report in 1989 and 1990: originally a genuine competing currency option, and then a parallel currency option involving a hard European currency unit (ECU) as the transitional European currency before full monetary union. With these proposals it envisaged a market-led response to the evolution of monetary developments within Europe. Such options were supposed to preserve the sovereignty of different monies and at the same time restrain the inflationary tendencies of the more politicized federal bank options.

Competing currencies can mean a number of things. As envisaged by the influential neo-liberal economist Hayek, for instance, it would mean that any individual or institution could in principle issue money. Money would then constitute the liability that someone was willing to hold; competition between issuers of money would be expressed in the form of which of the competing monies was used and held by economic agents.

Such a radical plan as this was not envisaged by the British government. It first proposed the idea that different national currencies of the EC members should be allowed to operate as legal tender in each country. If this were strictly the case, prices would have to be designated in (at the time) 12 different currencies in each country, and Community citizens would be able to purchase goods and services in any of these currencies. When this was rejected by the UK's partners it went on to suggest the development of a hard ECU as a competing currency to be allowed to operate alongside existing domestic currencies. (The ECU is a unit of account made up of a weighted average of the values of all the EMS member currencies.) The term 'hard ECU' was meant to designate a currency that would not depreciate against a basket of the other Community currencies, and particularly not against whichever was the strongest of those currencies. Inflationary pressures would thus be controlled by means of guaranteeing the value of the hard ECU, which could always be used in competition with any depreciating domestic currency.

Quite why the competing currency options were offered as an alternative to the Delors proposals was not at all clear to the UK's European partners, and they rather ignored them as a result. They tended to treat them as a delaying tactic only. But in the final hard currency form mentioned above, the UK counter-proposal gathered some support from those less wedded to the highly centralizing thrust of much of the

Commission's vision of the future Europe. A cynic might accuse the Commission of promoting its own political interests via such a centralizing strategy.

Clearly, the main worry expressed in the debate about future monetary policy in Europe was the fear of inflation. Here the status of the German economy and its monetary policy would play a crucial part. An added uncertainty involved the consequences of Germany's own political union in 1990. Interestingly the case of German unification demonstrates a number of the features of interdependency and their possible consequences for integration. German inflation could lead to European inflation. On the other hand, Germany could act as a locomotive for European growth if it imported more after unification. Thus it is clear that individual country economic sovereignty has *de facto* passed in Europe. The only issue is the *form* of the political structure that is to manage the new stage in economic relationships – the form of the political integration that will follow the economic interdependency, as Morse (1971) might have put it. In the next section we look at this issue in another context, but one that despite its differences parallels the European case in many ways. However, here it is the impact that a particular form of economic interdependency has had upon the internal political structure of a country that is examined.

THE CANADA–US FREE-TRADE AGREEMENT AND THE SOVEREIGNTY OF CANADA

In January 1989 the comprehensive free-trade agreement (FTA) that had been signed between Canada and the United States in 1987 began to be phased in. Over ten years this will eliminate all remaining tariff barriers on the bulk of the trade conducted between the two countries and will eliminate a good many of the non-tariff barriers as well (Canadian Department of External Affairs 1988). The question this raised for Canada was how that country might preserve its domestic independence and sovereignty in the face of such a powerful economic neighbour. In 1987 the US took 77 per cent of Canada's exports and was the source of 68 per cent of its imports. The US and Canada conduct the world's largest bilateral trade in goods and services. The US is also the largest foreign investor in Canada (and Canada is a substantial investor in the US).

A long and bitter political struggle emerged over the FTA in Canada which was only settled by a general election in October 1988 where the agreement was the main point at issue. The Progressive Conservative Party, headed by Prime Minister Brian Mulroney (who had negotiated the agreement), won the election and the FTA was secured.

The concern in Canada over the FTA emerged in a number of contexts. The first of these involved Canadian culture. One important way in which Canada claimed it had defined itself in distinction to the ever present US was through developing a distinctive cultural configuration. Quite how that cultural configuration was to be described, and indeed whether it actually existed at all, became a major point at issue in the debate within Canada. It is indicative of a wider set of issues in the contemporary global political environment: the resurgence of specifically cultural forces and their impact.

This registered in Canada in two distinct forms: the future of its cultural industries and its particular political culture. These two features were how the cultural configuration was eventually defined in Canada.

As far as the cultural industries were concerned – comprising book publishing, newspapers, television and radio broadcasting, various arts and entertainment activities etc. – these were explicitly exempted from many of the FTA's final provisions and their ownership structure was explicitly preserved in Canadian hands. On the question of its political culture, this referred to the kinds of institutions and political structure that typify Canadian public life. Here nothing explicit could be done since, the argument went, these were not implicated in the FTA at all, as indeed they were not in any direct sense.

However, indirectly this political culture was implicated in the debate, and the consequences of the FTA for the future of this part of Canadian culture would seem to be highly problematical. Here we being to explore another dimension under which the FTA debate was conducted: the impact of what is ostensibly a limited and purely economic trade agreement on the wider domestic political environment.

Canada is a federal state. It has a relatively weak federal government at the centre in Ottawa and a set of relatively powerful provincial governments with quite diverse political traditions, outlooks and so on, and which face a diverse set of economic conditions and constraints. The history of the Canadian political structure is one involving attempts by the federal government to prevent centrifugal forces, emanating mainly from the provinces, from overwhelming the Dominion as a whole. This has been confounded by: (1) the existence of the US economy as an alternative focus for a good many of the provincial governments and economies, particularly in the west; (2) the concentration of population and economic activity along a narrow band close to the US border; (3) the existence of a large and important non-English-speaking province, Quebec, with an altogether different culture from the rest of Canada.

All of these elements have made it doubly difficult to weld Canada into an entity with a cohesive identity (let alone into a unity). To some extent, the political culture celebrated by many Canadians involves just this diversity, which can display positive liberating aspects as well as negative destructive ones. The FTA may have served to insert a new element and phase into this enduring flux of political aspiration and reaction.

Take the case of Quebec. Quebec was a strong supporter of the FTA. This is a province with a recently developed, prosperous and dynamic manufacturing and service economy. It was less concerned with any renewed cultural and political challenge by the US that might accompany the FTA. It thought its French language and culture would protect it from these incursions and that it would benefit from the more open trading relationship with the US. Indeed, the Quebec government saw the FTA as a way of distancing the province further from what it perceived as the even more intrusive activity of the federal government in Ottawa. It would provide a lever to prise Quebec freer from the English-speaking culture of the rest of Canada. Some saw in this an even more sinister aspiration: to use the FTA as a means of spinning Quebec clear of the Dominion altogether and launching its independence from Canada and the USA. Such aspirations may have been strengthened by the collapse of the Meech Lake proposals for constitutional reform in 1990. These would have constitutionally recognized Quebec as a separate culture within the Canadian Dominion.

If we now look at the provinces of west and central Canada, these also saw the benefits to be had from the FTA. Closer economic ties with the US were built into the agreement in the case of lumber, energy and mineral extraction in particular, something the western provinces specialize in. Again they saw this as a way of removing the influence of the Ottawa government in their decision making and increasing their own regional economic autonomy.

The areas most against the agreement were Ontario and the maritime provinces in the east. Ontario comprises the traditional heartland of the Canadian economy, generating some 70 per cent of its manufacturing economic activity and exports in 1988. This was perceived to be under the greatest threat from the FTA as it enabled US goods to enter Canada free of tariff, possibly undermining the Ontario economy as a result. The maritime states felt threatened by US fishing interests in particular.

All in all, then, there was a very mixed bag of reactions to the FTA from different parts of Canada, which was compounded by the way it tended to polarize society. Broadly speaking the left and organized labour were against the FTA while the right and business interests were for it.

Another distinctive feature of Canadian political arrangements in contrast to the US was heavily implicated here. This involved the differential importance and impact of organized labour on the national political arena. In Canada the ideology of the labour movement – social democracy, broadly speaking – has been an important feature shaping the form of the Canadian state and the kinds of activity it has been prepared to finance or provide. There has been much social legislation involving the public provision of services. Schooling, support for health care, rights in work, unemployment and welfare benefits, comprehensive pension schemes, regional and farm subsidies and so on, are part of the accepted landscape of Canada's social life, whereas these are to a large extent absent in the USA. Those against the FTA argued that these elements in Canadian life would increasingly come under threat as the implications of the FTA worked themselves out.

How might this arise, however, given that these elements were in no way directly involved or implicated in the agreement? Again this is difficult to specify with any accuracy. It relies upon an analysis of the myriad of subtle ways international economic relationships can impinge upon domestic economic and political forces. For instance, for the FTA to work in Canada's favour it must maintain its international competitiveness, particularly against the USA. From the point of view of the business community in Canada, social welfare programmes represent an additional cost they must bear; given that these programmes are less well developed in the US, this was seen by the Canadian business community as putting an added obstacle in the way of Canadian competitiveness *vis-à-vis* the US. Thus pressures began to emerge for these programmes to be cut back in Canada. Those organizations that lobbied hard for the FTA, like the Canadian Manufacturing Association, the Business Council on National Issues and the pro-Canada Network, began to raise issues along these lines in 1989. They argued for a cut in social programme spending and a reduction in the national debt. To some extent these calls for a retrenchment on state activity, in the name of their beneficial effects with respect to the FTA, were met in the April 1989 federal budget which began a cutback on welfare benefits.

The general point here is that political forces gather momentum on the basis of victories. For the bulk of the business community the FTA was seen as a clear victory and they began stepping up pressure on other areas not directly involved as a consequence. When and where these could be directly linked to the FTA, all to the better from the business community's point of view.

It is in this way that we can begin to understand how the political sovereignty of the Canadian state may be, at least in part, subtly compromised by international economic arrangements like the FTA. Now, it might be added, it would be naive to expect otherwise; indeed, was not sovereignty compromised long before the FTA, given the kinds of processes discussed elselwhere in this chapter and Canada's already close economic integration with the US? Clearly, this is likely to be the case. The pretence is to argue otherwise, though this still seems to be the case to an unexpected extent in Canada. Under these circumstances the problem becomes one of recognizing and accepting the realities of the modern globalizing economy – accepting that traditional notions of economic sovereignty are no longer sustainable – and going on to devise new institutional mechanisms to manage those new realities. In the FTA case it is perhaps surprising that little new institutional innovation accompanied the implementation of the FTA (there is a disputes mechanism, though how effective this might be remains open to question). One possible reason for the absence of a more thoroughgoing institutional development between Canada and the USA (not something absent in the EC case, by contrast) involves the attitude of, and the trade policy being conducted by, the US on a much wider front. This is discussed in the next and concluding section.

CONCLUSION

Over much of the post-war period the role of the USA within international economic relations has been to foster and uphold a liberal free-trade order via the institutional mechanisms of *multilateralism*. The GATT is a clear and outstanding example of this approach. But with the decline of US economic power and the rise of alternative centres of economic strength, such as the European Community and Japan, the US has begun to change its strategy in the globalizing economy. It still remains committed to a multilateral approach – witness the pressure it exerted to begin the latest round of GATT negotiations, the Uruguay Round, dealing with the liberalization of trade in agricultural products, trade related investment issues, and intellectual copyright matters – but at the same time it initiated a programme of *bilateralism*. To this end it has concluded a series of bilateral trade agreements with favoured nations, probably the most important of these so far being with Canada. This can be seen as a form of insurance policy for the US and, given its still overwhelming strength in relation to these other economies, it has tended to dictate terms to them (Canada being a case in point).

The problem the US faces is the possible breakup of the multilateral order, in which it continues to occupy a central position, as the other centres of economic (and increasingly political) power possibly become more inward looking and protectionist. Thus there remains a distinct possibility of the global multilateral order breaking up into a more regionalized order – dominated by a tripartition of the US, the EC and Japan.

Under these circumstances, the problem for the US is to strengthen its hand. The creation of a more closely interdependent North American trading block would meet this requirement, and provide the US with an insurance policy should the fragmentation actually occur. To this end it has concluded the FTA with Canada and was actively seeking another similar agreement with Mexico to the south. If this were successful the US would buttress its position with a truly continent-wide economic power block without having to go through any of the integrationist measures that were so exercising Europe in the 1990s. In a sense, then, the US is also conducting its own limited form of *unilateralism* on the North American continent, with the hope that this might be extended to the wider globalizing economy beyond as the US regains its economic strength via these and other measures. Thus the US is conducting a competitive international economic struggle as at the same time it is seen to cooperate with its neighbours; it is competing through cooperation in this instance.

An implication here is that cooperation, or coordination even, is not necessarily neutral in its effects on the parties involved. In game-theoretic terms, solutions to these kinds of situations can be classified as zero summed, positive summed or negative summed. In a zero-sum game, what one party gains the other loses, so there is no overall gain in welfare. With positive-sum games, both parties gain at least something. In the case of negative-sum games, by contrast, both parties lose. The question is which of these outcomes is most likely in situations of the FTA type? The official ideology is that both parties will gain (positive summed) and the Canadian government argues that Canada stands to gain the most. However, it may be that the US gains the most if the kind of scenario sketched out above does develop. One further possibility, however, is that the game will become negative summed, so that neither the US nor Canada gains overall. This would be the case if the strategy fails and Canada is tied into an arrangement that it finds difficult to break away from.

Similar comments could be made about the EC initiatives. Which countries will gain or lose as the EC integration process progresses, or whether all stand to gain at least something, is not at all clear. Perhaps in this case as well it will be the most powerful country that stands to gain the most, but then that country also bears a high risk itself in leading the coordination and policing the system. A fine balance in gain or loss terms characterizes any country that either strives for hegemonic leadership or has it thrust upon it in the modern globalizing economy (so-called leadership games). Sovereignty is thus divisible within this world; it has arrived. The problem now is for governments to come to terms with this.

The main point highlighted by Morse's (1971) pioneering analysis was that statehood was no longer absolute and indivisible. The forces of interdependence have outweighed those of the traditional concern with maintaining sovereignty. The globalizing economy, in as much as such an economy yet typifies international economic relations, has led to a new systemic interdependence where issues of autonomy and the effectiveness of state management of the domestic economy need to be rethought. While we should not exaggerate the extent and pervasiveness of these globalizing tendencies – there is still room for a good deal of effective domestic economic management in my view – it is the case that the modern context for this has irrevocably changed. The challenge is to develop an institutional complex to adequately deal with this new situation, not to insist that it has yet to arrive.

References

Canadian Department of External Affairs (1988) *The Canada–US Free Trade Agreement*. Ottawa: Minister of Supply and Services.

Committee for the Study of Economic and Monetary Union (1989) *Report on Economic and Monetary Union in the European Community (Delors Report)*. Luxembourg: Office for Official Publications of the European Community.

Keohane, R.O. (1984) *After Hegemony: Cooperation and Discord in the World Political Economy*. Princeton: Princeton University Press.

Morse, E.L. (1971) *Modernization and the Transformation of International Relations*. New York: Free Press.

Stopford, J.M. and Turner, L. (1985) *Britain and the Multinationals*. Chichester: Wiley.

Thompson, G.F. (1990) *The Political Economy of the New Right*. London: Pinter.

Williams, K., Williams, J. and Haslam, C. (1990) The hollowing out of British manufacturing and its implications for policy. *Economy and Society*, 19(4), 456–90.

11

The Autonomy of Third World States within the Global Economy

DAVID POTTER

INTRODUCTION

This chapter, like others in this part of the book, is broadly about relations between the global economy and patterns of politics. More specifically, it concentrates on the following question: *are states becoming more or less autonomous within the global economy?* The global economy here is conceived in its broadest sense to include production and market relations not only in Europe and North America but also in what is loosely referred to as the Third World in Asia, Africa and Latin America.

Aspects of the main question have already been considered in this part. In chapter 8, on the international economy in the inter-war years, the important point is established that the question of state autonomy in relation to the formulation and implementation of economic policy is complex and highly ambiguous when particular historical cases are examined. For example, the chapter suggests that in the monetary system existing after World War I, a state's autonomy was quite limited in relation to its capacity to fix the value of its own currency without reference to international economic processes. In chapters 8 and 9, more generally, the authors have introduced some of the complications involved in trying to characterize the changing nature of the global economy this century. Of particular relevance is chapter 10, which essays the issue of whether a state like Britain is becoming more or less autonomous within the global economy. In this chapter I want to go over some of this ground again, but from a different perspective and in the different context of the global economy and Third World states. In this way, the chapter aims to contribute to your understanding of the main question about state autonomy in the global economy by suggesting how to answer it in relation to different types of state.

At the outset, it may be useful if I indicate what I think this particular question is about. Broadly speaking, I follow Skocpol (1985) in finding it helpful initially to conceive the *state* as a set of organizations (including civil and military apparatuses) broadly claiming control over a territory and a people. State *autonomy* refers to the extent to which a state 'may formulate and pursue goals that are not simply reflective of the demands or interests of social groups, classes, or society' (p. 9). The more independent the state is in formulating and pursing goals, the more autonomy it has. The more a state pursues the goals of others, say the ruling class or international capital, the less autonomy it has.The question in this chapter concerns the extent to which states are important in patterns of global politics – important in the sense of having the capacity to formulate and pursue their own goals. The question explicitly places the issue of more or less state autonomy within the global economy. If it is the case, for example, that economic relations generally are becoming increasingly globalized or transnational, then the question becomes one of examining the consequences of that increased economic globalization for state autonomy. Or, as economic transnationalism increases, does the autonomy of states increase, reduce or stay about the same? Answering the question helps us understand the changing role of the state in patterns of global politics, and the state's growing or declining importance in these patterns.

The first thing to say about this question is that there are complexities and difficulties involved in trying to answer it satisfactorily. The next section draws attention to some of these difficulties. Secondly, there are competing theories on the global economy, each one tending to produce a different answer to the question about state autonomy. The third section sketches these differences, while paying particular attention to dependency theory which tends to figure prominently, at least implicitly or as a subject for critique, in discussions related to the political economy of the Third World. The fourth section comments briefly on the changing character of the global economy and the emergence within it of newly industrializing countries in Asia and Latin America. The fifth section goes on to examine the idea of the autonomy of the state within this changing global economy. One of the surprises here is that some of these newly industrializing states on the so-called periphery of the global economy appear to be moving towards greater autonomy, while some states in the core (e.g. Britain) are becoming less autonomous. The sixth section then moves from these considerations to an examination of a case study of Peru which throws more light on global economic processes, state autonomy and domestic consequences. The final section returns briefly to the main question.

Problems with International Political Economy Questions

Are states becoming more or less autonomous within the global economy? The first thing to say about this question is that it falls squarely into the intellectual arena of international political economy, an area of study widely regarded as difficult if not impossible to conceptualize satisfactorily. As one student pointed out:

> It is hard enough to summarize in theoretical form the complex of political and economic relations obtaining within one nation-state. To devise a framework that will enable comprehensive yet comprehensible explanation of the maze of relationships within the global complex is an appalling challenge. Theorists working in this field surely deserve combat pay, and it is not surprising that . . . they have failed to produce satisfactory theories.
>
> (Staniland 1985, pp. 4–5)

There are several reasons why questions about the global political economy pose such problems. First, and quite apart from global complications, there is the basic relationship between the economy and politics. At first glance, the relationship may look fairly straightforward. The economy comprises a society's mode of production and exchange, including its market relations. Politics at a nation-state level involves (amongst other things) the process of steering that society, that process involving the transformative capacity of the state, including the state's power to intervene in social events (e.g. attempting to implement laws). It is not difficult to see that these two are related.For example: (1) markets are affected by political actions of the state; (2) political actions of the state are affected by what is happening in markets. That is all right as far as it goes, but such statements are useless for explanatory purposes. All they do is assert a connection between politics and the economy. The difficulty, however, lies in specifying the nature of these connections and how they work. Scholars exploring such problems tend to find one of two things happening: either their attempts to formulate explanatory generalizations become so abstract, in their efforts to cover all cases, that their generalizations are of no use in trying to understand real events in the economy or polity; or they end up with detailed descriptions or case studies of real events, e.g. the cocoa trade in Ghana, which explain little beyond the particular case examined. It is hardly surprising that scholars have failed to produce a satisfactory theory of the global political economy.

Secondly, the difficulties of coping with questions about global relations between economics and politics are compounded by the growing importance and complexity of such relations. Few dispute that transnational economic relations are growing in importance:

> The increasing role of transnational flows of goods and capital has been a universal feature of post-war economic growth for all countries that participate in the capitalist world system. In the poorest countries, development has meant shifting from relatively autarkic subsistence production to the export of primary commodities into international markets. For industrializing Third World countries the achievement of an increasingly differentiated domestic economy has meant, first, the increasing domination of leading industrial sectors by transnational corporations (TNCs) and, more recently, an ever-heavier reliance on international finance capital. In centre countries, such as the United States, leading industrial and financial corporations derive an increasing proportion of their profits from foreign activities, and the productive investment undertaken by these corporations is increasingly foreign rather than domestic.
>
> (Evans 1985, p. 192)

Increased economic activity in the global arena is matched by the increasing involvement of the state in the economic relations of many countries. Such increasing involvement is especially noticeable in many countries of Asia, Africa and Latin America, where the pressures for economic development are such that governments are drawn increasingly into economic relations, both domestic and international. In short, the sheer complexity and growing importance of the global political economy poses a challenge for students of the subject.

Thirdly, there is the difficulty of cultural variety and non-global values. For example, international bankers in London or New York and their counterparts in Colombo, Nairobi and Montevideo may share the assumptions of development economics, but the values involved in the notion of economic growth may seem both strange and inappropriate to many others not yet part of these international networks. I refer here to peoples who live and work well away from Third World cities in local political economies not premised on economic growth and competitiveness. In my experience, some of the most civilized and sensible people encountered anywhere live in Third World countries well away from Third World cities, and even at a distance from the roads that run to these entrepôts of the global political economy. There is a certain moral arrogance about the very idea of trying to conceptualize one global political economy. The exercise tends to presume a moral imperative – some universal conception of a good life towards which everyone is striving and to which development economics and sensible state politics will bring us all in due course. Operating on such universal assumptions as guides to description and analysis can lead one astray. The global existence of cultural heterogeneity thus adds further to the difficulties involved in trying to cope with international political economy questions.

One could go on in this vein, to which the exasperated reply might be: if the main question in this chapter is so difficult, why bother with it at all? My point is not that the question is so difficult that obtaining a reasonable answer to it is impossible. It is that a simple and clear answer is not immediately available. Indeed, the sole purpose of this chapter is to suggest ideas and illustrations relevant to a reasonable answer. One thing that emerges from the exercise is that the question needs careful exploration and a willingness to accept uncertainties and tentative formulations. To some extent, the question can be seen as rhetorical: much can be learned from exploring its complexities, even if we accept that finding a certain answer may elude us.

COMPETING THEORIES

Are states becoming more or less autonomous within the global economy? Political economy questions like that are difficult to cope with not only for the reasons already indicated. Any tentative answer to the question is also going to be shaped by the particular theory or school of political economy being used. Since one needs a theory to cope with the question and there are several competing theories of schools of thought, there can be no one right answer. The purpose of this section is to identify briefly the position each of the main theories tends to take regarding the autonomy of the state in the global economy.

Four theories of the global political economy have been outlined by Staniland (1985). Staniland refers to them as schools: liberal, realist, interdependence and dependency schools. They differ somewhat in nomenclature and otherwise from the three paradigms of global politics which run through this book: realist, liberal-pluralist and neo-Marxist. Staniland's four schools, however, are not unrelated to the three paradigms.

Liberal School

The (free) market is pre-eminent and has shaped 'both overall patterns of international relations and the policies of particular states' (Staniland 1985). States have therefore had little autonomy in relation to the market and, as the market has become more globalized, states have continued to have little autonomy.

Rather inconsistently, liberals concede that political considerations can come increasingly to the fore and create economic problems for the (free) world market. Thus, in the long run, 'a world federal government will appear as the only rational method of coping with the world's economic problems' (Staniland 1985).

It is not clear where to locate the liberal school in the three paradigms of global politics. Liberal assumptions about free and rational individuals are important in pluralism, however, and I would tend to put the liberal school in there.

Realist School

The world had become increasingly dominated by nation-states, each struggling for dominance and security. States have been pre-eminent globally and have largely determined economic relations at both international and domestic levels. Powerful states like the USA have had a lot of autonomy in relation to the economy and continue to have a lot despite the increasing globalization of economic relations. Weaker, more subordinate states like Iceland have less autonomy. Indeed, it is state action and the broad distribution of power in the world which have largely determined the character of the global economy.

The realist school lines up with the realist paradigm of global politics.

Interdependence School

The global political economy is increasingly one of complex interdependence in which the nature and effectiveness of power vary depending on the nature of any particular issue and of the particular participants involved. Nation-states are not conceived as single, undifferentiated entities, because there is usually considerable conflict within the state between different officials and departments as to what national objectives and state policies are or ought to be. A multiplicity of global economic policy arenas have developed, each one involving a separate set of actors from both within and outside the apparatus of the state. In this conception of political economy, the idea of the autonomy of the state is compromised. Nevertheless, one can say that governments exist and 'are not mere puppets' (Staniland 1985). But their autonomy is severely constrained and, as economic interdependencies multiply, governments become even less autonomous *vis-à-vis* the global economy.

The interdependence school falls broadly into the pluralist paradigm of global politics.

Dependency School

Staniland's summary is on the following lines. The economies of Asia, Africa and Latin America on the periphery of global capitalism are dependent on the advanced capitalist countries of Western Europe and North America at the centre or core of the system. Both trade relations and capital flows are asymmetrical, shifting the economic surplus to the core and undermining the resource base of the periphery. This economic inequality determines the nature of the state in classic dependency theory. Core states are powerful, whereas peripheral states are weak, penetrated, dependent. States in the periphery, therefore, have very little autonomy in relation to the global economy in which they are entangled.

There are lively debates within the dependency school. Kitching (1982) would argue that dependency writing concentrates mainly on the blockages or impediments to capitalist development in Latin America. Surplus transfer out of Latin America in the interests of international capital is the basic mechanism at work. Ruling classes in Latin America are tied by economic interest to international capital, and play a managerial or intermediary role within their own country for international capital by using their 'control of state power to protect the interests of multinational capital' (Kitching 1982). Latin American states therefore have little autonomy in relation either to their own ruling class or to the global (capitalist) economy›

Dependency theory is heavily influenced by Marxism, and forms part of the neo-Marxist paradigm of global politics. But it is worth remembering that non-Marxist influences have also been important in dependency theory. Also, dependency theory is only part of Marxist political economy, which is a far broader church.

Summary

In sum, the different schools appear to take the following positions, roughly speaking, regarding state autonomy *vis-à-vis* the global economy:

Liberalism   Little autonomy.
Realism   Strong states very largely autonomous; weak states less so.
Interdependence/pluralism   Little autonomy; states do not really act as states.
Dependency   Some autonomy in core states; virtually no autonomy in peripheral states in Latin America and elsewhere.

We shall examine dependency theory more fully in later sections of this chapter.

There are two lessons to be drawn from this summary of different schools. The first is the vital one about answers to questions concerning the global political economy. The question here is: are states becoming more or less autonomous within the global economy? The initial answer is that it depends on the theory you are using; some theories say more state autonomy, some say less. That is only a start; there is much more to say by way of answer, including comparative evaluation of competing answers, further refinements (which we are coming to) and so on. But recognition of such theoretical differences is an essential first step in coping with such questions.

The other thing amounts to a huge disclaimer and note of caution. It is essential to appreciate that the brief summaries of the four schools are highly simplified versions. These theories are far more complex and sophisticated than the summaries reveal. Also, there are many different, even conflicting, theories within each of these schools. This is never more true than in the case of the dependency school. Some of the complexities and conflicts within the school are considered later.

THE CHANGING CHARACTER OF THE GLOBAL ECONOMY

Before concentrating on state autonomy, a brief comment is in order regarding the rapidly changing character of the world capitalist system. Conventionally, a broad distinction has been made between the economically advanced countries of Europe and North America (and Japan) at the core of the system, and economically underdeveloped (or developing) countries in Asia, Africa and Latin America on the periphery of the system. To identify underdeveloped countries as occupying a Third World also draws attention to broad economic distinctions in the world. The North–South terminology is another version.

Such conventional distinctions are becoming increasingly useless as guides to the nature of the global economy. Harris (1987), for example, in a book with the arresting title *The End of the Third World*, showed that four newly industrializing countries in Asia, the so-called Gang of Four (South Korea, Taiwan, Hong Kong and Singapore), had far higher rates of sustained economic growth in recent decades than countries in much of Europe and North America. Brazil and Mexico were examples of newly industrializing countries in Latin America during the period, although their impressive growth rates slumped sharply in the late 1980s. Other middle-income countries like Malaysia and Indonesia were also catching up fast. Comparative economic statistics always pose problems. However, for example, the old-established core of the world economy, in North America and Western Europe, produced 78 per cent of the world's manufacturing output in 1960; only 21 years later their share had dropped to 59 per cent. During the same period, the share in manufacturing output of newcomers and middle-income economies jumped from 19 per cent to 37 per cent. The global share of manufacturing output of low-income countries (including China, India and most countries in sub-Saharan Africa) stayed about the same during the period (all these figures are from Harris 1987, p. 103). It is no longer useful to characterize the global economy as involving a dependent Third World at the periphery producing primarily raw materials like cotton and rubber for First World manufacture at the core. A better characterization is of a global manufacturing system in which many newly industrializing countries in Asia and Latin America are intricately involved as part of an increasingly specialized and interdependent division of international labour. It would be wrong, however, to overdo this transformation. There are still many poor countries in Asia, Africa and Latin America primarily producing food and raw materials, and many of these countries have been marginalized *vis-à-vis* these global economic processes.

Two important conclusions follow from this brief characterization of the global economy. The first is that any answer to the question about more or less state autonomy cannot assume that the global economy is some static formation; any state's relations with the global economy are going to change through time because global economic processes are dynamic in character. The second conclusion is simply that one cannot assume that because country X is in the Third World it therefore has Y amount of autonomy in relation to the global economy. There is tremendous economic variety from country to country; one should beware of accepting uncritically any general proposition about the autonomy of Third World states within the global economy.

THE AUTONOMY OF THE STATE

Are states becoming more or less autonomous within this changing global economy? There are a number of complications involved in trying to answer any questions about state autonomy, and I want to draw attention to some of the more important ones.

The first is the complication related to using the term 'states'. The question 'are states becoming more or less autonomous' appears to imply that states are some uniform ensemble of institutions and processes broadly claiming control (or the monopoly of the use of force) over a territory and a people. A moment's reflection makes one realize that states are not uniform. They are immensely various when considered generally. There are different types of states and political regimes – e.g. liberal-democratic, military, communist mobilization – and within any one type each state has a unique and complex pattern of institutions and processes allocating values and resources according to different principles. Some states have a large public sector, others a small one or virtually none at all. Such complications behind the bland word 'states' must be constantly borne in mind when considering questions about any particular state's autonomy. Any particular state's autonomy therefore cannot be taken for granted as part of some general propostion; there are bound to be some unique features.

Secondly, state autonomy and state power are very closely related but need to be kept distinct conceptually. States are autonomous when they are free to decide on and pursue their own goals. States are powerful when they also have the capacity to achieve their goals, despite opposition, through the working of control and compliance relations in which they are involved. Frequently, autonomous states are also powerful states, but this need not be so. A state can have almost no autonomy (e.g. instead of having and pursuing any goals of its own it simply pursues the goals of the dominant class) and at the same time be immensely powerful domestically in achieving the goals set for it by others. Conversely, a state can be largely autonomous in setting and pursuing its own goals, but be unable to achieve its goals successfully because its power capacity is too weak. Many authors elide, or virtually equate, the concepts of state autonomy and state power, and certainly it is frequently unnecessary to make the distinction repeatedly and explicitly throughout an analysis. After all, states are unlikely to decide on their own goals and begin to pursue them unless they know they also have the power to achieve them. Furthermore, even to begin pursuing goals can involve engaging in power relations. But sometimes states misjudge their power, e.g. governments may think they have enough power to achieve their goals but be wrong. That is, the amount of their autonomy may not match the amount of their power. It is because of such considerations that it is worth remembering that state autonomy does not necessarily equal state power.

Thirdly, the autonomy of states in relation to the global economy can vary on *different dimensions*. The complication is that any particular state within the global economy may be largely autonomous in relation to domestic social groups or classes and at the same time be only minimally autonomous in relation to dominant groups or classes in other, more advanced countries. The surprising consequence of this is that any one state can be both more and less autonomous at the same time! It can be more and less autonomous as long as no clear distinction is made between the different groups and classes to which the state relates. For example, states in economically backward countries can be largely autonomous in relation to domestic groups while at the same time they can have little autonomy *vis-à-vis* transnational corporations, whereas in highly industrialized countries the situation may be roughly the reverse.

Fourthly, states are made up of a collection of different entities (e.g. institutions, policy arenas), and one part of a state may be more or less autonomous than another *vis-à-vis* the domestic economy or the global economy. For example, it may be the case that a department of economic affairs has little autonomy in relation to powerful business groups in society, while the police department and other agencies involved in maintaining internal (domestic) security have more autonomy. This provides a further difficulty in attempting any simple answer to a question about the autonomy of the state, and would be an important point for pluralists in the interdependence school.

The fifth complication is an extension of the previous two. Any state or proportion of a state, in relation to the domestic or global economy, is unlikely to retain the same amount of autonomy *through time*. State autonomy is not a static relationship; it changes historically. Therefore, any answer to a question about the relative autonomy of the state must build in, or at least acknowledge, the feature of change through time. The newly industrializing countries of the Third World that Harris (1987) talks about provide a good example. It is now widely accepted that when the process of accelerated economic growth in such countries began some decades ago it was led not by free enterprise or foreign capital but by the deliberate and persistent efforts of the state in such countries (Hong Kong has been an exception). In short, the autonomy and power of the state in relation to the domestic economy was very large indeed. However, as such states became more successful in pursuing industrialization and economic growth, domestic private capital gradually became more powerful and gradually integrated with external markets and the global economy; these developments have led to the declining power and autonomy of such states in shaping their domestic economies, because they too had to follow the trends of the world markets. Thus, states which may be largely autonomous at the start of the industrialization process may become gradually less so through time.

Sixthly, in addition to amounts of state autonomy changing through time, different states at any one time may have different amounts of autonomy depending on their location within the global economy. States at the core of the global economy may have more, states on the periphery may have less. As you know, your answer to the question of whether a state has more or less autonomy is influenced by the paradigm or school of thought you employ. This sixth point is, broadly speaking, one that emanates from a dependency approach, since it assumes there is a global system made up of core and periphery, within which states are located. The liberal school, as you know, sees all states, regardless of their location, as having rather little autonomy in relation to the market. (So also does the interdependence/pluralism school, although for different reasons.) Realists would tend to take the view that all states, regardless of location, tend to be very largely autonomous in relation to the domestic market.

Finally, whether or not location is important, it is generally agreed that all states have usually had at least a little autonomy in relation to the domestic economy in order to perform some functions essential to the continuing existence of the global economy. States have supervised territories and inhabitants, provided infrastructure, guaranteed the stability of exchanges, guaranteed the order and safety of participants through the use of police, army and health service, provided for the eduction and training of the labour force and controlled them when they threatened to get out of hand. Without all this, there could have been no capital accumulation, no profit making, no global capitalist economy. In short, the global economy requires states exercising at least some power over their inhabitants.

Seven complications have been identified related to the general idea of the relative autonomy of the state within the global economy. They are:

1 The word 'state' needs careful handling; states can take quite different forms.
2 State autonomy is not the same thing as state power.
3 State can be seen as more and less autonomous at the same time if no distinctions are made between different dimensions of autonomy.

4 An institution within a state may be more autonomous than another institution with the same state.

5 Amounts of state autonomy can vary through time.

6 Amounts of state autonomy at any one time can vary depending on the state's location in the global economy.

7 All states require at least some autonomy in order to perform important functions for the global economy.

Being aware of such complications can help to improve the scope and penetration of answers to questions about state autonomy. Suppose, for example, I was asked the question: are states in newly industrializing countries like the Asian Gang of Four and Brazil and Mexico becoming more or less autonomous within the global economy? My answer would run something like this. First, such states have had little autonomy in relation to the global economy in the sense that it has been impossible for any such state to influence the overall structure of world capitalism. Secondly, such states have had considerable autonomy in relation to their domestic economies (within the global economy) in the early stages of industrialization and accelerated economic growth, but their enlarged autonomy has been decreasing as they have become more developed and integrated into global capitalism. Thirdly, such states have had considerable autonomy and power in relation to controlling their own territory and inhabitants, including the domestic labour force, and they continue to have considerable (if not enhanced) autonomy and power in such arenas of domestic politics.

What kind of an answer is that? Liberal? Realist? Interdependence/pluralist? Dependency? As is usually the case, any one answer does not fit neatly into any one of the schools outlined earlier. The answer is certainly not liberal, nor is it fundamentally realist or pluralist. But neither does it sit comfortably within dependency theory. The conception of an interdependent, interacting global manufacturing system is at odds with the idea of a Third World of peripheral countries exchanging raw materials for manufactured goods from First World core countries. There is rapidly emerging a new world capitalist economy far more complex than the one previously identified as made up of First World industrialized countries and Third World non-industrialized countries. There are instead what amount to national specializations in the international division of labour that produce the products emanating from the global manufacturing system. The state plays a vital role in the determination and control of the national specialization domestically. States have more or less autonomy and power in relation to their national arenas and, generally, the less developed the national arena the more autonomous and powerful the state tends to be in that arena. Overriding these distinctions, however, is a basic premise in dependency theory that all nation-states are entangled at least to some extent with the global capitalist system.

Back to the main question again: are states becoming more or less autonomous within the global economy? All the component parts of the question have now been discussed in a general way: the changing character of the global economy, the idea of state autonomy (and the complications that go with it), and the issue of more or less autonomy (upon which different schools of political economy tend to take different positions). What we have not yet done in a detailed way is to explore relationships between the component parts. For example, how does a particular transnational economic process affect the relative autonomy of a particular state? Such an exploration requires us to move from the general to the particular.

A Case Study: International Bank Loans and State Autonomy in Peru

In this particular case, Barbara Stallings (1985) looks at the effects of international bank loans on the relative autonomy of the state in Peru. I think her essay can be considered a classic in the dependency literature, and it is perfect for our purposes here. First, it focuses squarely on the idea of the autonomy of the state, bringing it to life via a concrete illustration. Secondly, it concentrates on the most important type of global economic process that affects Third World states – private bank loans from banks in advanced industrial countries. Again, she provides specific illustrations to increase our understanding of distinct processes that make up the global economy, a subject normally treated in abstract and rather general terms. Thirdly, she sets out at the beginning of her essay to answer an important question we have not yet considered: why are Third World states drawn into, and constrained by, global economic processes?

Her answer runs roughly, I think along the following lines

1   Any state requires two things in order to exist at all: *resources*, including financial resources (e.g. obtained through taxation); and at least some *political support* (or acquiescence) from groupings in the society in which it is located. These resources on which the state depends are produced initially in the economy, which itself is heavily influenced by a dominant class or other controlling group. For example, in a capitalist economy the 'state must rely on the capitalist class to bring about an acceptable level of economic activity both because of the state's requirements for finance and because of its need for growth in order to maintain political support' (Stallings 1985). So states are dependent on, and have special links with, dominant classes in the economy.

2   States are dependent on dominant classes, but they must also have at least a little autonomy in relation to these classes, a little room for manoeuvre. This is so because states must make choices, and any choice is bound to affect adversely at least one small group within the dominant class. Some states will have more autonomy than others. At the extreme, a state may be so autonomous that it decides on, and pursues, an overall political project that opposes the fundamental interests of the dominant class. In short, there are *degrees of state autonomy*.

3   States from time to time struggle for more autonomy. How does state autonomy increase? There are basically two mechanisms. One is for a state to strengthen its *organizational capacity*, including its police and military forces. The other is for the state to augment its *financial resources* by either increasing its take from the domestic economy or obtaining additional finance from abroad. In Third World countries, the latter process is especially important.

4   There are dangers in seeking *foreign capital* for additional resources. Doing so may increase the state's autonomy *vis-à-vis* the dominant domestic class while simultaneously making it less autonomous in relation to groups who dominate in the global economy. So 'foreign capital can help expand state capacity as well as limit it' (Stalling, 1985). An important consideration affecting the relative autonomy of a state seeking financial assistance abroad is the type of foreign resource involved.

5   There are two main types of foreign resources which have a direct bearing on the issue of autonomy. One is *direct foreign investment*, which tends to restrict autonomy

because the investor maintains control. The other is *loans*, which tend not to restrict autonomy because, by their nature, loans are an investment made to earn income without there being much control over their use. Private rather than public loans are best for a Third World state setting out to increase its autonomy. Private bank loans, for example, can go directly to the state itself, in large volume, with few strings attached. Such banks pay little attention initially to how their money is spent as long as fees and interest payments are forthcoming. At the same time, in due course even private foreign creditors can severely limit the choices available to Third World recipients of such loans because, for the recipient, 'the debt that accumulates as the counterpart of the loan is particularly difficult to service given the unfavourable terms on which private credits are usually provided' (Stallings 1985).

As the Peruvian case illustrates, such international economic processes 'can then interact with domestic politics in such a way as to seriously endanger the government's autonomy and even its very existence' (Stallings 1985). A good example is the fall of the Leguia government in 1929. US bankers suddenly cut back on new loans to Peru as money was diverted to the US stock market where speculation had gone wild. 'Since an ever-larger portion of Leguia's expenditure had come to be financed by foreign loans, the sudden cut-off led to a decrease in state activity, which, in turn, undermined Leguia's autonomy from the domestic class structure and eventually led to his over-throw' (Stallings 1985). In such ways do global economic processes determine patterns of domestic politics. This fate of the Leguia government in 1929 provides a fine example of the way in which economic developments in one country can penetrate the state in another country and profoundly affect its politics.

A similar series of events took place involving the military governments of Peru from 1968 to 1980 in their relations with the domestic class structure and the global capital markets. It is instructive to examine this case in some detail. Stallings (1985, pp. 275–80) tells the story as follows.

The Military Governments, 1968–80
The failure of the Belaunde government [1963–8] to carry out most of the structural changes it had promised – particularly the agrarian reform – led to increasing discontent in Peru, including a guerrilla movement in the central highlands. The military became heavily involved in putting down guerrilla and peasant uprisings and, in the process, became more aware of the poverty and backwardness of the country, which, in turn, were seen as a major threat to national security. Since neither the civilian government nor private capital seemed able to resolve these problems, the military itself decided to take control of the state. They envisioned a long-term rule during which the economy would be strengthened, the country made more independent, and the incipient political rebellion eliminated. However, in spite of the nationalistic rhetoric of General Juan Velasco Alvarado, who led the coup in October 1968, the military government shared a number of important characteristics – and problems – with the Leguia and Belaunde regimes of the past.

From the National Development Plan for 1971–5, three main goals of the Velasco government can be identified. One goal was rapid economic growth with special emphasis on industrialization. Given that the Peruvian oligarchy had not proven itself capable of promoting a strong industrial sector and an independent economy in general, the goal of economic development was interpreted as requiring a much greater state role in the economy, including the ownership of key sectors. Another goal was greater equity through the redistribution of land, higher taxes on the rich, and profit sharing plus higher wages and benefits for workers. Finally, a third goal was greater national autonomy through nationalization of certain firms, greater control over foreign investment, and diversification of trade and credit flows (Peru 1971).

These goals were summed up in the nation of the Peruvian model as a 'third way' to development, *ni capitalista ni comunista*. This was the theme of the Velasco government, which lasted from 1968 to mid 1975. Like the Leguia years, the Velasco regime can be divided into subperiods. In the first, 1968–71, there was again a political move against the oligarchy and an attempt to stimulate the support of the emerging industrialist class. Because this support was not sufficient, in the second period, 1972–5, the state itself became the chief entrepreneur based on international bank finance. The overthrow of Velasco in mid 1975, and the rule of General Francisco Morales Bermudez from 1975 to 1980, provided a gradual transition to a less autonomous state and the eventual return of the dominant class to power.

The Peruvian oligarchy based its economic power in land and finance; important ideological influence also came from ownership of the country's main newspapers. The Velasco regime attacked them on all three fronts. The agrarian reform was the most important. Holdings were eventually limited to fifty hectares of irrigated land on the coast and to thirty in the highlands, with land turned over to former tenants and workers as cooperatives. Compensation was paid in twenty year bonds that could be exchanged for stock in industrial enterprises created by the government. Emphasizing the political nature of the reform, the exemptions provided under the Belaunde law for the large coastal plantations were eliminated; efficiency was no longer justification for monopoly (Booth 1983). Likewise the major banks and newspapers were taken over (Havens et al. 1983).

Two characteristics were especially important in the first group of reforms. First they were 'cheap' in the sense of not requiring large amounts of financial resources to carry them out. The major requirements were organizational capacity and political will. Second, the reforms were not anti-private sector but were intended to open up space so that a more modern private-sector group could step in, especially the industrialists.

The industrialists, however, proved reluctant to participate. Indeed, the issue of support from all parts of the society was problematic from the beginning, as was natural with 'revolution from above'. On the one hand, the closed decision-making style of the military alienated many who in objective terms benefited from the reforms. On the other hand, difficulties arose from the very nature of an autonomous government that refused to go along with *any* class fraction's own view of its interests. The industrialists, for example, were especially opposed to the Industrial Communities, which were aimed at providing workers with a stake in the system by giving them a share in profits and a say in management (Ferner 1983). But the government also refused to create close political links with the working class. A few attempts at top-down political organizing were made, but the government continued to be largely isolated throughout its twelve years.

When it became clear that the industrialists were not going to invest in the amounts that had been expected, the state itself took on the dominant role in capital formation through the establishment of some fifty public enterprises. This was the beginning of the second phase of the Velasco regime when the state began to act in its own interests. The investment process was expensive in financial terms. Building up the public enterprises required a great deal of capital, much of it foreign exchange. It was here that foreign capital became important, but it was not easy to obtain. One of the military government's first acts had been to nationalize the International Petroleum Corporation; the corporation sought the assistance of the US government, which then instituted another financial blockade. In concrete terms, this meant that direct foreign investment dried up, and Peru received almost no loans from AID [the US Agency for International Development] or the Export-Import (Exim) Bank between 1969 and March 1974, when the conflict was resolved. The Exim loans were especially crucial, since they were considered an essential prerequisite for some of the large-scale development projects to obtain other financing. Loans from multilateral agencies were also conspicuously few due to US vetoes. Between 1968 and late 1973, Peru received only one loan from the World Bank. Getting credits from the Interamerican Development Bank (IDB) was slightly easier, but a significant portion of the IDB loans were in response to a serious earthquake in Peru in 1970.

There appeared to be only one source to which the government could turn – the international capital markets, which had also been crucial for Leguia and Belaunde. Again private capital turned out to be more progressive than public loans because of its more apolitical character. Unlike the Belaunde period, the commerical banks operating through the Euromarkets had now become the most important source of finance for Third World countries. This trend started in the early 1970s, as a simultaneous economic downturn in all the advanced capitalist countries deprived the banks of their traditional blue-chip customers. It was exacerbated after the 1973 oil price increases as the Organization of Petroleum Exporting Countries (OPEC) began depositing their surplus revenues with the international banks, which in turn had to find borrowers willing to absorb these funds (Stallings 1986).

Realizing that Peru was going to need good relations with the private bankers, the government took early steps to prepare the ground. When it assumed control of the domestic banking sector in 1970 (including Chase Manhattan's Banco Continental), it sought favour with Chase – and presumably with the rest of the financial sector – by buying its shares for five and a half times their stock value (Hunt 1975). In addition, Peru's mineral wealth, including its expected oil exports, made it seem a good credit risk in spite of the government's leftist rhetoric. Consequently, Peru was able to escape the official credit blockade by turning to the Euromarkets.

This international borrowing capacity became increasingly important for the military government for several reasons. First, as a result of its increasing activities, the government began to run a large budget deficit. This was the consequence of rising expenditures, both current and capital, and the fear that raising taxes to offset them would increase political opposition ... Second, the balance of payments was also beginning to move into deficit. In 1974, for the first time since the military took power, the trade balance went into the red as imports increased sharply. Increasing debt-service payments, largely attributable to the stringent terms on private bank loans, also added to the balance-of-payments difficulties. In the mid 1970s, debt service was absorbing over 20 per cent of export revenues; by 1978 it would have been over 50 per cent without the refinancing that took place that year. The main reason for both deficits was that the government began to need increasing amounts of money to finance its investment program.

The growing balance-of-payments and budget problems, combined with rising inflation, provided the justification for the August 1975 'coup within a coup'. General Francisco Morales Bermudez, Velasco's prime minister, who had briefly served as Belaunde's finance minister, took over as president. Although Morales characterized his regime as a continuation of his predecessor's, it was obvious that the change meant a move to the right. Repression increased, leftist military officers were forced to retire, and more orthodox economic policies were introduced. This new direction was reinforced and exacerbated by the international financial agencies.

With a balance-of-payments crisis still threatening in 1976, the Peruvian government took the unusual step of approaching a group of private banks for a large loan rather than going to the International Monetary Fund. Although the bankers agreed to a $400 million balance-of-payments loan, two conditions were imposed. One was an orthodox stabilization program that the banks would monitor; the other was more favourable treatment for foreign investment. However, the banks proved incapable of substantially reducing the government's deficits; the IMF reassumed its traditional role and negotiated a stabilization agreement the following year. As the economy slowed, and many of the Velasco reforms began to be rescinded, the living standard of a large part of the population fell substantially. The political consequence was increased opposition to the government, including strikes and political demonstrations.

By 1978, as a result of their economic predicament, together with rising opposition, the military decided to return the government to civilian control. A constituent assembly was elected to write a new constitution, and in mid 1980 the military formally stepped down as Fernando Belaunde Terry was sworn in as president a second time. Belaunde's program and policies had changed significantly from those followed in the 1960s – though perhaps mainly because of changed circumstances. The autonomy of the state was substantially reduced as the dominant class moved more directly into power once again and as the government made determined efforts to lower the economic role of the state. It should be made clear, however, that the dominant fraction was no longer the agro-export oligarchy of old, but industrial and mining sectors with strong multinational connections. To a significant extent, Belaunde's goals of modernizing the Peruvian economy and promoting capitalist development had been accomplished by the military, so he no longer saw the need for the state to assume an autonomous stance.

Stallings's account provides illustrations of a number of the points made in this chapter about state autonomy. For example, the transition from more to less autonomy after Morales replaced Velasco illustrates how the autonomy of the state can change through time. The complex way that states can be both more and less autonomous at the same time is also illustrated here; the Peruvian state, we are told, related differently to the international financial agencies, the international bankers, the industrial and mining sectors of the domestic capitalist class, peasants and workers. The case study also shows why struggling to achieve more state autonomy can be so important for a political leadership; Velasco needed more autonomy from dominant classes in Peru in order to pursue his fairly radical political project. Perhaps the most striking thing about this case is the way it shows how global economic processes can profoundly affect domestic politics. Velasco's political project in the National Plan required for its success increased autonomy from dominant classes, so he borrowed from the international bankers to obtain the capital needed for his project. However, eventually escalating debt servicing payments and balance of payments difficulties provided the justification for the Morales coup. This in turn led to less planned development and more political repression, escalating political opposition to the Morales regime, the return of civilian rule under Belaunde, and the writing of a new constitution. In short, we see in this example one slice of the interdependence of the global economy and the political process.

CONCLUSION

This chapter has suggested a number of aspects that need to be borne in mind when dealing with any general questions related to the issue of more or less state autonomy within the global economy. It may be helpful if I note the main ones once more by way of conclusion:

1 There are major difficulties with general political economy questions like this and it is helpful perhaps to treat them as to some extent rhetorical. That is, much can be learned from exploring their complexities even though certain answers may elude us.
2 There are competing schools or theories in this subject area – liberal, realist, interdependence, dependency – and each one tends to produce a rather different answer to questions about state autonomy.
3 The concept of state autonomy presents at least five major complications: (a) the bland world 'states' hides a wide variety of political forms, and there is no prototype; (b) state autonomy is not the same thing as state power; (c) states generally can be more *and* less autonomous at the same time, in relation to different external entities; (d) different institutions or policy areas within a state may each be more or less autonomous; (e) state autonomy can vary through time, that is a state may have been more autonomous in the past.
4 Bearing these complications in mind, there does seem to be evidence to suggest that the autonomy of states, in relation to domestic economic forces, may vary depending on their level of development and location in the global economy. For example, states in newly industrializing countries on the periphery of the global economy may be more autonomous than states in advanced industrial societies at the core, and as industrialization efforts succeed, state autonomy may recede.
5 However, any such generalizations about state autonomy must be treated with extreme caution because one tends to find a number of exceptions when particular examples are examined. For instance, underdeveloped agrarian economies dependent on international capital appear in many cases to have little autonomy in relation to

domestic ruling classes, but there are other cases like Peru where considerable state autonomy has been achieved from time to time.

Finally, a brief comment is in order regarding what the discussion in this chapter may tell us about the continuing importance of states in evolving patterns of global politics. In sum, the chapter can tell us rather little because systematic comparisons have not been made with other, non-state levels or forms of politics that may be emerging as more important. However, it is reasonably clear that, as markets and economic relations are becoming increasingly globalized, all states are not becoming correspondingly less important in terms of their autonomy. Some are, some are not. And even where state autonomy is minimal in relation to international capital, state power has been and remains absolutely essential in that global context. States supervise territories, provide infrastructure, educate and control the labour force. States continue to perform these absolutely essential political functions for those who profit within the global economy.

References

Booth, D. (1983) The press reform in Peru. In D. Booth and B. Sorj, *Military Reformism and Social Classes: the Peruvian Experience, 1968–80*, New York: St Martins Press, 141–85.

Evans, P.B. (1985) Transnational linkages and the economic role of the state: an analysis of developing and industrialized nations in the post-World War II period. In P.B. Evans et al. (eds), *Bringing the State Back In*, Cambridge: Cambridge University Press, 192–226.

Ferner, A. (1983) The industrialists and the Peruvian development model. In D. Booth and B. Sorj, *Military Reformism and Social Classes: the Peruvian Experience, 1968–80*, New York: St Martins Press, 40–71.

Harris, N. (1987) *The End of the Third World: Newly Industrializing Countries and the Decline of an Ideology*. Harmondsworth: Penguin.

Havens, A.E. et al. (1983) Class struggle and the agrarian reform process. In D. Booth and B. Sorj, *Military Reformism and Social Classes: the Peruvian Experience, 1968–80*, New York: St Martins Press, 14–39.

Hunt, S. (1975) Direct foreign investment in Peru: new rules for an old game. In. A. Lowenthal (ed.), *The Peruvian Experience*, Princeton: Princeton University Press.

Kitching, G. (1982) *Development and Underdevelopment in Historical Perspective: Populism, National-ism and Industrialization*. London: Methuen.

Peru (1971), Prediencia de la Republica, *Plan nacional de desarrollo para, 1971–75*, vol. 1, chapter 1.

Skocpol, T. (1985) Bringing the state back in: strategies of analysis in current research. In P.B. Evans et al. (eds), *Bringing the State Back In*, Cambridge: Cambridge University Press, 5–37.

Stallings, B. (1985) International lending and the relative autonomy of the state: a case study of twentieth-century Peru. *Politics and Society*, 14, 257–88.

Stallings, B. (1986) *Banker to the Third World: US Portfolio Investment in Latin America, 1900–85*. Berkeley: University of California Press.

Staniland, M. (1985) *What is Political Economy? A Study of Social Theory and Underdevelopment*. New Haven: Yale University Press.

12

Conceptualizing the Global Economy

ROGER TOOZE

INTRODUCTION: PURPOSES AND QUESTIONS

This chapter is in two halves. The first half focuses on how the three main paradigms described in this book explain the nature of the global economy and its relationship with global politics. The purpose of this critical analysis is, first, to lay out the skeleton of the argument; second, to describe and unpack the core ideas and assumptions; and third, to expose these assumptions to critical examination.

The second half of the chapter draws out some comparisons between the paradigms as to how well they each explain the phenomena and questions in which we are interested, namely the relationship between the global economy and global politics. The process of comparison necessarily raises the question: what are the criteria of evaluation, or how do we evaluate these conceptual frameworks? Chapter 4 has already discussed the criteria for comparison in relation to US interventionism in Central America, in this case comparing the explanations of realism and neo-Marxism, and we will return to and extend this discussion in the second half of this chapter. As you will have seen from chapter 4, the process of comparison and evaluation is difficult and challenging, and raises a number of key theoretical problems, but it is absolutely necessary if we are to move forward in explaining and understanding the global economy. This half of the chapter links the study of the global political economy to social science in general and raises a number of points for you to consider. Above all, it is intended to make you aware of and think about the kind of questions that go beyond a common-sense basis for understanding the global political economy; for, as we shall see, to rely on common sense in these matters is often to accept unconsciously and uncritically the dominant explanation which serves a particular interest, as do all orthodoxies.

THE CENTRAL QUESTION

The central focus of this paper is on the question: *what is the relationship between the global economy and the character of contemporary global politics?*

Each of our three paradigms provides a different set of answers to this question. In this section we will consider the broad outlines of these different answers, noting their key features. While you are considering these outlines remember that each presents an ideal type, a pure distillation of the world view embodied in the paradigm which individuals and groups may or may not hold in full, and which may thus seem extreme and rather narrow.

Realism and Neo-Realism

For realism the nature of the global economy reflects the lack of overarching authority and is, at base, conflictual. That does not mean to say that it is continually characterized by conflict because states cooperate, recognizing their common national interests in maintaining order and some semblance of rule governed behaviour. Much cooperative behaviour takes place within a hegemonic framework (see chapter 9), where the hegemonic state creates and maintains a particular form of order in the inter-national/global economy. However universal the order seems, for example the post-war liberal order, it is essentially in the hegemon's interest; when circumstances change (say when US goods are no longer competitive or US domestic industry is hit by imports), the support for the liberal order is challenged. The key actors in the global economy are nation-states (i.e. national economies ultimately serving the national interest as defined by government) and realism has a particular conception of the state as an organic whole. Where foreign direct investment takes place, creating transnational corporations, the TNCs are viewed as extensions of state power or as additional foreign policy instruments. The global economy for the realist owes its structure and processes as much, if not more, to the political framework as to any separate economic and technological forces. And this view, as well as providing a distinctive analysis of the contemporary system, also provides a particular history of the world economy, in terms both of patterns of hegemony, i.e. long cycles of dominance by a single state and imperialism, and of increasing cooperation between states for common economic benefit. Finally, the undoubted goal of economic activity within the context of a global economy is the maximization of national wealth. But the global economy, and the benefits it brings in terms of increased production, trade and wealth, must be managed to achieve the maximum economic benefit *consistent with* the maintenance of national autonomy.

The relationships between the global economy and politics are very clear for realism: in essence, politics determines economics. For the realist, this is a statement that can be verified by reference to evidence from the real world, and represents the objective reality of the global political economy. This reality is most frequently characterized as a zero-sum situation in which one state's gain is another state's loss. It is also the underlying principle of the continued survival of the global economy. The basic need for political units is to achieve security (military, economic, psychological) and this fundamental need comes first in priority. From this we can derive the logic of politics determining economics, not only to maintain territorial integrity but also to achieve economic security. The global economy is itself a product of realist economic policies and hegemonic structures. However, *by its very existence* it makes the achievement of economic security more difficult but more necessary. Edmund Dell, a former (UK) Secretary of State for Trade, argues that: 'It is modern interdependence that has compelled national governments to identify economic security as a prime requirement of policy. The instinct for national economic security impels governments to seek to retain in their hands the greatest possible control of national economic destinies' (1987, p. 16).

Hence, although production, trade and technology, particularly transport and communications technology, make possible the existence of a global economy, its composition, international structure and specific characteristics are explained by the political, in the sense of those features being determined by states interacting in an anarchic order. Hence the most significant changes for the global economy are those in the distribution of power among states, the rise and fall of great powers.

Liberal-Pluralism

The liberal-pluralist paradigm (which I will refer to as LP) generates a very different view of the nature of the world economy. However, before we look at this, a word of caution is in order. Because the LP view, in its principal features, is by and large the conventional academic view of the global economy, embodied in mainline economics and conventional wisdom, it has a special status in society: it is taken to represent the reality of the global economy, against which other views and paradigms are judged and evaluated. We will confront this problem later in this chapter, but for the moment it makes identifying the outlines of an LP view even more important because many of its features we take for granted, or we are socialized into not questioning. This does not mean that I, or you, will necessarily not accept the LP view, just that we need to make implicit assumptions explicit before we can consciously agree or disagree with them.

The nature of the global economy for LP derives from the conception of economic relations as essentially harmonious. Within a national economy, individuals following their own self-interest will, *within the framework of a free market* and assuming a particular form of state, collectively increase the amount of wealth available to their society, and in this way convert individual selfishness into the general good. Moreover, the principles of a free market also tranlate into a political structure which emphasizes the individual and individual freedoms. This principle, translated to economic relations among nations, means that trade based purely on LP economic criteria (i.e. free trade) is harmonious, both nationally and internationally. Hence by extension the greater the amount of trade, the greater the economic specialization and the greater the wealth generated. The global economy is therefore a natural unit as it provides the greater opportunities for *efficiency* gains, through global production for a global market. More than this, the creation of high levels of interdependence not only ties states together in a beneficial way, and hence further reduces the causes of conflict, but also begins to break down the realist state by setting up communities of interest that are transnational. Within the global economy the key actors are firms and households, who form a complex and expanding web of harmonious relationships mediated through the market. Government has the key but limited function of providing security and maintaining law and order domestically and globally. A plurality of actors is necessary to prevent any group or organization (such as the state or a large corporation) from wielding monopoly power and being able to structure the market to its own benefit. The increasing internationalization of production, finance and services is to be encouraged because of the economic benefits it brings.

The LP view of the relationship between the global economy and politics is not straightforward. Conceptually there is a clear separation between economics and politics, giving politics a lesser but important status, that of ensuring the specific political conditions necessary for efficient economic activity. But economic activity itself is not considered to be political in any way. It is above politics and is considered to have a higher rationality. So, for example, once the political conditions for the post-1945 economic order were set up at Bretton Woods it was widely expected that the institutions would operate as non-political, merely carrying out technical functions. One of the reasons for the separation is that free-market economic behaviour is considered rational, whilst politics is considered irrational, with political intervention in the economy introducing many costs which reduce efficiency. Hence, efficiency demands a minimum of political intervention from a state that is represented as an aggregation of private interests, a plural competition among interest groups. The other reason for the practical separation is the assumption that conflict can be managed by international economic agencies because it takes place within a system which generates continual economic growth. In other words, the global economy is viewed as a non-zero-sum situation, in which conflict can be managed because bargains can be struck between entities on the basis that everyone could gain.

While the LP paradigm accepts the existence of states and allocates them certain roles in the global economy (the maintenance of peace) and of a specific global economic order (labelled 'free trade' but including the movement and location of capital and the regulation of the institutions of capital), there is a certain tension between the global economy and *international* politics. If the political system remains dominated by states and the interstate system, the structure of politics becomes increasingly anachronistic from the point of view of economics because it prevents the full realization of the efficiency gains of a global system. Thus the LP paradigm gives a higher priority to economic values and structures than to the political; efficiency gains would be highest *if* the structure of politics reflected that of economics, i.e. we had a world government! In the meantime the complexity of the global economy must be managed, normally through the process of international cooperation and coordination, and the economy itself encouraged to grow to ensure the maximization of benefits and their appropriate distribution.

Neo-Marxism

The neo-Marxist paradigm shares with realism a central assumption about the nature of the global economy: that it is inherently conflictual. In both paradigms the conflict is *structural* because of the framework within which interstate economic relations take place. In realism it is the framework of an anarchic world order, whilst for neo-Marxism it is the framework of dominance-dependence that is constituted by global capitalism. Again, the global economy does not always seem conflictual, but that is because the patterns of domination are sometimes very subtle, involving language and consciousness as well as material exploitation. The global nature of modern capitalism is the logical and historical culmination of capitalism as an economic system, and the global level reproduces and intensifies the conditions of capitalist production: that the key actors are classes, and that economic relations are structured for the benefit of class interests. Global capitalism is not just multinationals and high levels of economic interdependence between national economies; it is an integrated system, a whole, with a built-in dynamic which continually brings about change as the system expands, as it must. For individuals, groups and states, wealth and economic growth are determined by their position within the structure of global capitalism, not only as members of a national economy but as actual and potential members of the capitalist class. This produces not only a vertical structure of dominance-dependence between core and periphery, but a horizontal structure of class relations whereby groups in the periphery (usually, but not always, pre-existing elites) are coopted into the system the more their national economy is structured by and is dependent on global capitalism.

Neo-Marxism covers a wide range of writings and it is sometimes difficult to extract general principles from within this paradigm. And one of the distinctions we have to make to understand neo-Marxism is that between instrumental (classical) and structural (neo) Marxism (see chapter 4). In the instrumental version the state, and its institutions, is a direct expression of class interests, and policy merely reinforces and reflects the interests of the capitalist class. By contrast, for structural Marxists the state can have an *independent* role within the framework of the capitalist system as a whole. In this version of Marxism the state is involved in an effort to deal with economic and political contradictions that are inherent in a capitalist system. Our neo-Marxist paradigm broadly reflects the structural Marxist position, but bear in mind that not all Marxists writing today are neo-Marxists. Modern Marxist thinkers, particularly Antonio Gramsci, have extended the structural understanding of the state within the system of capitalism and, whilst accepting the material basis of the system, have emphasized the importance of culture and the role of legitimating ideas that both generate consensus and mystify and cloak the objective relationships within capitalism. In this way neo-Marxism looks very different from classical Marxism.

Given the above view of the state, the relationship between the global economy and politics indicated by this paradigm is clear: politics is a reflection of economics, of the structure of global capitalism, rather than of the immediate needs of national class interests. Economics ultimately determines politics in the fundamental sense that political institutions and relations exist only as an extension of economic relations, although the framework for these economic relations is global rather than contained within the state.

THE REALIST PARADIGM

In this section of the chapter our purpose will be to flesh out our understanding of the realist paradigm in relation to the global economy.

How does the realist view of the global political economy explain what we need to explain – the relationship between the global economy and contemporary global politics? The core assumption of the centrality of the state (which is larger than the sum of its parts) for both national and international purposes imposes a particular framework on global political and economic relations. First, it constructs an international economy, rather than a world or global economy, where *significant* economic relationships are between and among states, that is national economies. And the most important economic relationships are those among the richest and most powerful states, with the interesting exception of those less developed countries (LDCs) who supply key raw materials. In these cases disruption of supply becomes a threat to the economic security of the core states and political measures are normally taken to ensure that the impact of disruption is minimized. The purpose and direction of this international economy is determined by the dominant state(s) in line with the demands of domestic politics. As David Calleo shows in his *Imperious Economy* (1982) and Jeremy Mitchell discusses in chapter 9 in this book, much of the history of the post-1945 system is made up of the US attempt to internationalize its domestic structure and processes. This is a characteristic of all hegemonic states. Second, the assumption of the centrality of the state incorporates an associated assumption on the extent of the autonomy of politics and the autonomy of the national economy. Apart from setting up the state as the key mediator between the global economy and the national economy, it reinforces a distinction between national and international and denies, not the existence of trans-national relations, but their effective political impact upon the state. Hence this paradigm recognizes the importance of the internationalized money markets but assumes sufficient political autonomy (of the Group of Seven members, for example) to enable states to control the consequences of such structures, either through collective action such as policy coordination, or through policy taken by the leading states individually.

For realism, then, the structure of the global economy is determined by state power and the way in which state power is externalized through hegemony. Hence changes in the relative power position (political, economic and strategic) of the hegemon have an impact on every member of the hegemonic system, to the extent that each state is integrated into the hegemonic system.

Not surprisingly, the subsidiary concepts coming out of the realist core assumptions also embody particular state-based conceptions of economic and political reality. The best example of this is the concept of hegemony as discussed in chapter 9. A realist conception of hegemony is based on the changing material power and relative economic position of the hegemonic state. An analysis based on this realist conception of hegemony would lead to the conclusion that the US is losing or has lost hegemony and therefore different global structures are necessary and are in fact emerging. However, if hegemony is conceptualized in a different way, a different conclusion is possible. If we use the conception of the world political economy developed by Susan Strange (1988), which identifies four prime structures, we can conclude that because the US still dominates these structures it still has hegemonic power. Or, if we conceptualize hegemony as more than material power to include the power of ideas and culture, as is suggested by Gill and Law (1988), we can conclude that the US still has hegemony, although its leaders and politicians do not perceive this to be the case. If the substantive conclusion is that the US is still a hegemonic power, the belief by its leaders that it no longer has this power itself becomes a factor explaining the current problems in the world political economy. It is important to see the limitations of a realist concept of hegemony based on the measurement of material capabilities and on a state-centred conception of the global political economy.

THE LIBERAL-PLURALIST PARADIGM

It is in some ways more difficult to tie down the LP view of the relationship between the global economy and global politics. This is partly because of the implicit assumption that LP makes of the inherent rationality of economic behaviour as compared with political, and partly because the liberal view which forms the basis of LP contains some inconsistencies in its logic. Hence political responses to economic challenges are seen as irrational, interfering and promoting inefficiency. The role of politics is to minimize disruption, to provide a stable political environment for economic activity and to manage the transition to a world market and world production – for only at the global level will the benefits of efficiency be realized. The global economy and the state are in a facilitating alliance, where politics is an enabling structure and a set of processes, but where the goals of the whole system are set by the values of the economy. In addition, the nature of the relationships is a product not only of the way the LP paradigm conceptualizes the global economy in market terms, but also of the way in which politics is construed. As we have seen from chapter 1, the disaggregation of the state and the interstate system into a large number of actors and policy arenas is a notable feature of the LP paradigm. This disaggregation mirrors the structure and process of an ideal market in economics: a large number of actors, many arenas of activity, and no one actor able solely either to determine outcomes or to change the nature of the structure, that is the market system itself. It is interesting, therefore, to note that this paradigm seems more adequately to be able to explain periods and events in the global political economy which take place when there is no *effective* hegemonic power (for whatever reason), such as the period between the two world wars analysed by Richard Bessel in chapter 8. Moreover, the resurgence of the LP paradigm in its contemporary form coincided with the American realization of the breakdown of the post-war Bretton Woods system, a system which had, in practice rather than by design, relied on American hegemonic power.

The LP view, as are all the paradigms, is open to many interpretations, criticisms and revisions, but for the purpose of this chapter only a few central features need to be examined. Let us here start with the core assumption of the relationship between politics and economics, because so many of the concepts of the LP paradigm that relate to the global economy flow from this one assumption. In the predominance that LP gives to the economic, it downplays other values derived from society. LP reproduces what Karl Polanyi calls the 'economistic fallacy', where the separation of economics from other aspects of society is assumed to be given for all societies rather than a specific historical creation. As a result it naturally downplays the importance of social and political values and structures, particularly and most importantly nationalism and other political ideologies. As a result, economic values are assumed to dominate all societies. This point is very well illustrated when we look at the LP view of development, which assumes not only that all societies can be understood outside their historical context, but also that all societies wish to emulate Western capitalist societies in the economic goal of a society with high mass consumption.

One of the consequences of this unique role given to economics is to identify the market economy, in our case the global economy defined and limited by the existence of a global market, as a natural expression of social life, not only separated from but *above* politics. And it is this feature of LP, the ideological depoliticization of economics, that makes it most open to question and criticism. This critical assessment makes the LP analysis (and complaint), that economics and international economics have become politicized by interdependence and other developments, appear rather naive in its assumption that they were never political in the first place.

The emphasis on a plurality of actors in the global political economy has the important effect of at best understating and at worst ignoring the wider context within which action takes place. Action and actors only have import and meaning within a pre-existing structure, for example the US hegemonic structure. This point is well illustrated by considering the progress of the LDCs in achieving a new international economic order: where the LP paradigm would identify specific negotiations between key actors (which are, of course, important) it tends to ignore the underlying values of the existing system, and it is precisely these underlying values that the LDCs challenge. In general, the pluralism of LP tends to take insufficient account of structures. We see this clearly in the definition of the state as *no more than* the aggregation of plural interest groups, whereas realists would give a key role to the state as an organization in its own right, with definite interests distinct from the plurality of other interests. Similarly in the global political economy there are assumed to be no *overarching* structural conditions which broadly set the context for action, yet we have seen that this is not the case for many who participate in the global economy. Most individuals and groups and the majority of states have to accept the existing structure of the global economy as it impinges on their lives; they do not have the power to change either rules or outcomes.

THE NEO-MARXIST PARADIGM

The neo-Marxist paradigm contains a clear statement of the relationship between the global economy and the pattern of global politics. As we have seen, the structural economic forces of capitalism condition and ultimately determine the nature, structure and content of politics. The scope for political autonomy for states within the capitalist system is thus limited by the structural features of global capitalism. It might appear that states and other groups have extensive autonomy, but the boundaries of political action are set by the capitalist system. Moreover, the long-term purpose of politics is also set by the system. As you might expect from our discussion of the dominance of politics over economics within realism, this conclusion is directly the opposite of the position taken by realism. Realism sets out the state as the dominant structure, with political goals and frameworks that condition and limit economic autonomy. For neo-Marxism the state, the interstate system and the institutions of the interstate system all reflect the interests of an international capital, and the economic problems these entities are attempting to manage derive from the contradictions inherent in the long-term development of capitalism. Within the economic crisis there are two political struggles going on: at the superficial level, the struggle between national sections of international capital to increase their share of the global product within the existing system, and at the same time to expand this system; and at the fundamental level, the struggle between capital and labour to defend or change the nature of the system itself (see Hymer 1975 for this point). The superficial struggle is important as it extends and deepens the system. However, the extension and deepening of the system present a problem for states, particularly at the core. The internationalization of national capital takes much economic activity outside the control of the state (not unlike the LP argument). This creates what Kolko has described as 'a constant contradiction between nationalism and the integration of the world economy' (Kolko 1988, p. 81) which presents itself as an intractable problem of domestic and international economic management for states.

As the capitalist system expands globally, state forms and national economies are drawn into the periphery. This happens at different times and with very different results for each state, depending on a range of factors. To the extent that the peripheral state is integrated into global capitalism its autonomy is reduced and it is obliged to enter the first type of struggle, a struggle in which it is in a dependent relationship to the core. However, integration into global capitalism does not work only or even primarily at the national level. Different sectors of peripheral states become integrated at different times and some sectors are marginalized by the whole process, creating a dual economy. This differential integration breaks down national political forms as the pattern of social relations of production that are inherent in capitalism quickly replaces non-capitalist social relations.

Although there are many varieties of neo-Marxist theories, all of which differ in their emphasis and in the distinctions they make, the above summary hopefully does no variety an injustice. The neo-Marxist conception of the global economy and its relationship to politics is grounded in the philosophical basis of historical materialism. Essentially this translates into the principle that the satisfaction of material needs and wants through economic activity is the determining aspect of human existence. Society, politics and ideas all follow from the way in which material needs are met. Without going through the full outline of the neo-Marxist interpretation of historical materialism, it should be reasonably clear how important this assumption is for the neo-Marxist view of the global political economy. We can identify variations of interpretation and different strands of thought, but they all start from this view of history. But, most importantly, this view of history, as with *all* paradigmatic assumptions, cannot be proven or demonstrated to be true in any absolute sense, and cannot be disproven either.

One particular and important problem generated by the determination of politics by economics is the question of the autonomy of the state. It is worth reminding ourselves of the neo-Marxist position. As Kolko (1988) points out, there is a wide range of opinion within this paradigm on the nature of the state. But what most seem to agree on is that the state is *subordinate* to the capitalist system, although not necessarily a direct instrument of the capitalist class. In this matter Kolko has no doubts: 'It would appear that in the present period that, far from being autonomous, the state is barely even separable from capital as a category of analysis.' This means that even giving the state an analytical identity, that is even talking about it as a separate entity, is in this view to give the state more significance than it deserves. As we have seen, this view is not typical of neo-Marxism, but few neo-Marxists would give the state the kind of autonomy that our two other paradigms attribute. The neo-Marxist view of the state is clearly at odds with both of the other paradigms and gives a very different explanation of the development and structure of the post-1945 global political economy.

COMPARING PARADIGMS

Once we accept that our understanding of the global economy is a product of the assumptions and theories we hold, and that we hold these assumptions and theories because understanding is a social process which generates the paradigms we use, comparing and evaluating paradigms becomes much more difficult. Deciding between paradigms is not reducible to logic or empirical evidence and conclusions alone, because:

> There is no appropriate scale available with which to weigh the merits of alternative paradigms; they are *incommensurable*. To favour one paradigm rather than another is in the last analysis to express preference for one form of life rather than another – a preference which cannot be rationalized by any non-circular argument.
>
> (Barnes 1982, p. 65)

This point is a fundamental one and is worth further thought. If paradigms are incommensurable, that is they have no common measure, how do we then decide on the merits of a paradigm? We have seen from chapter 4, in relation to evaluating explanations of US interventionism in Central America, that *evaluating* an explanation is difficult and requires the use of a meta-theory, that is a theory of evaluation itself. We shall return to the notion of a meta-theory of evaluation, but before this it is important to make a few points that derive from the incommensurability of our paradigms. First, no one paradigm can provide the universally accepted explanation; this is not me being dogmatic and refusing to accept an overarching view but an inherent characteristic of paradigmatic knowledge. Hence, a search for the ultimate paradigm is both misguided and perhaps dangerous because it implies that there *is* one true view of reality. Second, conflicting paradigms, as we have here, are an integral part of the reality of the global political economy and cannot be analysed out into one superparadigm; conflicting and complementing ideas will always be with us. Third, each one of us will compare and evaluate one of the three paradigms from a position *within* the same or another paradigm. In other words, we cannot stand above or apart from some kind of paradigm which forms the basis of our own values and understanding. This last point is fundamental to any evaluation of our competing paradigms.

These observations do not mean that we accept or reject paradigms purely on the basis of personal preference. There are critera we can apply which will at least identify the strengths and weaknesses of a paradigm, if not its overall merit. These criteria are derived from the philosophical basis of understanding international relations and, like most Western social science, employ a particular though widely accepted notion of 'how we know what we know'. The basis of 'how we know what we know' is known as epistemology, and the epistemology of international relations here provides the meta-theory which enables us to state a number of criteria which we shall use to evaluate our paradigms. From a broadly accepted epistemology we can initially identify these criteria as follows:

Consistency Two aspects of consistency are important: internal and external. Internally, to what extent does the paradigm provide explanations that are consistent in their internal logic? (This can be approached initially through formal rules of logic.) Externally, does the paradigm account for the facts of the case being explained?

Coherence   The extent to which any interpretation or account of a social or political phenomenon provides a clearly argued and reasoned narrative.

Comprehensiveness   The extent to which a paradigm accounts for the available facts and how many facts remain to be explained. Generally, the more comprehensive a paradigm the less the range of facts unaccounted for.

Scope   To what extent can a paradigm explain new or changing situations and phenomena which were *not* included in its original assumptions? (This is a criterion that I would add to the generally accepted three Cs given above.)

In comparing and evaluating our three paradigms we need to use *all four* of the above criteria. It is not sufficient, for example, for a paradigm to be coherent and internally consistent if it does not explain what we need or want to explain. Similarly, a paradigm might seem to offer a perfectly good and comprehensive explanation but be logically inconsistent in its explanation.

With these criteria in mind, let us now return briefly to a comparison of the three paradigms using the following questions derived from Gilipin's (1987) analysis.

What is the Nature of Economic Relations?

This is a core question, and from it derives each paradigm's notion of the global economy. Both realism and neo-Marxism see economic relations as ultimately inherently conflictual, although cooperation takes place for instrumental reasons, whereas for LP they are essentially harmonious. We are certainly experiencing the conflictual nature of economic relations in the contemporary global political economy, although it is also possible to see that with an expanding broadly based global economy economic relations could be harmonious. However, because LP assumes harmonious relations it is hard pressed to supply explanations for the evident conflicts we have today.

What are the Major Economic Actors?

Here the three paradigms differ completely in emphasis and identification. The realist state is replaced by a multiplicity of actors for LP, predominantly corporations and households with a facilitating and mediating state; whereas the actors for neo-Marxism are of a different kind, classes with a subordinate state and state system. These specified actors do not mean that the paradigms in question do not admit the existence of other actors, only that these actors are the significant ones. Hence each would admit the existence of international organizations such as the IMF, but each would interpret them differently. The key question for us is where does the state fit? We cannot ignore the state, yet the internationalization of economic activity, which all the paradigms accept, has created changed objective circumstances for the state. But we also cannot ignore the existence and power of the corporation in the global economy. The concentration of economic power that the corporation represents clearly requires us to take account of such actors, again even if they can be interpreted differently: as an extension of state power for the realist, as a transnational economic actor among a range of such actors for LP, and as an extension and manifestation of the global capitalist system for the neo-Marxist.

What are the Major Characteristics of the Global Economy?

First, is the economy global? Perhaps yes, but each tends to define the extent of global differently. Realism has tended to confine the global to the (ideological) West (i.e. includes LDCs not aligned with the East) with non-inclusion of the centrally planned economies (CPEs), although this has changed. LP tends to see global as defined by the extent of the market. This includes some CPEs, but others only slightly; it also includes most LDCs, although very large numbers of people in these economies are not part of a monetized market economy. Neo-Marxism defines the global economy by the expansion of capitalism and the integration of states into the system; it is ambivalent on the CPEs but includes most LDCs.

Second, what are the main problems of the global economy? Each paradigm identifies a form of crisis in the global economy. The realist crisis is one of declining hegemony with a consequent loss of control for states and increasing instability for the global economy. The LP crisis is managing complexity and interdependence in an increasingly complex and unstable system beset with rapid technological change. Finally, the neo-Marxist crisis is one of the historical evolution of the capitalist system; the internationalization of production, which characterizes modern capitalism, reproduces the inherent contradictions of capitalism in a global form. Only the neo-Marxist focuses directly on the problems of the LDCs, whose populations constitute 80 per cent of the world total.

What is the Nature of the State?

We have already dealt extensively with this question, but it is fair to say that it is given the most searching analysis by the neo-Marxist, for whom the continued power of the state and its relation to capital constitute an important theoretical and practical problem. Neither realism nor LP subject the concept of the state to searching analysis, preferring instead to assume respectively a dominating organic whole (via the concept of national interest) or an accommodating plurality in which the state is deemed to have no interests of its own.

What is the Relationship between Economics and Politics?

This key question is not answerable in as straightforward a manner as we would perhaps like, because the advocates of each of our paradigms have attempted to make them as comprehensive and as consistent as possible. And in so doing the posited relationship between economics and politics, which is the basis of each paradigm's view of the global economy, has become more complex. For example, it is clear that for classical Marxism the relationship is unquestioned: economics *determines* politics. But the attempts of Marxists, or more accurately historical materialists, to deal with the complex forms of modern global capitalism has produced a neo-Marxism which has a more ambivalent view of the relationship. Now, neo-Marxists give limited autonomy to politics and political institutions, moving away from a strict and immediate economic determinism. However, in the longer term politics is still *subordinate* to economics, that is the long-term goals and possibilities are set by economics, and economics (specifically the structure of global capitalism) provides the context for politics. Similarly, neo-realism has moved away from the strident political determinism of the state and its needs that characterized an earlier view, to encompass structural forms of economy and interdependence in which other actors and a broad range of relationships are significant. But our realist paradigm still stresses the domination of politics over economics, the imperatives of the *interstate* system over the demands of the global economy. The relationship between economics and politics posited by the liberal-pluralist paradigm is more complex. Because of the particular separation of politics and economics envisaged by the LP paradigm, politics is seen as a necessary enabling activity; LP economics is predicated on a particular political context, with a specific and limited role for the state. In this paradigm the structures and forms of liberal economics should *determine* politics in the long run, because of the inherent rationality of economic activity.

Summary

Taking an overview of each paradigm from the above questions is helpful in drawing together an assessment of their ability to explain what we are interested in. Realism provides us with a clear and deceptively simple framework in which economic power is a necessary component of state power and economic forces are subordinate to national and international political demands. Hence the history of the global economy is one of the rise and fall of great powers, whose hegemonic rules have brought some stability and whose decline brings instability. Change in the international system is a product of change in the hegemon. For this paradigm, the fundamental problem facing the contemporary global economy is declining US hegemonic power, and the way that the US and its allies respond to this problem will determine what will happen. Neo-Marxism is equally as clear in its formulation of the problem, but denies the possibility that states can manage their way out of the crisis because the crisis is systemic; unless the nature of the capitalist system is changed, resolution is impossible. Thus only a temporary accommodation can be achieved through political means. For neo-Marxism, change is produced by economic and technological forces, and the fundamental problem facing the global economy is to resolve the contradictions which reproduce exploitation throughout the whole system (within and between states) but more noticeably in the LDCs. Finally, liberal-pluralism is less clear cut in some respects. The history of the post-war economy is one of increasing interdependence and pluralism because of rapid economic change and expansion. In order for the state to coexist with the global economy and for its citizens to benefit from the increased material wealth produced, complexity has to be managed without sacrificing the economic benefits gained so far. In the contemporary global economy, international cooperation seems to offer the solution to the crisis, but any long-term resolution involves international policy cooperation that must inevitably further erode the autonomy of the state. Remember that policy *coordination*, unlike cooperation, necessarily involves changing domestic policies to fit with internationally agreed system goals.

EVALUATING PARADIGMS

In his study of the international political economy, Gilpin (1987) takes a number of features and problems identified by his interpretation of the Marxist ideology and grafts these on to his own realist paradigm of the political economy of international relations, for example the process of uneven growth. This is a good illustration of an important preliminary point: paradigms of the global political economy can *overlap* and can *inform each other*. Following from this we can illustrate the relationship between paradigms of the global economy by figure 12.1, where each paradigm is represented by a circle. The paradigms overlap because they identify common features and phenomena of the global economy, but they do so on the basis of different premises and assumptions about the nature of the world (in other words they have a different ontology). The area of overlap, shaded in the diagram, is however not fixed, partly because the paradigms themselves are not fixed statements of explanation, but alter over time and with modification and are thus subject to different interpretations. In effect, what actually constitutes the main explanations and claims of a paradigm is itself disputable. The overlap is also not fixed partly because the global economy itself is changing, and changing in different ways. One good example of the overlap is the incorporation into the realist paradigm of the condition of interdependence, initially characterized by the liberal-pluralist paradigm. The state is faced with the evolving condition of interdependence and has to deal with this as part of the existing structure of the global economy. Similarly, the neo-Marxist view increasingly has had to come to terms with the political autonomy of the state, although, as we have seen, this is a much disputed matter. In this way it is possible to identify a number of features that are identified by two or all three paradigms. Moreover, as the paradigms are developed to take account of objective changes in the global economy, such as the internationalization of banking in the 1970s, they sometimes fade into one another at different points, particularly in areas that are clearly undergoing change. However, and notwithstanding this latter point, I would argue that they still retain a fundamental difference in the basic explanation that is posited of the relationship between the global economy and the pattern of contemporary global politics.

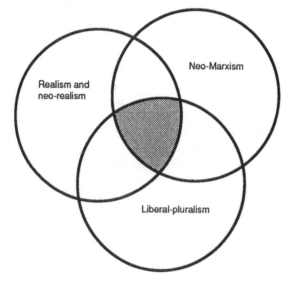

Figure 12.1 Overlapping paradigms: shaded area represents identified features of the global economy common to all three paradigms

Even though we do have some clear areas of overlap in the identification of important features and problems, we are still left with the problem of evaluation. How do we evaluate which is the best *explanation*? And here it is explanation we are after because we are concerned to understand cause and effect. In the process of evaluation of paradigms of the global economy, we immediately confront the implication that, once we set up knowledge as conditioned by paradigms, *all* knowledge becomes paradigmatic. In this sense, knowledge is paradigmatic either because it fits into and supports the dominant or broadly accepted paradigms (realism, liberal-pluralism and neo-Marxism, among the advocates of which there is a struggle for dominance) or because it challenges any one or all of these and attempts itself to become *the* paradigm. In other words, the process of evaluation paradigms is *itself* conditioned by one's own paradigm. It is impossible, in the final analysis, to stand outside paradigms, and any judgement that an individual makes about paradigms, is made from a position *within* a paradigm. The key here is that paradigmatic knowledge is consensual knowledge among those attempting to understand the phenomena under investigation. That is, it is knowledge produced through a social or group process of agreeing 'what is', continually juxtaposed with the group's experience of the objective world.

Now, it should be reasonably clear what our next task is: to review each of our paradigms for consistency, coherence, comprehensiveness and scope as a necessary step to giving them the status of acceptable and competing (i.e. of equal validity) paradigms. For, if one of the paradigms is more or less consistent, more or less coherent, or more or less comprehensive than the others, or if one clearly has greater scope, there may be a case for either not accepting that paradigm or giving it preference over the other two.

Some, like Gilpin, (1987), conclude that each paradigm has strengths and weaknesses, and this conclusion is right. It is possible to incorporate elements of each paradigm into an eclectic explanation, as does Gilpin. However, some of you may find this process very unsatisfactory (as I do) and may be wondering whether we can progress any further in this matter. I find it unsatisfactory for two principal reasons. First, our choice of paradigms and what we consider to be the strengths and weaknesses of a paradigm is conditioned by a particular conception of reality that, as Gilpin rightly points out, is non-falsifiable in a scientific sense. Therefore, the choice of paradigm ultimately is not about the scientific criteria that we have discussed, because *each paradigm can probably meet these criteria*. Providing the paradigm meets these criteria as a necessary condition, the choice must be related to the political, social and economic values embodied in the paradigm. All this makes the perhaps totally unwarranted assumption that the choice of paradigm is a rational and conscious exercise: how many of us think the way we do because of our upbringing, our economic life chances or our culture? Do we accept one paradigm over another because we are socialized into certain values?

Secondly, even if we can rationally choose or construct the best paradigm to explain what we want to explain (here, the relationship between the global economy and the pattern of contemporary politics), I feel that our methods of evaluating paradigms (our epistemology) are inappropriate for what we want to do. This is because our epistemology and our three paradigms are based on the separation of subject and object in the process of political action and the analytical processes of understanding, explaining and evaluating. This means we assume that we, as human beings, can stand *outside* political action. I do not believe that this is an adequate basis for understanding. And

I think we have to address this problem in order to progress in our understanding of the relationship between the global economy and the pattern of contemporary global politics.

Liberal international political economy is more than an academic perspective dependent for its explanatory power on its coherence, consistency and comprehensiveness. My argument here is that the liberal paradigm itself has become part of the objective reality of the global political economy, and thus is a core element of structural power in the global political economy. Indeed, it is becoming clear that the liberal paradigm is being replaced as the set of dominant ideas by realism, particularly in the policies of the hegemonic (or declining hegemonic) state, the US. From this comes the point that our paradigms are themselves part of the power structure and have to be viewed in this political sense.

Accordingly we need a distinction between two kinds of paradigms and theories. The first is problem solving, that is the theories accept the broad historical context within which they are located and are principally useful in explaining problems within that context. The second kind comprises those theories that try to explain their own historical context and in so doing begin to explain their own emergence as paradigms. Robert Cox (1986) labels these critical theories, in contrast to the problem solving theories which take their historical context as given, as a starting point, without trying to explain how the problems came about. The extent to which a paradigm and the theories it produces is critical, in the sense used here, links to the paradigm's ability to explain phenomena beyond its original context as well as its ability to explain *itself*.

Now, what does an evaluation of our three paradigms look like when we apply such an extended meta-theory of evaluation? The criteria still include consistency, coherence and comprehensiveness, although we should be aware of the essentially contingent nature of any conclusions we draw. In addition, we need to consider whether our paradigms offer two things. The first, at the level of meta-theory, is an account of their own emergence and context as ideas. That is, do any of our paradigms conceptualize ideas as part of the structure of power? To what extent are they *reflexive*? This is of fundamental importance because the paradigm itself must be seen as part of the political structure and has to be understood and evaluated as more than a set of academic ideas separated from political action and subject to rational choice. The second, at the level of substantive explanation, is an account of phenomena that goes beyond its original historical context. In other words, what is the *scope* of the paradigms? Do our paradigms offer a critical analysis, one that is aware of the broad historical context of the problems?

With regard to these two new related criteria, only neo-Marxism and, in a much more limited sense, neo-realism take into consideration the role of ideas and hence their *own* roles as paradigms. Liberal-pluralism does not consider ideas as power, and nor does it attempt to give an explanation of its own emergence. In terms of scope, liberal-pluralism seems to me the most limited of our paradigms. It is principally focused on problem solving within a specified context. Both realism and neo-Marxism offer a broader analysis than LP, but realism is confined to the interstate system as a context whilst neo-Marxism attempts to locate the state system within an even broader framework. What both realism and neo-Marxism clearly illustrated when we use these extended criteria of evaluation is that the US as the post-1945 hegemon used the ideas of liberal-pluralism to maintain and extend its own position in the global political economy because the ideas of LP at that time served the interests of the US, as well as a number of other states.

If we use all five criteria of evaluation we will get a better judgement of the adequacy of the three paradigms. Whilst none of our paradigms fully meets the demands of the five criteria, neo-realism and neo-Marxism seem to provide a better explanation of the relationship between the global economy and global politics.

References

Barnes, B. (1982) *T.S. Kuhn and Social Science*. London: Macmillan.

Calleo, D. (1982) *The Imperious Economy*. London: Harvard University Press.

Cox, R. (1986) Social forces, states and world orders: beyond international relations theory. In R.O. Keohane (ed.), *Neo-Realism and its Critics*, New York: Columbia University Press.

Dell, E. (1987) *The Politics of Economic Interdependence*. London: Macmillan.

Gill, S. and Law, D. (1988) *The Global Political Economy: Perspectives, Problems and Policies*. Brighton: Harvester Wheatsheaf.

Gilpin, R. (1987) *The Political Economy of International Relations*. Princeton: Princeton University Press.

Hymer, S. (1975) International politics and international economics: a radical approach. In L. Lindberg (ed.), *Stress and Contradiction in Modern Capitalism*, Lexington, MA: Lexington Books.

Kolko, J. (1988) *Restructuring the World Economy*. New York: Pantheon Books.

Strange, S. (1988) *States and Markets*. London: Pinter Publishers.

Part IV

Modernity
and
the Transition
to a Global Society

13

Modernization, Globalization and the Nation-State

MICHAEL SMITH

Introduction

Writers, politicians and the course of international affairs remind us constantly that politics everywhere is connected with politics everywhere else. Through a variety of processes and channels, power is now exercised at a global level in a variety of spheres and with a bewildering variety of political effects. Indeed, many of the earlier chapters of this book have dealt with precisely these phenomena, pointing out the ways in which economic, technological and military power have extended their range and their impacts. This process of extension has had its effect not only on the empirical reality of world politics but also on the way analysts and practitioners conceive of the global arena. There is greater awareness of common entanglement and of the interconnectedness of events and problems, but at the same time this has given rise to new areas of debate about the development of the international system and the ways in which global political issues might be managed.

In this chapter, the aim is to provide an assessment of three central elements which contribute to global politics in the round:

1 The notion of globalization: the idea that, through a series of mechanisms, the world has become more closely interconnected, and by implication that it will continue to become more closely interconnected. But what have been the crucial mechanisms in this process? When did the process start, and why? Is it inevitable that the process will continue, or can it be halted and even reversed?

2 The concept of modernization: the cluster of trends and processes, at the national and the international level, which has produced new forms of economic, social and political organization and which has encouraged the development of global communications, production and exchange. But how far does the phenomenon of modernization extend? Does it not produce and reproduce forms of inequality and conflict, as opposed to collaboration and progress? Does modernization enhance or diminish the possibility of solutions to global problems?

3 The role of the state: although central to the traditional conception of international

politics, this is thrown into question by the emergence of global processes and perceptions, and is challenged by the transnational logic of modernization. But is the state not also the building block of a global politics? Despite its limitations, is its power not also enhanced by the processes of technological, economic and political change which have taken place? How might the ambiguous position of the state affect the attempt to manage global issues and achieve some kind of global order?

These elements are potentially all-encompassing, but they form an essential part of the attempt to conceptualize global politics. They also define the arena for spirited debate among the protagonists of different perspectives on global politics, and the later parts of the chapter will address the major features of the debates which have emerged.

GLOBALIZATION

One of the most obvious features of globalization is the fact that it reflects a lengthy process of historical development characterized by intense political competition and reflecting the exercise of power in a variety of forms. George Modelski (1972) conceives of the globalization process as a series of waves represented by the impacts of different and successive civilizations. Significantly, though, he sees the political unification of the world as emerging directly from only one civilization – that which centred upon the nation-states of Europe. These states differed from their predecessors in a number of crucial respects, which not only made the political unification of the globe possible, but also ensured that it followed certain patterns and took certain forms. In the first place, these states possessed an unprecedented range of power, reflecting a comparative advantage in naval and military technology. Not only this, but they drew strength from their statehood itself, which provided them with the means to mobilize and concentrate their power and a form of ideology with which to support it and motivate their citizens.

The quasi-ideology of independent statehood, combined with the force of nationalism, thus provided the basis on which the great maritime colonial empires of the seventeenth to the nineteenth centuries were founded. To this extent, then, the world was politically unified, since the politics of the European powers were projected on a global scale and the institutions of Western civilization were exported to the rest of the globe. It is open to question, though, what was the depth as opposed to the breadth of this process. The global politics of the European powers can be seen as only one of a number of layers around which political activity was centred, and likewise the growth of a global community was in many respects superficial.

The historical process of globalization is an essential prerequisite for a notion of global politics. In some respects, it might be better to see this not as an independent process but primarily as the strengthening of the global reach of European states, and particularly of states in what we now know as Western Europe. These states could mobilize a number of assets in dealing with other parts of the world, and three in particular were crucial. First, there was the ability and willingness to use large-scale violence, often based on technological supremacy. Second, there was an assumed cultural supremacy which was often translated into political and social institutions. Finally, as already noted, there was maritime power and organization, which married up in many cases with military and technological power. The global power of the Europeans rested not only upon raw strength but also on organization and institutions, a crucial factor when it comes to the translation of potential advantage into actual domination.

Although the Europeans came to dominate, the process of expansion was not simply a one-way projection of power. The politics of globalization had important effects on the European states themselves, since they had to organize for world power, and in the process they were transformed internally. In a way, this poses a chicken and egg problem: did these societies succeed at the global level because they had changed internally, or did their global responsibilities lead to domestic change? Whatever the true direction of the process, it is clear that the emergence of the great European colonial empires was accompanied by several significant trends in domestic statehood: the growth of bureaucracy and military organization, the expansion of government budgets, the development of corporate commercial organization and the consolidation of the technological and scientific base for state activity.

The process of globalization was also not without its broader paradoxes. In particular, whilst it may have unified the globe politically, it also created intense divisions and tensions. In many parts of the world, existing institutions and orders were overthrown, but no global institutions and order arose to replace them. A large community was created, but this community was riven by conflicts and open to disruption, not least by the European states on whose power it was founded. Modelski expresses this paradox in the form of a question: 'Globalization ultimately raises the question of whether the large community, indeed the community of mankind, can be a good community' (1972, p. 56). If there is a global community, it is important to ask in whose interests it operates, and whether it represents an indisputable advance over less extensive forms of political organization.

Globalization has thus had an uneven and ambiguous impact upon the world arena. Despite wide-ranging changes, it is argued by many writers that the process of globalization is fluid and unfinished: in effect, that global politics represents a transitional world, containing elements of many cultures, political practices and power structures. Roger Masters (1969) draws the conclusion that world politics contains factors of instability underlined by the decentralization of power and by the essentially uneven impact of economic, social and political change. Perhaps most significantly, he also argues that the crucial catalyst in determining the state of global politics is that of culture, and the existence of a multicultural world without the regulating influence of a global state or government:

> The international political system currently includes radically different political cultures...national systems which face the task of integrating different political cultures are subject to strains that are absent in more homogenous societies; *a fortiori*, this problem is even greater in a system which permits many antagonistic political cultures to organize themselves into autonomous nation-states. In general, therefore, it could be argued that self-help and structural decentralization tend to produce a greater degree of instability in world politics than in most primitive stateless societies.
>
> (p. 115)

Although this conclusion might tend to support a view of world politics as a form of anarchy, Masters also concludes that the emergence of intermittent structures of collaboration between nation-states in the global context provides a basis for some predictability and order. Perhaps most importantly from the point of view of the argument here, it also provides a basis for the argument that globalization has produced a global politics based upon the nation-state. This argument now demands investigation.

A Global System of States

As can be seen from the preceding discussion, the role of the state in global politics is inherently ambivalent. On the one hand, the state can be seen as the vehicle for the global spread of economic and technological progress, but on the other, it can be presented as the source of violence and repression, and as a fundamental barrier to the unification of the world. Equally, it can be argued almost in the same breath both that the state is being or has been weakened by the changes relating to globalization, and that it has been strengthened by precisely those changes. The forces of technological, economic or military power can be seen both as bursting the bounds of the national state and as providing it with yet further strength to control its citizens and its social life. In order to explore these apparent paradoxes, it is necessary first to take the state at face value – to assess its role as a building block of the global system, and to analyse the implications this has for the processes of global politics. This position will be challenged later, but at this stage it is important to see where it leads.

In the traditional study of international politics, and in its practice, the state assumes pride of place as the central component of the international system and the source of its most significant actions and interactions. The realist paradigm of world politics expresses this position, with its focus on the elements of statehood: sovereign territoriality, authority and legitimacy, recognition, control of citizens and their actions. Although the realities of statehood can and do diverge from this ideal type, the assumptions reflect powerful perceptions about the pervasive strength of states and their historical domination of the global political arena. The state, it appears, is a source of order and authority domestically, and a major concentration of power in the world outside its boundaries – only equalled or excelled by other states. In many ways, this position has a quasi-ideological tinge, justifying and rationalizing the organizational and political supremacy of the state and reflecting what Eric Nordlinger (1981) calls a state-centred rather than a society-centred approach to political power and policy making. The state is thus seen as autonomous not only in relation to its domestic base but also in relation to the international arena.

What do these qualities and assumptions tell us about the process and the impact of globalization? It is clear that the state as an organizational and political form has conquered the globe, since virtually all of the planet – and even some extra-terrestrial areas – is claimed or occupied by states of one kind or another. But this very pervasiveness of statehood has important moderating effects on the abilities of states to exercise their autonomy and influence upon each other. J. D. B. Miller (1981), whilst taking a firmly state-centric approach to global issues, emphasizes also the large elements of interconnectedness both between states and between domestic and international political processes. Whilst stating very firmly that 'the world of states is the world we live in', he goes on to identify three features which he sees as running through all politics. These features – inequality, interests and government – are central to his view of the international political process. Inequality he sees as a prime fact of international life; interests, for his purposes, are effectively summed up as the aims and activities of states; and government, whilst it may seem an inappropriate concept in a world of governments, consists not so much of formal institutions and procedures as a set of processes by which inequalities and interests are brought together and reconciled. These ideas raise a number of problems to do with the measurement of inequalities, the aggregation of interests and the nature of government as process rather than government as institutions, but they do imply that it is possible to see global politics as politics between states on the global level.

Whilst global politics between states is a possible concept, it is clear also that according to Miller this is not the crude realist politics of states in collision. The essence of his position is the idea that politics between states is a process of negotiation between those pursuing definable interests – a kind of trade in which the currency is national power and in which authority is produced through agreements and understandings arrived at by sovereign states. At times, it appears that some states can effectively act as sovereigns over their competitors on the basis of their superior strength, but even then the process has substantial elements of give and take as well as dominance and submission. Miller does not assume that all states are necessarily well ordered or equally solid; nor does he see the possibility of war as ever-present, since the dealings between states are predominantly civilized and responsible.

This is a subtle interpretation of the roles played by states and governments, and one which can be illustrated in many ways from the global arena. It helps to explain, for example, why even the superpowers have to proceed in many situations by negotiation and diplomacy rather than through coercion and force. Equally, it gives insight into the gap which frequently emerges between technological supremacy and state power, and into the necessity and difficulty of negotiated agreements in an era of rapid technological change. In the realm of economic power, it helps to explain why such power is often best deployed in negotiations and bargaining between governments rather than through unilateral actions, even by dominant powers.

States are thus a vital and vigorous force in global politics, but their significance may have changed to reflect the realities of increasing interconnectedness and coexistence. This does not eliminate an awkward and persistent tension between the two faces of the state: at the national level, the state is the source of authority, legitimacy and order, whilst at the international level it is often the source of conflict and disorder. Although this problem cannot be pursued in detail here, it is important to note that the global reach of states and statehood has its inevitable dark side. The state is unquestionably a popular way of organizing human efforts and activities, not least among those peoples who have gained independence during the post-1945 period, but its popularity raises in a persistent way the tension between competition and collaboration. Whilst Western commentators might tend to assume that states are responsible and moderate, this can be seen as betraying their cultural bias in a way which blinds them to the continuing necessity for the exercise of power and the pursuit of national as well as international interests.

The relationship between globalization and the state is thus an uneasy and ambivalent one. It also relates closely to another area of tension, between the forces of continuity and those of change, which has preoccupied writers on global politics. In particular, the notion that modernization has transformed both the state and the global system has become a focus of debate and controversy. This is the next area for discussion here.

THE IMPACT OF MODERNIZATION: A TRANSFORMATION OF THE GLOBAL SYSTEM?

The global system, particularly that of the twentieth century, has been subject to continuous and wide-ranging processes of change. As noted earlier in this chapter, the nature and impact of this process of change has been ambiguous, and this has had inevitable effects both on the practice and on the academic analysis of global politics. The argument so far has emphasized the essential continuity of much of the global system – a continuity built upon and expressed in the role of the state – but this is only one side of the argument. To many, it is more plausible to talk not in terms of continuity or even those of incremental change, but in those of transformation. The assumption is that there has been radical and discontinuous change in the global arena, and that this change is to all intents and purposes irreversible. A central catalyst and driving force in this process has been the impact of modernization, which has affected the nature and exercise of power and has brought about a major challenge to understanding of the contemporary world. In particular, the impact of modernization has fundamental implications for the relevance and role of the state.

The idea of modernization or of becoming modern has preoccupied many thinkers and politicians, especially in the Western world, and many attempts have been made to explore both its components and its consquences. Three manifestations of the idea can be identified, each of them relevant to the processes of globalization and the position of the state. First, there is the perception that modernization is a process of change from which there is no going back, and one which transforms the nature of national societies. Second, there is an implicit comparison between national societies, reflecting the assumption that some societies are more modernized than others, and that the cultures and practices associated with modernization are unevenly distributed across the globe. Third, there is an assumption that although different national societies or particular regions may exhibit to a greater or lesser degree the symptoms of modernization, the whole of the globe experiences its effects.

This, though, begs the question 'What is modernization?' At the most general level, it might appear to be almost identical with change or progress. As George Modelski implies when discussing globalization, it is possible to be much more specific and to point to links between modernization and military power, or economic growth, or technological prowess, or technological supremacy (Modelski 1972). It is also clear that the notion of modernization reflects in many respects an essentially Western perception of the nature of economic, social and political advance. A particularly clear exposition of this position, and of its implications for global politics, is to be found in the work of Edward Morse (1976), who is concerned both to chart the symptoms and effects of modernization and to identify some of its internal tensions and contradictions. Morse sees himself as an adherent of a perspective which focuses on the elements of change in global politics rather than on continuities, and expresses his position thus:

> Proponents of this perspective would argue that as a result of the conditions fostered by the advent of industrialization, the rise of high mass consumption societies, the emergence of mass politics and other concomitants of the process of modernization, none of the traditional assumptions concerning the norms and structures of diplomatic behaviour has gone untouched. Furthermore, they would

say, the scale and scope of change in these environing factors have been so great that traditional statecraft has been and is continuously transformed. As a result, classical treatments of statecraft no longer serve to explain international political behaviour. Traditional assumptions concerning the use of force, the role of economic diplomacy, the processes of foreign policy decision making, or the norms embodied in the international legal order are...part of a paradigm of international affairs that is no longer adequate for explaining contemporary conditions. Rather, we seem to be in an era without a general concurrence on a paradigm that would serve to explain the changes that the international system has undergone.

(p. xvi)

This paragraph not only defines some of the key components of modernization, but also identifies some of the key reasons for the debates about its impact. For Morse, perhaps the two most important elements in modernization are the development of industrialization and the growth of the modern state. The growth of the state framework for human activity, and the changing nature of that activity itself, have led to an accelerating pace of change not only within the advanced industrial societies but also in the global arena. This linkage is crucial. At the level of the national society, modernization is associated with demographic change, with increases in living standards and the welfare state, with shifting patterns of economic activity and employment, with urbanization, with new patterns of culture and new levels of educational attainment and aspiration. Alongside these have gone changes in political behaviour and expectations, which have given the state more authority and legitimacy through the extension of the franchise, but which have also greatly increased the power of the state apparatus. The state is also buttressed by the growth of technological power, and not least by a massive increase in its military and coercive capacity.

But the transformation wrought by modernization is not merely contained to the national level. Indeed, it is effectively unsustainable without engagement and activity at the international level. As Morse and many others have pointed out, one implication of modernization has been the decline of national self-sufficiency and the growth of international interdependence. The widespread application of science-based technology to industry (and, incidentally, to warfare and weapons), the growth of global markets, and the politicization of ever growing areas of human activity, have led to a global transformation which has simultaneously extended and undermined the authority of the nation-state.

The widening and weakening of the state is only one – albeit the most important – of a number of paradoxes which Morse sees as flowing from the revolution of modernization. In essence, he sees the present global system as transitional, with elements of the old existing alongside the novel featues of an interdependent and transnational world – the revolution and transformation of which, he writes, is thus an incomplete one. Interdependence and transnationalism are inevitably accompanied by attempts on the part of states to reassert themselves, and new areas of activity thus become politicized. Whilst world politics is increasingly global in scope and effects, there is persistent fragmentation, not only between states but also within them. In turn, those responsible for taking political or economic decisions find themselves increasingly unable to keep up with the pace of change in their environment, and thus their capacity to make informed or effective decisions must be open to doubt. To be a modernist like Morse is thus not inevitably to be an optimist about change or to espouse the idea that progress is a necessarily a good thing. Issues of management and control are raised by the radical nature of modernization and change, but they are not easily resolved even where they are recognized.

It is partly due to the incompleteness of the revolution of modernization and its paradoxical effects that there is controversy about the implications of the process. As Morse argues, the pace and extent of change have led to a situation in which there is no agreed paradigm for the analysis of global politics, and the existing paradigms find themselves wrestling with problems of a new and intractable kind. This is the starting point for a more detailed examination of the responses from different schools of thought.

MODERNIZATION, TRANSFORMATION AND THE STATE: COMPETING RESPONSES

The Realist Response: States in a Changing Global Arena

On the face of it, the challenge posed to realist thinking by a focus on modernization and transformation is far-reaching. At the most fundamental level, a confrontation between the essential continuity assumed by realists and the profound discontinuity proposed by modernists such as Morse seems to imply an irreconcilable split. Indeed, this perception is precisely the reason for the attacks mounted on Morse and others by some traditionalist writers (see Bull 1979, for example). The protagonists disagree about the nature of the participants in world politics; the realists are concerned predominantly with states, whilst the modernists focus on a more complex and pluralistic set of actors. They disagree about the issues: on the one side, the traditional focus on national security and independence; on the other, the stress on economic and welfare issues. They disagree about the political process: on the one hand, interstate competition and collaboration; on the other, transnational activity that is often outside the control of governments. Finally, they disagree about the outcomes of global politics: the traditional realist view focuses on the competition for power and the balance of power, whilst the modernists concentrate on the complexity and uncertainty which demand new mechanisms of management and new institutions.

Does this mean, though, that the realists have nothing to say about a transformed world beyond a blind rejection of its consequences? In fact this is very far from the case, and a number of neo-realist writers have attempted to reformulate realism for the world of the 1990s. They have done so by exploring the implications of the new circumstances with which states are confronted, by assessing the ways in which states can adapt to them, and by exposing the possibility of a continuing central role for the state in the global arena. For example, Robert Gilpin (1981) has identified three central dimensions of change in the global arena, which would largely be agreed by modernists such as Morse: the nuclear revolution, the interdependence of national economies, and the emergence of a global society. Gilpin would part company with Morse on the scale and scope of these changes, since he sees them as changes of form rather than of essence, and he would also place greater faith than Morse in the capacity of states to cope with them through creative statecraft. Wolfram Hanrieder (1979) has argued that such creative adaptation has extended the influence of the state into new areas;

far more of the world's economic and social activities are now penetrated by state influences, and although the state is not always in full command of what is going on, its presence in itself is important.

Authors such as Gilpin and Hanrieder would also agree with modernists that the global political process has changed in ways that demand innovation from states. To put it bluntly, the balance of interstate activity has shifted from competition towards collaboration (with echoes of what writers such as Miller say about the negotiation of interests; see above). Gilpin sees this as an example of the ways in which states can learn, whilst Hanrieder places great stress on the fact that external cooperation is vital to the internal success of many states in the economic and social (but also often in the military) spheres. Transnational activities, after all, frequently express the needs of the domestic state. The focus of politics has changed, and so has the aim of much state action: away from the high politics of national security, and towards the low politics or distributional politics of welfare and other economic issues. As the politics have changed, so have governments, to establish their presence and stake their claims in the new arenas. As both Gilpin and Hanrieder would admit, however, the changing nature of governments and the growth of mechanisms of collaboration are largely features of the Western developed world, rather than the Third World or regions such as Eastern Europe, although both of these (and particularly the latter after the changes of 1989 and after) are penetrated by the revolution of modernization.

Those who have adapted the realist paradigm to new circumstances have been labelled neo-realists. Particularly in the USA, the 1980s saw attempts by analysts to explore the ways in which states can adapt to the demands of cooperation and the loss of self-sufficiency without sacrificing their claims to be sovereign self-interested actors. Their viewpoint extends beyond an analysis of state behaviour of the political process to a new formulation of the ideas of world order. In particular, it emphasizes the ability of states to cooperate and to shape the structures within which political activity takes place. This is not to argue, for example, that the risk of war has been eliminated; rather it is to argue that the domain of collaboration for all states has increased, and that the costs of deviant behaviour – either through the use of force or through such mechanisms as trade protectionism – have become much greater. It would be quite possible on this basis to conclude that the transformation of world politics, far from eroding the influence of the state, has greatly extended it, and that this has gone alongside an extension of its role in the domestic economy and society. These arguments would not, of course, convince those who subscribe to either the liberal-pluralist or the neo-Marxist paradigm.

The Liberal-Pluralist Response: Beyond the State

Although the realists and the neo-realists have proved capable of reformulating and adapting their approaches to accommodate at least some of the changes brought about by modernization, it is hardly surprising that the revolution of modernization has found its strongest echoes in the liberal-pluralist camp. Morse argues very strongly that many modernized states have lost control of their foreign relations, and although he does not go so far as to declare the state redundant, he certainly sees it as beset by problems as well as facing new opportunities. Perhaps it is no coincidence that he and others were writing in the mid 1970s, when the confidence of many Americans in their state had been shaken by the combined impacts of Watergate, the Vietnam War, the collapse of the dollar and the oil crisis. In such circumstances, it must have been very tempting to see world politics as complex and uncontrollable, for that is what it was in many respects.

Whatever the reasons for the ascendancy of liberal-pluralism as orthodoxy in the field of global politics during the 1970s, it must be admitted that this approach sits well alongside the perceived implications of the process of modernization. The participants in global politics suggested by a modernist perspective – a wide range of subnational, transnational and other groups – are very much those of the liberal-pluralist universe. Much the same could be said in the area of issues, where liberal-pluralists stress precisely the technical, welfare problems that feature on the new agenda of the modernists. The political processes suggested by Morse and others are those of bargaining and accommodation rather than coercion and force, and these are central to the liberal-pluralist conception of the world, both domestically and internationally. Furthermore, the world of complex interdependence envisaged by the liberal-pluralists and sustained by a proliferation of international or transnational organizations is an outcome implicit in analyses of modernization and of the need to maintain order in an increasingly unpredictable world. Many writers have noted this need, either in general or in specific areas such as those of technological change or economic globalization.

This is not to imply that there are no difficulties in relating the liberal-pluralist paradigm to the conditions of a modernized world. One conceptual problem is fairly obvious: if everything is so complex, and everything is connected to everything else, how can the analyst or the practitioner formulate a clear view of what is important? Connected with this is the problem of control: in conditions of bewildering complexity, is it possible to calculate the consequences of one's actions, or to formulate strategies which are capable of implementation on any basis other than 'it all depends'? A third issue concerns the nature of world order: do not the conditions of a modernized and interdependent world make world order impossible to achieve, no matter how much it may be seen as desirable? It is important to note that these are not merely empirical questions; they are inescapably normative, and thus they raise strong emotions of an often irreconcilable kind.

Liberal-pluralist authors nonetheless rest many of their arguments on assumptions related to the revolution of modernization, and on the imperative for new ways of acting in the transformed world. The emphasis for many such authors is on discontinuity rather than continuity in the global arena: although they may talk about the same phenomena as realists and neo-realists, they do so from a position which leads them to very different explanations and evaluations. The revolution identified by many liberal-pluralists is as much a revolution in thinking as in the empirical reality of the world, and although this may not yet be complete, its inevitability is taken largely for granted. For instance, writers such as Richard Mansbach and Chris Mitchell argue that the ultimate conclusion of a reconceptualization of global politics will almost certainly be a withdrawal of loyalty from the state by important groups of citizens (Mansbach et al. 1976; Mitchell 1984).

This means that a critical issue for many liberal-pluralists is that of change in the global system: why does it occur, how extensive is it, where is it leading? According to Mansbach and his colleagues, one of the most significant effects of modernization has been the recognition that states can no longer contain or control some of the most important functional systems in the arena; established national authorities are simply inadequate to the tasks with which they are confronted, and which significant groups of their citizens expect to see performed. States are unable either to channel and express these demands, or to suppress them, and in this situation there is a major role for processes of transnational communication and expression, which are increasingly available on a decentralized basis through the impact of new technologies. Mitchell takes this line of argument further, by contrasting coercive relationships (largely associated with the state) and legitimate relationships, which more accurately reflect the needs and aspirations of the individuals and groups involved in them. Global politics is seen as the product of action by a very wide range of participants, not simply states and their representatives, whilst the new participants reflect the growth of new tasks and new constituencies which demand and support them (Mansbach et al. 1976).

From this proliferation of groups and organizations there results what Oran Young (1972) has described as a mixed-actor system in the global arena. Young sums up the implications of such a system as follows:

> The basic notion of a system of mixed actors requires a movement away from the assumption of homogeneity with respect to types of actor, and, therefore, a retreat from the postulate of the state as the fundamental unit of world politics. Instead, the mixed-actor view envisions a situation in which several qualitatively different types of actor interact in the absence of any settled pattern of dominance–submission (or hierarchical) relationships. In such a system, questions regarding political stature, competencies, rights, obligations and so forth cannot be dealt with in terms of a simple rule indicating the supremacy of one type of actor, and, therefore, they must be worked out on an *ad hoc* basis with different results for different types of relationship.
>
> (p. 36)

This approximates to what Mansbach et al. would term a complex conglomerate system (1976), which is characterized by a host of overlapping and coexisting relationships. Clearly, one feature of these more diverse relationships is that they present both the analyst and the practitioner with a potentially bewildering range and number of possible connections and consequences, and thus broaden the scope for both opportunism and accident in global politics. Another feature, emphasized by Chris Mitchell, is that there needs to be some means of judging not just the nature of the relationships, but also their legitimacy (1984). For Mitchell, this is the crucial issue: to what extent does any given connection result in an exchange which satisfies the needs of those involved, as well as broader requirements of global order? The key element here may be the mutual responsiveness of the participants – the extent to which they can form accurate and sensitive images of the situation and of each other. While states and governments are not incapable of demonstrating these qualities, it would be fair to say that Mitchell sees states as inherently coercive organizations which are very unlikely to develop any real empathy with those demanding change.

The complex conglomerate system is thus heterogeneous and dynamic. According to many pluralist writers, though, it is also strong and resilient, and the basis of a durable global order. For Mitchell, therefore, the cobweb of relationships between diverse actors, which reflects overlapping systems of action and exchange, produces a basis for a more legitimate global order. For Mansbach et al. there is corresponding strength in a system of 'diffuse, flexible and situationally specific alignments' (1976, p. 43). The global order thus produced is not the product of state dominance (and thus by implication a form of oppression), but rather an expression of the mutual responsiveness already noted. It is one of the functions of the revolution of moderniz-ation to bring such groups into contact where they might otherwise not have been, and to form transnational alignments which can have significant political consequences. Often, these alignments and the interests they express will take a concrete organizational form; equally often, however, they will be transient and addressed to specific issues or situations.

Such ideas as these are in clear contrast to those of the realists and neo-realists. Whereas for them the necessity for order is satisfied by the collaboration or the muted competition of states, this is seen by many liberal-pluralists as an obstacle to the realization of basic human values such as justice or equality. In place of this state-centric conservatism, they demand recognition of the fact that the world does not always conform to state boundaries, and the creation of structures that enable the better realization of economic and humanitarian objectives. The impact of modernization has led to the growth of many non-state structures and processes, but it has yet to be proven conclusively that the world beyond the state is a benign one. This is one starting point for neo-Marxist approaches to the problem.

Neo-Marxist Responses: Modernization and its Contradictions

In some ways, Marxism can be seen as a type of modernization theory, since it focuses on the ways in which capital and the means of production combine to create particular social and political forms – among them the world economy and the global political system. In other ways, however, it is clear that neo-Marxist approaches take a completely different standpoint from those that emphasize modernization, either as the basis for an extension of the state's presence or as the foundation of a potential system of global justice and equality. To be specific, there are three major differences in the ways in which neo-Marxist writers have interpreted the process of modernization and its impact on the global system.

The first area of difference concerns the role of the state, particularly in relation to the development and organization of capital. While the state may provide a convenient shell for the growth of national capital, one of the features of an increasingly modernized world is the transnational nature of capital, expressed through such organizations as the multinational corporations (MNCs). Therefore, it cannot be taken for granted that the interests of capital and a given state will coincide, particularly where the state concerned is relatively weak and underdeveloped.

This leads to the second area of difference: whereas realists or liberal-pluralists, in different ways, can be seen to stress the concept of autonomy, either for states or for non-state groupings, neo-Marxists emphasize the autonomy of transnational capital which leads to the exploitation of both states and non-state groups. The world according to Marxists is one of uneven development, and thus one in which the changes attached to modernization bring profoundly unequal benefits and disadvantages to different classes and nations.

It follows from this (and this is the third area of difference) that there are fundamental contradictions within the global system, which condition the possibilities of achieving order and ensuring future stability and justice, and thus play a crucial role in shaping the dynamics of global politics. These contradictions are, if not actually created, greatly heightened by the impact of modernization, since this enhances the efficiency with which the inequalities and contradictions of the system are transmitted from the dominant to the dependent and the exploited. By creating a global economy, which is the fundamental component of the global system, transnational capitalism structures the context within which the state and other groupings operate.

Such an argument does not mean that political structures such as those of states are unimportant for neo-Marxists. After all, historically, it has been the civil state which has enabled capital to grow, to concentrate itself and to acquire mobility in political space. In talking about the global expansion of capital and its transnational expression, questions inevitably arise in relation to the political composition of the global arena, and this leads on to questions about the possible growth of transnational or global political structures to accompany the range and scope of capital and its movements. Such themes are taken up, for example, by Robin Murray (1975), whose ideas have been central to neo-Marxist writing about capital and the global system. Perhaps the key element in Murray's thesis is the notion of the territorial non-coincidence between capital and the state in the era of transnational capitalism, which has important consequences for states in the industrial world. This argument is paralleled by a number of Third World writers, who focus on the ways in which transnationalization affects the less developed countries. Osvaldo Sunkel and Eduardo Fuenzalida, for example, point to the ways in which Third World countries are penetrated by techno-industrial oligopoly capitalism (1979).

Seen in this light, the development of transnational capitalism raises questions about the adequacy of the state either to nurture or to contain the power thereby generated. The clearest expression of this tension comes from Murray, who identified six central state functions relevant to the needs of capital (1975). It is vital to Murray's argument that these state functions need not be performed by national states. Rather, they represent a set of requirements that can be met through many channels, such as international organizations or (in the case of the European Community, for example) by supranational bodies. What they amount to is a specification of the conditions that the owners of transnational capital wish to see met so that the social and political order facilitates their operations. As Sunkel and Fuenzalida also point out, these functions are performed in the world economy by a number of First World organizations such as the IMF or the OECD, allied to the strength of certain states (particularly the USA) and the transnational community of those entangled with the great corporations or financial institutions. From the point of view of the Third World countries, this set of networks and institutions has fundamentally damaging effects, since it reduces their ability to pursue autonomous or appropriate development strategies. The problem may also exist for the advanced industrial countries, but the terms on which capital and the state meet are very different.

What does this mean for the impact of modernization in the global arena and the world political system? In the first place, it means that much of what impresses the realists or the pluralists becomes open to question. The power and influence of the state, and its potential for interstate collaboration, are not rendered meaningless, but they are put into a very different context, in which the fundamental power relationships are those between capitals and capitalists. Even the use of force and military threats by states, it could be argued, only assume significance when they are placed within the context of transnational military orders sustained by the technological and financial power of transnational capitalism. As Murray points out (1975), the global extension of capitalism may mean that states are used as agents for the achievement of its objectives, but this is by no means certain. The transmission belts of the transnational community and its accompanying culture will produce political effects from an essentially non-state or non-governmental process of diffusion and interaction. Whilst this may appear at first sight to have much in common with the arguments put forward by some liberal-pluralists, there are fundamental points of divergence. In particular, the question of legitimacy which is raised by many pluralists has a totally different meaning for the neo-Marxists, since they see this as an issue predetermined by the power of transnational capital and only resolvable by a major shift in the terms on which that capital operates. In other words, capital decides what is allowed and, barring revolutionary upheaval, the rules will reflect the requirements of the capitalists.

This raises the question of global order, which is given great importance by both realists and liberal-pluralists (see above). For neo-Marxists, there is a central distinction to be made between 'order" in general terms and 'the order' which exists at any point in time. The order is a reflection of the objective conditions prevailing in the world political economy, and thus is not an abstract set of principles or aspirations; it is organically connected with the distribution of economic power and with the contradictions inherent in global capitalism. In the contemporary era, therefore, it is to be expected that the global order will reflect the transnational spread of capitalism, and that it will express the demand for the performance of state functions at the global level. It is not impossible for states to perform these functions – indeed, for a long time and in many ways the USA has done so – but there are many alternative channels such as the MNCs themselves, international organizations and the network of interdependencies between open national economies.

One important consequence of an emphasis on transnational capitalism, which distinguishes the neo-Marxists sharply from both realists and liberal-pluralists, is their attention to structure and its influence on action. Whereas realists would see the needs of states as shaping the international order, and liberal-pluralists would stress the formative influence exerted by specific groups or networks, for neo-Marxists it is the other way round. For them, it is the incorporation of groups, including the state, into the world economy which has the potential to shape not only their external relations but also their internal affairs. In other words, the place occupied by a group in the global political economy will dictate to a considerable extent its freedom of action, its definition of objectives and its specific actions. Whereas the international order might be seen by realists as reflecting state independence and sovereignty, and by pluralists as reflecting complex interdependence, the neo-Marxists would emphasize a more or less overt exploitative dependence arising from the structural dominance of transnational capitalism.

The net result of the situation thus described is a series of fundamental contradictions in the world economy and the global order, which are closely linked to the process of modernization. Why then does it not collapse? According to neo-Marxists, it might well do so at some stage, but a notable feature of the transnational capitalist order has in fact been its resilience and ability to adapt to new challenges. In part, this has flowed from the capacity of dominant states (particularly the USA, and perhaps soon Japan or the European Community) to shape the world economy to the needs of capital. Another element in the equation is the ability of the capitalist states to sell their model of modernization and development to Third World countries and to recruit supporters for it among ruling elites there. Finally, there is the fact that for the dependent countries the sheer cost of a collapse or of a withdrawal from the structure would inhibit them from taking the decisions which might in the long term be for their benefit. Thus, although the structure might eventually collapse of its own accord, this is likely to be a long-term development, and a major source of pain and disruption in itself.

GLOBALIZATION, MODERNIZATION AND THE STATE: SOME CONCLUSIONS

It is apparent from the argument in this chapter that the relationship between globalization, modernization and the state is both intimate and often paradoxical. Globalization is a process which has often seemed to depend upon not only state power but also the power of specific states, such as those of Europe in the nineteenth century. Nonetheless, some of the major components of globalization can be seen as only loosely linked with state power, and as having a logic of their own – for example, in the areas of economic and technological development. The consequences of globalization can also be expressed in terms of paradox and tension since, as Modelski (1972) suggests, there is no conclusive evidence that the large community created is necessarily a good thing; indeed, there is important evidence to the contrary, pointing to the disruption of regional and local orders and the clash of cultures or political and economic systems. Whilst the state has spread globally, sustained by material power but also a set of values expressed in the notion of statehood, the evidence for its decline or continued vigour is essentially contradictory.

Similar ambiguities attend the concept of modernization. Although it can be seen as a force for progress and for the incorporation of societies into the global community, many of its results are best seen in terms of tension and either actual or potential conflict, as the forces of tradition stand against the tide. The global system is changing, but there is no certainty about the direction of change or the kind of world it will produce. The coexistence of centralization and fragmentation, of nationalism and transnationalism, of traditional and modern, is a characteristic feature of the world as it approaches the twenty-first century. Modernization is thus as likely to be a source of disruption as a source of development, a source of important questions rather than a reliable guide to a simple model of progress.

In particular, the notion of modernization raises three sorts of questions. First, there are questions relating to the nature of modernization. Is it simply a projection of Western concerns on to the global level? Is there more than one model of modernization? Is it a concrete condition, or simply a set of aspirations and values? Is it an inevitable stage of social, economic and political development, or can societies effectively opt out from or reverse it? Second, there are questions relating to the specific content of modernization. Is it possible to develop objective indicators of the degree of modernization achieved by different – and diverse – societies? Is modernization necessarily transnational and an attack on the autonomy of states and their governments, or can it be used by them? What about societies which are only partly modernized, and where the presence of these features is counteracted by powerful forces of tradition? Third, there are questions relating to the impact and implications of modernization. What is the balance between continuity and transformation, given that no complete break can be made with the past? Since modernization is uneven in its impact, does it ameliorate or exacerbate the conflicts and tensions in the global arena? Is the process essentially uncontrollable, and thus a source of uncertainty or potential disaster?

These are questions not just about a concrete phenomenon, but also about the world views of scholars and policy makers. Not surprisingly, therefore, the notion of modernization and its links to globalization is an area of analytical and political debate. Different paradigms of global politics see the process and its implications for the role of the state in very different lights, and draw opposing conclusions from the same bodies of evidence. In this way, the debate about globalization, modernization and the state stands as a symbol of the transitional state of global politics itself.

References

Bull, H. (1979) The state's positive role in world affairs. *Daedalus*, 108(4).

Gilpin, R. (1981) *War and Change in World Politics*. Cambridge: Cambridge University Press.

Hanrieder, W. (1978) Dissolving international politics. *American Political Science Review*, 72(4).

Mansbach, R.W., Ferguson, Y.H. and Lampert, D.E. (1976) *The Web of World Politics*. New York: Prentice-Hall.

Masters, R. (1969) World politics as a primitive political system. In J. Rosenau (ed.), *International Politics and Foreign Policy*, New York: Free Press.

Miller, J.D. (1981) *The World of States*. London: Croom Helm.

Mitchell, C. (1984) World society as a cobweb. In M. Banks (ed.), *Conflict in World Society*. London: Simon and Schuster.

Modelski, G. (1972) *Principles of World Politics*. New York: Free Press.

Morse, E.L. (1976) *Modernization and the Transformation of International Relations*. New York: Free Press.

Murray, R. (1971) The internationalization of capital and the nation-state. *New Left Review*, 67.

Nordlinger, E. (1981) *On the Autonomy of the Democratic State*. Cambridge, MA: Harvard University Press.

Sunkel, O. and Fuenzalida, F. (1979) Transnationalization and its national consequences. In J. Villamil (ed.), *Transnational Capitalism and National Development*, Brighton: Harvester Wheatsheaf.

Young, O. (1972) The actors in world politics. In J.N. Rosenau et al. (eds), *The Analysis of International Politics*, New York: Free Press.

14

Modernity and Universal Human Rights

JOHN VINCENT

Politics and Human Rights

Whatever our paradigmatic preference we take rights, in the West, to be a natural starting place for thought about politics – politics here being the public arrangements we make for the governance of society. The first explicitly political act many of us undertake is the exercise of a *right* to vote after we have reached the age of majority. Before that, we might have acted politically, though not necessarily self-consciously so, by, for example, claiming a right not to wear uniform in the sixth form at school, or exercising a right to eat lunch in a pub at the age of sixteen provided we were accompanied by an adult, or (moving to domestic politics) insisting on the right to have a rise in pocket money on every birthday. After eighteen, we go on engaging in rights talk: we say we have a right to the rate for the job; or claim a right to participate in taking a decision which affects us; or point to our right to be left alone. Political talk is often talk about rights: about whether we have them, how we exercise them, and what good purposes they provide for. It might seem reasonable, then, from a Western standpoint, to make listening to an international conversation about *human* rights one of the principal means of identifying the emergence of global politics.

But the language of rights which seems so natural to us in the West might seem more or less alien to other cultures in which obligation or duty habitually come first. In view of this, the conversation between the cultures on the question of rights might be rather halting and rudimentary. And even when a non-Western culture accepts that rights are a proper subject for discussion in world politics, they might mean by rights notions so different as to lead us to doubt whether there is much in common beyond mere vocabulary. Moreover, the extent of this minimal commonality may itself be criticized as an indication of the extent to which Western ideas have been foisted on others, so that talking the language of rights is actually a measure of continuing Western cultural imperialism despite the disappearance of the old colonies.

The idea of a common vocabulary when it comes to values in world politics, and what the using of this vocabulary indicates about the reality of a political community stretching across the globe, is the subject matter of this chapter. What do ideas and values tell us about the nature of global politics that we do not already know from the discussion of power and force – the habitual starting places for enquiry about international as distinct from domestic politics?

The idea of a *right* can be divided into the following five main elements: (1) a right holder (the subject of a right) (2) has a claim to some substance (the object of a right), which he or she might (3) assert, or demand, or enjoy, or enforce (exercising a right) (4) against some individual or group (the bearer of the correlative duty), (5) citing in support of his or her claim some particular ground (the justification of a right) (Gewirth 1982, p. 10).

The idea of a *human* right makes each of these elements apply to every human being. Who is the subject of a human right? Everyone – though, as we shall see later, there may be debate about the unit that is being identified as the 'one' in 'everyone'. What is the object of a human right, what is it a right to? It is the something fundamental which makes possible the enjoyment, by anyone, of all other rights. How are human rights typically exercised? By an appeal to this something fundamental which everyone equally should enjoy. Against whom are human rights held; who bears the obligations correlative to them? Everyone else. And what particular ground is cited in support of a claim to have a human right? The ground that this is what being human requires; that this is what is due if a minimally decent life is to be lived.

To make this definition less abstract, let us apply it in the case of a particular human right about whose existence there is little debate, namely the right to life:

1 Everyone has such a right; we are all the subjects of it. There is, of course, debate about when precisely we become the subjects of it – at conception, or at birth, or somewhere in between – and also about the circumstances in which we might forfeit it by, for example, taking the life of another.
2 What is it a right to? At least to security against its violent deprivation and to subsistence in order that it may be sustained, though it may be argued that the former places fewer demands on the rest of us than the latter.
3 How is it typically exercised? By appealing to it as something everyone ought to have when it is plainly not being met, as when something akin to genocide is being committed in Campuchea, or when famine is producing a similar outcome in Ethiopia. Of course, making an appeal is not the same thing as having it met.
4 Who bears the obligations correlative to the right to life, of for example Campucheans or Ethiopians? Everyone – but, it may be argued, some more than others.
5 And what is the ground for the assertion of a right to life? The rather obvious one that being human entails being alive. However, it may be argued that merely being alive is not itself a value to be cherished unless it is accompanied by other values; hence the cry of the American revolutionary 'give me liberty or give me death'.

The caveats in this list suggest that, even in the case of a right that few find controversial, there is considerable debate about what the political implications of having a right are. So while it is helpful to identify the elements of a right, and of a human right, and to see them in place in the case of a particular right, because this allows us to get our bearings in the discussion of the values that are fundamental in the consideration of all politics, global or local, it does not exhaust the enquiry. This is because each of the elements in the idea of a human right is itself an arena for a debate about the nature and content of values in politics. Thus each of our elements of the right to life begin a political argument, or several. When does a foetus have a right to life? Does the world owe everyone a living? How is the right to life best vindicated? What obligations do the citizens of one society owe to those of another? On what grounds might a right to life be held to be prior to a right to liberty? And if we broaden the focus to encompass a general debate about human rights in world politics, the list that might be produced is similarly controversial. Who is the proper subject of a human right: an individual, or a tribe, or a nation, or a state? And if all four, how are they connected and in what order of priority? What are rights the rights to: merely to be left alone, or to be provided with something? How is a right most successfully exercised: defended in a court, proclaimed on a banner at the head of a column of marchers, or fought for on a battlefield? Who does bear the correlative obligations: governments or individuals, the First World or the Third, them or us? What is the final justification: natural law, human dignity, religion?

It is a feature of the discussion of human rights in world politics that the lists are rather long. It is possible to simplify the discussion of human rights in world politics by referring to the clusters of rights that have been the subject of the discussion of the matter at the United Nations, in regional organizations, and in academic reflection on the world. There are three such clusters: civil and political rights; economic and social rights; and collective rights. However, these are not mutually exclusive; economic rights, for example, could also be collective rights. Civil and political rights include the rights of individuals to life, liberty, security of the person, privacy and property; the right to marry and found a family; the right to a fair trial; freedom from slavery, torture and arbitrary arrest; freedom of movement and to seek asylum; the right to a nationality; freedom of thought, conscience and religion; freedom of opinion and expression; freedom of assembly and association; and the right to free elections, universal suffrage and participation in public affairs. Economic and social rights include the right of an individual to work and for a just reward; the right to form and join trade unions; the right to rest and leisure, and to periodic holidays with pay; the right to a standard of living adequate to health and well-being; the right to social security; the right to education; and the right to participation in the cultural life of a community. Collective rights include those of nations to self-determination, of races to freedom from discrimination, and of classes to freedom from neo-colonialism.

Now if global politics were to be constructed as the politics of party as well as the politics of rights, these clusters or lists might form the kernel of the manifestos of the three great factions in contemporary world politics, labelled (in a usage which is now a commonplace feature of global politics) the First, Second and Third Worlds. Thus the West or First World, it might be said, takes the civil and political list to be the foundation of politics. The East or Second World advances the cause of economic and social rights. The South or Third World asserts the primacy of the rights of the collectivity.

This is a simplification of reality. There is considerable variation within the worlds as well as between them. And each of them pays attention in some degree to the lists preferred by the others. But we may make some progress in understanding the place of rights in world politics if we pay attention first to *party* – what it is that divides the factions from each other in point of their doctrine about rights – and then to the senses in which, despite these differences, there is in some degree a practical consensus among all societies on the question of human rights that makes the *universalism of human rights* more than mere rhetoric. The former question about party is the subject of the next two sections. The latter question about universality is the subject of the following section.

THE PARTIES: THE WEST, THE EAST AND THE THIRD WORLD

The standard definition of a political party is a number of persons united in maintaining a cause or policy against others maintaining a different one. Applied to world politics, 'party' applies to states and societies as well as persons. And it is used in this context much more loosely than in domestic politics – reflecting the rudimentary nature of the global polity. Indeed there is a sense, in this section, in which we are experimenting with the idea of party in world politics rather than merely describing it. If a party is a division of a whole we need immediately to identify two different wholes in which the division has meaning: the world *within* the state about whose governance our three parties have different ideologies; and the world formed *among* states about whose organization the same factions have different views derived in part from their preoccupations about rights in domestic politics. There is also a third whole, that of the emerging global polity, of which states and the life within them are only part, which will be the concern of later sections of the chapter. Here, we shall begin with the different formulas for *domestic* government.

The West

The Western conceit is that we invented human rights, that we have the best record in relation to them, and that the extent of their discussion in contemporary world politics is the measure of continuing Western dominance, at least when it comes to the language in which the political conversation is carried on. All these things may be true, as well as conceited, but it is also true that it is possible to discern a particularly Western view about human rights which distinguishes it from the ideas of the other parties in the discussion that we shall come to later.

In the West we think of human rights as being the property above all of individuals. Human rights for us mean the rights of individual human beings, and we are suspicious of any claim made on behalf of a group to have human rights unless the connection between it and individual rights is clearly demonstrable. This is a reflection of the history of the struggle for human rights in the West, from the Magna Carta to black liberation in the United States, as a struggle *against* the state. Rights were things pressed for against a reluctant state, and constant vigilance is thought to be necessary in protecting them against the ever present menace of state intrusion. The classical civil liberties – freedom of speech, freedom of movement, freedom of assembly, the right to a fair trial – all have this quality of being insisted on as sacrosanct, individual claims against the state.

It is also a reflection of the history of the struggle for human rights in the West, that civil and political rights are widely thought of as having a natural priority over economic and social rights. It is at the point of a threat to our liberty that we find the appeal to human rights most appropriate, and we habitually think that all that is required to vindicate that liberty is *abstention* or *forbearance* on the part of others, especially the state. A's right to liberty merely imposes an obligation of non-interference on B, not a more demanding requirement that B provide something for A. We shall have occasion to question this doctrine later, but it is a widespread one in the West.

A third feature of the Western approach to human rights in addition to that of its individualism, and its presumption in favour of civil and political rights, is its insistence on universality. If human rights are indeed *human* rights then they are claims available to every human being wherever he or she lives in whatever social circumstances. The principle of non-interference established between states for the convenience of their intercourse should not then be a wall behind which any barbarism is sanctioned by default because of an exaggerated interpretation of the liberty of states. In this regard the doctrine has always been present in Western international law (though more visible at some periods than others) that conduct which outrages the conscience of mankind triggers a right if not a duty of humanitarian intervention in the international community as a whole.

We might represent these three features of Western policy on human rights ('policy' here figuratively to go along with our use of 'party') – individualism, priority to civil and political rights, and universality – as mainstream Western thinking, or as that which constitutes the Western orthodoxy. There are, of course, also Western views which are not in the mainstream, and which might seek to counter the orthodoxy: the idea, for example, that collectivities produce rights from the experience of social interaction and are not themselves the products of the myth of human rights; or the notion that civil and political rights are bourgeois interests disguised as moral claims in order to hoodwink those not benefiting from them; or the heretical view that rights are fixed in time and place and reflect circumstance not universal priniciples, timeless and placeless, to which circumstance itself has to adjust. These ideas from the Western counter-culture crop up as orthodoxy in the East and in the Third World, as we shall see.

The East

The former state socialist countries of the East – the East here meaning the Soviet Union and its neighbouring Eastern European countries – have not led on the issue of human rights in international politics. Human rights are after all part of the vocabulary of liberalism not of socialism, and the cause of the latter is not necessarily advanced by borrowing the doctrine of the former. But the issue has not simply been ignored in the East, and the socialist countries have come up with a view about human rights which counters the Western position in each of the elements we dealt with above.

They do not, in the first place, start with the individual. The socialist revolution was the achievement of the group, the proletarian class, which acted and continues to act against exploitation. Constituted as the state, this class then provides for the rights of individuals, who then maintain their liberty *through* the state, as beneficiaries of the victories it has won, rather than *against* it as in Western doctrine. This approach to the matter allows us to understand the Soviet reaction to its dissidents, on whom Western attention is focused whenever the question of human rights in the Soviet Union is raised. The rights of these dissidents, like those of all other Soviet citizens, did not drop from the sky but were produced by Soviet society. It followed that constructive criticism was a right of all citizens, but not anti-Sovietism, which dwelt on only the negative aspects of society and failed to recognize its achievements. Individuals and the working of the system could be criticized but not the socialist system itself. The selfish individualism of the dissidents demonstrated their failures as citizens, and their alliance with anti-socialist interests outside the Soviet Union. In the light of this line of reasoning, official and popular hostility to dissidents in the Soviet Union is not surprising.

The nature of the state, in socialist theory, reflects the underlying economic relationship in any society. In socialist societies, power is in the hands of the working class, delivering to their citizens that fundamental economic liberty which comes from the removal of capitalist exploitation. Against the Western priority to civil and political rights, then, stands the Eastern insistence on the primacy of economic and social rights – the rights to work, leisure, health care, pensions, housing and education – without which civil and political liberty are empty and insulting. And because of the fundamental nature of the achievement of emancipation from capitalist exploitation, civil and political rights always remain subordinate to it. They cannot be used against the socialist system which guards the primary freedom.

On the question of the universality of human rights, the socialist countries do not in general deny that human rights are intended to be the birthright of everyone, though they tend to stress need and desert more than rights. They do, however, point out the sensitivity of the cultural context in which universal human rights are to be implemented, and claim that the question of implementation remains a matter that is within their domestic jurisdiction. So, as we shall see below when we discuss the debate between West and East on the place of human rights in the relationship between them, the socialist countries are more inclined, on this issue, to clutch closely to them the principle of non-intervention.

The Third World

The principle of non-intervention protects the rights of the collectivity – the sovereign state – and the Third World countries that have recently won, or regained, their independence are staunch defenders of it as the guarantor of their group liberty. Like the East, but unlike the West, the Third World takes the group to be the natural starting place for thought about rights. Thus, in traditional African political arrangements, the identity of an individual is intelligible only in relation to his or her incorporation into a group and to functions fulfilled within the group, in contrast to Western individualism in which distance from the group is one of its measures. In Islamic society too, which is discussed in chapter 15, it is the community, the *umma*, that provides for the integration of the human personality realized through self-abnegation and action for the good of the collectivity. In societies like these, obligations to the community are more prominent than rights won from it, and their approach to the idea of human rights is one that does not abandon this priority to social obligation. The talk of peoples' rights, the rights of groups and the principle of self-determination in contemporary international politics has been deeply affected by the prominence of ideas of collective rights in the political experience of non-Western societies; and this prominence tends to be accompanied by the idea that collective rights correlate with individual obligation. Hence the dispute with a Western tradition that tends to put the relationship the other way around.

The new states of the Third World have also been more aligned with the East than with the West in their view of the priority of economic and social rights over civil and political rights. The weight behind the idea of the proclamation at the United Nations of a right to development has been theirs, and they have assembled it in three characteristic forms. First, development is a collective activity; for example, individuals cannot provide their own clean water supply. Second, it is an economic and social process which might require in the short term the infraction of the classical civil and political rights, such as directing labour to development projects rather than allowing freedom of choice in employment. Third, civil and political liberties are something that may have to be postponed until a level of development is reached which might allow these comparative luxuries a place on the political agenda. The ideas put in this way have not had a clear run, and the Western powers have been particularly concerned to resist the idea that development is a process which is necessarily oppressive when it comes to the liberty of individuals. However, the economic and social circumstances of the Third World countries have made them the chief exponents of the second and particularly the third generations of human rights in the discussion of the subject at the United Nations: the first generation being the Western list of civil and political rights, the second the Eastern list of economic and social rights, and the third the Southern list of rights to development.

In all this the Third World countries have been, in some degree, the beneficiaries of the universalism implicit in ideas of human rights. Their independence was gained by reference to the principle of self-determination, and it has been buttressed since by interpretations of that principle that we have shortly to discuss. But they have also wanted to interpret the principle of self-determination not as a rule which allows them the *same* rights as everyone else, but as something which makes it obligatory for others to recognize their difference.

PARTIES AND RIGHTS: THE INTERNATIONAL POLITICAL DEBATE

We come now to the question of the international impact of these different ideas about the issue of human rights in the domestic politics of the parties that we have just considered. When they confront each other in international politics on the issue, what is the outcome? Let us consider this in relation to the two dominant polarities of contemporary international politics: that of East–West relations; and that of North–South relations.

East–West Relations

In the history of East–West relations the question of human rights has been associated above all with that measure of the high-water mark of *détente* – the Final Act of the Helsinki Conference on Security and Cooperation in Europe of 1975 – and with the follow-up conferences which have convened to consider its implementation. The Helsinki agreement gave roughly equal space to questions relating to security in Europe and the Mediterranean; to cooperation in the fields of economics, science and technology, and the environment; and to cooperation in humanitarian and other fields. This shape was determined by a deal done between a Soviet Union anxious to legitimize existing European frontiers, and thus its hegemony in Eastern Europe, and a West anxious to exact a price for the recognition of this situation as legitimate.

The deal was symbolized by the juxtaposition, in the Declaration on Principles Guiding Relations between participating States, of principle VI on non-intervention with principle VII on human rights. The non-intervention principle contained an extensive definition of the action from which the participating states were to refrain, including direct or indirect, individual or collective, armed or unarmed intervention in internal or external affairs. The human rights principle included in its title freedom of thought, conscience, religion or belief, and went on to produce a list of rights and freedoms longer than that comprising the types of intervention ruled out by the preceding principle. In the words of the Final Act, these two principles enjoyed equal status (along with the other eight). In diplomatic practice, the issue of human rights in East–West relations has been taken up with a discussion of the rival claims of principle VI and principle VII. It is this diplomatic practice that we are concerned with here. The policy question concerning the place of human rights is a deeper Western strategy we return to later.

In the official Western view, one as we saw earlier of the universality of human rights, principle VI was no barrier to the international discussion of human rights in the Soviet Union, or indeed to monitoring them, negotiating about them, or using influence to improve them. This view was based on two grounds. First, human rights were now a matter of international concern in virtue of the existence of a body of conventional and customary law on human rights that was referred to in the Final Act. So the plea of an area of domestic jurisdiction which the principle of non-intervention was designed to protect was not in this context acceptable. And, second, the classical conception of intervention in international law consisted not in *any* kind of interference in domestic affairs, but only in dictatorial interference which sought coercively to subordinate the exercise of sovereign rights to foreign interests. Lesser action, by implication, was not illegal. Discussion of human rights issues within signatory countries was not quite legitimate.

The human rights questions which the West pressed at Helsinki, and in the follow-up conferences, arise from their provisions for more human contact between East and West, freer information, and enhanced cultural and educational cooperation. And the human rights issues which received the greatest attention in the West included the search, arrest and trial of human rights activists and the misuse of psychiatry in their punishment; the continuing Soviet view of the right to emigrate as a privilege to be granted by the authorities rather than a matter of individual choice; the jamming in the Soviet Union of Western radio broadcasts; and the Soviet denial that there can be cultural communication and exchange without boundaries or barriers. The most depressing issue, from the point of view of what the West wished the outcome of the Helsinki process to be, was the harassment, arrest, exile and imprisonment of members of groups that were the children of the process – the Helsinki monitoring groups.

The Soviet response to all this was to insist at every turn on the principle of non-intervention. This did not involve a denial that human rights were a matter of international concern. This was something that the Soviet Union (and the Eastern European countries) had agreed to at Helsinki and elsewhere. But it did involve a denial that any foreign government, group or individual had any business overseeing the process of implementing human rights within the socialist part of the world; this was within the domestic jurisdiction of the state concerned. And what the Soviet Union has objected to, in general, about the Western initiatives on human rights was the lack in them of any semblance of balance between the various aspects of the Helsinki agreement, and between international security and individual rights. Balance, for the Soviet Union, involved seeing the dissidents for what they truly were: a tiny, isolated privileged and atypical segment of socialist society. In the Soviet view it was worse than a mere error of judgement on the part of the West to allow the interests of these dissidents to set the course of superpower relations.

The *détente* between the superpowers which led to Helsinki thus produced issues between them whose thrust is to undermine it. And the issue of human rights revealed fundamental differences between East and West in their understanding of the meaning of *détente*. In the West, the *détente* between East and West, exemplified by the Helsinki process, was thought to consist of a new style of international relations, resulting from diminishing ideological tension between the blocs, and a new subject matter of human rights added to the old concerns with trade and security. These elements, it was thought, would be revealed in the gradual opening up of the closed societies of the East. But for the Soviet Union, *détente* was to take place between governments, not between societies; and it would be revealed in businesslike relations between states based on the principle of non-interference. The result of these different interpretations of *détente* is that what the West took to be evidence of *détente* working, that is the progress made in the Soviet Union of the Western conception of human rights, was taken by the Soviet Union to be the very thing which undermined *détente* because it sought to subordinate Soviet domestic affairs to foreign interests. And what the Soviet Union took to be evidence of *détente* working – strict adherence to non-intervention – was taken by the West to be a surrender to the mere fact of Soviet preponderance in its part of the world. For this reason, some writers have despaired of human rights being a plank in the platform for global politics, and we shall return to this question in our conclusion. Meanwhile, let us look at the other main polarity in contemporary world politics.

North–South Relations

The Charter of the United Nations, established as the formal framework for international relations at San Francisco in 1945, is interpreted in the West (and in the East) mainly as a minimalist document to provide for the maintenance of peace and security among states. Its references to the sovereign equality of the units in international society, peace and security among them, and to collective action if an act of aggression which challenged the sovereignty of the units were to take place, are all procedures whose purpose is to maintain global politics as the politics of several sovereign states, rather than a more ambitious programme of cosmopolitan amalgamation. If it could provide some element of international order, well and good, but it was not remotely to be thought of as a world government even in embryo.

However, according to Ali Mazrui (1967), an African professor of international relations, the Third World conception of the United Nations Charter is very different from the one held by either the Eastern or the Western sections of the North – but especially that of the West. The Third World concept is closer to maximalism than minimalism. It interprets the Charter not as a deal done between states whose main interest is to interrupt each other's well-being as little as possible, but as a proclamation of global emancipation for the downtrodden: self-determination before sovereignty; liberty before peace and security; cooperation to produce justice and human rights before collective action to enforce order. In this vein, Professor Mazrui interprets the United Nations Charter as having become a global bill of rights, with self-determination a prominent right and a principle which the Third World would apply naturally to peoples and nations before individuals.

There is a rhetorical element in Ali Mazrui's work which makes his book something to read as itself a part of the struggle for liberation, and not merely as an academic interpretation of it. But it is possible to interpret the whole of the Third World position on human rights in contemporary international politics as following two phases in a strategy of emancipation, together with a third aspect which, while it might not constitute a phase of its own, illuminates the other two and helps us to understand the Third World attitude to human rights. The two phases and the third aspect can in turn be regarded as developments in the doctrine of self-determination.

The first phase is the ending of colonialism. Most of the member states of international society have achieved their independence from colonial rule since 1945, with the rush coming in the late 1950s and the 1960s. Having, by one means or another, brought to an end their colonial status and entered international society as full members, they have sought to buttress their position doctrinally so that there can be no going back. Thus there arose the famous Declaration on the Granting of Independence to Colonial Countries and Peoples, adopted by the General Assembly of the United Nations in 1960, in which the 'subjection of peoples to alien subjugation, domination and exploitation' was said to constitute a denial of fundamental human rights, to be contrary to the Charter of the United Nations, and to be an impediment to the promotion of world peace and cooperation. Inadequacy of political, economic, social or educational preparedness did not serve as a pretext for delaying independence. And immediate steps were to be taken in territories which had not yet gained their independence to transfer power to their people. This was the principle of self-determination in its clearest and most consensual form in contemporary international politics, the form which removes legitimacy from colonialism and makes the normal international actor the self-governing nation-state.

Independence having been won in a formal sense, the next step was to make sure that it was accompanied by substance. This was increasingly seen by Third World countries to require that economic sovereignty should stand beside independence. It is this idea that has prompted the set of claims associated with the new international economic order that the countries of the South have been pressing on the attention of the North since the early 1970s. And what has given coherence to this set of claims is the notion that the exploitation associated with colonialism did not end with empire but continues in the structure of economic dependence in which Southern countries still find themselves embedded. Hence their demand for payback – for the remedying of past and present injustices inherent in the structure of the world economy, and for something more like equality of benefit from participation in the contemporary international economy. The symbol of this phase in Third World emancipation was the Charter of Economic Rights and Duties of States adopted by the General Assembly of the United Nations in 1974 in which the rights of developing states were ranged against the obligations of developed states.

The third aspect of Southern emancipation has to do with cultural liberation, of which two elements may be mentioned here. The first is the idea, the phrase for which Ali Mazrui invented in *Towards a Pax Africana*, of 'pigmentational self-determination'. This is the principle, not of *national* self-determination in its political or economic aspect, but of *racial* self-determination. In Mazrui's treatment this is a principle that rulers and ruled should manifestly belong to the same race. It has not, as such, entered international law, but the thrust for racial equality of which it is evidence *has*, in the shape of the conventions on the elimination of racial discrimination and on the suppression and punishment of the crime of apartheid. The second element which may be mentioned as an illustration of the force of cultural liberation in contemporary world politics is that cluster of developments associated with what we call in the West (and which is examined in the next chapter) the Islamic revival. The idea of the purification of a system by purging it of the debased foreign elements summed up in the expression 'Westernization' has been important in the Islamic world during the last two decades, and it is appropriate to include it here as an aspect, the cultural aspect, of the principle of self-determination.

The Northern response to this Southern assault has, in general, been composed of a mixture of conceit and chagrin: conceit that the South has been embroidering what is after all the Western cloth of self-determination, but chagrin when the principle is turned against the West. In particular, the response to each element of the Southern corollaries to the principle of self-determination has been as follows: on the end to colonialism, concession; on economic sovereignty, some response to the rhetoric but little to the substance of fundamental change in the world economy; and on cultural self-determination, a mixture of scepticism and confusion.

Thus colonialism, in its classical sense of the acquisition of overseas territory by metropolitan powers which claim sovereignty over them, has some remnants in contemporary world politics, but they are regarded as the debris of a bygone age and do not occupy a legitimate place in the contemporary international system. The first phase of the principle of self-determination, the liberation of the colonies, is virtually completed; it is an emancipatory project consummated.

The second phase of the principle of self-determination, however, is in a very early stage of its development. The log of claims associated with the new international economic order, including more aid from the First World to the Third, the industrializ-ation of the Third World, generalized preferential trade arrangements in favour of the Third World, debt rescheduling or its conversion into grants, and equal access to Western technology, are not far advanced – except in the sense that consciousness of them in this generation may yield results in the next. This may be the importance of Western concessions to the rhetoric of Third World solidarity against it, but it has not yet produced practical results. But there has also been a counter-attack by the West in the shape of the basic needs strategy for development endorsed by such important institutions as the International Bank for Reconstruction and Development (the IBRD, widely referred to as the World Bank). This strategy is centred on individuals, particu-larly those at the periphery of developing societies, and as such it seeks to confront the collectivism of Third World claims and to see liberation as a project for individuals.

On the third aspect of the principle of self-determination, the question of cultural emancipation, it is difficult to characterize a general Third World position beyond the idea that the rediscovery of indigenous cultures and the rolling back of the lesser if not all Western values is a good thing. The Western response has been piecemeal: to the idea of pigmentational self-determination, scepticism about its application outside the obvious candidate, South Africa; to the idea of religious revivalism, a tendency to dismiss it as a lapse into barbarism.

We are driven by this analysis to the conclusion that human rights as an aspect of global politics indicate division in the world rather than solidarity, and that to understand their political significance we must look beneath the language of unity to the ideologies and the interests which separate one political community from another. We shall return to this disposition later in the chapter. But we must first hear from the other side, from those who find the language of human rights evidence of a global polity, pointing to certain institutions which show that in some sense planet earth is a parliamentary constituency.

THE EVIDENCE FOR UNIVERSAL RIGHTS

Despite the plurality of their interpretation, the language of human rights has caught on in contemporary international politics to such an extent that the appeal to them has become commonplace – not only in the mouth of protest where one might expect it, but also in the voice of the legitimation of state conduct where its presence seems less likely. But if human rights do provide a unifying language, what kind of unity do we have in mind when we use the expression? The object of this section is to investigate this question, trying out three different ways in which there might be said to be an actual unity in world politics and not merely an imaginary one.

Human Rights as Particular Rights

The first of these dwells on the language of human rights, noting its ubiquity, such that few societies are to be found in the contemporary world that do not use it in justification of their own actions or in criticism of others. Even China, a long-established civilization, but accustomed to thinking of values in terms of interlocking obligations rather than of rights, has had to use this language in its daily encounters at the United Nations. But China, like all other societies, uses the expression 'human rights' to describe *its* conception of what is due to all or more likely some (namely its citizens) human beings, and not some abstract extracommunal conception of what is in principle the inheritance of everyone. So our first attempt to produce unity out of diversity in relation to human rights is actually a very superficial enterprise. It notes that all or most societies use the language of human rights, but that they mean by it their own particular conception of rights – what it is to be human in their part of the world. This might seem an attractive approach because it allows 'human rights' to take on whatever is the local colour. But it does not help us with our problem – finding a concept of human rights which could apply to several societies.

Human Rights as Core Rights

The second route along which we might seek genuinely universal human rights confronts this question directly. It asks whether there is in fact a core of basic rights that is common to all cultures despite their apparently divergent doctrines about values. This question is consistent with the natural rights tradition in the West; according to this tradition we all have rights whose content can be decided on by the use of right reason, which, since reason is a human faculty, should produce fundamentally similar answers across all cultures. This provides us with an empirical question – a question about what actually happens, not what ought to happen – concerning patterns of practice across societies. If human rights set out what ought to be due to everyone in virtue of their humanity, how might we decide whether in fact all societies acknowledge these principles?

One way is to follow Barrington Moore's (1972) line of argument about the unity of human misery. While human beings find it difficult to agree on the meaning of human happiness, he suggests, they find it much easier to know when they are miserable. Presumably, he says, it requires no laboriously accumulated proof to demonstrate that human beings hardly every really enjoy being tortured or slaughtered by a cruel enemy, starvation and illness, the exactions of ruthless authorities who carry off the fruits of prolonged labour, the loss of beloved persons through the acts of others over which one has little or no control, and rotting in prison or being burned at the stake. This conception of the unitary nature of human suffering, at least in comparison with human happiness, Barrington Moore takes to be helpful in resolving some of the issues involved in assessing the role that moral judgement should play in social inquiry. It is equally helpful in establishing a cross-cultural starting place for ideas of universal conceptions of the wrong that is done by the imposition of unnecessary suffering on any human being.

Another way of answering the question 'Do all societies respond in a similar way to suggestions about the content of fundamental human values?' is to start not with some hypothesis, like Barrington Moore's, about the unity of human suffering, but with the investigation of the values held in the several societies making up world politics. The thrust here is inductive rather than deductive, starting from practice rather than first principles. As a result of a survey of world cultures it would attempt to provide an empirical answer to the question of whether there are any universal values. What this investigation might be expected to produce, if anything, is a lowest common denominator of basic or core rights, which, if found across all societies, would then have a proper positive claim to the label 'human rights'.

Another way of producing a list of genuinely universal human rights is not by finding out what is common to all cultures, but by taking something from each culture so that all of them will be satisfied in some degree with the end product. According to this notion, human rights that were properly universal would do something for the West, something for the East and something for the Third World, so that every group had something of a stake in the outcome. The difficulty with this procedure is that while it might in some sense reduce the ethnocentrism of declarations about them, it abandons in the process any notion of universal human rights. Drawing up a long list to accommodate everybody merely adds variety together. It does nothing to resolve the differences between one item or group of items on the list and another, and it would invite particular societies to consult only their sections of the document. It therefore makes no progress beyond our first solution, which had human rights as particular rights.

Accordingly, it may be more productive to investigate the question of the existence of human rights from the top down rather than from the bottom up. That is to say we should start, not with the several societies of which world society is composed, but with the society formed among those societies.

Human Rights and the Structure of Modernity

A third possible solution to the problem of establishing that there are indeed such things as universal human rights lies in the assertion that there exists in the contemporary world a single cosmopolitan structure which is spread across all indigenous cultures, and which carries to each of them what are, at least in some geographical sense, global human rights. This is the common structure of modernity (delivered by the process of modernization already examined in chapter 13) which has touched, some would say engulfed, all societies in virtue of the rise of a fundamentally global economy taken by technology to all corners of the world. States, regions, cities, families and patterns of life, it may be said, are all shaped by this structure. Cities grow with industrialization, families are oriented to forms of bread-winning determined by a global division of labour, and patterns of life are configured by production. All over the world, it may also be said, individuals have been pulled away by its operation from their traditional attachment to the local community. Someone who works on an automobile production line has his or her life shaped by a system that imposes similar patterns in Japan or Britain or the United States. In these circumstances the fact of the Japaneseness or the Britishness or the Americanness of the workers might mean less than the nature of the work. And in these circumstances, too, the spread of the philosophy of human rights can be rendered as the normative response to a single globalizing social process; and this is expressed in that body of doctrine that we have now to examine, the international law of human rights.

There has been a considerable thickening of the human rights regime since 1945. In the nineteenth century international law was treated as exclusively a law between states. States were its subjects, individuals merely its objects. So the human rights that belonged to individuals may have had some claim to the moral attention of the world, but were not regarded as part of the international law. But in the twentieth century the exclusion of the individual from the provisions of international law has been broken down. A number of developments illustrate this process at work:

1 The minorities treaties, a series of treaties associated with the establishment of the League of Nations after the First World War, imposing obligations on certain states with respect to minorities living within their jurisdiction.
2 Treaties giving rights directly to individuals, such as the Convention of 1907 setting up the Central American Court of Justice; the Mixed Arbitral Tribunals established by the Treaty of Versailles in 1919 to deal with debts owed by Germany to allied nationals; and the European Convention on Human Rights of 1951, giving access to all individuals in signatory states to an Europe-wide court (once domestic remedies had been exhausted).
3 The work of the International Labour Organization (ILO), set up after the First World War, which produced international standards of treatment for workers.
4 The International Military Tribunal at Nuremberg after the Second World War.
5 The provision for human rights and fundamental freedoms in the Charter of the United Nations as purposes which members pledged themselves to achieve.
6 The Universal Declaration of Human Rights, the International Covenants on Civil and Political Rights and on Economic, Social and Cultural Rights (these three together making up what is called the International Bill of Rights), and several other conventions and declarations sponsored by the United Nations.

All these developments bear witness to the increasing attention paid to human rights in contemporary international law, and to the extent to which standards are being set by the international community which are expected to be met, or at least aimed at, in each constituent part of that community. In the preamble to the Charter of the United Nations this expectation is recorded in the determination of the peoples of the United Nations not merely to save succeeding generations from the scourge of war, but also to reaffirm faith in fundamental human rights, in the dignity and worth of the human person, and in the equal rights of men and women and of nations large and small. The kind of language associated with revolutions within certain member states of international society, notably the United States (in its Declaration of Independence) and France (in its Declaration of the Rights of Man and of the Citizen), was now asserted on behalf of world society as a whole. It is this commitment that allows the interpretation of the United Nations Charter as a global bill of rights.

We shall come later to the question of whether this heroic interpretation of the United Nations Charter as a global bill of rights is indeed the text for our times. Meanwhile we may note, in a rather more mundane way, the acceptance of human rights as part of the general business of international society being signalled institutionally by the establishment (by the Economic and Social Council of the United Nations in 1946) of the United Nations Commission on Human Rights. It is states that sit on this Commission, and progress in it on the question of human rights is constrained by the preoccupation of states and of international society. But in the year of its own establishment, the Commission appointed a Subcommission on the Prevention of Discrimination and Protections of Minorities, whose members sit as experts and not as representatives of governments. Partly because it is uninstructed (that is, not the creature of governments), this body has become an important agency on the issue of human rights in general, and not just on its official concern with discrimination and minorities. And it has developed procedures which allow wronged individuals some access to its working.

Universal human rights have also been received regionally. Indeed, the United Nations itself has directly encouraged the establishment and development of human rights institutions at the regional level. This has been most notable in Western Europe, America and Africa. The European Convention on Human Rights, which came into force in 1953, has both a commission and a court to promote the cause of human rights in Europe, and it has established machinery by means of which individuals could bring complaints against their own governments once domestic remedies had been exhausted. The American Convention on Human Rights, which came into force in 1978, has similar institutions though they are as yet less well used. And the African (Banjul) Charter of Human and People's Rights adopted by the Organization of African Unity in 1981 has a commission concerned with the promotion of human rights throughout the African continent.

However, the establishment of human rights institutions at the UN or at the regional level is not the same thing as the implementation of human rights in each society making up the world community. This, as we have already seen in relation to the Soviet attitude to the Helsinki process, is because of the rearguard action being fought by the principle of state sovereignty. The strength of this action can be illustrated by reference to the question of the lawfulness of humanitarian intervention in the internal affairs of some delinquent state in order to vindicate some humanitarian purpose. According to positivist international law, that is the law sanctioned by the practice of states, there is very little support for a doctrine of humanitarian intervention. This is partly because of the strength of the prohibition against the use of force in international society (except in response to unlawful aggression) which is contained in article 2(4) of the United Nations Charter, and which no state openly confronts, and partly because of the preference states have to use the doctrine of self-defence to legitimize any force they feel obliged to use and not some more controversial appeal to humanitarian values.

This goes back to the predominant interpretation of the Charter of the United Nations as a framework for peace and security rather than as a declaration of global emancipation. States, even the new states, even especially the new states, are more concerned to protect the values associated with state sovereignty than to further the cause of human solidarity.

This absence of human solidarity, and of a disposition to intervene on its behalf, should make us cautious about associating human rights with a unifying common structure of modernity of which we have suggested international law is a normative manifestation. There are at least three difficulties about it of which we need to be aware. The first is that there is not one single animal called the common structure of modernity. The process of modernization might be said to produce two structures, as in the centre–periphery model and in the idea that modernization creates a dual economy in developing societies (we might associate this view with the neo-Marxist paradigm). Or it might be said to produce as many structures as there are societies, modernization affecting each differently and producing a blend of the global and local which is in each case unique (we might associate this notion with the liberal-pluralist paradigm). Or, with reference to our discussion of party earlier in this chapter, it might have three principal variants depending on the mode of production and the style of politics – Western, Eastern or Southern – in each of which there is a different doctrine of rights (and we might associate this attitude with the realist paradigm).

Second, if there is more than one structure associated with the process of moderniz-ation, then it might reasonably be argued that there is no basis for an appeal to that process itself to settle an argument about universal human rights. Calling up the international law of human rights as evidence for the existence of a global cosmopolitan structure of which all societies are part, and whose rules should then apply to them, might be said to fail because international law itself is subject to interpretation from the standpoint of this or that society.

A third objection to the idea of a common structure of modernity as an anchorage for universal human rights questions not its existence but its pedigree. A common structure, however superficial, might be conceded as existing, but the extent of it, it might be argued, is the measure of Westernization rather than of modernization. It is a species of imperialism, the argument might run, a charge the West seeks to avoid by calling it a world social process, or modernization, or an emerging global structure – all deodorized expressions for exploitation. In this kind of interpretation the inter-national law of human rights would be explained as a legitimation machine, widening and deepening the hold of Western conceptions of the good society. As a result, if emancipation is to take place, the Third World countries seeking to get out from underneath the downward seepage of Western culture need to invent or to recall a human rights vocabulary of their own which is different from that of the West.

Let us take in turn these difficulties about the association of universal human rights with a common structure of modernity. The first was the most radical. It suggested that there were plural modes of modernization, each of which might spawn a conception of rights most appropriate to its own proper functioning. The flaw in this objection is that it seems to suggest that the plural worlds are sealed off from one another, oblivious to and immune to external criticism. This seems doubtful empirically. It may be that there are three main tendencies, three parties or factions in contemporary world politics, each cleaving to a particular conception of rights as the thing which gives it its distinguishing colour. But we may observe these tendencies in contest against each other *within* the West, the East and the South as well as between the West, the East and the South. In short, if there are parties, parts of a whole, who contest with each other in terms of rival attitudes to rights, we should not lose sight of the whole of global politics and of the common language of rights, which make the debate among them intelligible.

The second difficulty with the argument for universal human rights as part of a common global structure was that this global structure was subject to interpretation by the primary cultural groups, over which the so-called world structure was arched. Thus the international law of human rights was in reality Western, or Eastern, or Southern, or some subdivision within these categories, and not some meta-law above the cultures. This difficulty is too crude. It is inescapable that Western, or Eastern, or Southern, or Hindu, or Muslim lawyers interpret international law from a Western, or Eastern, or Southern, or Hindu, or Muslim point of view. But it is plainly not true that they regard international law merely as the vehicle for their own cultural freight. A law among nations acceptable to all its members suggests the existence of some common ground, and not simply the outward thrust of domestic preoccupations. This common ground has then some autonomous existence, and it is the job of international lawyers to give an account of it. They might disagree about it. But this does not sanction the reductionist view that international law can be understood only at the level of the cultures participating in it. Because, for one thing, the disagreement might take place as much within as among cultures.

The third difficulty concerned the pedigree of the global structure of modernity. It may be true that the chief fact about modernity is its Westernness, and that the international law of human rights, like all international law, is more of an export of the West to the rest of the world than of the rest of the world to the West. It may also be true that the emancipation of the Third World requires the uncovering of authentic indigenous conceptions of human rights with which to confront the doctrines of the imperialists. Ironically, however, it may be argued that the emergence from Western dominance is advanced not by the assertion of the cultural relativity of all values, but rather by appealing to certain universal principles, such as that of state sovereignty, to roll back the hegemony of the imperialists. And even if the right asserted is a right to be different, it is one protected by a doctrine long familiar in the Western world, namely the principle of self-determination. According to the principle of self-determination, every nation enjoys the same right to be different.

The principle of self-determination is an apt illustration of that process, in the international law of human rights, by which a certain legal tradition has been received from on top and added to from underneath. It is a Western principle, at least as old as the French Revolution, which the new states have used to gain their independence and then, if the account earlier in this chapter is accurate, added to with particular economic and racial corollaries of their own. It may be that the whole of the international law of human rights repays interpretation from this point of view – as a body of doctrine received from the West, but added to by East and South in such a way that it is now truly a cosmopolitan corpus and not a mere promontory of Western imperialism.

Are There Universal Rights?

Let us recapitulate. There are three sociological procedures which might bridge the gap between cultural pluralism and the singularity of human rights. The first, asserting the universality of particularism, fails by making no real attempt on the task. However, in failing, it does serve to remind us that the model of a community in which there is an expectation that rights will be respected is local rather than global. The second procedure, that of a cross-cultural validation of natural rights theory, seems more promising, and the naturalist tradition provides useful bridging points (perhaps in the identification of basic rights) even if a modern social scientist might doubt if it could construct the bridge itself. The third argument, about the global cosmopolitan culture, has taken up the most space here because it may be the best indicator of the extent to which there are genuinely global politics; and in its normative aspect, as the international law of human rights, it suggests a social process by which global values are being worked out in an exchange between the cultures. So are there any of these global values, any universal rights? We suggested that self-determination was characteristically one of them, but that it was an ambiguous principle in being composed of elements that proclaimed difference and similarity at the same time.

HUMAN RIGHTS AND THE GLOBAL POLITY

We have now considered the question of human rights in world politics from the point of view of the parties divided by different conceptions of human rights and from the point of view of the reception of a common conception of human rights in world society as a whole. Our task now is to look at the tension between these two in the life of contemporary world politics. We shall investigate the matter in three arenas: in politics within states, in international politics, and in the emerging politics of planet earth.

Politics within States

At the level of politics within the state, the classical polity received from Greek political thought, we might ask the following questions. To what extent have states sought to advance, within their own domains, the values of cosmopolitan society at the same time as defending a right in their locality to be different in some degree from everyone else? And is the area covered by the values they have in common expanding at the expense of the area covered by what makes them different?

There are two aspects to this that we need to notice here. In the first place, many states have been founded precisely for the purpose of securing for their citizens the human rights that everyone ought to enjoy. The best-known examples of this, as we have already seen in another context, are the United States and France. But, more recently, many of the new states entering international society have taken their standards to be written into their constitutions from the Universal Declaration of Human Rights passed by the General Assembly of the United Nations in 1948.

Second, whatever the reasons for their establishment, states are having to come to terms with the expanding international law of human rights, in the sense of deciding on the extent of its domestic application. They have to take positions on the whole range of conventions from those on racial discrimination to that on refugees. There are several contentious issues here. One of them, which we have already encountered, is the question of whether the implementation of obligations to respect and promote human rights is itself a domestic or an international matter. Another connected one is whether international law applies directly to individuals in domestic courts even if it lacks the legal qualities of mandatoriness and definiteness. Another is the extent to which international conventions should be taken account of in the ordinary application of domestic law. But however difficult these issues are, it is plain that, because of the weight of customary international law on the matter of human rights, no state is in a position simply to put up the shutters against them.

The answer then to our first question, about the extent to which states have sought to advance cosmopolitan values within their own jurisdication, is that many have taken this to be their great political purpose, and that all of them have had to come to terms with them in some degree in virtue of their very membership of international society. The answer to the second question, about the progress made by cosmopolitan values in contrast to indigenous values, is less certain. If Britain's response to the values sponsored by the regime associated with the European Convention on Human Rights is any indication, we might describe this progress as slow but inexorable. But that is to appeal to the area in international politics where this process is at its most sophisticated. If, to return to an introductory question about the global polity, we look for form as well as foundation *within* states, we might detect more of the latter than the former, while conceding that even the latter is sketchy and uneven.

International Politics

Our discussion about the party politics of human rights in the contemporary world showed the extent to which, in public diplomacy among the powers, human rights have arrived as an issue about which to contend. At the East–West conferences carrying on the Helsinki process, and at the General Assembly of the United Nations, public positions on human rights are taken and loudly debated, and one may hear the same left–right battle taking place in world politics that we are familiar with in domestic politics. We may take up a sceptical attitude to this battle, for example by describing the high profile given to human rights by the Carter administration as the form taken by the anti-communist crusade at that time.

But this is not their only function. Human rights have also entered the more private diplomacy of bilateral relations, and the routine diplomacy of reporting from missions abroad. Thus the British foreign minister on a visit to countries in the Eastern bloc, or in the South, or indeed to Western allies (like Turkey), will expect to be briefed on particular human rights issues that come up in Britain's relations with those countries. Moreover, British diplomats abroad have become accustomed to making one item of their communications home a report on the human rights record of their host country. Reporting under this heading may of course be more or less lurid according to circumstances. But the point is that it has become a matter of routine, and is no longer regarded as something about which diplomats maintain a conspiracy of silence in order to maintain good relations among governments of very different political dispositions.

Human rights have also become part of routine diplomacy in multilateral relations, associated above all with the United Nations. This includes the work of the Human Rights Commission in Geneva; the activity of the political organs of the United Nations in New York, especially the General Assembly itself and its committees (notably the third committee on social, humanitarian and cultural matters, the fourth committee on trusteeship and the sixth committee on law); the task of monitoring the human rights agreements carried on by such bodies as the Human Rights Committee set up under the International Covenant on Civil and Political Rights; and (though it is not strictly diplomacy but a facilitator of it) the functions fulfilled by that part of the United Nations secretariat which is collected together in the Division of Human Rights.

Part of public diplomacy, part of the routine; this does not of course indicate the *weight* of the impact of human rights questions on the ordinary everyday business of international life. The high politics of security and welfare have not been dislodged from their pre-eminent positions by considerations of what is due to the individuals and groups who make life difficult for the diplomats acting for states. Nor, as we suggested in our discussion of rights and factions, does the mere discussion of human rights in international affairs indicate that the world is moving forward together on an agreed programme in regard to the treatment of individuals and groups everywhere. It might, indeed, indicate just the opposite.

The Emerging Global Polity

The levels of politics within the state and of international politics impress us, as students of political science, as the politics which are already in business. The advice to the Martian visitor, if he or she wishes to understand global politics in the late twentieth century, is that he or she acquaint himself or herself first with the state and then with politics among states. But if he or she is a peculiarly sophisticated visitor then we might wish him or her to come to grips with the emerging politics of the planet earth. There are three elements to this in regard to the connection with rights: the question of the emergence of *transnational* politics to accompany intrastate and interstate politics; the question of perceiving the planet as a political *whole*; and the question (connected to the other two) of *citizenship* of the planet and not mere occupancy of it. You should be able to see in this tripartite division our three questions about global politics recurring: first, connectedness; second, the broadening of the political process (to encompass the planet); and third, the idea of belonging together in a polity.

The emergence of transnational politics has been and will be discussed elsewhere in this book in relation to such matters as economic interdependence or dependence, and the sideways spread of ideologies. In the matter of rights, the transnational developments of interest are those exemplified by the establishment of such groups as Amnesty International. Amnesty International exists to promote freedom of opinion, the right to a fair trial, freedom from torture, and the abolition of the death penalty. And it exists to promote these values across the face of world politics; not in this state or that, but wherever they are under threat. Its method is the classical dissenting one of agitation; and it seeks results by mobilizing opinion on particular cases and bringing the weight of that opinion to bear on decision makers who might make a difference.

Amnesty International makes a point of being apolitical, or above the fray. Dealing even-handedly with human rights violations anywhere is part of its official doctrine. Its even-handedness is given expression by having each of its groups adopt prisoners of conscience from the First, Second and Third Worlds, and by not having them adopt such prisoners within their own countries. The genuineness of its even-handedness has been questioned by some of its critics, who have pointed out the Westernness of its values and the expectation that more adjustment is required outside than within the West to conform to them. But while it may be in some sense a prisoner of the civilization that produced it, it is plainly not the creature of governments, and the transnational, non-governmental network it has established is an indicator, however weak, of the emergence of global politics that are not simply the shadows cast by states.

Amnesty International, in this regard, plays some part in our second dimension of global politics, which consists in seeing the planet whole. But the spectacular contribution in recent decades to this perception has been that of writers such as Richard A. Falk (1981) who, in talking of an endangered planet, have rehearsed those threats to its survival which make us aware of its unity: the nuclear threat, both peaceful as in the case of Chernobyl and warlike as in the potential breakdown of deterrence; the running down of finite national resources; the population explosion; and the pollution of the atmosphere, and its consequences such as the famous greenhouse effect. These items are not the subject matter of this chapter. Their relevance to the rights issue is through the connection we made earlier, helped by Barrington Moore (1972), between the causes of suffering and the articulation of rights. If human rights are invoked as they characteristically are, at the point of real danger to deeply held human values, then we might expect the argument that the planet itself is endangered, if presented vividly enough, to encourage individuals to see their involvement in humankind not as a poetic abstraction but as a reality that can only be sustained if the individual rights and obligations are allocated in some global political calculation. And this leads on to the question of planetary citizenship. Sprout and Sprout (1971) wrote of the necessity for a *cognition* of global interdependence to follow the *condition* of it if there was to be a reasonable chance of survival.

A Global Polity?

The above discussion of a global polity is very speculative. Whether it will become a reality, with each one of us its citizens, is something that we may know only when we have achieved it. If that happens, then the era of international relations will be described in the history books as having intervened between the decline of empires and the formation of the planetary *polis*.

In this world, human rights have a part in domestic politics but one which generally takes second place to the rights of citizens. They feature now in the landscape of international politics but not in its foreground, which is composed of the immediate interests of states in their security and welfare. They also crop up in transnational politics as a result of the modern form taken by the old tradition of political agitation. Human rights show that there are global politics in the sense that we cannot give an account of world politics by reference to the world of states alone, but they have not delivered, if they ever will, the global polity which will have made of every human being a global citizen, such that *human* rights will have withered away and global *citizens'* rights become established. So in terms of our earlier definitions, human rights connect up a global society at least in terms of the spread of normative language. They expand politics beyond the state because they carry normative concerns about individual action into the society of states. And they have produced some foundation for a global cosmopolis, if not yet its forms.

Conclusions: the Direction of Change

For the reasons outlined above, about human rights being in the margin of international politics, we should hesitate to call human rights, as some writers have, the idea of our time. But there is some evidence that they have become the vocabulary of our time because human rights have increasingly become the common language in terms of which the states in their international relations discuss the values which they hold to be fundamental. Thus even if we take the party politics view of human rights in world politics to be more basic than the global society view (that is, if it is a language which divides more than it unites) we have to recognize, in the conversation *between* the parties, a conception of politics that is wider than that which one party to the discussion happens to believe.

In this very rudimentary sense, then, global politics exist in virtue of an implicit agreement among the parties that the conversation about values is worth having, that someone might be persuaded, that they do not make mere utterances in the void. To the argument that it may, nevertheless, be close to a dialogue of the deaf, we might reply that the sensitivities that states show to the criticism of each other indicate that they listen. This might indicate, in turn, the arrival of an expanded notion of legitimacy or right conduct in the international polity. It is not enough now (though it once was) for states merely to be sovereign, and to prove thereby their eligibility for membership in the international club. There is also a question of how they treat their citizens – which the case of South Africa reveals the most clearly – whilst at the same time showing the limits of international action. There is broad agreement that South Africa is an offender against a cosmopolitan notion of what human rights are and the conduct they require, but the survival of the South African system shows the weakness of the international community in disciplining offenders. Thus John Ruggie (1983) holds that the human rights struggle is condemned to work within a system that remains fundamentally inhospitable to the kinds of claims and challenges it represents.

These questions about legitimacy and South Africa raise two deeper issues. First, what is it that determines what the content of legitimacy is? That is, why has the discussion about human rights followed the course that it has taken? And second, should we endorse this or that direction of change?

One answer to the first of these questions is circumstance. Attention to human rights might follow the committing of human wrongs. This is the argument that human rights surfaced in international society because of Western revulsion at the evil done within its midst before and during the Second World War. We may refer also to a contemporary example of reaction to circumstance. The problem of refugees and migrants is a substantial one in every part of modern international society. States, and especially the popular target states for immigrants and refugees, have to form a view about the rights of these individuals because they are confronted with the problem in practice and not merely in theory. It is not a new problem. The right of asylum is an ancient recognition of one aspect of it, but the scale and scope of it in the contemporary world is a vivid illustration of the demands that individuals and groups are making of the club of states. And such is the pressure of migration and seeking refuge that states have, it might be said, a prophylactic interest in seeing to it that mass migrations are not sponsored by the wholesale disregard for human rights in one section of international society. So an interest in the human rights record of a neighbour, certainly, but also of a state the other side of the globe, becomes part of the calculation of *raison d'état*. Thus circumstances produce practices which are defended on the grounds of interest and harden over time into custom. In such an accidental way, it might be said, the conventions regarding human rights in international law are established.

A view more often heard in the Third World is that the place of human rights in contemporary international society is the outcome of the grafting of a Western tradition on to the rest of the world. The West, in the first place, sets the standards for everyone else – on slavery and the slave trade, then on economic and social rights in such things as factory legislation, then on the welfare state, and so on. Second, when it has the opportunity, it seeks to see to it that other societies conform to its standards – as in the idea that aid should be tied to the liberalization of the economies of the Third World countries. And, third, there is the notion that human rights are a kind of penumbra of empire; the thing itself has passed, but there is still an attempt to control political change in peripheral societies by a sort of cultural imperialism.

A third theory of the nature of change in regard to the content of ideas about human rights canvassed in international society is the opposite of the second. It sees the international law of human rights as an attempt on the part of international society to detach itself from what are purely Western values, rather than seeking to entrench them. In this interpretation, human rights become what is agreed between civilizations rather than what is imposed by one of them, and we have seen how this process might be worked out in the case of the principle of self-determination.

It is possible to build a bridge between these positions despite their apparent contradictions. It may be true that social rules emerge from the experience of coexistence. They may be responses to circumstance. But the circumstances themselves have a context, and it happens that the context of contemporary international politics is predominantly a Western one. However, if the modernization which was associated at its outset with Westernization continues, even in circumstances of relative Western decline, we may call it a universal social process in which it is difficult to identify the particular contribution of this or that culture. In this regard, the international law of human rights may be, as we have seen, an expression of this global process and not merely the American interpretation of human rights law writ large.

But what of the desirability of this direction or that? Is the cosmopolitanization of international society a good thing? Should we endorse, to the extent that we can identify that it is happening, the emergence of global politics? Not presumably if global political institutions delivered a tyrannical system in which the rights of individuals were more threatened than buttressed. Only a fanatical pluralist would wish movement in this direction. Nor if, as many conservatives argue (and here we may recall our paradigmatic realist), the global institutions of which human rights conventions are one have served to weaken order in international affairs by placing responsibilities on states that they have not shown themselves mature enough to administer. Nor if, as many radicals argue (echoing our neo-Marxist paradigm), the global system is in effect, and merely, the institutionalization of capitalism on a global scale. But to the extent that increasing attention to human rights liberates individuals and groups from sealed enclosure in what can be the stifling accommodation of the state, giving them a court of appeal beyond the state, this is a step towards the establishment of a world civil society of which we all might approve.

292   John Vincent

References

Falk, R. (1981) *Human Rights and State Sovereignty*. New York: Holmes and Meier.
Gewirth, A. (1982) *Human Rights: Essays on Justification and Applications*. London: Chicago University Press.
Mazrui, A. (1967) *Towards a Pax Africana*. Chicago: University of Chicago Press.
Moore, B. (1972) *Reflections on the Cause of Human Misery and on Certain Proposals to Eliminate Them*. London: Allen Lane.
Ruggie, J.G. (1983) Human rights and the future international community. *Daedalus*, 112(4), 93–110.
Sprout, H. and Sprout, M. (1971) *Towards a Politics of the Planet Earth*. New York: Van Nostrand Reinhold.

15

Islam as a Global Political Force

BRIAN BEELEY

ISLAM AND THE STATE

In the first centuries after the establishment of the faith, most Muslims lived in an Islamic world where the state was the political component of the whole cultural framework of Muslim society. In the early centuries, this unity of the Realm of Islam was expressed in the empire which ruled in South West Asia, Northern Africa and even Iberia in the name of the faith before that of a state. Later, this political-religious unity was lost as the Islamic Realm split into separate entities. More recently European imperialists took advantage of such divisiveness and contributed, by their intrusions, to the emergence of a mosaic of separate states differentiated in four main ways. Firstly, the size, situation and resource base of Muslim states divide them sharply into contrasting categories. Secondly, the pre-Islamic experience of Muslim communities has left its differentiating mark. Thirdly, the legacy of European control and influence has affected every part of the Muslim world. Fourthly, changes within Islam itself have differentiated Muslims by community and as individuals, by sect and by the intensity of commitment to the faith. This differentiation exists at the modern state level: Iran is predominantly Shi'a, whereas other Muslim states are largely *Sunni*; Saudi Arabia's law is based directly on that of Islam, while secular Turkey has imported much of its legal code from Europe. The differentiation also exists at the level of personal commitment to the status of Islam. Devoutly Muslim Turks protest against their state's national commitment to secularism, just as some Saudi Arabians lead Western lifestyles. It is possible to generalize very broadly about Islamic commitment if one is prepared to note the exceptions to every stereotype. Rural people tend to be more formally committed to Islam than are urban, though many city dwellers are recent immigrants from villages. Women tend to be more conservative in religious practice than are men. Those on whom the colonial legacy has made the greater impact may stress Western notions of state, justice and progress more than they do those of Islam.

In short, West-led modernization has impressed its distinctive state form on to Islamic areas while individual Muslims have been variously changed by contact with Western technology and lifestyle. There are now some 40 states where at least half

the people are Muslim (figure 15.1 and table 15.1). The nature of European encroachment in these areas has ranged from the long-term colonial in Asia, to more recent
incursions into Arab and African lands (table 15.2). In Iran and Turkey colonialism
has been non-formal. In the USSR, by contrast, it has been complete to the point of
political absorption – though Moscow's hold on its Muslim republics in Central Asia
and the Caucasus is now strenuously questioned. The challenge is now part of the
wider late-twentieth-century reaction to the fragmentation of the Realm of Islam (Dar
ul-Islam) resulting from Western encroachment. Muslins may aspire to the earlier
unity which they remember but, in reacting to their political fragmentation, they operate
within the global state system developed on the non-Islamic, Western model. It should
not surprise if the Islamic reaction is mixed, even contradictory, and if Islam may seem
to have a better chance of being a transnational ideal rather than a political force.

Indeed, given the variety of experience and local circumstance across the mosaic of
present-day Islamic states, it is reasonable to ask whether such entities can be both
nation-states *and* Islamic. Vatikiotis argues that the concept of nation-state is alien to
Islam because it works against the unity of the faith (1987, p. 38). Such an intrusive
nation-state gets some of the blame for the fragmentation of Islamic political organization where, traditionally, the *umma* (Muslim community) had been *the* basic unit.
Vatikiotis goes on to stress that in Islam ultimate political sovereignty is vested in God
so that governors derive their legitimacy from their acceptance of His word. For some
observers, however, 'the fact of the matter is that, in Islam, the nation-state is no less
possible, or no more fraught with problems, than it is in the non-Muslim world'
(Piscatori 1986, pp. 149–50). However, for this discussion, a decision in favour of one
or other side of the Islam–state debate is less important than a recognition that the
debate continues and that differing response to it can affect political action. And a key
element is the identification of *nation*.

In the Ottoman Empire up to 1923 there was no doubt about the identity of the
state in the sense of recognized territories, population and effective and legitimate
government. Indeed the status of each ruling sultan was reinforced by his also holding
the rank of caliph of Islam. However, a number of religious communities among the
Empire's citizens were considered each to have a special status as a nation (*millet* in
Turkish), with recognized leadership, organization and privileges. For example, the
sultan could negotiate with heads of *millet* communities which, for their part, had
control over education, group legal affairs and much else. Indeed such *millet* nations
had a form of autonomy without territory. The attempts by Greek and Armenian *millets*
to achieve territorial separation also, and to reject the ultimate paramountcy of the
sultan within the *state*, spelled the end for the multination *millet* system; it was swept
away with the Empire in 1923.

In the Ottoman case the distinction between nation and state was formalized on
grounds of religious affiliation, giving individuals a dual loyalty to nation (religious
community) and state (the Empire). For Muslims the ultimate community is the *umma*
of Islam. Whereas the Ottoman *millet* was a division within the Empire's citizenry, the
essence of the transnational *umma* to a Muslim is that it exists within and beyond the
boundaries of political states. Indeed, Islam has traditionally shown concern for the
relationship between Muslims who live in states where they constitute majorities and
those who live as minority groups in non-Islamic states. This is the distinction between
the Realm of Islam and the outer Realm of Conflict, though the former is now a varied
array of separate states with varied commitment to Islam. As for the Islam in the outer

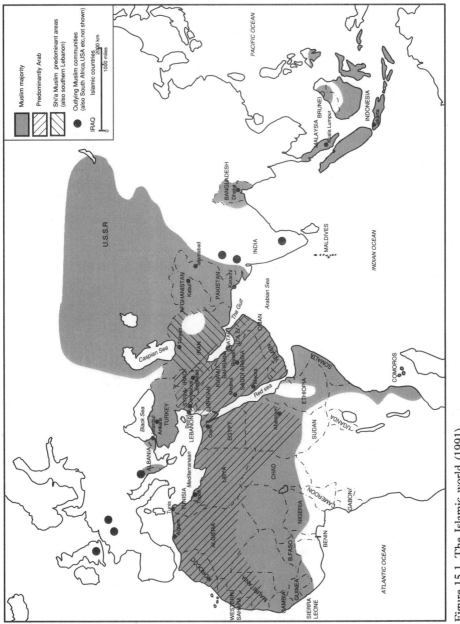

Figure 15.1 The Islamic world (1991)

Table 15.1 Islamic countries

Country[a]	Population Millions[b]	% Muslim[b]	Political independence	Previous colonial influence	Principal language	Membership of selected organizations[c]					GNP per capita $US[b]
Gambia	0.8	85	1965	UK	English	I	B		A	C	220
Senegal	7.0	91	1960	France	French	I	B		A	F	630
Guinea	5.2	90	1958	France	French	I	B		A		350
Nigeria	107.0	c.50	1960	UK	English	(I)	B		A	O	290
Mauritania	2.0	98	1960	France	French/Ar.	I	B	L	A		480
Mali	7.9	70	1960	France	French	I	B		A	F	230
Niger	7.4	88	1960	France	French	I	B		A	F	310
Chad	5.4	c.50	1960	France	French/Ar.	I	B		A	F	160
Ethiopia	50.0	c.50	1941	Italy	Amharic						120
Djibouti	0.5	95	1977	France	Somali/Fr.	I	B	L	A		1,118
Somalia	7.1	99	1960	Italy/UK	Somali	I	B	L	A		170
Comoros	0.4	98	1975	France	Fr./Comoran	I	B		A		440
Morocco	23.9	99	1956	Fr./Spain	Arabic	I	B	L	A		750
Algeria	24.0	99	1962	France	Arabic	I	B	L	A	O	2,450
Tunisia	7.9	98	1956	France	Arabic	I	B	L	A		1,230
Libya	3.6	98	1951	Italy	Arabic	I	B	L	A	O	5,410
Egypt	54.7	91	1922/1954	UK	Arabic	I	B	L	A		650
Sudan	24.9	72	1956	UK	Arabic	I	B	L	A		340
S. Arabia[d]	15.9	100	Old	—	Arabic	I	B	L		O	6,170
Kuwait[d]	2.0	85	1961	Ottoman/UK	Arabic	I	B	L		O	13,680

Qatar	0.4	95	1971	UK	Arabic	I	B	L	O	11,610
Bahrain	0.5	89	1971	UK	Arabic	I	B	L		6,610
UAE	1.9	94	1971	UK	Arabic	I	B	L	O	15,720
Oman	1.4	97	1971	UK	Arabic	I	B	L		5,070
Yemen[e]	12.1	99	1919/1967	Ottoman/UK	Arabic	I	B	L		580
Syria	11.7	89	1941	Ottoman/Fr.	Arabic	I	B	L		1,670
Lebanon	2.9	59	1941	Ottoman/Fr.	Arabic	I	B	L		240
Jordan[d]	3.9	92	1946	Ottoman/UK	Arabic	I	B	L		1,500
Iraq[d]	18.2	96	1932	Ottoman/UK	Arabic	I	B	L	O	2,940
Pakistan	108.0	97	1947	UK	Urdu/Eng.	I	B		C	350
Bangladesh	108.5	83	1947/1971	UK	Bengali/Eng.	I	B		C	170
Malaysia	16.9	55	1957	UK	Malay/Eng.	I	B		C	1,870
Indonesia	180.4	88	1949	Neth.	Indonesian	I	B		O	430
Brunei	0.3	63	1983	UK	Malay/Eng.	I	B		C	14,120
Maldives	0.2	100	1965	UK	Divehi/Eng.	I	B		C	410
Iran	53.5	98	Old	—	Farsi	I	B		O	3,766
Afghanistan	18.6	99	Old	—	Farsi/Pashtu	I	B			234
Turkey	55.7	99	Old	—	Turkish	I	B		T	1,280
Albania	3.4	70	1912	Ottoman	Albanian	I	B			740
India	800.0	11	1947	UK	Hindi/Eng.				C	330
USSR[f]	289.1	19	Old	—	Russian				C	4,550

Countries listed have 50 per cent or more Muslim population, except for India and the USSR which are included because they have the largest Muslim minorities. OIC members Benin, Cameroon, Gabon, Guinea Bissau, Sierra Leone, Burkina Faso and Uganda are not included because they have populations less than 50 per cent Muslim.

[a] Predominantly Muslim territories not listed are:

Mayotte (Comoros) (pop. 0.07 m, 98 per cent Muslim): a French Territorial Collectivity from 1976.

Turkish Republic of Northern Cyprus (pop. 0.2 m, 98 per cent Muslim): part of Republic of Cyprus from withdrawal of UK in 1960 to secession in 1974, recognized only by Turkey. The TRNC has observer status with the OIC.

West Bank and Gaza (Palestine) (pop. 1.6 m, 91 per cent Muslim): occupied by Jordan (West Bank) and Egypt (Gaza) after UK withdrawal from Palestine in 1948; occupied by Israel in 1967, Jordanian link severed in 1988. Member (as Palestine Liberation Organization) of the Arab League, the Organization of the Islamic Conference and the Islamic Development Bank.

Western Sahara (pop. 0.2 m, 100 per cent Muslim): occupied by Morocco after withdrawal of Spain in 1975. Membership of OAU disputed by Morocco.

[b] 1989–90 estimates.

[c] Membership of selected organizations:

I Organization of the Islamic Conference (OIC): Nigeria has observer status; PLO is a member; Afghanistan membership is in respect of the *mujaheddin* government (1989)

B Islamic Development Bank

L Arab League

A Organization of African Unity

O Organization of Petroleum Exporting Countries (OPEC)

C Commonwealth

F Franc zone

T Turkey is a member of the North Atlantic Treaty Organization (NATO) and the Organization for Economic Cooperation and Development (OECD), and is an Associate Member of the European Community (EC)

[d] GNP relates to position before Iraqi occupation of Kuwait, August 1990 to March 1991.

[e] North Yemen and South Yemen merged in 1990.

[f] USSR (1991) includes the Muslim republics of Azerbaijan, Kazakstan, Kirgizia, Tajikistan, Turkmenistan and Uzbekistan.

Table 15.2 Islam and European colonialism

	Pre-colonial		*Colonial*		*Post-colonial*	*Examples*
Long-term colonial	Competitive European involvement • plunder • trade	1600s	• conquest • control • investment	1957	• investment • multi- nationals	Indonesia: resource- rich, large pop.
Arab world	Limited European involvement Ottoman Empire	1830	• settlement (e.g. Algeria) • oil (e.g. Iraq) • strategic (e.g. South Yemen)	1971	• oil money • rapid industrial modern- ization	Qatar: oil- rich, small pop. Egypt: oil- poor, large pop.
Black Africa	Competitive European involvement • slavery • trade routes • forts, missions	c.1870	Competitive European involvement • raw materials • imperial prestige	1965	Continuing dependence • primary products • multi- nationals	Nigeria: resource- rich, large pop. Chad: resource- poor, small pop.
Non-colonial	Limited European involvement		Informal colonial- ism		Varying reactions • investment • multi- nationals	Turkey: secular, pro- West Iran: Shi'a, anti-West
Absorbed	Limited European involvement	c.1840	Conquest • Russific- ation		Non- independent	USSR: Muslim minority

Realm, two facts stand out. Firstly, the numbers involved are in some cases very substantial. India has nearly 90 million Muslims and the Soviet Union some 50 million. Secondly, numbers are increasing rapidly. The USSR foresees a very much larger Muslim element in its total population in the future, with implications not only within the country but also for Moscow's relations with Islamic states. In Africa the Muslim element in a number of countries is growing. In Europe, Muslim communities are now established in major industrial and urban areas, following two decades of labour migration from Islamic areas up to the mid 1970s. The largest of these is in Germany, which has 1.5 million Turkish Muslims. In the United Kingdom there is a similar number of Muslims from Pakistan, India, Bangladesh and other territories with which

Britain has had imperial links. Even larger numbers of Arab Muslims from North West Africa now live in France, and there is a community in the Netherlands of Muslims from Indonesia, the one-time Dutch East Indies. Some states may indeed be regarded as Islamic because the government and ruling establishment is Muslim even though a major part of the population is non-Islamic; Sudan is one important example of this type. Meanwhile, Uganda is one of those African countries where the government identifies with the Islamic group of states (in the Organization of the Islamic Conference, OIC) although only a minority of its people are Muslim.

Whatever the degree of their commitment to Islam, Muslim countries operate within a system of states which is both newer and wider than the faith. Although Islam is already global in its ideal, all-embracing completeness, it clearly is not global in the sense of acting as one in international relations. This is scarcely surprising given the variety of states and parts of states into which it has become fragmented. Islam extends the state in so far as Muslims identify politically with each other across state boundaries but not in terms of functional political union. In short, Islam operates multinationally in so far as Muslim states join in groupings such as the OIC and internationally in terms of conventional links between states whether Islamic or not. As an ideological basis for personal identification, the Islamic concept of *umma* links people rather than governments, regardless of state citizenship. Individuals may identify with the *umma* as well as with a state but the two cannot be organically articulated. There cannot be an Egyptian or a Malaysian *umma* – only an Islamic one. Yet not all Muslims identify with the *umma* in the same way because of sectarian and other splits within the faith. And the split between those Muslims who accept compromise with non-Islamic Western values and practices, and those who seek to reaffirm the traditional pattern of Islam, separates individuals as much as states. In short, the *umma* is an established, transnational norm mediated in places and within classes and groups by history, contemporary orientation and local circumstances.

Inevitably we turn to the proposition that paradigms based on Western experience and ideological priorities can be applied to Islamic states in so far as they are states because the modern state is itself Western in origin. In other words, the paradigms can accommodate political Islam when it operates within the West-led system of states. Where we focus on traditional, normative Islam, either in the past or in present-day reassertive forms, it is clear that a better explanatory paradigm is Islam *sui generis*. Such an Islamic paradigm in state terms starts from the acceptance that sovereignty is vested in God, the source of political (and all other) legitimacy, expressed through divine revelation. Islam was and is prior to the state. The future of the Islamic state (as of individual Muslims) is therefore to be based either on the restoration of traditional Islam or on varying mixes of traditional and Western as contemporary states accommodate and compromise. In such a mix the Islamic component could potentially be the operational framework for power. Alternatively it might only be an element among many in social control or, still less, the faith might be no more than a source of ideas about priorities.

ISLAM AND INTERNATIONAL POLICY

Muslims are today numerous and increasing, widespread and varied, and sometimes strident in the name of their faith. In trying to assess Islam as an ideology which transcends allegiance to the nation-state we can accept that it emerged as a comprehensive and prescriptive set of values and priorities uniting religious and political life. The *universality* of the Islamic world view is basic to Muslim thought, but it is for them specifically an Islamic universality and thus different from, say, Western ideals of equality. For Muslims there is a basic distinction between those places and people where Islamic writ holds and those where it does not. The apparent paradox of a war (1980–8) between Iran and Iraq, or of the latter's seizure of Kuwait in 1990, does not deny the ideal – even though all are Islamic countries – but argues that in such cases the state shows itself to be the primary point of reference, perhaps with its actions justified by participants in Islamic terms. Islam is an ideology in which political attitudes and actions are *part* of a total world view which may transcend allegiance to the state.

Does it follow, therefore, that Islam is *inter alia* a transnational political force creating and sustaining its own structures of political power and authority? A first response to this question could be 'potentially'. A more considered answer requires some assessment of the extent to which Islam can be expressed in political institutions backed by the power to achieve Islamic objectives. In theory, one possibility would be the ideal single Islamic state where questions about Islam versus the state would not be asked because the two were the same. More realistic in a later twentieth century which sees world territory allocated in state entities is the prospect of some kind of superstate Islamic association. Equally realistically, such a grouping might not expect to encompass Muslims under non-Islamic rule or indeed those predominantly Muslim states whose national commitment is to the secular.

As an actual or potential transnational political force, Islam has some important distinguishing characteristics. Firstly, it is clearly not a new phenomenon, and subjugation to European imperialism and incorporation into a world market system has not changed its essence. In so far as what is now re-emerging is Islamic practice modified by contact with non-Muslims, there can be said to be both old and new forms of Islam. Secondly, the old form is valid alongside the new in political terms because it is the ideal and can therefore constitute a basis for the legitimation of political structures and actions. Thus, for example, war can be acceptable if it is accepted as holy war – *jihad*. Thirdly, the comprehensiveness of Islam implies that what is seen by outsiders as *political* action on the part of Muslims may be more than political to those indulging in it. In this context Islam can be a transnational political force within a wider ideological framework.

How then can the policies of states towards other states be mediated by Islam? Could a set of values and ideals, such as those of Islam, constitute any form of authority above or between states? Here concern is with the pragmatic, with the behaviour of states on the international stage, because for Muslims Islam is the ultimate, ideal authority. We may not get far in answering the question because of the difficulty of determining whether Islam generates, legitimates or simply justifies policies and actions. But the question is worth asking if it helps to clarify the transnational impact of the faith.

Perhaps we can assess the Islamic impact on foreign policy by categorizing Muslim countries. All of them have been changed by the West, but no two countries have absorbed the same mix of Western inputs. One categorization can distinguish traditional, liberal and revolutionary, though countries may move from one alignment to another as did Iran after the 1979 revolution. Relations *between* Islamic states also change. Iraq went to war with Iran. Libya attacked Chad and tried to seize part of its territory. Morocco invaded Muslim western Sahara. Meanwhile Arab Syria aligned itself with non-Arab Iran against Arab Iraq. Egypt withdrew from war with Israel, to the dismay of Palestinian and other Muslims. East Pakistan broke away from the equally Muslim western part of the country to form Bangladesh. Clearly the transnational impact of Islam is interwoven with other strands – cultural (e.g. Arab), sectarian (e.g. Sunni–Shi'a) and linguistic (e.g. Urdu–Bengali). With such qualifications in mind, it would be surprising if Islamic states acted in concert in the name of the faith. One institutionalized grouping in which they do is the Organization of the Islamic Conference.

After earlier attempts to discuss problems shared by Muslim countries at summit level, the General Secretariat of the Organization of the Islamic Conference was set up in 1970 in Jeddah, Saudi Arabia. Later, government representatives added economic matters to the political relations, which had been their first concern, in the form of the OIC Standing Committee for Economic and Commercial Cooperation established in Mecca in 1981 at the Third Islamic Summit. A 1987 meeting of the committee involved 46 OIC member states, plus observers. A range of specialist agencies which have been set up by the organization shows the breadth of its concerns. They cover Jerusalem, relief work, the Islamic heritage, law, urban centres, commerce, research, vocational training, banking, transportation, press and broadcasting, and education.

The OIC is a grouping of sovereign states. Hence it differs fundamentally from the traditional concept of Islamic unity, the *umma*, with which all Muslims can identify as individuals. Indeed some OIC member states have substantial non-Muslim populations, just as there are Muslims in states outside the organization. The charter of the OIC holds that Muslim states may join in, but it avoids a definition. India, with one of the world's largest Muslim communities, was briefly a member. Uganda is one of several other countries accepted to membership although they have only minorities of Muslim citizens. Nevertheless, the OIC reflects an evidence desire for greater unity among many Muslims and gives a focus for the *umma* not available since the Caliphate was abolished in 1924. An apparent strength of the OIC is that it has retained the allegiance even of countries in conflict with each other (e.g. Iraq and Iran during the 1980–8 war). It is also an effective indicator of Islamic feeling on contentious issues. A 1980 meeting, for example, demanded the withdrawal of Soviet forces from Afghanistan. In 1984 the OIC called on both Iraq and Iran to stop attacking ships in the Gulf. A 1977 meeting condemned France for a referendum in Mayotte which kept that Indian Ocean island French and out of the Republic of the Comoros. Most numerous of all have been declarations about Palestinian rights and the status of Jerusalem.

The limiting factor in the OIC is that it has no power to implement its decisions and no specifically Islamic strategy towards the rest of the world. As such it is a cultural and religious entity which reacts and proclaims; it is not a bloc with any demonstrable impact on events. But it exists, appears to be durable, and is clearly effective as an intergovernmental forum for the exchange of attitudes and experience.

Economic Patterns: the Peripheralization of Islam

As long ago as the 1870s one Islamic state, the Ottoman Empire, called upon Muslims everywhere to support it economically and politically against penetration from Western powers. In this case pan-Islamism was government sponsored and designed to strengthen the Ottoman component of a West-led political system *within* that system. Bernard Lewis (1981) distinguishes this from the pan-Islamism based on individual leaders or groups, often with traditional doctrines. Efforts at the official type of pan-Islamism have, says Lewis, produced only limited results, though more than anything similarly achieved in the name of Christianity. The nineteenth-century Ottoman sultan was calling on Muslims to act in concert against outside (i.e. non-Muslim) power. In his role as caliph, the sultan wanted the Realm of Islam to confront the Realm of Conflict beyond. In trying to do this, the sultan knew that Islam included the economic along with concern for *all* aspects of life; he was not appealing to Muslims in terms of any specifically Islamic economic community. In the circumstances of the time, he was appealing to Muslims who were in most cases subjects of European empires anyway and thus not free to offer any response, Islamic or otherwise.

Although there is in practice no global Islamic economic structure, Islam makes statements about economic behaviour which can guide the actions of individuals or of states and – at least initially – avoid the injustices found in Western society (Kuran 1989). Ultimately all wealth and productive capacity is owned by God. The human agent with temporary access to that wealth is prevented from accumulating more than individual need by rules of taxation and inheritance. Muslims with resources are expected to use them for the common good, not to make profit from them for its own sake. Ideally, the beneficial *use* of wealth rather than its accumulation should be the objective of activity. Hence unearned interest on invested money is opposed in Islamic teaching because an individual should not profit simply from being the holder of resources which belong to God. Ultimately, the notion of material growth is not an Islamic one. Human material demands should be restrained to allow energies to be devoted to spiritual aims.

Rules and priorities set out in the *Qur'ān* and other sources of *Shari'a* law to guide individual behaviour can, by a process of analogy which is part of the continuing relevance of Islam in changed circumstances, guide the actions of individuals, of groups and of the state itself on behalf of its citizens. In some cases, the connection is quite direct. For example, a number of countries now have banks which operate without the payment of interest (Wilson 1990). They attract Islamic business by a form of shared risk taking. In ways such as this, Muslim governments can claim to be acting in accordance with Islamic guidelines extrapolated from the original rules. Equally they should resist the intrusion of un-Islamic priorities. But this is easier said than done, given the extent to which Muslim states – and individuals – have been integrated into a global system which they do not direct but in which they can choose to stress indicators prescribed by their faith or to accept, if only in a pragmatic way, that they are part of a West-led system in which they will compete on the terms prevailing in that system. Clearly, individuals within one state make very different decisions for themselves and for their state on the basis of their education, class, age, gender and sect.

The practical economic outcome for Islamic countries in the late twentieth century is that they do not constitute a bloc in the world economic system. The very variety of size, resources, population and trade within the Islamic state pattern is an obstacle to unity, quite apart from matters of Islamic interpretation or the extent of intrusion from the West. The range is from high-income oil exporting Gulf states, with GNP per head in some cases over $15,000 per annum, to Chad, a low-income food deficit African country with a GNP per head of $160. A few countries are high-income oil exporters with small populations, and most of these are Arab states. Countries in this favoured group, where average incomes are high, have profits from petroleum to invest abroad, notably in other Islamic countries where they command special influence in view of their disposable wealth. A network of relations between donor and recipient countries has been built up, with specially prominent roles for Kuwait and Saudi Arabia. A further category of middle-income oil exporters, with larger populations making demands on national oil revenues, ranges from South East Asian Indonesia, the largest Muslim state, to Arab Algeria and to Gabon in central West Africa. A few non-oil exporters also achieve middle-income status: Turkey is the best example of these, with its developing output in both manufacturing and agriculture.

Most Islamic countries have no income from oil, though some have non-fuel mineral resources in quantity. Malaysia, Turkey and Morocco are examples. A few (Pakistan, Turkey) are substantial sources of manufactured goods. Some produce large quantities of food but in only a few cases is there a substantial export surplus. In many cases large populations cannot be sustained from national resources and imported food comes mainly from non-Islamic countries. In short, most Islamic countries fall within the peripheral zone of the present world free-market system. Those with oil are able, at least temporarily, to buy themselves out of direct dependence. Those, such as Turkey, with industrial potential have a basis for economic self-determination. One, Iran, while rejecting the market system as it stands, remains dependent on selling its oil within that system.

Thus more than 40 Islamic states around the world today are not free to act as an economic bloc because of their dependent links with non-Muslim lands. So connections between Muslim countries are attractive precisely because they do cut across the established links. The Organization of the Islamic Conference stresses the development of trade between member states and looks for ways to expand levels of investment by Muslims in extractive industries and in manufacturing in Islamic countries. Capital surplus states, such as Kuwait and Saudi Arabia, invest some of their available funds in other Muslim countries precisely because the activity is *Islamic*.

ISLAM: MULTINATIONAL, INTERNATIONAL OR TRANSNATIONAL?

The notion of a periphery can be applied to the political as well as to the economic structure of the Realm of Islam in so far as countries with Muslim governments have substantial non-Muslim populations. Sudan has seen separatist struggle in its black, non-Muslim southern provinces since independence in 1956. In Malaysia the Muslim population feels increasingly threatened with domination by ethnic Chinese. In Lebanon and Cyprus, Muslim–Christian competition has led to *de facto* partition. Nigeria and Ethiopia are African countries where, as in Lebanon, the Muslim element of the population continues to grow, with the prospect of a Muslim takeover of the central control of the state. Palestine is a special case where an overwhelmingly Muslim majority has been overturned through the displacement of indigenous people by Jewish settlers.

These references to the Islamic elements of states are about the relative *size* of the Muslim population within a state. An attractive assumption is that states with a high percentage of Muslims operate internationally in assertively Islamic ways, especially where such states are also large in population and resource terms. But the earlier part of this discussion showed that the Islamic component in states is qualitative as well as quantitative. Thus, for example, in secular Turkey, where Muslims account for 99 per cent of the population, Islam has a circumscribed role in the legitimation of political expression and action.

The short answer to whether or not there is an identifiable Islamic bloc is 'no', since the candidate states vary so greatly in size, power and perception of national priorities, and because of the additional evidence of Muslim countries at war with each other. But questions about blocs and states are founded on Western experience and are about how far constituent units in the mosaic of Islamic states conform to Western notions of sovereign independence and nationalism. It is consistent with the logic of Islamic tradition that individual state units are political pieces of the whole that was and is the Realm of Islam. In other words, where European states might come together in a new grouping, such as the European Community, by separate and joint consent, Islam existed as a total Islamic-state entity *before* the pieces into which it has split. A Western style bloc of modern Islamic states is thus either precisely Western in genesis or a reconstituted form of the status quo ante.

This said, can Islam, as a transnational force rather than as a multistate bloc, create new structures of political power and authority between and within states? The Organization of the Islamic Conference is the largest grouping of states in the name of the religion, but it has more structure than power since member states continue to act as states however much they may proclaim common purpose. Transnationally, therefore, Islam scores 'yes' on legitimacy, 'somewhat' on structure and 'no' on political power. Multinationally it is to be credited with arguing cases within and between states, but more straightforwardly in the support of a Muslim group against non-Muslims. Examples are the OIC's championing of the causes of the Muslims of the southern Philippines and of the Palestinians.

The dichotomy between tradition and compromise facing Islamic states and individual Muslims involves a range rather than a one-or-the-other choice. Neither is possible as an extreme. No country could operate fully traditional Islamic forms ignoring the rest of the contemporary world, just as each person's choice is circumscribed by the national choices made by his or her state. Meanwhile, a state or individual which compromised *completely* with a non-Islamic world would be no longer Muslim. Between these logical extremes, however, states may opt for different mixes of tradition and compromise and such choices may be modified over time. There is also an inevitable mismatch between the pattern of choice by states and that by individuals. Thus men or women within a state may make personal choices markedly different from those made nationally in the name of their state. The scope for tension and conflict is as clear as it is potentially diverse.

Iran and Turkey are countries which have made very different decisions about Islam and the state. The differences are described briefly in the following sections.

Iran: the Revolutionary Option

The leaders of Iran's 1979 revolution rejected the Shah's monarchy primarily because it was Westernizing and, to that extent, un-Islamic. Its models and ideals were not those prescribed by Islam. However, the revolution has to operate in a world dominated by non-Muslim powers and by a West-led market system. Iran sold its oil abroad and bought the armaments needed for its war with Iraq wherever they could be obtained.

There was no paradox here. Khomeini's supporters believed that Iran had recovered its political self and could function in a world shared by the two Realms. Westerners, quick to call the Ayatollah a fanatic or fundamentalist in exchange for the Great Satan label which he hurled at the United States, were puzzled to find him abusing the USSR and Islamic countries too. Conventional Western good–bad labels, such as left-wing, moderate, extremist, seemed to sit unsatisfactorily on the internal and external revolutionary alignments of Iran.

Iran is one of several countries which have made well-publicized moves of a back-to-Islam nature; Pakistan, Sudan, Malaysia and Libya are others. Elsewhere Islamic political parties are looked upon as potential threats (one in Turkey was banned). Islamic laws and penalties are reported with apprehension in the Western press, which also looks askance at cases where women are obliged to wear Islamic dress. But no state level proclamations of a return to Islamic values and practices attracted as much Western attention as did those in Iran. After 1979, when television pictures of besieged embassies in Tehran accompanied reports of the overthrow of a pro-West leader, Iran was kept under intense media scrutiny because of damage to Western interests, because of the horrific Iran–Iraq War of 1980–8, and because many people outside Iran were fascinated by the emergence, as it seemed, of a new kind of state and society which promised to export its revolution.

Najmabadi (1987) represents the 1979 Iranian revolution as 'a sharp break with a whole set of previous concerns…[which]…embodies a radical redefinition of society's preoccupations'. He quotes Khomeini as saying that the countries of the West 'will not experience happiness, moral virtue, and spiritual exaltation. They will be unable to solve their social problems, because the solution of social problems and the relief of their own miseries require more solutions, solutions based on faith' (p. 204). Najmabadi points out that Iran's revolutionary leaders blame the present political fragmentation of Islam upon the divisive impact of Western colonialism, and he conveys the argument that this divisiveness was indeed a policy, rather than merely a consequence, because Western intruders perceived a need to discredit Islam as a basis for national, ethnic and political identity. Nineteenth-century Iran blamed its material backwardness on internal inadequacies, and Western models were brought in to reform the country. After 1979, however, the blame for Iran's ills was put on the very outside influences which had previously been invited in as a cure. The cultural imperialism of the West became the culprit. Social priorities were redefined and the emphasis was on cultural and moral campaigns, on cleansing Iranian society of un-Islamic Western imports. Economic issues were downgraded; stress on material growth was one of the alien imports anyway.

Khomeini's Iran thus rejected modernization if this were to be synonymous with Westernization. His view of Islam was itself the preferred model for modernization – though to the West the faith was self-evidently non-modern. Strangely, before the revolution Khomeini's name and teachings were not widely noted in Iran, although he had raised the idea of Islamic government 35 years before the revolution in his book *Uncovering the Secrets (Kashf al-Asrar)*. He was even then speaking out about the harm resulting from change on the Western model, pointing to decline across the board from state building to moral decadence.

Iran was one of the few areas which were never formal colonial dependencies. It retained an organized clergy facing what they saw as the relentless suppression of traditional (Islamic) social and political institutions. The clergy was therefore in a position to spread its case for the Islamic alternative among those who failed to benefit from the social and economic transformations of the 1960s and 1970s. To such people, many of them migrants to burgeoning urban areas, the clergy seemed to offer a prospect of equity and social justice apparently denied to them in the programme of economic development promoted by the Iranian monarchy with support from the West. But the revolution was against *both* the foreign policy of the Shah *and* its internal expression within the country (Ramazani 1983, pp. 9–10). The two added up to the now rejected Western model as far as the Ayatollah Khomeini and his followers were concerned. Khomeini regarded modern states as the products of man's limited ideas and was comprehensive in his rejection of the international political system as now constituted. His call for Islamic universalism was coupled with his conviction that Iran is well placed to lead the wider revolution as well as its own. In his rejection of both capitalism and Marxism, Khomeini opposed both superpowers. As an Islamic revolutionary he wanted to liberate Jerusalem from Zionism. More broadly he offered support to those whom he considered to be oppressed across the Third World, offering them a view of a new political future. The reality of Khomeini's first revolutionary decade fell short of the plan. No other states joined his revolution, though he could claim individual supporters in many countries. War with Iran during the 1980s remained a conflict between states, even Islamic states, rather than a second phase in the new spread of Islam. Khomeini's achievement was that he translated Islam, the religious factor, into political action in a way that was consistent with his traditional view of his faith. Any separation of the religious and the secular was for him unholy and so a theocratic state was his objective – and one which would later expand to free Muslim areas for the Realm of Islam. The government and management of Khomeini's republic was to be regulated by religious law subsuming political and all other law.

More than half a century before the Islamic republic was set up in Iran, a revolution in the opposite direction had occurred in neighbouring Turkey.

TURKEY: THE SECULAR ALTERNATIVE

'Secularism, and the difficulties it has faced in the world of Islam, lies at the centre of the problem of Islam and the nation-state' (Vatikiotis 1987, p. 76). Arguably, all Islamic countries are secular to the extent that traditional Muslim values and practices have given way to Western or modern ones. This encroachment at the expense of Islam lay behind the support for the revolution in Iran; Khomeini saw his task as *restoring* Islam where it had been displaced and *spreading* the proper Islamic order beyond Iran.

Turkey, in sharp contrast, accepted the Western model in 1923 when the then new republic, led by Mustafa Kemal Ataturk, opted for a secular state, albeit one where the great majority of the people were Muslim. In other words, where Khomeini believed that the problem was Westernism and the cure was Islam, Ataturk saw Islam, at least as it existed in Turkey in 1923, as an obstacle to the achievement of Western progress and modernization. The new Turkish republic did not privatize Islam in the country but took it over so that the state became responsible for maintaining organizational links between the religious institutions and the state bureaucracy (Toprak 1981). Ataturk wanted Turkey's religious institutions to be controlled by the people, not the reverse. Indeed, he stressed to his compatriots that the sovereignty of the republic rested with them, where sovereignty in the preceding Empire had been ultimately with God.

The religious basis of the link between citizenry and the Ottoman state had, however, been too deeply embedded in society under the Empire to disappear with the departure of the last sultan in a British warship from Istanbul. Initially Mustafa Kemal and the Nationalists had fought in the name of the sultan-caliph while, at the same time, denying his authoritiy because of his readiness to accept outside demands. When the Sultanate was abolished in 1923, the Caliphate continued for a further year. When it too was removed, the Realm of Islam went with it in a formal sense. Yet population exchanges between Turkey and Greece were on the basis of religion. Muslims, many of them Greek-speaking, moved into the new Turkish republic to replace Greek- and Turkish-speaking Christians going to Greece. Religion continued to define *personal* identity even under republican rule.

Muslim subjects of the Ottoman Empire had been part of the *umma*, the community of all Muslims, and they had been citizens of the state which was one political expression of that community. Ataturk saw the need to create a nationalist equivalent of the *umma* so that individual Turks could identify with the state before their faith. This is to restate the point that state legitimacy switched from the divine under the Empire to the popular after 1923. The *'ulema*, the corps of Islamic scholars who had interpreted Islam in the Empire (and thereby legitimated Ottoman political authority), were replaced after 1924 by secular parliamentarians. Members of the *'ulema* had been expected to interpret the Qur'ān and the Hadith Islamic traditions to provide Islamic answers to all questions faced by government. After 1923, secular interpreters looked at Ataturk's speeches and opinions to provide, perhaps by analogy and extrapolation, guidelines for Kemalist rule, as the *'ulema* had done for the sultan with holy writing and traditions. The theme of continuity through the radical change of state form and legitimacy can be seen in the appropriation, into republican ideology, of key concepts from the Ottoman-Islamic philosophy of knowledge. The new republican Kemalists were aware of the magnitude of the state transformation but saw the need to recognize the underlying political culture of Turks by making mechanisms of transition consistent with it (Tapper and Tapper 1991).

Certainly it is not hard to identify the continuity of Islam in Turkey nearly seven decades after the end of the Caliphate. Islam has emerged as focus of opposition to Kemalism, which is to say opposition to secular republicanism. This opposition became a feature of competitive politics after 1950, since when a small pro-Islamic party grouping has commanded varying electoral support. It has, however, to operate (according to the 1982 constitution) in a political landscape where calling for the establishment of an Islamic (or, incidentally, of a communist) state is illegal.

In formal terms the secularization of Turkey has been far-reaching. Western visitors find familiar points of reference in much of Turkish society – notably in the cities and larger towns, which look as though they have much in common with Europe. Yet pro-Islamic political activity persists, with calls for the revival of Muslim values and practices. Even secular state figures refer to 'our religion' as they welcome foreign delegates to meetings of the Organization of the Islamic Conference. Perhaps 'the Kemalist state has not succeeded in producing a continuing national version of Islam to legitimize its power' (Mortimer 1982, p. 157).

Others can argue that Islam, to the limited extent that it is resurgent in Turkey, represents a conservative element in the country now reacting to secularization and able to do so because Kemalist secularism in Turkey did not replace Islam. Neither did it push the faith into a subservient position. It *used* it: it did not destroy it. It follows that the Islam which figures in the political debate in Turkey today is more than a protest ideology with an imposing name. It *was* the dominant ideology and is still bigger than politics for those Turks who have not made the full compromise with European secularism. Thus Turkey now has complete compromisers, non-compromisers, and those between who try to reconcile both their European and their Islamic identities.

As far as Turkey is concerned, both Europeanism and Islam are transnational forces. Of course Turkey is a special case, given its history and setting, but so is Iran and each other Islamic country in terms of the compromise which each makes between the expression of traditional faith and global processes for which the motor power is West-led modernization.

ISLAM: THE POLITICAL OPTIONS

A number of processes have affected the nature of the state within the Realm of Islam. These are Islam itself, pre-Islamic legacies, the colonial input, and a state's present place in the Third World – which itself variously shows the impact of West-led modernization. To the extent that this modernization values material growth and the separation of the secular from the divine, then religion becomes non-modern at best and an obstacle at worst. Many Third World Muslim states have reacted against the West-led aspect of modernization but have done so within the terms of that modernization. For Ayatollah Khomeini resurgent, restored Islam was a form of modernization alternative to, and better than, the West-led version. Critics of Khomeini can point out that even if all the Islamic world were to follow Iran's lead, the faith could never be more than part – albeit a very big part – of a *global* polity. We know that the Realm of Islam is now less a global polity than it was, for Muslims, more than a thousand years ago.

A major element has been modernization itself, defined in the terms in which it has emerged in Western society where it has been associated with industrialization and with the concentration of production in expanding urban areas. Divisions of labour and specialization are determined by technological rather than social or kinship realities. The small nuclear family unit replaces the larger extended one. Mass consumption and mass culture reaffirm and reproduce modern values and objectives.

Such modernization, projected by the West upon the rest of the world community and variously absorbed by it, may be challenged by anti-modern ideologies. Green groups campaign against pollution and peace groups against war. Feminists and unions attack exploitation. Ethnic, class, linguistic and other culturally based groups define themselves in transnational rather than in national terms. Religious affiliation – such as to Islam or to sects within it – may displace state allegiance (or may threaten to do so) and so erode the distinctiveness of state identity.

One potential danger in a discussion of Islam from a non-Islamic vantage point is that it can emerge as an inherently static set of values and prescriptions which change only in response to outside stimuli such as colonial intrusion. Such a picture must be qualified because Islam has not lacked its own *internal* modernizing energies (Esposito, 1987, pp. 30ff). To this extent modernization can be *Islamic*, and is to be distinguished from modernization which sets aside Islam, or elements of it, in favour of non-Muslim alternatives (such as secularism). The important debate may be whether Muslims in the twenty-first century will have a real Islamic option in their modernization. This is different from saying that Islam can or cannot change. Possibly the most far-reaching model of modernization will be the West-led one, based on industrial, consumption-oriented values of equal individual rights, material progress and so on, organized within territorial states or groups of states. And perhaps this will establish the rules for the global human system in which non-Western models – even one with a billion subscribers, such as Islam – can expect at best some sort of autonomy rather than independence, and certainly not effective overall control. Muslims have become organized in territorial states, in many cases set out as such by non-Muslims, but retaining various degrees of affiliation to Islam and to Muslims across dozens of states. The nearest thing to a bloc of Muslim states, the Organization of the Islamic Conference, finds consensus on matters affecting relations between Muslim and non-Muslim states (the concern about Jerusalem is one example). But this consensus has not yet led to concerted action by Muslim states, even in crises as threatening as the Iran–Iraq War. Indeed, on matters where Islamic states are ranged against each other (the independence struggle against Morocco in the western Sahara, for instance) the state element dominates the Islamic element in policy making.

Evidently the rise of nation-states across the Islamic world now confronts Muslims with a problem of double identity which has to be resolved at state, group and individual levels. There is potential for conflict where individuals and groups make an identity choice different from that of the state in which they find themselves. For that matter, a basis for discord can arise within a group – or even between generations within a family. Individuals feel affinity to like-minded people in other states (e.g. Kurdish sentiment in 'Arab' Iraq). Shi'a Muslims identify with 'foreigners' of the same sect (as between Arab Shi'ites of Iraq and non-Arab Shi'ites of Iran). Secular-minded Muslims develop links across international boundaries easily, given modern media networks. The new ingredient in the late twentieth century for the faith–state debate is the increasing importance of the state in processes of globalization and modernization. In this context, Islam emerges as both unifying and divisive: unifying because individuals, groups and states can identify with the faith which they share with dozens of other states and hundreds of millions of Muslims, but divisive too because of the local variety of expression of Islam.

There is some movement towards the creation of transnational structures of political authority in the name of Islam – most obviously in the Organization of the Islamic Conference and in talk of mergers among Muslim states and of other concerted action. The existing state system appears to be the main constraint here, so that Islamic political institutions are groupings of separate states, Islamic towards the outside but conscious of state sovereignty within the group. Individual Muslims can identify their own preferences in the range between traditional faith and compromise, but such individuals have to decide whether or not to accept the limits set by the states in which they find themselves. Islam *can* replace nationalism as a basis for legitimacy and allegiance *if* it is permitted to do so by individuals, groups and states, but it shows no sign of replacing the state.

References

Esposito, J.L. (1987) *Islam and Politics* (2nd edn). Syracuse, NY: Syracuse University Press.
Kuran, T. (1989) On the notion of economic justice in contemporary Islamic thought. *International Journal of Middle East Studies*, 21(2), 171–91.
Lewis, B. (1981) The return of Islam. In M. Curtis (ed.), *Religion and Politics in the Middle East*, Boulder, CO: Westview Press, 9–29.
Mortimer, E. (1982) *Faith and Power: the Politics of Islam.* New York: Random House.
Najmabadi, A. (1987) Iran's turn to Islam. *Middle East Journal*, 41(2), 202–17.
Piscatori, J.P. (1986) *Islam in a World of Nation-States.* London: Cambridge University Press.
Ramazani, R.K. (1983) Khumayni's Islam in Iran's foreign policy. In A. Dawisha (ed.), *Islam in Foreign Policy*, Cambridge: Cambridge University Press, in association with the Royal Institute of International Affairs.
Tapper, R. and Tapper, N. (1991) Religion, education and continuity in a provincial town. In R. Tapper (ed.), *Islam in Modern Turkey: Religion, Politics and Literature in a Secular State*, London: IB Taurus, 56–83.
Toprak, B. (1981) *Islam and Political Development in Turkey.* Leiden: E.J. Brill.
Vatikiotis, P.J. (1987) *Islam and the State.* London: Croom Helm.
Wilson, R. (ed.) (1990) *Islamic Financial Markets.* London and New York: Routledge.

16

Global Politics in a Transitional Era

ANTHONY G. McGREW

INTRODUCTION

Global politics has entered a period of profound and unsettling change. The end of the Cold War, the beginnings of a transformation in Eastern Europe, the growing regionalization of the world economy, and the emergence of new axes of conflict and alignment, are amongst a series of recent developments which suggest that the world is on the edge of a new historical epoch. What were once regarded as the permanent features or structural characteristics of the global system, such as superpower rivalry, no longer appear to dominate global political life. The familiar and the permanent have been exposed as ephemeral or at least contingent. Moreover, established assumptions and certainties are continuously overtaken by events, whilst the contradictory impulses and volatility of global politics confront us daily. At the very moment commentators hailed the outbreak of peace in the world and politicians in the West debated the peace dividend, Iraq's annexation of Kuwait in August 1990 culminated in a major war. For some writers the incredible uncertainty and turbulence of the contemporary epoch signify that the global system has arrived at a historical turning point, that both the pace and scope of change have conspired to bring about a transformation in global structures and dominant forms of interaction (Rosenau 1990; Morse 1976). Yet others perceive, in the confusion of the present, essential continuities with the past (Gilpin 1981). Whether current developments, trends and patterns of interaction define the beginnings of a new epoch, a historic transformation, in global politics, or whether they distract our gaze from the historical parallels and underlying continuities with the past, remains a hotly contested issue within the international relations community. It is a controversy which finds a legitimate home in this concluding chapter. For this final chapter provides an overview, located firmly in the contributions to this volume, of the essential contours of global politics in the 1990s. It is both a review of the arguments and themes trailed throughout this volume, and an attempt to contextualize and evaluate the significance and direction of emerging trends and patterns of interaction in global politics.

THE GLOBAL POLITICAL SYSTEM

Whilst debate continues to flourish over the dominant forces shaping contemporary global politics, there is a more widespread acknowledgement that a truly global political system now exists. This point was given much emphasis in chapter 1 and has been reinforced by other contributions to the volume (chapters 6, 9, 13 and 14). Whilst this suggests that, in respect of its global scope, the present system is historically unique, this is not to argue that the world is becoming more politically integrated and harmonious. As many chapters have indicated, the present global system is riven by discord, cultural diversity, economic inequality and political fragmentation. Indeed, a number of the essential ingredients of the domestic polity are missing from the global political system. But the fact that it is not a recognizable polity, in the sense that it lacks established forms of government, should not lead us to neglect the profound significance of the emergence of a global political system. As Giddens observes, such a system 'is not just an environment within which particular societies like Britain develop and change. The social, political, and economic connections which cross-cut borders between countries decisively condition the fate of those living in them' (1989, p. 520).

To talk in terms of a global political system is essentially to return to the cobweb image introduced in chapter 1. Although this image is most frequently associated with liberal-pluralist analyses of global politics (such as those of Burton 1972; Mitchell 1984), its graphic depiction of differentiated systems and patterns of global interaction provides a simple device for conceiving the complexity of the contemporary global political order. Although proponents of different theoretical traditions might disagree about the fundamental features of that order, few would now dispute the existence of a global political system. Even Bull, that staunch defender of realism and the nation-state, accepts that 'there is now a wider world political system of which the states system is only part... By that world political system we understand the world-wide network of interaction that embraces not only states but also other political actors, both "above" the state and "below" it' (1977, p. 276).

But what are the characteristic features of this global political system? Five distinctive features of the contemporary global political system can be readily distilled from the contributions to this volume. Interestingly, these overlap with Frankel's (1988) analysis, and his categories have been exploited here. These five distinctive characteristics include: complexity and diversity; intense patterns of interaction; the permeability of the nation-state; rapid and cascading change; and the fragility of order and governance. Each of these will be elaborated briefly below.

Complexity and Diversity

Coming to terms with the overwhelming complexity and diversity of the global political system is a difficult intellectual challenge. As previous chapters have repeatedly indicated, it is not simply that there is now an extensive array of agencies and actors other than nation-states to take into account but also that the agenda of global politics is equally crowded. Alongside national governments the global political system embraces international organizations, bureaucratic fragments of governments, subnational government agencies, and a diverse ensemble of non-state bodies from transnational corporations to individuals, including social and class forces as well as transnational pressure groups and organized interests. But if this were not enough, there is also a vast range of political issues surfacing on the global agenda. It is simply no longer possible to argue that high policy matters, such as security, defence and the balance of power, dominate the global agenda as they might have done in the nineteenth century. For as Hanreider (1978) and others have argued, the global political process has experienced a domestication, with low policy issues (economic welfare, drugs, environment etc.) acquiring greater significance. This situation is compounded by the interlocking nature of many global issues, such that action in one sphere of activity can have dramatic consequences in other policy arenas. A good example of this is the complex relationship between the Third World debt problem and global environmental problems (like deforestation), made worse by actions taken to service that debt. It is also questionable whether the distinction between high and low policy issues remains particularly helpful when traditional conceptions of state power and security are being redefined to embrace economic and environmental security (Gilpin 1987).

Such complexity has been fuelled by the erosion of the bipolar structure of world power which dominated global politics until the 1960s. As Paul Lewis suggested in chapter 2, the global system has evolved into a much more multipolar or polyarchic order. The ending of the Cold War has merely confirmed the direction of earlier trends in the restructuring of global power relations. But if the East–West division no longer dominates global politics, it is too early to conclude that the era of superpower politics has come to a close. Indeed, during the 1991 Gulf War superpower diplomacy was a central feature of the crisis. What is evident is the existence of new sites of conflict which cross-cut old alignments and political divisions. For example the environment, the rise of fundamentalist Islam, and the struggle between rich and poor in the global community are amongst the more salient sites of ideological and material conflict in the global political system analysed in this volume.

Accompanying this erosion of bipolarity has been a certain regionalization of the global system. As a number of chapters have indicated, the strengthening of the regional layer in global politics has been stimulated in part by the intensification of processes of globalization. Recent developments within the European Community have been driven to some extent by global competitive pressures and the evident regionalization of the global economy. And as Grahame Thompson demonstrates (chapter 10), this regionalization is not simply confined to Europe or the Far East but is evident on the American continent, with the moves towards a US–Canadian–Mexican free-trade area. Between the nation-state layer and the global layer there is a set of regional dynamics at work which is reconstructing the nature of the global political order.

Whichever theoretical tradition informs our *Welstanschauung*, there can be little dissent from the general proposition pervading this volume that the modern global political system is defined by its complexity and diversity. As Kegley and Wittkopf have observed:

> Today's world is divided both ideologically and economically. Its opposing div-
> isions are armed militarily, and they often conflict violently. Yet along with these
> divisions we also find unprecedented levels of transnational cooperation. And
> overlapping all of them are a plethora of issues on the global agenda that breed
> conflict but require multilateral cooperation for their solution.
>
> (1989, p. 29)

Intense Patterns of Interaction

Throughout this volume, evidence concerning the intensity and scope of interaction between the states and the societies constituting the global political system has been given a prominent position. Whilst it has not been argued that the nature of this interaction is in any sense historically unique, or that its intensity has attained historically unprecedented levels, or that it represents the unfolding of some teleological historical process, it is undeniably of increasing political significance. This, as Morse (1976), Hanreider (1978) and Halliday (1988) have understood, is a consequence of the nature and form of the modern nation-state, particularly its relationship to domestic civil society.

Patterns of transnational interaction and interconnectedness between national societies assume a special salience in the context of the modern nation-state, since such relations or activities have the potential to enhance or disrupt the state's ability to discharge effectively the functions demanded of it, either by its citizens or by dominant elites. This is particularly the case where the level of interconnectedness establishes structural relations of dependence or interdependence between states. As David Potter and Mike Smith remind us (in chapters 11 and 13 respectively), the intensity and scope of patterns of global interaction are very unevenly experienced, with some states and societies more tightly enmeshed in the global system than others.

As well as highlighting the levels of interaction between states, the contributions to this volume have identified the multiplicity of channels of contact between societies. Besides traditional diplomatic relations, states are also enmeshed in all kinds of transgovernmental networks, intergovernmental relations and international regimes, as well as transnational relations and networks which cut across national societies. It is therefore not simply the intensity of interactions between states in the global political system which is distinctive but also the differentiated forms which such interaction takes.

The Permeability of the Nation-State

Given the extensive patterns of global interconnectedness identified in this volume, it seems hardly surprising that states and societies are extremely permeable to external forces. By definition such interconnectedness implies that domestic developments in one society are in some sense contingently related to developments within other societies in distant parts of the globe. As Smelser argues:

> One of the hallmarks of human history in the late twentieth century is the increasing internationalization of the world: in production, trade, finance, technology, threats to security, communications, research, education and culture. One major consequence of this is that the mutual penetration of economic, political and social forces among the nations of the world is increasingly salient; and it may be that the governments of nation-states are progressively losing degrees of direct control over the global forces that affect them.
>
> (quoted in Rosenau 1990, p. 21)

This structural linkage between the domestic arena and the external arena has been a recurring theme in each of the contributions to this volume. A number of chapters have focused explicitly upon different manifestations and dimensions of this linkage, including the connections between the domestic and global determinants of superpower rivalry (chapters 2 and 4); the political consequences and ramifications of technologically driven transboundary problems (chapters 6 and 7); and the global diffusion of ideologies and modes of social organization (chapters 13, 14 and 15). This interpretation of the domestic and the international has profound political consequences not just for how particular policy issues are managed but also for more fundamental matters such as the structuring and restructuring of domestic and international society. Chapter 5, for instance, argued that military rivalry between the two superpowers has not only reshaped their domestic societies but also imposed its own logic upon the global military order. In the economic domain the integration of Eastern European economies into the global economic order will have the most profound consequences for these societies, since it will demand the restructuring of many domestic political, social and economic institutions. As Frankel observes: 'The linkage between domestic and international affairs has grown greatly in both directions. On the one hand, rapidly growing domestic needs and demands have become increasingly dependent upon international politics; on the other, international politics has become increasingly affected by domestic conflicts' (1988, pp. 219–20).

This structural interpenetration poses a threat to the nation-state in terms of its autonomy or its capacity to control developments within its jurisdiction, but it also poses a theoretical challenge for the social sciences more generally. For it undermines many traditional approaches to the study of society, the economy and the polity which treat these categories as bounded entities and which deny the interplay between the exogenous and endogenous forces of order and change. Such a challenge invites a considerable retooling or rethinking of basic concepts within the social sciences, together with a re-examination of the fundamental unit of analysis which has been taken for granted for so long, namely the nation-state.

Rapid and Cascading Change

As chapter 13 emphasized, the present global system is subject to rapid and pervasive change. Perhaps the most dramatic ilustration of this point is the complete transformation in superpower relations which occurred in the late 1980s. Less than a year after the revolutions in Eastern Europe, both superpowers formally acknowledged 'the end of the era of division and conflict which has lasted for more than four decades' and agreed that East and West 'are no longer adversaries' (CSCE 1990). But it is not simply the rapidity of change which is significant but also the fact that events in one domain of global activity stimulate a chain reaction across other domains.

Rosenau (1990) refers to this latter phenomenon as cascading change or cascades, to capture the dynamic but unpredictable fashion in which events in one part of the world spill over into different issue areas, different political arenas and different legal jurisdictions and cross-cut different national systems and subsystems. By introducing the concept of a cascade, Rosenau delivers an important insight into the dynamics of change in the global political system. For it is not simply the rapidity or intensity with which change occurs that is distinctive, but equally the complex dynamics which such change sets in motion because of the interconnected nature of the modern global system and the existence of global communication networks. Thus he argues that:

[The] importance of distinguishing cascades…lies in the way issues are transfsormed as a cascade encounters collectivities in its flow. As a cascade gathers momentum and drags in wider circles of actors, the values it encompasses and the consequences it portends change, and each change adds further complexity and dynamism to the interdependent structures that link the actors. Like the so-called butterfly effect in meteorology, an event in one part of the world can ultimately have unexpected repercussions in remote places…Thus, for example, …efforts to control drug usage in the United States expand into the politics of Panama and introduce a new dimension into US relations with many other nations in the Americas.

(p. 302)

In each of the four main parts to this volume, some attention has been given to how change in these respective spheres conditions the nature of global politics. Part I, for example, examined how the dynamic of superpower rivalry inserted itself into regional politics in different parts of the globe. In part II the ramifications of technological innovation in expanding the agenda of global politics and stimulating new forms of cooperation and coordination were given special emphasis, as were its ramifications for the legitimacy of the nation-state itself. Part III explored how change in the global economy impacted upon global politics and national autonomy. And finally in part IV the focus shifted to an exploration of modernizing processes and their implications for the continued viability of the nation state.

It is the particular combination of the rapidity and scale of change, the relative ease with which change cascades through the global system and subsystems, and the virtual instantaneous global diffusion of change (facilitated by the multiplicity of channels of communication between societies) which distinguishes the contemporary global political system from its historical precursors. According to Brezinski: 'We are living through an era of the most extensive and intensive political change in human history… Our generation is living through a genuine global political awakening' (quoted in Kegley and Wittkopf 1989, p. 3).

The Fragility of Order and Governance

The final distinctive feature of the contemporary global system is the existence of primitive institutions and processes of global governance. Even the most conventional realist analyses would accept that, despite the anarchical nature of the global system, hegemonic powers and mechanisms such as the balance of power do impose and maintain a limited form of order at the global level. An obvious illustration of how order is maintained by major powers is the Gulf War of 1991. This involved an international coalition of military forces, led by the US but acting under the auspices of the United Nations, forcefully ejecting Iraq from Kuwait and restoring the latter's sovereignty. Thus while anarchy may be a valid description of the global system, it does not equate with the total absence of global order, or the complete lack of any processes of international governance. Moreover, as a number of chapters in this volume have argued (chapters 6, 9, 10, 11, 13 and 14), there do exist global processes and institutions of governance which seek to regulate global affairs and to manage an expanding range of global problems. Although the form and character of this governance is quite different from the authoritative actions of sovereign governments within their own territorial boundaries, the fact is that the global system 'is none the less – and arguably to an increasing extent – governed' (Smith 1989, p. 61).

Despite the existence of a primitive polity, processes of governance at the global level are inherently more fragile, contingent and unevenly experienced than is the case within most national political systems. Since nation-states are defined by their sovereign status, any institution of global governance or management must by definition lack that ultimate authority which is a characteristic of the relationship between the state and civil society in the domestic domain. As a consequence, international regimes and institutions of global management tend to lack the authoritative means to ensure compliance with their decisions. But, as chapters 6 and 9 suggested, the authority of global and regional structures of governance can vary considerably across issue areas and across time. Although a growing number of issue areas and an expanding array of global activities are within the jurisdiction of global regimes, regional organizations and international institutions, the political authority of these governing structures differs enormously. Thus while the European Community can be considered a quasi-supranational organization, because of the majority voting mechanism and its legal powers over member states, very few other international regimes or institutions have equivalent power or authority over member governments. Any discussion of global order and governance must therefore recognize its essential fragility.

GLOBALIZATION, THE NATION-STATE AND THE GLOBAL POLITY

In the previous section some of the distinctive characteristics of the contemporary global political system were highlighted. This representation reinforces the cobweb image introduced in chapter 1, and is supported by the snapshots of global politics offered in subsequent chapters. But this picture of the system tells us very little about the logics and dynamics which underpin its global reach.

Globalization

Hardly a single news bulletin passes without some report of developments in distant parts of the world. Indeed listening to, reading or watching the daily news cannot but fail to impress on us a certain global awareness. But beyond this fairly superficial awareness lies a faint recognition that somehow our own lives are affected by or implicated in activities or decision-making occurring across the globe. This, according to Giddens (1990), is a striking feature of social life in the modern era. Globalization, he reminds us, 'should be understood as the re-ordering of time and distance in our lives. Our lives, in other words, are increasingly influenced by activities and events happening well away from the social context in which we carry on our day-to-day activities' (p. 520).

To talk of globalization is to recognize that there are dynamic processes at work constructing and weaving networks of interaction and interconnectedness across the states and societies which make up the world community. Throughout this volume an attempt has been made to provide a critical and systematic investigation of these key globalizing processes as well as their consequences for global politics and the viability of the nation-state. In chapter 1 globalization was defined in terms of two discrete dimensions, 'scope (or stretching) and intensity (or deepening). On the one hand it defines a set of processes which embrace most of the globe or which operate world-wide; the concept therefore has a spatial connotation. Politics and other social activities are becoming stretched across the globe. On the other hand it also implies an intensification in the levels of interaction, interconnectedness or interdependence between the states and societies which constitute the world community. Accordingly, alongside the stretching goes a deepening of global processes. Furthermore, it was argued that there exist four key processes of globalization which have been responsible for the forging of a global political system and a corresponding global politics. These four globalizing forces are great power competition; technological innovation and its diffusion; the internationalization of production and exchange; and modernization or the dynamism of modernity (Giddens 1990, p. 16). Each was critically examined in parts I to IV respectively with a view to how each has contributed to the globalization of politics.

In identifying and analysing the dominant processes of globalization which have inaugurated the era of global politics, several authors in this volume have been careful not to elide globalization with the emergence of a world society or idealistic notions of world unity (chapters 6, 11, 13 and 14). This is a crucial point, since too many contemporary analyses confuse globalizing processes and consequent interconnect-edness with the unfolding of some predetermined historical logic which is culminating in one world. This, in view of the evidence drawn upon within this volume, is a somewhat eccentric representation of contemporary realities. There are also four other important qualifications about globalization which have surfaced in previous chapters and which are worth recalling at this juncture.

Firstly, a number of chapters have sought to remind us that processes of globalization have to be located historically, that global politics was not born in 1945, and that the contemporary epoch is not necessarily unique in terms of levels of globalized interaction between societies (chapters 8, 9 and 13). As Modelski (1972) has argued, processes of globalization have a longer historical reach than the post-war era. Wallerstein (1980) too, in his studies of the emergence of a world economy, makes a similar point by locating the origins of the modern world system in seventeenth-century developments. Yet this historical dimension to globalization should not lead us to deny some of the distinctive dynamics and features of the contemporary global order. According to Bull, what 'is in any sense new or recent in the world political system of the nineteenth and twentieth centuries is its global or world-wide character; and, of course, it is only in this recent period [post-1945] that the states system has itself become world-wide' (1977, p. 278). Moreover, it can be argued that it is the actual conjunction of, and complex interaction between, the four dominant processes of globalization which figure prominently in this volume which makes the present epoch somewhat historically unique.

Secondly, care must be taken to distinguish globalization from notions of interdependence. As John Vogler has argued in chapter 6, interdependence is a distinct concept which cannot be elided with interconnectedness or globalization. Whilst processes of globalization may generate interdependencies between communities, equally they can, as David Potter has signalled in chapter 11, generate relationships of dependence and reinforce existing inequalities in the world system. Accordingly, globalization should be taken to refer simply to interconnectedness and should not be confused with notions of interdependence.

Thirdly, in a somewhat similar vein, it is invalid to infer that globalization necessarily correlates with harmony in global politics. It does not by necessity encourage an intensification of international cooperation, or presage the emergence of a world society or world government, or imply the end of the nation-state. These are amongst a range of potential consequences, but by no means form the only menu on offer. Indeed Bull (1977) recognized that the intensification of world interconnectedness stimulates both conflict and cooperation. Accordingly it is crucial to understand that globalizing processes generate the conditions for intense conflict as much as for greater cooperation and harmony in global politics. Globalization, as chapter 1 noted, is essentially dialectical: it generates opposing forces wherever its effects are experienced. Whilst the intensity of global interaction undoubtedly creates certain favourable background conditions and requirements for enhanced global cooperation and structures of collective management, such an outcome, as a number of chapters have indicated (chapters 2, 6, 9, 12, 13 and 14), is by no means inevitable. Whilst globalization may be a necessary ingredient in creating a more integrated world community, it is not by itself a sufficient condition for doing so. One of the reasons for this lies in the highly uneven nature of processes of globalization.

Fourthly, globalization has to be qualified in terms of its differential reach and the fact that its consequences are not uniformly experienced across the globe. Processes of globalization vary considerably with respect to their global reach and the extent to which they penetrate different regions of the globe. Thus some regions are more deeply implicated in global processes than others and some are more deeply integrated into the global order than others. Even within nation-states some communities are enmeshed in global networks whilst others lie completely outside them. And this unevenness is replicated across different issue areas; for instance, the same nation may well be highly integrated into one set of global activities but be hardly implicated at all in others. Coming to terms with the unevenness of globalization is an essential ingredient of a more critical appreciation of its dynamics and consequences. It is not experienced uniformly across the globe or even within the same nation-state or local community. As chapters 3 and 4 illustrated, superpower rivalry has had a differential impact upon the politics of various regions around the globe. Similarly, in the contributions to parts II and III of the volume significant variations were noted between different regions and communities in terms of how deeply they are enmeshed in the global technological and economic orders. And in chapter 13 Mike Smith gave considerable emphasis to the essentially uneven character of processes of globalization and modernization.

In reviewing how the contributions to this volume have qualified our understanding of the nature of globalization, the above four points have emerged. These should be helpful in stripping globalization of its hidden normative connotations. Moreover, a more sophisticated appreciation of the complexity of globalization is essential to any account of contemporary global politics. Whether globalization is to be welcomed or opposed opens up a further set of issues concerning its ramifications for existing social and political structures and practices, most obviously the nation-state.

Globalization and the Nation-State

Three specific aspects of the nation-state in its global setting have received particular attention throughout this volume: the autonomy of the nation-state; its changing roles and nature; and the question of its decline or transcendence. What stands out from the rich discussion of these issues in this book is a sense of agreement that processes of globalization have had and continue to have dramatic consequences for the modern nation-state. Nor, as has been discussed previously, do the proponents of different theoretical traditions deny the significant ways in which the state and state power have been deconstructed and reconstituted by globalizing forces (Gilpin 1981; 1987; Rosenau 1990; Kolko 1988; Cox 1987). In this section some generalizations will be offered concerning the centrality and functioning of the modern nation-state within the present global political system.

Extensive consideration has been given in parts I to IV of this text to the complicated issue of state autonomy. In chapter 11 David Potter provided a clear discussion of nation-state autonomy, identifying it as the capacity of states to formulate and pursue their own goals. And in chapters 3, 7, 10, 13 and 14 further consideration was given to how global forces impinge upon state autonomy. What emerges from this analysis is a refinement of the original conceptualization of autonomy.

Clearly states have always operated under constraints of all kinds; none has ever been free to act completely independently from external pressures. However, it is frequently argued that globalization has imposed tighter limits on the exercise of state autonomy across a range of policy areas. Thus autonomy can be defined in terms of the state's capacity to act independently, within circumscribed parameters, in the articulation and pursuit of domestic and international policy objectives. State autonomy can be further differentiated with respect to both its scope and the domains within which it can be exercised. By scope is meant the level or intensity of constraints on state action, whilst domains refer to the areas of state activity or policy arenas within which such constraints operate. This conceptual refinement not only allows an important distinction to be made between sovereignty – the *de jure* use of power through supreme legal authority or competence within a defined territory – and autonomy, but also offers pathways towards a more sophisticated understanding of the relationship between globalization and the nation-state.

What emerges from this discussion, combined with the previous analyses in chapters 3, 10, 11 and 13, are three fairly broad generalizations about state autonomy. Firstly, the case studies in this volume suggest that the structural consquences of globalization are such as to deny the relevance or practicality of autarky – strategies of self-reliance or virtual independence – in the modern global system. This immediately restricts the menu of foreign and domestic policies from which state authorities can choose (see chapter 7 in particular). Secondly, state autonomy varies considerably between different forms of nation-state, as well as across time and between different issue areas. Thus hegemonic states may have greater autonomy than peripheral states, whilst the same state could well have greater autonomy in some issue areas than in others. State autonomy therefore has to be differentiated in relation to types of states and sectors of activity. To make broad generalizations about it is a risky exercise. Thirdly, as noted previously, globalization is a term which covers a dynamic set of processes whose effects are not felt uniformly across the globe. Thus globalizing tendencies may lead to some states facing an erosion of autonomy whilst others acquire greater autonomy.

If state autonomy has been compromised by processes of globalization, the nature and role of the state in world affairs has certainly not been left unscathed. But it would be foolish to draw any general conclusions about this without first acknowledging that the global system incorporates a wide diversity of nation-state forms. It embraces advanced capitalist states, such as the US, Germany and Japan, as well as post-communist states such as Poland and Hungary, micro-states such as Kiribati, and disintegrating states such as the Lebanon and others. The point here is that to provide any meaningful statements about the impact of globalization on the nature and role of the state demands an initial caution that the term 'nation-state' covers a diverse assortment of state forms such that any generalizations are subject to obvious qualifications.

Having noted that, three fairly uncontroversial points can be made. Firstly, it is quite clear that in the post-war period most states have significantly expanded the regulation of domestic and foreign affairs. Even in the post-communist states it is the form of state intervention in social life which is subject to revolutionary change rather than a complete rejection of state interventionism *per se*. Moreover, the emergence of a highly interconnected global system means that many of the nation-state's traditional functions (defence, economic security, health etc.) cannot be fulfilled effectively without some resort to forms of international cooperation, coordination or collaboration. Secondly, states face powerful pressures from their citizens and domestic groups to regulate those transnational activities which directly impinge upon their interests and livelihoods. Such pressures, as in the environmental or economic issue areas, generate a significant momentum for the expansion of international regimes and international regulatory frameworks at the regional or global levels. Thirdly, technological advances and more intense patterns of global interaction have generated a whole series of collective problems which cannot be resolved without recourse to intergovernmental regulation (see chapters 6, 9 and 10 in particular). The role and functions of the state are thus being internationalized, and in some cases the state apparatus is internationalized too (see chapters 9 and 13).

If there is a modicum of agreement on the expanding role of the nation-state in global politics, it nonetheless conceals major schisms with regard to its long-term viability. This takes us forward into the controversial question of the decline or transcendence of the modern nation-state. In chapter 13 Mike Smith highlighted the paradox in the fact that states have been expanding their jurisdiction and acquiring greater functional responsibilities, yet in order to perform the tasks demanded of them they have become increasingly enmeshed in international regimes and institutions which by definition restrict national autonomy. Rosenau (1990), together with Morse (1976), considers the erosion of state authority to be one of the more dramatic and revolutionary consequences flowing from the intensification of globalization in the post-war epoch. Yet for most neo-realists, such as Krasner and Thompson (1989) and Gilpin (1987), the increasing enmeshment of states in global and regional structures of collective management enhances rather than undermines state power and autonomy. (This latter is a kind of enpowerment thesis deriving from the literature on collective action, which stresses how the power of individual agents can significantly expanded through cooperative and collective action, e.g. workers forming a trade union.) There is a vigorous intellectual debate here, and interestingly one which cuts across the three theoretical traditions which have framed this study of global politics. It would thus appear that in the contemporary global political system there is a powerful tension between the state's attempts to manage, through intensive international cooperation, those global forces which impinge upon its activities and the concomitant loss of authority and sovereignty which accompanies such a strategy. Whether this tension is resolved in favour of the strengthening or the transcendence of the nation-state is a debate which is continued in the final section of this chapter, which is concerned with the interplay between the forces of continuity and change in global politics.

A Global Polity?

There is an apparent contradiction in describing the global system as ordered and subject to processes of governance when in fact there exists no single locus of public authority or government at the global level. Yet as a number of chapters have implied, authoritative decision making and the maintenance of global order simply take a different form to that with which we are familiar within the domestic polity. As Miller (1988) concedes, what creates confusion is the (understandable but nonetheless erroneous) tendency to adopt an excessively formal, legalistic and institutional understanding of government when in fact there are broad similarities between the actual processes of governance in the domestic and global spheres. This distinction between government (as an institutional entity) and governance (denoting the processes of governing) is vital in considering how order is created and maintained in the global system. It is also relevant to the issue of whether global politics can be argued to occur within a corresponding global polity, however primitive such a polity may be.

Within the domestic polity there exist accepted rules and authoritative political institutions which govern society. In addition to these basic foundations there also exists a shared culture and a set of broadly accepted basic values which underwrite the legitimacy of political practices, institutions and order. These features are the essential building blocks of the domestic polity; they are also features which are much less in evidence at the global level. Cultural diversity combined with massive inequalities, and the lack of any overarching authoritative institutions and rules, suggest that, at best, the notion of a global polity is somewhat idealistic. Yet even in the most advanced and democratic national polities the sense of cultural unity, and the legitimacy of political institutions and practices, are subject to stresses and contradictions. The ideal is not necessarily reflected in the reality. Accordingly the global polity might best be conceived not simply as a much weaker form of the domestic polity but rather as a more unique entity which has quite distinctive governing arrangements. The fact that there is no world government beyond the nation-state does not warrant the conclusion that there are no effective political mechanisms by which order is established and maintained at the global level. In this context the distinction between government and governance becomes critical.

Much emphasis has been placed in previous chapters on the nature and processes of governance in the global system. In chapters 3 and 4 the discussion indicated how superpower hegemony and the balance of power acted as mechanisms through which global and regional order was established and reproduced over time. In part II, chapter 6 explored how technologically induced collective problems led to the creation of international regimes and collective management arrangements at global and regional levels. Chapters 9 and 12 examined the nature and different accounts of the government of the global economy. And finally in chapter 14 specific attention was focused upon the global legitimacy accorded to cosmopolitan values, such as human rights, and their role in creating the foundations of a universal citizenship and global polity. From these contributions it is possible to argue that the global system is increasingly governed, although the form which that government takes is quite distinct, but not entirely dissimilar, from that which occurs within the stereotypical domestic policy. According to Smith, 'world society is inherently diverse and multilayered, and the global polity we have is not a replica of the cosy, stable and predictable politics of the well-ordered national state ...but it is nonetheless – and arguably to an increasing extent – governed' (1989, pp. 61–2).

In analysing the nature of governance in the global polity, the three paradigms or theoretical traditions provide a valuable starting point. From the discussions in chapters 4, 12 and 13 it is possible to distil an overview of how each of the paradigms accounts for processes of governance and the reproduction of order in the global system. Table 16.1 summarizes the position of the three paradigms in relation to four key aspects of global governance: Who governs? What is governed? What are the distinctive processes of governance? What is the outcome of governance?

Global politics describes the existence of global political processes which transcend

Table 16.1 Governance in the global political system

	Realism and neo-realism	Liberal-pluralism	Neo-Marxism
Who governs?	Major or hegemonic powers operating through nation-states	Governments, IGOs, INGOs, markets, and diversity of groups	Dominant transnational classes and technocratic elites
What is governed?	High politics, war and peace, the system of states	Fluctuating agenda of global economic, social political and ecological issues; low and sectoral politics	Global economic order, global relations of production and exchange, national socioeconomic orders through global agencies, class relations
Processes of governance	Balance of power, diplomacy, hierarchy and superpower dominance	International regimes, IGOs, the global market, negotiation, bargaining and compromise, the management of interdependence	Transnational capital and its agencies, the exercise of capitalist ideological, cultural and economic hegemony
Outcome of governance	Order within anarchy, stability, maintenance of hierarchy, preservation of states system	Fragmented and polyarchic order, decentralized and democratic forms of governance, heterarchy as opposed to hierarchy, a world society	Maintenance of the rule of capital, perpetuation of global structure of dominance and inequality, a global class system, a world capitalist system

Source: adapted from Smith (1989)

the traditional boundaries between domestic and international politics. It is distinguished, as recalled from chapter 1, by a stretching, deepening and broadening of the political process and the exercise of power. Global politics thus articulates a dominant reality of modern political life, the signal emergence of a primitive and fragile global polity.

GLOBAL POLITICS: TRANSITIONAL ERA OR HISTORICAL TRANSFORMATION?

'Perhaps at no other time in history has a consideration of the changes taking place in world politics been more urgent than now' (Kegley and Wittkopf 1989, p. 4). It is somewhat trite to observe that we live in an age in which contingency and uncertainty define global political reality. Since 1989 there have been a series of historic developments across the global political landscape, from the ending of the Cold War, the collapse of communism in Eastern Europe, the prosecution of a major war in the Middle East, the revival of European political integration, to the greening of international relations, the spectacular lurch towards democratization across the globe, and the diffusion of the North–South conflict, to recall but a few. Yet these surface events may themselves be simply a reflection, in part, of more profound structural changes (emanating partly from those very globalizing processes which have been the focus of this volume) which have been under way for some time. As Kennedy has observed, the global system 'is subject to constant changes, not only those caused by the day to day actions of statesmen and the ebb and flow of political and military events, but also those caused by deeper transformations in the foundations of world power, which in their time make their way through to the surface' (1988, p. 536). Do the dramatic developments in global politics we are witnessing today therefore herald the arrival of a new epoch in world history?

Certainly much of the contemporary speculation on the cumulative ramifications of global developments suggests that the world is confronting one of those historical turning points, a *fin de siècle*, which, like the Second World War, delineates one epoch from another in the collective consciousness. But does such speculation have any value, or is it simply idle chatter? In this final section some attempt will be made to identify potential patterns in the patchwork of contemporary change as well as the potential trajectories which change might be taking. Such speculation has the benefit that it helps clarify our own assumptions about the forces shaping the existing global order, the status quo. Moreover, as Frankel rightly asserts 'to prevent a tyranny of the present, one needs both to study its historical origins and to probe into the possibilities for the future' (1988, p. 232). But have the contributions to this volume delivered any possible clues as to the possibilities for the future? Can we identify the potential trajectories of global change?

In chapter 13 considerable emphasis was given to the nature and ramifications of change in the global system. From this discussion and other contemporary analyses it is possible to distil five discrete *trajectories of change*. What is curious about these trajectories is that none maps easily on to any of the three paradigms or traditions exploited throughout this volume. This is undoubtedly because within each theoretical tradition there exists a serious debate about the prognoses for global politics. These five trajectories are labelled: the world transformed; the primacy of continuity; the world in crisis; the bifurcated world; and global politics in transition. Each interprets the trends and current developments within the global system as prefiguring radically different kinds of global political futures.

The World Transformed

At the heart of this interpretation of current trends is the assumption that the basic structure of the global system and the post-war global order are experiencing a metamorphosis (Morse 1976). The decline of both superpowers; the fragmentation of both power blocs; the emergence of multipolarity and new ideological cleavages; the intensification of global interdependence; the requirement for global and regional structures of government; the growing significance of transnational organizations and forces; the integration of all states into a single global economy; and the existence of a global society; all these developments are taken as evidence that the world is undergoing a profound transformation. As a consequence, the future direction of global politics is envisaged as an evolutionary shift towards a more complex configuration of power, in which the nation-state will become of declining significance as its functions are transferred to new global and regional administrative structures, whilst national allegiances will be compromised in the process. Such a world will not be without conflict. Rather conflict will occur within the constraints of a more cooperative world order in which there will be authoritative mechanisms of global decision making. This is a model of the future which gives primacy to the integrative potential of the globalizing processes which have been at the core of this study of global politics. It is a model which, on the basis of current trends and events, envisages the transformation of the world into a truly global society with a correspondingly effective global polity.

The Primacy of Continuity

A radically different vision of the future emerges from those, like Gilpin (1981) and Bull (1977), who, whilst recognizing many of the same developments noted above, conclude that the future will continue to be very much like the present. This model of the future rejects the above notion that a discontinuity, a break with the past, has arrived in global politics. On the contrary, it predicts a basic continuity whilst accepting that the surface appearances of global politics (which states rise and which decline) will undoubtedly be subject to considerable change. This model of the future is very eloquently described by Gilpin:

> World politics is still characterized by the struggle of political entities for power, prestige, and wealth in a condition of global anarchy. Nuclear weapons have not made the resort to force irrelevant; economic interdependence does not guarantee that cooperation will triumph over conflict; a global community of common values and outlook has yet to displace international anarchy. The fundamental problem of international relations in the contemporary world is the problem of peaceful adjustment to the consequences of the uneven growth of power among states, just as it was in the past. International society cannot and does not stand still. War and violence remain serious possibilities as the world moves from the decay of one international system toward the creation of another.
>
> (1981, pp. 229–30)

The World in Crisis

Rather than a world of continuity, there are those authors such as Bozeman (1984), Wallerstein (1980), Kolko (1988) and Porritt (1988), who envisage the future as an intensification of the global contradictions and global crises of the present. This is a model of the future which highlights the unsustainable contradictions in the global economic order; the world population crisis; the encroaching ecocrisis; the deepening cultural and ideological fragmentation of the world; the disintegration of global order; the intensity of global insecurity; the ever present threat of global armageddon; and the crisis of the territorial nation-state. It is a very pessimistic vision of the future, one which gives primacy to conflict, tension and political fragmentation brought about by processes of globalization. But, equally, it stresses the possibilities or opportunities for dramatic political change to avert the worst consequences of impending crises.

The Bifurcated World

According to Rosenau (1990), global politics is increasingly bifurcated into two distinct domains or systems of interaction, each with its own particular logic and dynamics of change: the interstate system and the multicentric system. He argues that contemporary developments confirm the existence of two worlds of global politics:

> The state-centric system now coexists with an equally powerful, though more decentralized, multicentric system. Although these two worlds of world politics have overlapping elements and concerns their norms, structures and processes tend to be mutually exclusive, thus giving rise to a set of global arrangements that are new and possibly enduring, as well as extremely complex and dynamic.
>
> (p. 11)

Moreover, the present epoch is conceived as a historical breakpoint because global politics has entered an era of profound turbulence in which the discontinuities and the anomalies make history and traditional theories of global politics largely irrelevant to an understanding of the contemporary global condition. Rosenau suggests that:

> The very notion of 'international relations' seems obsolete in the face of an apparent trend in which more and more of the interactions that sustain world politics unfold without the direct involvement of nations or states. So a new term is needed, one that denotes the presence of new structures and processes while at the same time allowing for still further structural development. A suitable label would be *postinternational politics*. The social sciences are now pervaded by analyses of postindustrial, postcapitalist, postsocialist, and postideological society, post-Marxism and postmodernism, the post-Christian era, and many other such 'posts'. Profound changes in world affairs can surely, then, be regarded as constituting postinternational politics.
>
> But use of this label involves more than conforming to fashion. Postinternational politics is an appropriate designation because it clearly suggests the decline of long-standing patterns without at the same time indicating where the changes

may be leading. It suggests flux and transition even as it implies the presence and functioning of stable structures. It allows for chaos even as it hints at coherence. It reminds us that 'international' matters may no longer be the dominant dimension of global life, or at least that other dimensions have emerged to challenge or offset the interactions of nation-states. And, not least, it permits us to avoid premature judgement as to whether present-day turbulence consists of enduring systemic arrangements or is merely a transitional condition.

Accordingly, the term will henceforth be used to designate the historical era that began after World War II and continues to unfold today. It is a shorthand for the changes wrought by global turbulence; for an ever more dynamic interdependence in which labour is increasingly specialized and the number of collective actors thereby proliferates; for the centralizing and decentralizing tendencies that are altering the identity and number of actors on the world stage; for the shifting orientations that are transforming authority relations among the actors; and for the dynamics of structural bifurcation that are fostering new arrangements through which the diverse actors pursue their goals. Postinternational politics is that hitherto unimaginable scheme, a generic conception of how the human links that span the globe have been affected by the complexity and dynamism that are coming into view as the present millennium draws to a close.

(pp. 6–7)

Global Politics in Transition

The combination of dramatic developments on the surface of contemporary global politics and the intensification of underlying secular trends (such as globalization) has suggested to some that the world has entered a transitional era. Evidence for this comes from the coexistence of unprecedented and accelerating global change alongside the inertia of tradition and powerful continuities. In this model, the near future will be an unfolding of this present transitional era. It will be a continuation of the current struggle between: global integration and global fragmentation; the intensification of international cooperation and international competition; military bipolarity and economic multipolarity; universalism and particularism; transnationalism and nationalism; and transnational capital versus labour. The present and the near future are thus conceived as a historical transition, located as we are between a certain past and an uncertain distant future.

This transitional character of the contemporary era is vividly exemplified in the crumbling of the post-war global order evidenced amongst other things in: the relative decline of both superpowers; the emergence of new centres of economic and political power such as Japan and Europe; the demise of the two great power blocs; the regionalization of the global trading system; and the displacement of US hegemony in the global economic order. But these surface developments coexist alongside significant structural changes in the global system, brought about by secular trends such as the intensification of globalization. This is captured in Kissinger's comment that: 'We are stranded between old conceptions of political conduct and a wholly new conception, between the inadequacy of the nation-state and the emerging imperative of global community' (quoted in Kegley and Wittkopf 1989, p. 25).

In this transitional era model, the future pattern of global politics appears to be inherently uncertain except that it will mark a historically distinctive, although not complete, break with the present. Such is the essential nature of transitional eras.

GLOBAL POLITICS IN A TRANSITIONAL ERA

One of the main themes of this volume has been the relationship between globalization and the continued viability of the modern nation-state. As has been argued in this chapter, this is a complicated and hotly contested matter made even more complex by the nature of the transitional era in which we live. Nevertheless it is possible in conclusion to agree with Joseph Frankel that:

> We are undoubtedly faced with a major crisis of the territorial sovereign state in its traditional form. No state is any longer self-sufficient or safe within its boundaries, not even the superpowers, let alone the new mini-states; all are facing a diminution of their sovereignty. Nevertheless, it is hard to see how the present division of mankind into states could lose its importance in the forseeable future. This supposition readily leads to one possible future – an international system continuing much as it is now, but with states probably somewhat readier to coordinate their activities at the cost of further inroads into their sovereignty, and new non-state actors and transnational activities further supplementing their activities. Envisaging such a future is, however, no more than a simplistic, and naive, projection into the future of the trends of the present and the immediate past.
>
> (1988, p. 229)

References

Bozeman, A. (1984) The international order in a multicultural world. In H. Bull and A. Watson (eds), *The Expansion of International Society*, Oxford: Oxford University Press.

Bull, H. (1977) *The Anarchical Society*. London: Macmillan.

Burton, J. (1972) *World Society*. Cambridge: Cambridge University Press.

Cox, R. (1987) *Production, Power and World Order*. New York: Columbia University Press.

CSCE (1990) *Conference on Security and Cooperation in Europe*, Joint Declaration, Paris, 19 November.

Frankel, J. (1988) *International Relations in a Changing World*. Oxford: Oxford University Press.

Giddens, A. (1989) *Sociology*. Cambridge: Polity Press.

Giddens, A. (1990) *The Consequences of Modernity*. Cambridge: Polity Press.

Gilpin, R. (1981) *War and Change in World Politics*. Cambridge: Cambridge University Press.

Gilpin, R. (1987) *The Political Economy of International Relations*. Princeton: Princeton University Press.

Halliday, F. (1988) State and society in international relations: a second agenda. *Millennium*, 16(2).

Hanrieder, W. (1978) Dissolving international politics. *American Political Science Review*, 72(4).

Kegley, C.W. and Wittkopf, E.R. (1989) *World Politics – Trend and Transformation*. London: Macmillan.

Kennedy, P. (1988) *The Rise and Fall of Great Powers*. London: Unwin Hyman.

Kolko, J. (1988) *Restructuring the World Economy*. New York: Random House.

Krasner, S.D. and Thompson, J.E. (1989) Global transactions and the consolidation of sovereignty. In E.-O. Czempiel and J.N. Rosenau (eds), *Global Changes and Theoretical Challenges*, Lexington: Heath.

Mitchell, C.R. (1984) World society as a cobweb. In M. Banks (ed.), *Conflict in World Society*, London: Simon and Schuster.

Modelski, G. (1972) *Principles of World Politics*. New York: Free Press.

Morse, E.L. (1976) *Modernization and the Transformation of International Relations*. New York: Free Press.

Porritt, J. (1988) *The Coming of the Greens*. London: Collins.

Rosenau, J. (1990) *Turbulence in World Politics*. London: Harvester Wheatsheaf.

Smith, M. (1989) A global polity? Paper 23, *D312 Global Politics*, Milton Keynes: Open University.

Wallerstein, I. (1980) *The Politics of the World Economy*. Cambridge: Cambridge University Press.

Index